WITHDRAWN

Praise for *Jobs in Paradise*

"How about a summer job in an exotic place? Author Jeffrey Maltzman has found a lot of ways to turn summer employment into the adventure of a lifetime."
—*Today* show

"A terrific book—tells you the who, what, why, where, when, and most importantly how, to get jobs in paradise! Everybody should grab a copy if for no other reason than to just imagine what it would be like to live and work in paradise. It kept me up most of the night reading the book just checking out places I've always wanted to go! Get a copy!"
—"The Paul Strassell Show,"
KOTA, Rapid City, S.D.

"Worthwhile tips . . . and who knows, if your [summer] tour of duty as an aerobics instructor goes well, you may never have to return to Akron."
—*Akron Beacon Journal*

"210,000 jobs in paradise and Maltzman lists every one and how to get them. All the information is here. Over 400 pages of information. A fascinating book. I'm impressed!"
—KFI Radio, Los Angeles

"Great reading!"
—WWDB Radio, Philadelphia

"A straightforward listing of job opportunities in mountain lodges and beach resorts in the United States, Canada, the South Pacific, and Caribbean. The Tropical Island section is fun just for the day-dream factor."
—*San Diego Union*

"Lots of good inside information."
—CJCA Radio, Edmonton, Canada

"*Jobs in Paradise* gets an A+ on relevance of the subject matter to our students, completeness and organization of the information, and overall readability of the book. A valuable addition to our library."
—Kathy Campbell, Coordinator,
Stanford University Student Employment Services

D0095601

JOBS IN PARADISE

The Definitive Guide to Exotic Jobs Everywhere

REVISED EDITION

Jeffrey Maltzman

HarperPerennial
A Division of HarperCollins*Publishers*

This book was originally published in 1990 by Harper & Row, Publishers.

JOBS IN PARADISE (REVISED EDITION). Copyright © 1990, 1993 by Jeffrey B. Maltzman. All rights reserved. Printed in the United States of America. No part of this book may be used or reproduced in any manner whatsoever without written permission except in the case of brief quotations embodied in critical articles and reviews. For information address HarperCollins Publishers, Inc., 10 East 53rd Street, New York, NY 10022.

HarperCollins books may be purchased for educational, business, or sales promotional use. For information please write: Special Markets Department, HarperCollins Publishers, Inc., 10 East 53rd Street, New York, NY 10022.

FIRST EDITION

Library of Congress Cataloging-in-Publication Data
  Maltzman, Jeffrey.
    Jobs in paradise / Jeffrey Maltzman. — Rev. ed.
      p.   cm.
    ISBN 0-06-273186-6
    1. Vocational guidance—United States—Directories.
2. Occupations—United States—Directories. 3. Recreation—
Vocational guidance—United States—Directories. 4. Tourist
trade—Vocational guidance—United States—Directories. 5. Seasonal labor—United States—Directories. 6. Summer employment—United States—Directories. I. Title.
  HF5382.5.U5M345   1993
  331.7'02'02573—dc20   92-53297

96 97   RRD   10 9 8 7 6 5

To My Family

Contents

ACKNOWLEDGMENTS

Special thanks to Craig Nelson and Jennifer Hull of HarperCollins and to my agent Doe Coover, without whose energy, enthusiasm, and creativity this book wouldn't have been written. Most of all, my love and gratitude to my girlfriend Ana for her never-ending support, and to my parents and brothers Forrest and Reed, who shared their travels with me and helped proofread my drafts (even while on their vacations!). To my researchers, Tami Timmer, Lisa Adler, Cynthia Muccillo, Jane Bailie, Gene Robertson, Brenda Pascoe, and Katie Curry, a million thank yous! My heartfelt appreciation to those countless friends who lent moral support and helped out with a thousand favors, small and large: Bob Hessinger, Jimmy and Beth Trilling, Miguel Smith, and Steve and Maggie Pitchkolen. For going above and beyond the call of duty in sharing their unique knowledge and expertise with me, thank you to Singleworld Cruises & Tours' Wendy Lowenstein, Disneyland's Richard Ramsey, the Western River Guides Association, and the International Association of Amusement Parks and Attractions. For teaching me the joy of writing, a veritable plethora of thank yous to Barry Bergstrom, David Lewis, Emmett Jordan, and the rest of the *Campagnile* gang. Finally, a special note of gratitude to my partners Larry Kaye and Brad Rose of Kaye, Rose & Maltzman for giving me the time to revise this book.

A special note of appreciation to the countless employers, employees, and trade organizations who provided me with invaluable information and insight.

INTRODUCTION

I couldn't believe my luck when I first landed a job as a social director for singles cruises aboard "the love boat." Eight years, 167 cruises, and a Stanford law degree later, I decided to write *Jobs in Paradise,* the definitive guide to cruise ship, resort, and more than 200,000 other dream jobs across the United States, Canada, the South Pacific, and the Caribbean.

On the Fourth of July in 1979 my life changed. It was a few months after my high school graduation and college still loomed as a distant mirage in the endless summer. I was driving a shuttle bus at San Francisco International Airport. For eight hours that day I looped around the scenic whirlpool of congested airport traffic, avoiding taxis, lost motorists, and horn-blowing late businessmen. After my shift, I went into the office to punch out my time card. A weary secretary stopped me as I was halfway out the door and mentioned that I had received a phone call from the operations manager at Singleworld Cruises & Tours. I returned the call and my life changed. The good news was that they wanted to offer me a job leading groups of single travelers between the ages of eighteen and thirty-five on ten-day tours of California and seven-day cruises to Alaska aboard the SS *Rotterdam.* The bad news was that if I wanted the job I had to be in Alaska to catch the ship within twenty-four hours. I phoned home to tell my folks, quit my job as a shuttle bus driver, packed my bags, and never looked back!

From that day forward, I vowed never to settle for a boring job again. While friends spent their college summers flipping burgers at the local McDonald's, I cruised Alaska, the Caribbean, Bermuda, Mexico, Europe, and the Orient. When cruise ship life became too confining, I worked as a camp counselor and lifeguard in Malibu, California. In more recent years I took time off from law school to live and work in Honolulu, Hawaii.

The path to my life of hedonistic pleasure was not always paved with gold. Along the way I left behind a mountain of form rejection letters, unanswered applications, and false hopes. Countless friends have described how their attempts to find an ideal job led to lives of indentured slavery instead. Phil Friedman's summer job in a national park sounded ideal. The employment application promised clean living in the beautiful High Sierras with plenty of time for hiking, rock climbing, fishing, and exploring. Instead, Phil found himself slaving over a hot grill at minimum wage while being forced to pay exorbitant rent to live in mandatory employee dormitories that were not suited for human occupation. He lasted six weeks.

You can last longer and be a great deal happier than Phil. *Jobs in Paradise* reveals the inside scoop on what resort and cruise ship employers look for in employees and explains how to land your dream job. Detailed listings are included for specific seasonal and full-time job openings at hundreds of resort hotels, ski areas, state and national parks, whitewater river rafting companies, hot air ballooning companies, travel and adventure outfitters, and aboard cruise ships, charter yachts, and sightseeing excursion boats.

I hope that with the information included here, you too can find your *Job in Paradise*. Good luck and have fun!

—Jeffrey Maltzman

FINDING A JOB IN PARADISE

Each year thousands of sleepy beach and mountain towns are transformed into bustling tourist meccas. As the number of tourists multiply, so does the demand for seasonal employees. These employees are the lifeblood of the resort industry. Without seasonal and long-term workers, the beaches, ski slopes, cruise ships, and resort hotels would all have to close. And any vacation facility, no matter how beautiful, is only as good as its staff.

If you have ever thought it would be fun to live in paradise but didn't think you'd be able to find a job or a place to live—think again! Resorts from Hawaii to the Florida Keys, from the Rocky Mountains to the Hamptons, and from Alaska to New Zealand are desperately seeking affable, competent personnel.

The recent shortage of resort and tourism employees makes this a job seeker's market. Many resort town employers have raised salaries by 35 to 50 percent in the past year in an effort to attract needed help. Resort areas such as Cape Cod have established employer-sponsored community organizations to advertise for seasonal resort employees. Even the ever-popular Disneyland has begun to offer subsidized housing for summer employees in an effort to attract qualified applicants from around the country.

The listings in this book provide everything you'll need to find your job in paradise.

All information in this book has been supplied by the employers. While every effort is made to assure accuracy, neither the author, the publisher, nor their agents, employees, or representatives can be responsible for errors or omissions made herein. Be sure to confirm all important details and working conditions before accepting employment.

How to Use This Book

Most of us have dreamed of spending a month, a season, or a few years living and working in paradise. Whether you consider paradise to be the alpine mountains of the Rockies, the scenic shores of Hawaii, the frigid tundra of the Arctic, or the deck of a sleek cruise ship in the Caribbean, this book will tell you where the jobs are and how to get them.

In this chapter you'll learn the inside secrets of landing the job of your dreams. The basics of cover letter and résumé writing, as well as the fine art of interviewing, are explored. You'll learn when to send a photo with your application, when to write and ask for the official application form, and when simply to send a résumé. Resort and tourism employers look for unique and special traits in their employees. You'll learn through profile interviews with major employers and recent paradise employees how to tailor your application to meet their needs.

The second part of the book lists tens of thousands of jobs in resort areas around the world. Each listing explains how and where to apply, what positions are available, what to include with your application, how many new employees are hired annually, and what traits and qualifications employers look for in applicants. The listings include jobs with ski areas, resort hotels, lifeguard services, tour companies, whitewater rafting outfits, stables, national park concessionaires, hot air balloon companies, passenger cruise ships, adventure travel enterprises, and more.

Each job listing includes:

- a brief description of the employer
- total number of employees and approximate number of new employees hired annually
- list of positions for which applicants may apply
- job requirements, if any
- employee perks (i.e., free ski passes, free housing, etc.)
- insider tips, including descriptions from personnel directors of the qualities they seek in employees, and salary information when available
- detailed application instructions including the name of the personnel director, address, and phone number

The jobs are as diverse as lifeguards on Waikiki Beach and gravediggers in Martha's Vineyard. The employers range from Club Med to Squaw Valley Ski Area, from Fun Water Tours of the Virgin Islands to Alaska's Denali Park Hotel.

The listings are organized by the type of locale in which the company is found:

High Adventure Run silent and run deep or soar with the eagles. This section includes listings for everything from a deep-sea tourist submarine company in the Caribbean to hot air balloon companies in California's Napa Valley. Mountaineering and wilderness survival programs, fishing, and even safari guide companies are included.

Mountains Readers in search of clean living in the mountains will discover hundreds of employers in areas from the Sierra Nevadas to the Hamptons, from the Canadian Rockies to New Zealand's Remarkables.

Tropical Islands For those who yearn to explore uncharted islands, this section provides listings for countless jobs at resort hotels, SCUBA and snorkel tour operators, charter boat companies, and more on islands from the Florida Keys to Hawaii, and from the Virgin Islands to the Great Barrier Reef islands.

Snow and Skiing For readers who dream of spending their lunch breaks skiing, this section includes listings for hundreds of ski areas, resort hotels, Nordic ski chalets, ski schools, ski mountain photography companies, and other employers in the vicinity of ski areas.

Coasts and Beaches Listings for SCUBA and snorkel tour companies, beach and coastal hotels and resorts, and beach boardwalk shops. Includes beaches from Florida to Maine on the Eastern seaboard and from California to Canada in the West.

Rivers and Lakes Listings for jobs with whitewater river rafting companies and at river and lakeside resort hotels throughout the United States, Canada, Australia, and New Zealand.

Deserts For those tired of frozen winters, this section provides listings for resort hotels and other employers in the desert areas of the United States.

Tour Escorts Listings for companies hiring tour escorts to lead everything from swinging singles tours through Europe to senior citizen bicycle treks through Vermont.

Amusement and Theme Parks Interested in playing Mickey Mouse or training a whale for a summer? This section has tens of thousands of full-time and seasonal jobs at theme parks from San Diego's Seaworld to Orlando's Disney World.

Cruise Ships These listings cover more than 40,000 jobs working aboard major cruise ships and excursion boat companies plying both domestic and international waters. A brief introduction to life at sea and subsections on the worldwide travel and the crews of cruise ships are included.

A cross-index by geographic area is provided as an Appendix at the back of this book. In an effort to divide the employers between the chapters, employers are listed in the chapter that most closely coordinates with their business. Additionally, since many jobs fit into more than one chapter category, a mini cross-index is included at the end of each chapter.

Within each listing, a section on "Perks" details such fringe benefits as Yosemite Park and Curry Company's employee housing and meals and the free employee ski pass program at Park City, Utah. "Perks" covers the employee intramural sports league at Disneyland as well as the free SCUBA certification course offered to employees by Virgin Island Diving Schools of St. Thomas.

"Insider Tips" in each listing includes information and hints provided by employers and employees. It reveals how long you must be available for work to be considered for a job at a Great Barrier Reef island resort and what to stress in an application for children's counselor aboard Carnival Cruise Lines. Employers explain when prior experience is required and when they are willing to train someone without any experience. Employees provide tips on subjects from Rocky Mountain National Park's employee dress code enforcement to the employee drug policy at Volcano House National Park in Hawaii. This section offers basic "do's and don'ts," honestly outlining both the pluses and the minuses of working for each employer, thus allowing readers to make certain that their idea of a dream job meshes with that of their employer.

Each employer listing starts out with a brief description of the company's business. These descriptions were gathered through a combination of personal on-site visits by the author, visits by *Jobs in Paradise* research assistants, mail and phone surveys, and promotional brochures and employee recruitment literature published by the companies. While every effort has been made to assure the accuracy of the information given here, most information came directly from the employers. As a final check for accuracy, all the companies listed in the book were given an opportunity to review their listings before publication. However, be aware this information is subject to change: The name of the personnel director may have changed. Companies modify their rates of pay. An employer that once provided employee housing may no longer do so. Thus, before accepting any job, be sure to verify all important details.

HOW TO IMPROVE YOUR CHANCES OF LANDING A JOB IN PARADISE

While it is true that jobs in paradise are highly sought after, they are *not* impossible to get. If you can swim, your local Red Cross office can certify you as a lifeguard in a few short weekends or evenings. With a Red Cross certificate you can be a lifeguard on beaches from Hawaii to Key West or the Jersey Shore. If you want to further increase your chances of landing your dream job, another few short Red Cross courses can earn you CPR and advanced first-aid certificates.

Are you interested in a job leading whitewater rafting excursions? In many instances, that same Red Cross certificate is all you need when sending in your application. The listings in *Jobs in Paradise* include numerous rafting companies that offer river guide courses and then offer jobs to the students who perform best in the course.

Are you interested in spending a summer teaching SCUBA diving in the Caribbean? The book includes listings of numerous dive operators, including a few who even hire instructors who have never been SCUBA diving! With the information included here, you'll learn how you can earn a SCUBA instructor certificate while you work.

Carefully read through the job titles. In addition to the usual assortment of typical resort jobs, you'll find some unusual entries. For example, look at the job openings in the "Dunk Island Australia Resort" listing. This Great Barrier Reef hotel hires the usual bar staff, restaurant staff, housekeepers, and front desk clerks. However, the island also hires staff to coordinate the nightly entertainment and daily activities programs, nurses, hairdressers, barge captains, and even five farmers to run its self-contained dairy and horse corral!

Everyone knows Disneyland hires attraction operators, ticket sellers, and maintenance staff, but did you know that the Magic Kingdom also has positions for kennel attendants, pony breeders, craftsmen, and firefighters?

Other listings tell you how to apply for work as a host on a civilian sightseeing submarine in the Virgin Islands or as a gravedigger on Cape Cod.

See, you'd better read them all.

PROFILE OF JOHN SAGE

"Appearing to be settled into the community is important when looking for a job after arriving in paradise."

> **HOMETOWN:** Berkeley, California
> **SCHOOL:** Stanford University (B.A., American Studies)
> Harvard Business School (M.B.A.)
> **JOBS:** Parking Valet (San Francisco)
> Nightclub Bouncer (Lake Tahoe, California)
> Maintenance Worker (Lake Tahoe, California)

John Sage landed a job in beautiful Lake Tahoe, California, without any advance preparation. "I decided at the last minute to spend my summer working at Tahoe. I moved up there without the slightest job lead. However, I managed to find both housing and two part-time jobs within a week. The key was finding a place to live. It would have been impossible to find a job without an address and phone number. If you show up at an employer's doorstep without an address or phone number they won't seriously consider you."

Resort town employers are turned off by applicants they don't feel will stay. They have been conned by employees who claim they are in the city to stay and then quit after a few weeks of fun.

If you are afraid to commit to renting an apartment and paying to hook up a phone before you have a job, there are several ways to appear settled without actually having an address. Most cities have answering services to which you can subscribe at a modest cost, providing you with a phone number to list on applications. For a local address, rent a post office box.

As for John's experience working at Lake Tahoe, "while my bouncer and maintenance jobs at Tahoe probably didn't play a major role in getting me admitted to Harvard Business School, my summer there was one of the best I ever had."

PROFILE OF BRENDA HOLMAN

"Be realistic—a job in paradise is still a job."

HOMETOWN: Eufaula, Oklahoma
SCHOOL: Eufaula High School
JOBS: Summer Cheerleading Camp Counselor
Restaurant Hostess (Arrowhead Lodge, Oklahoma)
Waitress (Arrowhead Lodge, Oklahoma)

When Brenda Holman landed her dream job as a restaurant hostess (and later as a waitress) at the acclaimed Arrowhead Lodge she was ecstatic. The lodge was located in a beautiful wooded mountain area filled with lakes, deer, and other wild animals. To Brenda, the long curvy road that led to the lodge was her ticket to paradise. "I pictured my job at Arrowhead as the perfect summer position. I would be working in a beautiful mountain resort and meeting people from all across the state."

What Brenda didn't realize is that a job in a spectacular resort is still a job. "While there were parts of the job I loved, it was *hard* work! Having access to all the amenities of the resort was wonderful, but it seemed there was rarely time to use them." Brenda's story is reminiscent of many resort employees. If you look at your job in paradise purely as a vacation, you'll be disappointed. However, if you think of it as a job first and as a chance to live and work in a wonderful place second, you'll do well. "People on vacation are usually real nice and in a great mood. They are doing fun and exciting things and I really enjoyed getting to know our guests. Staff members who work at a resort may eventually get to try everything that the guests enjoy. However, it may take an employee a month to fit into his or her work schedule what a guest could accomplish in one week. As long as you realize that going in, you'll have a great time."

APPLYING FOR THE JOBS

The Cover Letter

Each job listing concludes with a brief explanation of how to apply. While a few employers require you to write and request their official application form, most welcome applicants to send a cover letter and résumé. (Regardless of how you apply, a short cover letter should always accompany your application.)

The purpose of your cover letter is to introduce you to the employer. It serves to tell the employer which specific job you seek and whether or not you will consider other positions if they are offered. Your cover letter should call attention to your relevant job skills and creatively emphasize how your skills will benefit the employer.

As tempting as it might be to write on the funky fluorescent pink paper your college roommate gave you last Christmas, forget it! A cover letter should always be neatly typed in a professional business format on good quality 8½" × 11" white bonded paper. (An example of a basic cover letter is shown in Example 1, p. 10.)

Your cover letter creates the employer's first impression of you. You want the letter to demonstrate in both form and style that you are a neat, organized, efficient, and intelligent applicant. Submitting a letter in fancy script type or on purple paper is a clear sign to an employer that you don't know how to behave in a professional environment.

A cover letter should be attention-getting, short, and concise. It should never exceed one page; often a far shorter letter will suffice. Begin your letter by introducing yourself and stating the position for which you are applying. If you want to increase your chances of being hired, specify other positions you would consider. Most employers believe an ideal applicant is someone who knows what position he or she wants but is open to considering other jobs that better suit the employer's needs.

Next, your letter should specify the date you can be available to start work and how long you are willing to commit yourself to the position. The more flexible you can be in your start and finish dates, the better your chances of being hired. Possible phrases to explain your starting dates might read:

1. As I am currently finishing my junior year at Anystate University, I could be available to start work after (date).

2. While I would prefer to start work after (date), I can be available immediately if necessary.

3. I can be available immediately should you need someone on short notice.

If you are going to be in the area where the employer is located for any reason (vacation, etc.), mention when you expect to be there and request a personal interview. While most of the employers in this book do not require a personal interview (many conduct phone interviews), a personal interview usually increases your chances of landing your dream job.

Next, explain how you believe your qualifications meet the employer's needs. Most of the employer listings in *Jobs in Paradise* detail what qualities the company looks for in applicants. Thus, use your cover letter to detail how your résumé reflects those qualities. The important key here is merely to highlight your résumé. Don't bore the employer by simply rehashing what is already on your résumé.

Just because you have never worked as a front desk clerk at a resort before doesn't mean you lack the qualifications for the job. If you have past work experience with the public, or experience dealing with money and figures, point that out. Obviously, both people skills and money-handling experience would be important traits that any employer would consider valuable in a front desk clerk applicant.

Finally, conclude your letter by thanking the employer for his or her time in considering your application and express a hope for a prompt response. Never tell an employer that you will call in a certain number of days to discuss your application. While such follow-up phone calls are generally a good idea, mentioning a call in your letter can make you seem overly pushy and aggressive to some employers.

The following cover letter is a sample of the letter Vince Redman used to land his job as a shore excursion manager aboard Norwegian Cruise Lines' SS *Norway*.

EXAMPLE 1

VINCE REDMAN
P.O. Box XX
Anytown, USA

Date

Dear Sir or Madam:

Enclosed is a copy of my personal résumé briefly outlining my background and qualifications for your consideration. I am seeking a challenging position of responsibility as a shore excursion manager on a cruise ship where my experience and abilities as a tour director and coordinator can be effectively utilized. Any entry level crew position will also be considered.

Please note on my résumé both my training and background. I have practical experience in selling, organizing, and implementing tours for groups ranging in size from two to a thousand or more.

I am confident that I can do a professional and productive job for you on one of your ships if granted the opportunity.

I would appreciate the opportunity for a personal interview with you. I may be reached at the above address or by calling (phone number).

I appreciate your time and consideration and look forward to hearing from you soon.

Sincerely,

Vince Redman

Enclosures: Résumé
. Photograph

The Résumé:
Your Life in One Page

For most people, nothing is more frustrating than trying to condense their life onto one sheet of paper. However, professionals everywhere will tell you that where résumés are concerned, one page is the limit. Consider this rule to be written in stone: *Your résumé must not be longer than one page.*

Before you start panicking, there are several tricks to help you fit more onto that one page. For example, using elite type instead of pica type on most typewriters will allow you to fit almost 12% more information onto the page. Better yet, have your résumé professionally typeset. A typeset résumé serves two purposes: It looks more professional and can fit almost double the information on each page. If you are serious about pursuing your dream job, the $25 to $45 it will cost to have a résumé typeset is well worth the investment.

The sample resumes on pages 15 and 16 demonstrate two effective styles (see Examples 2 and 3). Example 2 is a short and concise résumé that attempts to list only the barest of outlined information. The résumé of Example 3 is more detailed and includes not only a list of experience and qualifications, but detailed statements explaining the applicant's qualifications.

If you choose to use the second, more detailed style of résumé, try to use action verbs to describe your past experience. Action verbs grab a reader's attention. They have force and demonstrate that you are a "leader" type of person. Typical action verbs that appear in résumés include *developed, presided, arranged, researched, planned, coordinated, directed, managed, supervised, implemented,* and *trained*. An example of action verb usage in a job description might be:

ASSISTANT MANAGER; ACME RESTAURANT, *Anytown, USA.* Hired and trained restaurant personnel. Implemented and organized new system for employee scheduling. Supervised all aspects of customer satisfaction. Responsible for accounting for more than $5,000 in receipts nightly.

You can use action verbs to describe your past work experience and to detail your educational background.

ANYSTATE UNIVERSITY, *Anytown, USA.* Candidate for B.A. degree in Communications (degree expected June 1991). Presided over class social committee. Researched the effects of television advertising on teenagers.

THE RÉSUMÉ HEADING: Résumé experts disagree whether or not to label your résumé with a bold "RÉSUMÉ" at the top of the page. As a general rule, any employer with half a brain will recognize a résumé for what it is. Thus there is really no need to waste space with a title. The one exception is if you do not want your current employer to know that you are searching for another position. In this case, labeling your résumé "CONFIDENTIAL RÉSUMÉ" signals a potential employer not to contact your present boss.

Your résumé should start with your full name, address, and phone number (with area code). Don't use nicknames or suffixes such as "Jr." The address and phone you list on your résumé should be accurate and current. If you are away from home frequently or are afraid your roommate won't give you messages, use an answering service or an answering machine with a crisp, businesslike message. Try not to use your Talking Heads cassette as background music to your answering machine message. A post office box is useful if you don't have an established address or if you move frequently.

Aside from the heading, the other categories of information on a résumé are fairly routine. As a general rule, all résumés should include headings for "Education," "Experience," "References," and "Interests." Other optional sections include "Job objective," "Personal information," and "Other." The following pages will help you draft your résumé entries for each section.

EDUCATION: List all schools attended starting with high school. Your most recent school should appear first with previous schools appearing in reverse chronological order. If you have graduated from a school, be sure to note what degree you earned (e.g., high school diploma awarded June 1984; B.A. in Communications awarded June 1987). If you are still in school, your entry should state what degree you expect to earn and when (e.g., high school diploma expected June 1991; B.A. in Communications expected June 1993). If you did well in school, feel free to indicate your grade point average. If you received any awards or were elected to any positions while in school, include this information and highlight it. Obviously, if you do not feel that including your grade point average will help your résumé, omit it.

EXPERIENCE: The experience category on your résumé is where you should list all your prior work experience. List all jobs starting with your present or most recent positions. All previous employers should be listed in reverse chronological order. In addition to actual employers, you can include any volunteer work, community service, or other experience you feel is pertinent. For example, if you are short on work experience but served as a scout troop leader, list that as experience and emphasize your organizational and leadership qualities. While some career counselors suggest this section be entitled "Work Experience" or "Employment Experience," the more general title "Experience" is broader, allowing you to include volunteer and social experience.

REFERENCES: Depending on how long your résumé is, you can either list your references by name, address, and phone number or merely state "References available on request." Before listing a person as a reference on your résumé, obtain their permission to do so. References can either be former employers or respected members of your community who know your abilities and character. Your mother, while probably an enthusiastic supporter, is a poor choice.

INTERESTS: This final section gives you a line or two to list a few of your hobbies, interests, and favorite activities. The purpose of this section is to set you apart from other applicants by demonstrating your individuality. If you enjoy hiking, tennis, and sailing, say so. If you prefer writing poetry and cooking, list that. Should you later have either a personal or phone interview, your interests often become a point of focus for discussion with the employer. If you have an unusual hobby or interest you should not hesitate to list it. One of my good friends enjoyed drawing with charcoal in his free time. The last line on his résumé was "aspiring charcoal artist." While this might seem like a rather bizarre entry, he found that every potential employer with whom he interviewed spent at least a few moments talking about what charcoal drawing was like. If you can get an employer interested in you as a person on any level, you are halfway to landing your job in paradise.

JOB OBJECTIVE: As noted above, a job objective section is optional on a résumé. If space is a problem, this is the first section you should cut. Since your cover letter should address what type of position you are looking for, there is really no reason to repeat that information on your résumé. Also, as you may be simultaneously applying for several different types of jobs with different employers, a job objective statement might force you to print several different versions of your résumé. If you decide to include a job objective statement, show that you are a dedicated and serious candidate by writing something like:

> **JOB OBJECTIVE:** To locate a challenging and rewarding position in the adventure travel industry where my background in working with people of all ages can be utilized effectively.

PERSONAL INFORMATION: Once again, this is an optional section. While some applicants list their age, marital status, and health, this type of information is generally more a hindrance than a help. Information that you might want to include in this section is any first aid or lifesaving certificates that you hold.

OTHER: This last optional category is a catchall that allows you to list any additional information you think will help your case. If you won your local beauty pageant, were an eagle scout, served as chairperson of your church youth group, or have any other honors that don't seem to fit into any other category, list them here.

EXAMPLE 2

JANE DOE

P.O. Box 1212, Anytown, USA 12345 (602) 555-1212

OBJECTIVE

A rewarding position as a **Shore Excursion Leader** on a cruise ship where my training and experience in the hospitality industry could be used to mutual benefit.

SUMMARY OF QUALIFICATIONS

- Possess sound training and successful experience as a professional tour guide and coordinator.
- Able to work well with people on all levels and from a variety of backgrounds.
- Possess excellent knowledge of the intricacies of selling and organizing tours for groups and individuals.
- Effective communication skills . . . particularly adept at rapid and accurate analysis of people and situations.

PROFESSIONAL EXPERIENCE

Tour Director

ABC Tours
Phoenix, Arizona   *February 1986 to Present*
Responsible for organizing and coordinating outdoor tours in and around the resort areas of Arizona, including trip coordination, billing, food and beverage, organized activities, follow-up and customer satisfaction.

Tour Director

Desert Travel   *January 1988 to Present*
Supervise and lead tour groups to Palm Springs area, coordinating all logistical aspects of the tour, including billing and accounting.

EDUCATION

Northern Arizona University, Flagstaff, Arizona
Bachelor of Science, Business and Graphic Communications, December, 1986

PERSONAL

Single   Born 5-21-60   Excellent Health
American Citizen   eager to travel, international or domestic.

INTERESTS

Skiing, golf and travel

EXCELLENT PERSONAL AND PROFESSIONAL REFERENCES FURNISHED ON REQUEST

EXAMPLE 3

JOHN B. DOE

Present Address:	Permanent Address:
P.O. Box 6747	509 Anystreet
Anytown, CA 12345	Anytown, CA 12345
(415) 555-1212	(415) 555-1212

EDUCATION: **Stanford University,** *Stanford, California*
B.A. degree in Human Biology, 1983. Course work includes psychology, biology, public policy, and English.

WINTER BREAK EMPLOYMENT:
1982 (4 weeks)
Jr. Activities Host, *High Seas Cruises, San Francisco, California*
Programmed and conducted daytime activities for children aboard SS *Royal*. Evening duties included general cruise staff responsibilities. Extensive passenger contact.

SUMMER EMPLOYMENT:
Summers,
1983
1982
1981 (6 weeks)
1980 (4 weeks)
Cruise Escort/Tour Conductor, *Acme Travel System, New York City, New York*
Company's sole representative on cruises and tours to Alaska, Bermuda, the Bahamas, California, and Mexico. Responsible for all aspects of client satisfaction. Planned and implemented social activities and shore excursions. Extensive passenger contact.

Summer
1981 (7 weeks)
Intern, *Public Defender Service, Washington D.C.*
Assisted staff attorney in representation of indigent defendants. Informed clients of legal rights. Interviewed government and defense witnesses.

Summers,
1979
1978
1977
Camp Counselor, *YMCA, Anytown, California*
Responsible for 10-40 youths age 7-18 at day, residential, and caravan type camps. Duties included maintaining health and safety of children, programming activities, teaching swimming, crafts, sports, archery, and fishing.

SCHOOL TERM EMPLOYMENT:
3/81–3/82
Advertising Representative, *The Stanford Daily, Stanford, California*
Duties included solicitation of new accounts as well as the service of existing ones. Responsible for more than $25,000 in revenues annually.

ADDITIONAL INFORMATION: Eagle Scout, Boy Scouts of America.
Member Stanford University Marching Band.
Interests include backpacking, skiing, sailing, scuba diving, river rafting, racquetball, and photography.

Letters of Recommendation

While almost none of the employers included in *Jobs in Paradise* specifically requests applicants provide letters of recommendation, a letter sent with your application can often make the difference between a form rejection letter and a job offer. Personnel directors in popular resort areas are often besieged by dozens of unsolicited applications each week. An application that comes complete with a photocopy of a letter of recommendation saves the personnel director the time, trouble, and expense of trying to track down references merely listed on your résumé. For best results, try submitting one or two photocopied letters of recommendation with your application in addition to listing other references on your résumé.

PROFILE OF VINCE REDMAN
SHORE EXCURSION MANAGER, SS *Norway*

"A professional résumé and photograph make the sale."

HOMETOWN: Douglas, Arizona
SCHOOL: University of Arizona (2 years)
Northern Arizona University, B.S. Business & Graphic Communications
JOBS: Bartender
Waiter
Ski Rental Technician (Fairfield Snowbowl)
Ski Instructor (Fairfield Snowbowl)
Tour Director (leader of trips through Southwestern USA)
Tour Director (leader of corporate incentive trips throughout the USA)
Waterbed Salesperson
Shore Excursion Manager (SS *Norway*)

According to Vince Redman the key to landing any job in paradise is to have a "professional-looking résumé and photograph." And Vince should know. He has held such coveted jobs as ski instructor, tour director, and shore excursion manager aboard the longest cruise ship in the world. "I had my résumé prepared by a professional résumé writer and then had it typeset on the best quality paper I could find. Along with my résumé, I would always send a formal studio 5" × 7" photograph and brief cover letter." Obviously, Vince's system worked. "I've never been turned down for a job I really wanted," Vince explains. "When a personnel manager sees a professional-looking résumé and a bright smiling clean-cut face, they give you a call."

Vince uses his résumé and photograph to get the personnel manager's attention and then he follows up with an interview. Both phone and personal interviews have worked for the SS *Norway*'s current shore excursion manager. "For my job aboard the *Norway*, I was going to be in Miami on vacation and requested a personal interview in my cover letter. When I arrived in Miami I simply walked into Norwegian Cruise Lines' office and to my surprise they hired me on the spot."

Vince's second secret has been to target his application toward a specific job. "I always request a specific job for which I believe my background qualifies me. I use my cover letter to explain how my experience will make me a valuable asset to the company. However, in the event that the specific job I sought was not available I generally state that I would be willing to consider any other job the personnel director thought appropriate for me. For example, when applying to work aboard the SS *Norway*, I wrote: 'I am seeking a challenging position of responsibility as a shore excursion manager on a cruise ship where my experience and abilities as a tour director and coordinator can be effectively utilized. An entry-level crew position will also be considered.'

"My ski resort jobs were great and they were the easiest to get. Anyone can get hired at a ski resort. Most people, if they have a bright smile and pleasant personality, can get hired instantly. However, I know an awful lot of ski resort employees who got hired by stating in their applications that they had relevant experience that they didn't in fact have." While the deceit that some of Vince's friends practiced may have proved effective, his success in landing exotic jobs by means of a professional-looking photograph and résumé should convince you that honesty and professionalism can land almost any job.

A letter of recommendation can come from a past employer or any respected member of your community who knows your character and abilities. You'll find that most former employers are all too happy to write you a generic letter praising your virtues and ignoring your faults. When you ask someone to write a letter, don't be afraid to ask them to address specific traits that you think are important in landing your dream job. Most of the job listings given here include a brief statement by the employer describing what qualities they seek in employees. These are the traits that you want addressed in a good letter of recommendation.

While each employer has a slightly different idea of what traits make a perfect applicant, most include honesty, willingness to work hard, maturity, sense of humor, neat appearance, professionalism, and an energetic friendly personality on their wish list.

The bottom line answer to the question of whether to include letters of recommendation with your application is simple: If you can get a good, enthusiastic letter from a former employer or person who knows you well, send it! This advice holds true regardless of whether or not the employer requests references in their *Jobs in Paradise* listing. A good letter of reference can never hurt your application and will often make the difference in landing your dream job.

Smile! A Photograph Is Worth a Thousand Words

Many people are offended by an employer's request that applicants send a photograph of themselves, and several states have made this practice illegal. Some contend that employers use photographs as a subtle form of racial or ethnic discrimination. After all, what use is there in prohibiting employers from requesting an applicant's race or ethnic background if they can clearly see it in a photograph?

Although discrimination is not unknown in the tourism and hospitality industries, after discussions of this problem with hundreds of employers, I am convinced that it is very rare. In fact, many employers seek diversity in their staffs.

Most employers simply want a photograph to help them associate faces with the hundreds of résumés they receive. If they can attach a face with your résumé, they are much more likely to remember your application when the next job opening rolls around.

Perhaps the main reason employers request photographs is that almost all tourism and hospitality employers want clean-cut, wholesome-looking employees. Since interviews are often impossible for applicants who live hundreds of miles from a job site, a photograph reassures an employer that the person they are considering is clean-cut and knows how to dress properly.

The bottom line is that if you live too far away from the employer to interview in person, you should always send a photograph with your application or résumé. Regardless of whether or not the employer specifically requests a photograph in the *Jobs in Paradise* listing, you should send one. While many employers are willing to interview applicants by phone, they at least like to be able to see who they are talking to. Note that while some states make it illegal for employers to request a photo, it is never unlawful to voluntarily submit one.

Your photograph can be either a regular glossy print, a 5" × 7", or an 8" × 10". While face only or waist-up photographs are the most commonly accepted, cruise lines often request full body shots.

When having your picture taken, either use a professional studio photographer or have a friend with a good camera take an entire roll of you so you can choose the best shot. When considering what to wear in the photograph, remember that most employers are looking for that "all-American boy or girl next door image." Richard Ramsey of Disneyland's employment office advises applicants to "dress like the people at the company you are applying to." While that doesn't mean that Disneyland applicants should necessarily walk into the employment office dressed as Mickey Mouse, they should wear something casual yet conservative. When Vince Redman applied for a job as a shore excursion manager for Norwegian Cruise Lines (NCL) he dressed in a blue blazer and beige slacks, the same basic outfit that NCL's shipboard staff wears. "I wanted them to look at me and picture me as an NCL employee. By wearing something close to the NCL uniform, I helped the employer picture me working for him," explains Vince. A woman could create this same image by wearing a beige skirt with a blue blouse or sweater.

While a photograph alone will never land you a job, it can greatly help your application and, unless you belong to the "they will have to take me as I am" school, it will rarely hurt.

The Shotgun Approach to Applying

As you can probably guess, many of the jobs described in this book are highly sought after and competition to get them is keen. Thus, your best chances of landing a position lie in sending out as many applications as possible and in being politely persistent with follow-up phone calls and letters.

The number of applications you should send out is a personal decision and will vary according to your level of experience, your availability, and your willingness to commit for a fairly long term of employment. Another factor in determining how many applications to send is what position you are seeking. If you insist on applying only for "glamour positions," be prepared for lots of rejections before you land a job. However, if you are willing to take any position the employer might offer, you'll find a job much more quickly. Finally, some resort areas are overwhelmed with applications while others are starving for potential employees.

The shotgun approach to applying for a job means sending out a number of applications at once, at least fifteen. However, those fifteen applications should be spread over employers in different regions. For example, if you decide you want to work at a ski resort, you should apply to ski areas in several geographic areas at once (for example California, Colorado, and Vermont). Additionally, you might consider requesting your dream position from some of the employers while stating a willingness to accept an alternate position from others.

The Card File System

While the shotgun approach to a job search is the best method of assuring that you land a position, it is also extremely difficult to organize. Often applicants who send out large numbers of applications fail to properly follow up with letters or phone calls. To help organize your job search, try using the card file system described below, which is fairly simple to create.

For each job application, create a 3" × 5" index card. On the card note the name and address of the company you have applied to, the specific position you requested, the name of the personnel director (if available), and the date you mailed your application. If the *Jobs in Paradise* listing for a company tells you how soon applicants can expect a response, put that information on the card as well.

The next step is to write on the back of the card the date on which follow-up action is required and a brief notation as to what action is needed. For example, if a job for which you have applied specifies that applicants can expect a response in two weeks, put a follow-up date two weeks in the future on the back of the card for a follow-up letter or phone call. If the company profile doesn't indicate how soon responses are given, follow up fourteen days after you mail your application (allow twenty days for applications mailed to other countries). If you still do not receive a response after your initial follow-up, flag that card for another follow-up call or letter every two to four weeks. This occasional call or letter to the company will help ensure your résumé remains in their active file. Also, it tells the potential employer that you are truly serious about the position, and all employers have a preference for enthusiastic employees.

Once you have created your cards, organize them chronologically according to the date that follow-up action is required. By creating a card file system, you will avoid forgetting to follow up on one or more of your applications. The card file system also provides an easy reference source for recalling the last date you contacted the employer. This helps avoid the opposite pitfall of following up too frequently and becoming a pest. While some employers admitted that they have hired staff members who called frequently to get them off their backs, such hirings are rare. As a general rule, you want to remind the employer that you are still interested and keep your application in the employer's mind. On the other hand, you don't want to call so often that the employer cringes at the sound of his or her phone ringing.

Don't Forget the Follow-Up Call

An employer receives your application and is interested. Unfortunately, he doesn't have a current opening for you. Although you will probably receive a reassuring letter telling you that your résumé will be kept on file, the ball is now in your court. The sad truth is that all too often, while the employer really does want to hire you, he may receive several applications from other qualified people and have those fresh in his mind when the next position becomes available.

If you want your application kept on the top of the employer's application file, you'll have to call periodically to remind them that you are still interested. When calling, ask for the personnel director or the individual to whom you addressed your application. Use the phone call to make certain that the employer knows you are still interested. If the employer seems interested, ask if they have any idea of when a position might become available. The profile interview with Dunk Island Australia Resort employer Michael Haberland demonstrates how effective and important this follow-up phone call can be.

Interviewing Made Easy

While most of the jobs listed in *Jobs in Paradise* do not require a personal interview, you should try to interview whenever possible. An interview, whether by phone or in person, serves to reassure an employer that you have the social and speaking skills necessary for working with the public. It is your people skills that the interviewer is testing. As Disneyland recruiter Richard Ramsey explained, "An employer can always teach any necessary job-related skills, but people skills can't be taught."

The personal interview also gives you the additional opportunity to demonstrate that you know how to both dress and groom prop-

PROFILE OF MICHAEL HABERLAND
OPERATIONS MANAGER,
DUNK ISLAND AUSTRALIA RESORT

"A promise to stay is an applicant's best shot."

When Michael Haberland decided to spend his three-month summer break working as a bartender on one of Australia's Great Barrier Reef islands, he had no idea that seven years later he'd be managing one of those scenic resort islands. "It's not a bloody holiday and sometimes the work is hard, but living on a tropical paradise with a great staff and an international clientele is well worth it," he recounts. Dunk Island Resort receives more than sixty applications a week without ever advertising for staff help. "Sometimes it seems that everyone who visits our island dreams of living and working here.

"Like most resorts, we view our staff as ambassadors for both our island and Australia. We look for a clean-cut staff with a bright, pleasant personality." Although the resort receives almost twenty-four applications for each vacant position, most of them are immediately discounted because the applicant wants to stay only a month or two. "It's not worth it for us to hire someone who tells us from the outset that they're leaving in a few weeks. By the time they are settled in and are fully trained, they'll be gone." To be seriously considered, applicants most often state that they hope to stay for an eight-month minimum. According to Michael, a promise to stay is an applicant's best shot at landing a job.

Haberland encourages applicants to call and check on the status of their applications. "If you received a letter indicating that we are interested in you and are keeping your application on file, a phone call every six weeks or so will let us know that you are still interested."

Michael concedes, "We once hired a girl from New Zealand who had phoned us every day for six months to check on the status of her application. We figured we had to give her a job just so she could pay her phone bill!"

PROFILE OF JEFFRY MARK RUNDELL
CRUISE DIRECTOR

"Persistence pays off."

> **HOMETOWN:** Pensacola, Florida
> **SCHOOL:** Louisiana State University
> **JOBS:** Radio Announcer
> Bartender
> Disk Jockey (MV *Atlantic*)
> Cruise Staff/Cruise Director (SS
> *Galileo* and SS *Britanis*)

Be persistent is Jeff's number one tip to any aspiring applicant. "Most of the people I know who work aboard ship got their jobs by pestering the cruise lines until it was easier to hire them than to continue putting them off! Also persistence pays off because cruise lines often tend to hire at the last minute." In Jeff's case his application timing was impeccable. "I Federal Expressed a résumé and a demo tape of my disk jockey skills to the ship's entertainment agent and they called me the day they received it. I joined my first ship three days later!" Jeff's story is not unusual. Many new cruise ship employees tell stories of being given only a day's notice that they had been hired. It takes an adventurous, outgoing personality to pack up one's belongings and head off to the high seas with only a few hours to reflect on one's decision!

Cruise ship living seems to suit Jeff to a tee. "I've never regretted my decision to work at sea. This is the ideal job for travel, meeting new and exciting people, and putting an end to the mundane rigamarole of shoreside, day-to-day existence." However, despite the many advantages of shipboard life, Jeff warns of the limits of cruise ship jobs. "The toughest part of any ship job is having no regular contact with your family and friends." Nonetheless, Jeff wouldn't trade in his cruise staff job for any other. "Be prepared for a drastic change of lifestyle and just roll with the changes and enjoy!"

erly. While many of the jobs you apply for may be too far away to allow for a personal interview, you should try to meet the employer whenever possible. Many college students seeking summer employment arrange for personal interviews during their spring break vacations. A few summer employees interviewed during the researching of *Jobs in Paradise* even indicated that they used their Christmas vacations to interview with distant employers.

When interviewing in person, dress conservatively. Even if you are applying for an outdoor-type job such as a whitewater river guide, conservative dress is appropriate. While a coat and tie are not necessary for many resort area job interviews, you should always be dressed in neat and clean clothes. Never wear shorts or a T-shirt to a job interview.

The personal interview is your chance to make a positive first impression on the employer. Stein Erikson Lodge Personnel Director Cindy Dahle explains, "I look for applicants with social skills. When you meet me, shake my hand. When we are talking, smile."

Regardless of whether your interview is in person or by phone, always speak with confidence in yourself and your abilities. It is your task to convince the employer that your skills, enthusiasm, and energy can be a valuable asset. Your skills and dedication are conveyed through your self-confidence as much as through your words. Your energy and enthusiasm are judged by your alertness and interest level. You can let an employer know you are seriously interested by asking intelligent questions. To do this effectively, learn something about the company before you interview. Use your questions to let the employer know that you know something about his or her company. In other words, do your homework!

Ask about your potential job duties and responsibilities rather than about your salary and perks. The time to ask about wages and perks is after the employer has made you a job offer, *not before.* Other good questions include what opportunities for future advancement and training are available—but be cautious. As Stein Erikson Lodge Personnel Director Cindy Dahle noted, "I want to be sure that an applicant is seriously interested in the job being offered, not just the possibility of another job in the future."

Finally, if you interview in person, don't fidget or watch your hands. Look the interviewer in the eye when you speak. While normal hand gestures are fine, avoid holding your hands over your mouth. Your gestures and stature should reflect your self-confidence.

Other Items to Send

For application instructions that conclude with "send SASE," applicants should send a self-addressed, stamped envelope with their application. When a listing includes the designation "send SARP," applicants should send a self-addressed, stamped response postcard. A SARP is designed to allow employers to respond conveniently and easily to your application. You can have these postcards printed inexpensively at any local copy or printing center or you can handwrite them on blank postcards that can be purchased from any post office.

Enclosing an SARP with your application greatly increases the chances of receiving a reply to your application. Many employers are too busy to reply to every unsolicited application. This postcard makes it easy for an employer to tell you the exact status of your application.

"Passport, Please"

While the majority of the job opportunities described in *Jobs in Paradise* are located in the United States and Canada, some foreign employers are also included. Foreign employers are only included when they have indicated a willingness to hire foreigners who have proper work permits and visas.

Although, while researching *Jobs in Paradise,* I met scores of Canadians working in the United States and just as many Americans working in Canada, it is difficult to do so legally. However, there has been some talk recently that the United States and Canada may enter into an agreement that would allow easier access to jobs across the border. U.S. citizens looking for the latest information on job opportunities in Canada should contact the Canadian Embassy, 501 Pennsylvania Avenue NW, Washington D.C. 20001; telephone (202) 682-1740. Canadians interested in working in the United States should contact

PROFILE OF CINDY DAHLE
PERSONNEL DIRECTOR,
STEIN ERIKSON LODGE, PARK CITY, UTAH

"Impress me during your interview."

Unlike many resort area employers, the Stein Erikson Lodge almost always requires a personal interview before making a job offer. Personnel Director Cindy Dahle is responsible for interviewing the lodge's many applicants.

"While an applicant's experience is important, the key is their customer relations skills. The first impression an applicant makes is the most important. I want an applicant who smiles during the interview and shakes my hand when they walk in the door. I'm also impressed by an applicant who has the good manners to send me a thank-you note after an interview."

Ms. Dahle understands that requiring a personal interview causes difficulties for some applicants. "If someone sends in an application from out of state, I would be willing to talk to them on the phone before asking them to fly out. I can usually give someone some inclination as to their job chances before they travel all the way here."

Follow-up phone calls are also very important to Cindy. "I suggest applicants follow up on their applications with a phone call every month or so before the peak season begins. Once we are in the middle of our high season, an applicant might want to call every one or two weeks."

The other advice that Cindy offers to applicants is to complete their application forms fully and be specific about which jobs they are interested in. "I don't want to see an application form that keeps saying 'see résumé' on it. It makes my job easier if an applicant takes the time to answer each question on the form, even if that same information appears on their résumé. Moreover, an applicant should be specific as to what position they want here. An applicant who simply applies for 'any available position' is very difficult to evaluate," explains Cindy.

PROFILE OF RICHARD RAMSEY
DISNEYLAND CASTING OFFICE

"People skills can't be taught."

Richard Ramsey in a man with a mission. His mission: to find the best and brightest college students from across the country and initiate them into the Disney family. Through Disney's College Relations Department, Disneyland and Disney World attempt to give students who live far from either the California or Florida parks an opportunity to work as a Disney cast member. "At Disney we don't have employees. Our staff members are cast members who either work 'on stage' (in the public view) or 'back stage' (behind the scenes)."

Although skills are important, Disney is also concerned with finding people who believe in the company's commitment to creating the finest in family entertainment and are sincerely eager to make others happy. As Ramsey explains, "People skills are really the key to landing a job here. We can teach someone to dress properly, we can teach the skills necessary to work in a Disney park, but people skills are extremely difficult to teach." According to Ramsey's advice the essential element in landing a Disney job is to demonstrate that you have the ability to work well with the public and as a team player. It's that bright Disney smile that is essential in any applicant.

Although Ramsey believes that anyone can be taught how to dress for a job, "a proper and conservative appearance are extremely helpful in impressing an interviewer. I generally advise applicants when interviewing to wear what the company employees wear."

"A Disney entry on a résumé always looks good. We are known around the world for our dedicated and friendly staff. We want cast members who will share the spirit of Disney . . . the Disney philosophy and commitment to entertaining our guests and creating 'The Happiest Place on Earth!' "

Name of Employer

STAMP

Your Name
Address
City, State, Zip Code

SAMPLE FRONT OF POSTCARD

EMPLOYER RESPONSE CARD

[ ] We have received your application and will notify you as soon
as a decision has been reached.

[ ] Please phone_____ (name) at
_____ (phone #) for a phone interview.

[ ] We are sorry but we do not have any current openings. We
will keep your application on file for future reference.

[ ] Thank you for your interest. Unfortunately your qualifications
do not presently meet our needs.

[ ] Other _____
_____

SAMPLE BACK OF POSTCARD

the U.S. Embassy in Canada at 100 Wellington Street, Ottowa, Ontario, K1P 5T1, Canada; telephone (613) 238-5335.

While space does not permit a detailed discussion of the regulations and restrictions for working in every possible country, there

are several excellent sources of information. The Council on International Education Exchange (CIEE) publishes a book entitled *Work, Study, Travel Abroad—The Whole World Handbook*. The book is an invaluable source of information on the various requirements for working abroad. The book is published by St. Martin's Press and is available at any major bookstore or through any of the following CIEE offices:

New York CIEE Office
35 West 8th St.
New York, NY 10011
(212) 254-2525

Los Angeles CIEE Office
1093 Broxton Ave.
Los Angeles, CA 90024
(213) 208-3551

Chicago CIEE Office
29 E. Delaware Place
Chicago, IL 60611
(312) 951-0585

Austin CIEE Office
1904 Guadalupe #6
Austin, TX 78705
(512) 472-4931

Minneapolis CIEE Office
1501 University Ave. SE
Room 300
Minneapolis, MN 55414
(612) 379-2323

Boston CIEE Office
729 Boylston St.
Boston, MA 02116
(617) 266-1926

CIEE also offers a wide variety of programs for U.S. students to work abroad. When you participate in the CIEE program, they take care of obtaining all the necessary work permits and visas. CIEE currently offers programs for Americans to work in a wide variety of countries including Australia, New Zealand, France, Germany, England, and Ireland. For information on CIEE's foreign work programs, contact them at any of the offices listed above.

The Job
Listings

High Adventure

~~~~~~~~~

ANNAPOLIS SAILING SCHOOL
(Long Island, New York; Annapolis, Maryland; St. Petersburg, Florida; Charleston, South Carolina; St. Croix Virgin Islands; Clear Lake, Texas)

Seasonal (Summer)

Do you long for the freedom of the wide blue sea? This large sailing instruction school specializes in three- to nine-day-long yachting courses. Some courses involve living aboard the boats while cruising long distances; others involve day sailing out of the company's seven schools. Annapolis Sailing School currently runs 24-foot sloops and large cruising yachts including O'Day 37's and Gulf Star 50's and 60's.

SPECIFICS: Annapolis hires over 200 staff members including sailing instructors and boat maintenance and prep people for its Long Island locations. Most positions are seasonal, lasting from May through September. Rainbow instructors teach day sailing on 24-foot sloops and require sailing experience but no special licenses. Rainbow instructors earn $30 to $40 per day. Live-aboard cruising instructors require U.S. Coast Guard licenses and earn $50 to $60 per day. Boat maintenance/boat prep positions are available at $5 per hour with no special experience necessary. (Salaries subject to change.)

INSIDER TIPS: "Persons with a strong interest in sailing as well as sailing experience have the best shot at a position with us. A neat, clean, and sober appearance is extremely important. Responsibility and reliability are necessary qualifications as well as a friendly and outgoing personality."

PERKS: Employees may rotate to other branch offices (listed below).

TO APPLY: Applicants should send résumés and references that can be checked (photo optional) to Personnel Manager, Annapolis Sailing School, P.O. Box 3334, Annapolis, Maryland 21403; (301)267-7205. Be sure to indicate which location you are applying for. The company has branches at Annapolis, Maryland; St. Petersburg, Florida; Charleston, South Carolina; St. Croix, U.S. Virgin Islands; and Clear Lake, Texas. A personal interview is usually required; applicants may interview with the nearest branch office.

ATLANTIS SUBMARINES INTERNATIONAL
(St. Thomas, U.S. Virgin Islands)
Year-Round

For those who have always wanted to run silent and deep, here is the opportunity. Sub-Aquatics is one of the few high-volume tourist submarine companies in the world. Their Atlantis submarines carry twenty-eight to forty-six passengers on sightseeing dives 150 feet below the ocean surface. The company currently operates tourist submarines in Hawaii, St. Thomas, Barbados, the Grand Cayman islands, and Guam. Sub-Aquatics also plans to expand to other tropical locations in the near future.

SPECIFICS: Atlantis Submarines now employs approximately 175 workers at all sites. With the addition of their Hawaii operation this number will increase significantly. For landlubbers, Atlantis Submarines offer land-based positions in administration (ticketing, reservations, and bookkeeping), sales, and marketing. Those who have dreamed of venturing "down under" no longer need travel to Australia. Marine and diving experience is necessary for Atlantis Submarines' passenger attendants. Other underwater submarine positions include pilots and copilots. The company is willing to train copilots who have an interest in submersibles and a background in marine electronics. Pilots must meet the same requirements and have their Captain's license and submarine certification. For those who are intrigued by the deep blue sea but would rather stay on top of it, the company hires skippers to operate small passenger ferries between the submarines and shore. Skippers must have a current U.S. Coast Guard captain's certificate, mechanical experience, and negative drug test results.

INSIDER TIPS: Atlantis Submarines prefers applicants with a strong interest in the submersible field. Management notes, "we are not interested in transient applicants who want a vacation in the sun. St. Thomas and Hawaii locations can only hire U.S. citizens."

PERKS: Excitement and adventure alone could put this employer on the top of your list. Where else can you enjoy the beauty and serenity of the undersea world every day without even getting wet? Although you could join the navy, their submarines don't have windows! Management reports an excellent benefits package. This growing company offers numerous opportunities for promotion and transfers to new locations.

TO APPLY: Applicants for passenger attendants, skippers, or all land-based positions should send a cover letter, résumé, photo, and SARP to: Operations Manager, Atlantis Submarine, Havensite Mall Building #6, St. Thomas, U.S. Virgin Islands 00802; (809) 776-2896. Pilots and copilots should apply to: Sub-Aquatics Development Corporation (tm Atlantis), ATTN: Rick Shafer, 191 W. 6th Avenue, Vancouver, British Columbia V5Y 1K3, Canada; (604) 875-1367. Pilots may also send résumé to St. Thomas address as above.

BACKROADS
(Berkeley, California)

Seasonal (Summer) and
Year-Round

For more than twelve years, Backroads has been offering the ultimate in active vacations. Backroads' three-color brochures describe its biking, walking, and cross-country ski trips operated. The company specializes in camping and inn trips that take advantage of Backroads' fleet of nineteen custom-designed trailers. Trips cover regions as diverse as California and Vermont to China and Bali. In all, more than fifty-two itineraries are offered. For cyclists with special interests, there are mountain bike trips, singles trips, family trips, and even Napa Valley mud bath and wine tasting trips.

SPECIFICS: Backroads hires about twenty-five new tour leaders each year to fill its one hundred and forty-person staff (eighty tour leaders plus sixty office employees). Approximately eight hundred applications are received annually. Jobs are available for both summer seasonal (leaders) as well as year-round (office) employment. Summer staff start work between May and July and work through either September or October. All applications for summer employment are due by April 1.

INSIDER TIPS: According to Backroads, the key to the company's success is the "energy, charisma, and natural leadership qualities [of their employees] plus an exhaustive, nonstop training program that teaches finesse in the culinary skills, expertise in bicycle repair, plus proficiency in driving, public speaking, and first aid. Our leaders are unquestionably the best trained in the field. Backroads prides itself on a style of service and warm hospitality that reflects the winning personality of every Backroads staff member."

PERKS: Backroads provides housing and meals while leaders are on trips. Employees may use the company's fleet of bicycles. Dedicated staff members often receive tips from guests at the end of a trip.

TO APPLY: Applicants should either write for an official application form or send a cover letter and résumé to Kris Anderson, Backroads, 1516 5th Street, Berkeley, California 94710-1713; (510) 527-1555.

BALLOON AVIATION OF THE NAPA VALLEY
(Napa, California)
**Seasonal (Summer) and
Year-Round**

With the sun still over the horizon and the patches of fog just beginning to dissipate, the pilot guides our brightly colored balloon slowly toward the ground. "No mean horses or angry neighbors—prepare to land!" He pulls a lever to slow our descent and glides gently toward earth. Balloon Aviation of the Napa Valley (BANV) is one of California's largest commercial hot air balloon companies. The company operates both BANV and another Napa balloon company, Adventures Aloft. Passengers are treated to early morning sunrise flights over California's famous vineyards, followed by champagne celebrations.

SPECIFICS: The company's seven to nine balloons require a crew of forty-four aeronauts to staff. Positions are available for balloon pilots, ground crew staff, and champagne celebration hostesses. Pilots must have a FAA balloon pilot license and have extensive balloon experience. The company offers pilot training for a cost of approximately $3,000. (The minimum age for flight training is fourteen years.) Ground crew members are responsible for setting up and tearing down balloons and following the airborne groups in chase vans. Champagne celebration hostesses are responsible for setting up and organizing the post-flight champagne celebrations. Jobs are available for both year-round and seasonal (April through November) employment.

INSIDER TIPS: "Due to the shortage of large landing areas in the Napa Valley, pilots must have extensive balloon experience in difficult landings. Ground crew staffers must be big, husky high school and college guys or girls who are capable of moving the large, heavy balloons. Hostesses check in our passengers, take payments, and organize the logistics of our post-flight celebrations." Most ground crew staff do this for love of the sport, not for the money. There is almost no turnover in pilot positions.

PERKS: All employees enjoy free flights during the company's low season.

TO APPLY: Applicants should send a cover letter, résumé, and photograph to Matt Stahlecker, Director of Ground Operations, Balloon Aviation of the Napa Valley, P.O. Box 3298, Napa, California 94558; (707) 252-7067. A personal interview is required for all applicants.

CALIFORNIA SAILING ACADEMY
(Marina del Rey, California)
Seasonal (Summer and Winter) and Year-Round

If you've dreamed of spending your days sailing the blue waters of the Pacific, California Sailing Academy (CSA) could have just the job for you. CSA has more than one hundred sailing yachts and teaches everything from one-day introductory courses to multiday open ocean courses in advanced sailing and ocean navigation. While most courses are taught at the company's Marina del Rey base, courses frequently take overnight yacht charters to nearby Catalina Island.

SPECIFICS: California Sailing Academy receives approximately twenty applications each year for its three or four annual job openings. The CSA staff totals ten employees. Jobs are available for both summer and winter seasonal work as well as year-round employment. Applications are accepted for boat cleaners (no experience necessary), boat maintenance staff (excellent mechanical skills required), sailing instructors (excellent sailors with lots of sailing experience), and office staff. Wages vary according to position and experience.

INSIDER TIPS: California Sailing Academy has a wide variety of positions available ranging from boat cleaner to professional sailing instructor. CSA instructors are all professionally trained and certified. They take their jobs seriously and are concerned about a student's sailing progress. All instructors hold American Sailing Association certification as well as U.S. Coast Guard licenses.

PERKS: All staff are entitled to free sailing instruction and free use of the company's large fleet of boats.

TO APPLY: Applicants should either write for an official application form or send a cover letter, résumé, and photograph to Paul Miller or Jeanne Leighton, California Sailing Academy, 14025 Panay Way, Marina del Rey, California 90292; (213) 821-3433. Management responds to all applications in two to four weeks.

CAPTAIN ZODIAC
(Islands of Kauai, Maui, and Hawaii, Hawaii)
Seasonal (All Seasons) and
Year-Round

Captain Zodiac offers unique zodiac raft expeditions to some of Hawaii's most secluded and spectacular coastlines. The company operates fast-moving zodiacs on sightseeing, whale watching, snorkling, dolphin watching, and backpacking expeditions. On some days the seas are calm and suited for relaxing sightseeing, while other days bring rough and wild water ideal for thrillseekers and adventurers.

SPECIFICS: Captain Zodiac employs up to ninety staff members during its annual summer and winter peak seasons. Jobs are available for both year-round as well as seasonal staff. While seasonal personnel are hired for any three-month or longer period, the January through March whale watching and summer sightseeing seasons are the busiest. Applications are accepted for zodiac captains, zodiac crew, and sales personnel. Captains must have U.S. Coast Guard skipper's licenses and crew members are required to have valid first aid and lifesaving certificates.

INSIDER TIPS: The company looks for dedicated personnel with a true aloha spirit. Captain Zodiac staffers are known for their friendly and interesting personalities. All staff members must be excellent at customer relations and be able to deal with up to 250 passengers per day. Captains and crew must be able to work outdoors in the sun on a daily basis.

PERKS: Free trips and guest passes are available at management's discretion.

TO APPLY: Applicants should either write for an official application or send a cover letter, résumé, photograph, and xerox copy of all relevant licenses and certificates to Personnel, Captain Zodiac, P.O. Box 1776, Lahina, Maui, Hawaii 96767; (808) 667-5862. For positions in Kona write P.O. Box 5612, Kailuah-Kona, Hawaii 96740; (808) 329-3199. For jobs at the company's Kauai location address applications to P.O. Box 456, Hanalei, Kauai, Hawaii 96714; (808) 826-9371.

COUNTRY CYCLING TOURS
(New York, New York)
Seasonal (Summer) and Year-Round

Country Cycling Tours offers a wide variety of bicycling and walking tours through the United States, Europe, China, the Mid-East, and the Caribbean. The company's American trips cover areas such as Cape Cod, Vermont, Pennsylvania, Massachusetts, and the Great River Road leading to New Orleans. European treks include areas such as Holland, France, England, and Ireland. Caribbean cycling trips whisk guests away to the warm sunshine of Guadeloupe.

SPECIFICS: Country Cycling Tours (CCT) receives eighty to one hundred applications each year for its twenty to thirty job openings. The company's staff totals between forty and fifty employees. While there are a few year-round positions, most jobs are summer seasonal, lasting from June through September or October. According to CCT staffer Gerald Brooks, "We are looking for applicants to guide cycling and walking tours in the United States and Europe." Wages vary according to the applicant's commitment.

INSIDER TIPS: CCT looks for accomplished cyclists and walkers with excellent group support skills and a knowledge of bicycle repair. "CCT tour leaders are responsible, knowledgeable, safety-conscious, and fun-loving men and women. Our leaders come from all walks of life. Most have traveled extensively. Whatever they do, they share a love for bicycles and bicycle touring and for walking and the outdoors. They are interesting people who are interested in [our guests]. We're proud of our staff." Applicants who are able to interview in person are given first consideration for job openings.

PERKS: The company pays for all travel expenses for guides.

TO APPLY: Applicants should send a cover letter and résumé to Gerald Brooks, Country Cycling Tours, 140 West 83rd Street, New York, New York 10024; (212) 874-5151. All applicants receive responses, according to CCT management.

CRUISER BOB'S ORIGINAL HALEAKALA DOWNHILL
(Island of Maui, Hawaii)
Year-Round

If you've been searching for a job that you can literally cruise through, look no further. Cruiser Bob's operates daily bicycle trips down Haleakala volcano. In a mere ten hours, a Cruiser Bob's cycle trip covers more than 38 miles and a 10,023-foot vertical drop in elevation. While many companies have tried to imitate these exciting excursions, Cruiser Bob's is still the undisputed king of the volcano.

SPECIFICS: The company has approximately thirty-six employees at any given time. The most frequent job openings are for van drivers, who pick up groups at local hotels, drive them up the volcano, and then follow the cyclists down the mountain in chase vans. Van drivers start at $6.00 per hour plus benefits and are trained as cruise leaders if they stay with the company long enough. All tour participants must be at least five feet tall and able to ride a 26-inch mountain bike.

INSIDER TIPS: Management reports that cruise leader positions are generally long-term, career-oriented jobs. Cruise leaders must be extremely safety conscious and know the volcano intimately. Most employees start as van drivers. Cruiser Bob's prefers drivers familiar with Maui roads, history, and scenery, but will consider newcomers to the island if they are well versed in island sites, roads, and history. Employees must know (or learn) the location of all 147 major hotels on the island. Most importantly, staff members must be extremely responsible. All applicants must have a PUC medical certificate and a clean driver's record. A State of Hawaii First Responder Certificate is very helpful. First Responder courses are frequently given through the YMCA and fire and police departments in Hawaii. The course lasts forty hours and generally costs about $125.

TO APPLY: Applicants should apply in person to Cruiser Bob's, 505 Front Street, Lahina, Maui 96761; (808) 579-8444.

FOUR SEASONS CYCLING
(Williamsburg, Virginia)

**Seasonal (Summer and Fall) and
Year-Round**

Adventure travel is a fascinating business and Four Seasons Cycling presents a unique opportunity to become part of this fast-growing industry. This medium-sized bicycle touring company specializes in trips through Europe and the U.S. mid-Atlantic and southern regions. Four Seasons strives to provide high-quality relaxing vacations with overnight stays at small historic country inns between days of bicycle riding and exploration.

SPECIFICS: Four Seasons Cycling hires four to five new bicycle tour guides each year to fill its staff of eight tour leaders. The company receives more than seventy-five applications annually. To be considered for a guide job, applicants must have both CPR and Red Cross First Aid certificates *before* applying. All applicants must be willing to work from April 1 through November 15. Guides can expect to earn between $4,000 and $5,000 for fifteen weeks of actual work during this period.

INSIDER TIPS: "We want outgoing people who are athletic, highly organized, and detail-oriented. Employees must be able to handle the often unpredictable world that is the travel industry. Good bicycle repair skills, first aid, and an ability to relocate to Williamsburg, Virginia, are also pluses." For serious consideration, applicants should be interested in working at least two years and must be willing to come to Williamsburg for a personal interview.

PERKS: Travel expenses (food and lodging) are covered while leading tours. Bicycles, clothing, and other necessities are available at a discount for full-time leaders.

TO APPLY: Applicants should request an official application form from Jorn Ake, Four Seasons Cycling, P.O. Box 203, Williamsburg, Virginia 23187-0203; (804) 253-2985.

GHOST TOWN SCENIC JEEP TOURS AND RIVER RUNNERS LTD.
(Salida, Colorado)
Seasonal (Summer)

Ghost Town Scenic Jeep Tours/River Runners Ltd. is one of the largest adventure travel companies in Colorado. The company specializes in whitewater trips down the Brown's Canyon and Royal Gorge portions of the Arkansas River and unique four-wheel-drive jeep trips to some of Colorado's long-forgotten ghost towns. Horseback riding, pack trips, and camping are also offered.

SPECIFICS: Ghost Town Scenic Jeep Tours/River Runners receives two hundred applications and hires seventy-five new employees annually. The company employs a staff of more than two hundred. All jobs are summer seasonal and start and finish dates are somewhat flexible between May 1 and September 15. The application deadline is April 15 and employees are hired as needed throughout the year. Applications are accepted for river rafting guides, jeep tour guides (must be at least twenty-five years of age and have Colorado class "S" drivers license), bus drivers (same requirements as for jeep drivers), and office staff (minimum age eighteen, excellent skills with numbers). Starting wages range from $40 to $70 per day.

INSIDER TIPS: "We look for friendly, dependable, responsible, honest applicants who are not afraid of long hours and hard work."

PERKS: Many employees receive customer gratuities. Employees may use the company's equipment on their days off with management approval.

TO APPLY: Applicants should write for an official application from River Runners Ltd., 11150 Highway 50 West, Salida, Colorado 81201; (719) 539-2144 or 539-3788. A photograph must accompany all applications. Management reports responding to all applications within one week.

GRIZZLY RANCH
(Cody, Wyoming)
Seasonal (Summer)

The Grizzly Ranch is not a luxury resort or fancy dude ranch. Rather, the ranch provides a few fortunate guests with a chance to live a true ranch lifestyle. Morning begins with a large ranch breakfast, after which each guest is given his or her own horse and saddle—horseback riding through miles of trails is the favorite activity. Other activities include overnight wilderness pack trips, tennis, hiking, and fishing. The ranch overlooks the rugged peaks of Grizzly Ridge and the Wapiti Valley and is located between Cody, Wyoming, and Yellowstone National Park.

SPECIFICS: The Grizzly Ranch receives fifty applications each year for its five annual job openings. The ranch staff totals seven employees. All positions are summer seasonal and begin between May 15 and June 1. Applications are accepted for ranch cook, cook's helper/waitperson, housekeeper, wrangler, packer, yard worker, and irrigator/farm hand. There is no application deadline and employees are hired throughout the year as needed. Starting salaries range from $400 to $650 per month plus room and board.

INSIDER TIPS: "We are looking for interesting, personable men and women who will treat all of our guests with respect and consideration. We want people who can maintain their enthusiasm and drive throughout the season and work with minimum supervision. Do not apply if you are dishonest, unreliable, afraid to work long hours, or unwilling to make the extra effort to assist someone else in order to get a job done." Long hair for men is not permitted. Use of illegal drugs is strictly prohibited. All applicants must be at least seventeen years old.

PERKS: Room and board are provided for all ranch employees. Most staff receive gratuities from guests.

TO APPLY: Applicants should write for an official application from Rick Felts, Grizzly Ranch, North Fork Route, Cody, Wyoming 82414; (307) 587-3966. A photograph must accompany all applications. Due

to the large number of applications received, management is unable
to respond individually to each.

HELLS CANYON ADVENTURES
(Oxbow, Oregon)
Seasonal (Summer)

Hells Canyon Adventures operates whitewater rafting and jet boat
tours through Hells Canyon on the Snake River at the Oregon/Idaho
border. Jet boat trips involve shooting passengers through the river
canyon in highly maneuverable, high-speed jet boats. Slower scenic
jetboat trips are also available.

SPECIFICS: Hells Canyon Adventures receives between three and six
applications for its four to six annual employee vacancies. The company employs two full-time and four to six part-time staff members.
All jobs are summer seasonal beginning in early May. Applications
must be completed by March 31. Available positions can include jet
boat pilots, whitewater rafting guides, equipment maintenance persons, and trip packers/food preparation persons. Starting wages
range from $4.00 per hour to $50 per day, depending on the position.

INSIDER TIPS: Gary Armacost, president of Hells Canyon Adventures, describes an ideal applicant as someone who "likes the outdoor
life and is willing to work a variety of jobs at staggered hours.
Employees must be able to get along with co-workers and should be
honest, reliable, and hard working."

PERKS: Staff members receive free meals (some positions only) and
housing in shared crew quarters. Staff members are welcome on the
river trips on their days off and are eligible for an end-of-season
bonus program.

TO APPLY: Applicants should send a cover letter and résumé to Gary
Armacost, President, Hells Canyon Adventures, P.O. Box 159,

Oxbow, Oregon 97840; (503) 785-3352. Management reports responding to all applications within approximately thirty days.

McGEE CREEK PACK STATION
(Mammoth Lakes, California)
Seasonal (Summer)

McGee Creek Pack Station offers horseback riding excursions into the spectacular wilderness areas surrounding California's Mammoth Lakes. The company specializes in day rides, overnight full-service pack trips, and "drop" treks into the high Sierras.

SPECIFICS: McGee Creek Pack Station receives forty to fifty applications each year for its ten-person staff. Approximately five new employees are hired annually. All jobs are summer seasonal and run from early June through mid-September. Applications must be completed by May 1. Applications are accepted for day ride guides, packers, backcountry cooks, crew cooks, and stable hands. Starting wages range from $700 to $1,200 per month plus room and board.

INSIDER TIPS: "We work long, hard hours, but the environment, companionship, and outdoor lifestyle with horses and mules make it all worthwhile. We look for hard-working, dedicated, mature applicants with excellent horsemanship skills, superb public relations skills, and a level-headed nature."

PERKS: Housing and meals are provided for employees. Tips are common for some positions.

TO APPLY: Applicants should either write for an official application or send a cover letter and résumé to Lee Roeser, McGee Creek Pack Station, Rt. 1, Box 162, Mammoth Lakes, California 93546; (619) 872-2434. Management reports responding to all applications within two weeks.

M W RANCH, INC.
(Hudson, Colorado)
Seasonal (Summer)

Return to the Old West of 1874 on the crew of the authentic Tusas Trail cattle drive. The M W Ranch offers four-week-long authentic Western cattle drives each summer. This unique ranch offers an opportunity to live as the "drovers" did over a century ago as they pushed their long herds of cattle across the plains to market. Meals are cooked on wood stoves and guest drovers enjoy a trail rodeo and nightly campfire celebrations. Camping is under the stars or in tents. These cattle drives cover more than 60 miles of high plains, gentle prairie, and forested alpine ridges in southern Colorado and northern New Mexico.

SPECIFICS: The M W Ranch hires three to four new staff members each year to fill its nine regular positions. All jobs are seasonal, lasting only during the four annual drives (two in late June, one the last week of August, and one the first week of September). The company reports receiving plenty of applications but few from applicants with horsemanship or ranch abilities. Available positions include chuckwagon cook (must be able to drive a team of horses in rough country and cook over a wood fire for a party of twenty-five or more), wranglers (must be able to manage up to forty head of horses on picket lines, repair tack, perform light veterinary work, and teach horseback riding), and camp boss (must have excellent outdoor skills, be able to set up campsites, and drive a ¾-ton truck with a 16-foot flatbed). Starting wages range from $125 to $800 per week plus on-site expenses.

INSIDER TIPS: The M W Ranch looks for "clean-cut, literate, neat, well-spoken applicants with qualified horse experience and previous guest operations experience. Age and sex are not factors. An extensive amount of 'image' by the staff is involved in re-creating an authentic cattle drive. These are not dude ranch activities nor guided trail rides."

PERKS: On-site housing and meal allowances are provided for employees. Staff members frequently receive gratuities from guest drovers.

TO APPLY: Applicants should write a letter noting all relevant experience to Bill Diekroeger, Owner, M W Ranch, 19451 195th Avenue, Hudson, Colorado 80642; (303) 536-4206. Although not required, a photograph is requested with your letter. Management reports responding to all applications within two weeks.

NATURE EXPEDITIONS INTERNATIONAL (NEI) (Eugene, Oregon)

Seasonal (All Seasons)

Nature Expeditions International (NEI) operates approximately twenty-five various wildlife and cultural expeditions worldwide, each of which has numerous departure dates. Learning is the core of every expedition and expert trip leaders are hired to provide facts, interpretation, and perspective. While an NEI expedition is a vacation, it is also an adventure. NEI treks explore unique natural areas far off the beaten path. Trip participants are given the opportunity to observe wildlife at close range, experience unfamiliar cultures, and share in the excitement of trekking, rafting, snorkeling, camping, and sailing. Expeditions range in length from nine to thirty-two days and include such diverse itineraries and topics as Alaska wildlife, Hawaii natural history, Oregon country, and Southwest Indian country (all in the United States), as well as Amazon expeditions, Andes/ Amazon and the Incas, Ecuador and the Galapagos Islands, ancient Mexico, Baja California gray whales, West Indies natural history, Rwanda and Kilimanjaro walking safari, Annapurna walking expedition, Nepal discovery expedition, Australia natural history, and South Pacific discovery.

SPECIFICS: NEI hires approximately ten to twenty new guides each year. All positions are seasonal and specific working dates depend on trek departure dates. Hiring is done as needed throughout the year. Applications are considered only from individuals with a minimum of a master's degree and two years of college teaching experience. All guides must have expertise in the area their group visits.

INSIDER TIPS: Most trek leaders have either a master's degree or a Ph.D. in biology, natural history, or anthropology. While a minimum of two years of teaching experience is required, most guides have been teaching for three to five years. In-depth experience in the host country being visited is essential and typically means having either lived, worked, or served in the Peace Corps there. NEI looks for individuals with outstanding leadership potential or experience and good group rapport who genuinely care for people. Last but not least, the company seeks people who are sensitive to both people and the environment. As NEI staffer David Roderick wrote, "Applicants with travel experience without a solid academic background are a dime a dozen." As of publication, the company was actively seeking guides for treks to the Amazon (Brazil/Peru), Nepal/Bhutan/Kashmir, and Burma/Thailand.

PERKS: Trek guides are paid $50 to $100 per day plus expenses, which include air and group transportation costs.

TO APPLY: Applicants who meet the minimum requirements cited above should send a cover letter, résumé, and photograph to David Roderick, Nature Expeditions International, P.O. Box 11496, Eugene, Oregon 97440; (503) 484-6529. The company attempts to respond to all applications.

OREGON TRAIL WAGON TRAIN
(Bayard, Nebraska)
Seasonal (Summer)

"Return with us now to those wondrous days of yesteryear" is the watchword of the Oregon Trail Wagon Train. In addition to operating chuckwagon cookouts and Wild West history courses, the company specializes in re-creating wagon train treks across the Oregon Trail from the great prairies to the Rocky Mountains. Wagon trains travel just as they did in 1850. Life on the trail is simple and free . . . and very rugged.

SPECIFICS: The Oregon Trail Wagon Train hires summer seasonal staff to fill its twelve-plus-person staff. The company reports receiving approximately five applications for its one or two annual vacancies. While everyone on the trail does a bit of everything, the company hires camp cooks, maintenance workers, teamsters (draft horse drivers, not the modern truck driver version), wranglers, canoe guides, and trail entertainers (guitar, fiddle, banjo, etc., players). Summer staff members must be available to work from June through September.

INSIDER TIPS: According to Wagon Master Gordon Howard, jobs with the Oregon Trail Wagon Train involve "long hours and hard work." The Wagon Train looks for "outdoor-type people who enjoy hiking and are able to get along well with all people." A genuine interest in Western history is also important. As medical help can be a great distance away, persons with medical conditions requiring immediate medical assistance should not apply.

PERKS: This company offers a rare opportunity to live and work just as the cowboys did over a century ago.

TO APPLY: Applicants should send a cover letter, résumé, and photograph to Gordon Howard, Wagon Master/Manager, Oregon Trail Wagon Train, Rt. 2, Box 502, Bayard, Nebraska 69334; (308) 586-1850. Management reports responding to all applications within two weeks.

PACIFIC CREST OUTWARD BOUND SCHOOL
(Portland, Oregon)
Seasonal (Summer)

Outward Bound was formed in 1941 to teach British merchant seamen how to handle the hardships of wartime life on the North Sea. The men were taught boat handling and rescue techniques as well as physical fitness and the importance of working together as a group. Today there are five Outward Bound schools in the United States plus twenty-four others throughout the world. The schools run wilderness educational courses in mountaineering, backpacking, camping, rock climbing, and whitewater rafting. The Pacific Crest school operates in California, Oregon, and Washington. The school offers courses to all types of individuals ranging from corporate executives to juvenile criminal offenders.

SPECIFICS: The Pacific Crest Outward Bound School receives 250 applications for its fifty-five annual job openings. The school has a total staff of 200. All jobs are summer seasonal (year-round positions are available for experienced Outward Bound personnel). Working dates vary according to the type of program being run. River program staffers lead seven-day courses from April through October on Oregon's Deschutes and Rogue rivers. Mountain program staffers work on eight- to twenty-two-day excursions in California, Oregon, and Washington from May through September. Other programs include Mountain/River Combo (May through September), and Venture (June through August). The company's employee information letter describes the various programs and the unique attributes of each program's leaders. There is no specific application deadline and employees are hired as needed throughout the year. Applications are accepted for chief instructors (salary $62/day and up), instructors (salary $42/day and up), assistant instructors (salary $30/day and up), logistics staff (salary $900 to $1,100/month plus housing), and logistics managers (salary $1,100 to $1,300/month plus housing).

INSIDER TIPS: All instructors must have a current advanced first-aid certification or equivalent, a current CPR certificate, and be at least twenty-one years of age and in excellent physical health. Additional requirements for instructors are previous outdoor expedition experience, an ability to lead novices in both simple and difficult outdoor terrain, high self-esteem, and strong mountaineering or river running skills.

PERKS: Employee perks include participation in an employee equipment discount program, credit union membership, eligibility to apply for the company's expedition fund, a United Kingdom Outward Bound staff exchange program, access to a medical insurance plan, and an ongoing skills-enhancement program.

TO APPLY: Applicants should write or call and request the "Working for PCOBS" informational letter and an official application from the Pacific Coast Outward Bound School, 0110 SW Bancroft Street, Portland, Oregon 97201; (503) 243-1993. For information on other Outward Bound programs across the USA, write Outward Bound, 384 Field Pt. Road, Greenwich, Connecticut 06830.

RED SAIL SPORTS
(Hawaii, Grand Cayman Island, Aruba and the Bahamas)
Year-Round

Red Sail Sports operates water sports and activities centers at numerous hotels throughout Hawaii and the Caribbean. Red Sail activities range from snorkling and sailing to SCUBA diving and horseback riding. This Hyatt-affiliated company relies upon a winning mix of uncompromising standards, first-class service, and state-of-the art equipment to guarantee its success. With a little advance notice, this company even arranges for underwater weddings for SCUBA divers!

SPECIFICS: Numerous positions are available for year-round person-nel at all of the company's locations. Applications are accepted for beach attendants, sailing instructors, SCUBA and snorkling instruc-tors, boat captains, sales managers, area managers, and office staff.

INSIDER TIPS: Red Sail Sports is noted for its professional, friendly, clean-cut crew. All employees are dedicated to providing the utmost in top-notch service to all guests.

PERKS: While specific perks vary according to position and location, most employees are permitted to use the company's water sports equipment when off duty.

TO APPLY: Applicants should send a cover letter, résumé, and photo-graph to Personnel Manager, Red Sail Sports, 909 Montgomery Street, Suite 601, San Francisco, CA 94133; (415) 981-4411.

SHOTOVER JET, LTD.
(Queenstown, New Zealand)
Year-Round

Shotover Jet's excursions haven't been labeled the world's most ex-hilarating jet boat ride for nothing. Imagine all the thrills and spills of whitewater rafting down a narrow, churning river gorge. Now imagine that same trip at breakneck speed in a huge, custom-designed, high-powered jet boat and you have Shotover Jet! The company's boats take more than 60,000 visitors a year through the towering rock gorges near Queenstown, New Zealand, and combine thrills and chills with historic sites and spectacular scenery.

SPECIFICS: Shotover Jet employs a small and dedicated staff of boat drivers, van drivers, maintenance men, and administration staff. Safety is the company's main concern and boat drivers are trained for up to 200 hours before taking their first group of passengers down the river.

INSIDER TIPS: Due to the high profile of this exciting company, positions are at a premium. To have any real chances of landing a job you would probably need to interview in person, but a job with Shotover would be well worth the trip to Queenstown. Management is looking for mature, safety-conscious applicants who can work well in the tourist industry. Van driver and administration positions are the easiest to get.

PERKS: Living in Queenstown and working on one of the most exciting excursions anywhere.

TO APPLY: Applicants should contact Shotover Jet, Ltd., P.O. Box 189, Queenstown, New Zealand; phone: (0294) 28-570.

SKI GUIDES HAWAII
(Island of Hawaii, Hawaii)
Seasonal (Winter)

Where else on earth can you ski in the morning and tan on a tropical beach in the afternoon? Contrary to most visitors' impressions, Hawaii has a small but bustling ski industry operating 13,796 feet above sea level on the windswept peak of Mauna Kea volcano. Mauna Kea is the world's highest mountain, reaching skyward 33,000 feet from its base deep below the warm Hawaiian surf. Be prepared for a wild and exotic skiing experience. There is no comfortable ski lodge here. There aren't even any official ski lifts and nobody needs a trail map because there are no trees to separate ski trails. Ski slope access is by Ski Guides Hawaii's fleet of four-wheel drive vehicles. For ski enthusiasts, ski runs average over five miles with vertical drops of up to 4,500 feet per run! Ski Guides Hawaii's treks are among the most unusual skiing adventures anywhere. The company operates both downhill and cross-country (Nordic) ski tours.

SPECIFICS: Ski Guides Hawaii hires sales staff, vehicle operators, ski guides, and ski instructors. No specific prior experience is required for sales staff or drivers. Ski guides and ski instructors must have a valid Red Cross first-aid card.

PERKS: Perhaps the most valued perk anywhere, Ski Guides Hawaii offers the chance to ski free while gazing out over the blue Pacific Ocean!

TO APPLY: For more information applicants should contact Mauna Kea Ski Corporation's Ski Guides Hawaii, P.O. Box 2020, Kamuela, Hawaii 96743; (808) 885-4188.

SKI UTAH
(Salt Lake City, Utah)

Seasonal (Winter)

Ski Utah operates a unique program for advanced skiers that offers a guided day of skiing through five different ski areas. The program, licensed by the U.S. Forest Service, provides a day of skiing at the Park City, Brighton, Alta, Snowbird, and Solitude ski areas. Skiers travel with guides via back country routes connecting the five ski areas. The unique routes used by Ski Utah cover some of the most spectacular unspoiled scenery in the entire Wasatch Mountain range.

SPECIFICS: Ski Utah hires seven back country ski guides each season. Available positions include lead guide and interconnect guides. All guides must have both emergency medical technician (EMT) training and experience in avalanche control and rescue.

INSIDER TIPS: Applicants must be in excellent health. Advanced skiing ability is, of course, an essential job prerequisite. These jobs are in extremely high demand and are only for the most highly trained and skilled skiers.

PERKS: The primary perk is the ability to ski at five of Utah's finest ski areas plus access to spectacular and rarely visited back country terrain.

TO APPLY: For employment information, contact Ski Utah at 150 West 500 South, Salt Lake City, Utah 84101; (801) 534-1779.

SOBEK EXPEDITIONS, INC.
(Angels Camp, California)
Year-Round

Sobek is one of the nation's leaders in unique worldwide adventure trekking and whitewater expeditions. The company markets, sells, and operates its own unique trips around the globe. Some expeditions are considered "soft adventure," combining the excitement and discovery of exotic travel with the ease of a well-organized tour and first-class accommodations. Others trips are more challenging, combining exotic locales with primitive amenities. Typical destinations include Indonesia, Borneo, Africa, Nepal, India, Peru, the Galapagos Islands, and Hawaii's volcanos. Sobek is based in Angels Camp, home of Mark Twain's famous Calaveras County jumping frog competition.

SPECIFICS: Sobek hires up to five new tour escorts each year to fill its twenty to thirty escort positions. Although work is seasonal, depending on which trips one leads, the company seeks only applicants interested in a long-term employment relationship.

INSIDER TIPS: According to Sobek, "due to the nature of our rafting trips, we require a minimum of five years of professional river experience. Land trek expedition leaders must be knowledgeable in the particular region being visited and be very comfortable with both people and nature."

PERKS: Salaries and perks vary according to both experience and the particular trip being led.

TO APPLY: Applicants should either write for an official application or send a cover letter and résumé to John Yost, Box 1089, Angels Camp, California 95222; (209) 236-4525. A self-addressed stamped envelope should be included with all correspondence.

TONQUIN VALLEY PACK TRIPS
(Brule, Alberta, Canada)
Seasonal (Summer and Winter)

Tonquin Valley Pack Trips provides horseback treks into Canada's Tonquin Valley in Jasper National Park. The trips are ideal for horse lovers, fishermen, nature photographers, and outdoor enthusiasts. Cabin-style accommodations as well as a mountain chalet are available. The company provides all meals and supplies boats for guests to use on the Amethyst Lakes.

SPECIFICS: Tonquin Valley Pack Trips receives approximately twenty applications for its seven annual job openings. All jobs are either summer or winter seasonal. Summer seasonal staff must be available to work from at least June 1 through September 15. Applications are accepted for cooks (experience required), chambermaids (no experience necessary), and wranglers (must have a valid first-aid certificate, be able to pack a horse, and be willing to study for a Park Guide's license). Applications are accepted throughout the year. Starting wages range from CAN$800 to $1,000 per month plus room and board.

INSIDER TIPS: The company looks for applicants in good health (non-smokers only) who have an interest in horses, the outdoors, and people. A willingness to learn is essential. Applications are accepted from both Canadian citizens and non-Canadians with proper work visas. Wranglers must either have a knowledge of horseshoeing or be willing to learn.

PERKS: Room and board are provided for employees. According to management, staff tips average CAN$200 to $300 per month.

TO APPLY: Applicants should send a cover letter, résumé, and photograph to Wald & Lavone Olson, Tonquin Valley Pack Trips, General Delivery, Brule, Alberta T0E 0C0, Canada; (403) 865-4417. Management reports responding to all applications within two weeks.

WAGONS WEST
(Afton, Wyoming)
Seasonal (Summer)

"Wagons ho!" cries the trailmaster and your trip is off. Wagons West re-creates those wondrous days of yesteryear with authentic covered wagon treks through the foothills of the Grand Tetons in Jackson Hole, Wyoming. The wagons are lead by teams of gentle horses and guests may choose to either ride in a covered wagon or follow on horseback. Evenings are spent camping under the stars, sharing a campfire/dutch oven-cooked meal and listening to the "old-timers" share tales of the Wild West. The company operates trips each year from early June through early September.

SPECIFICS: Wagons West receives approximately fifty applications for their ten seasonal staff positions. In a typical year, about half of their ten staffers will be new employees. All jobs are summer seasonal from June 1 through September 1. Applications are accepted for wagon drivers (teamsters), wranglers, cooks, and campfire entertainers. There is no application deadline and hiring is done as needed throughout the year.

INSIDER TIPS: "From our years of outfitting wilderness pack trips, we realize that many people wish to have a genuine outdoor experience but cannot spend the time or do not feel qualified to undertake such a strenuous expedition. From the recognition of the needs of these nature lovers, Wagons West has developed."

PERKS: Meals and housing are provided for all employees.

TO APPLY: Applicants should write for an official application and submit a photograph to L. D. Frome, Owner, Wagons West, Box 47, Afton, Wyoming 83110; (307) 886-3872.

WILDERNESS TOURS
(Beachburg, Ontario, Canada)
Seasonal (Summer)

Wilderness Tours is one of Canada's largest adventure travel companies. The company's primary excursions are whitewater rafting trips on the Ottowa River in eastern Ontario, kayaking trips and courses, and jet boat rides up Montreal's St. Lawrence River.

SPECIFICS: Wilderness Tours hires approximately fifty new staff members each summer to fill its 200 positions. The company receives more than 250 applications annually. Wilderness Tours also employs twenty-five year-round employees. Positions are available for summer seasonal river guides, photo/video staff, and food service personnel. Summer staff should be available to work from May through Labor Day. Applications for summer work must be completed by February 15.

INSIDER TIPS: "This is a great summer job. Our small core of year-round staff and handpicked summer recruits live and breathe the whitewater lifestyle. They're dedicated to bringing [guests] an unparalleled river program. Our 600-acre facility is a whitewater resort complete with tall pines, sandy beaches, sports fields, wooded campground, restaurant, sauna, and other modern facilities."

PERKS: One of the company's unique perks is free kayaking lessons for all staff members. A small fleet of kayak equipment is maintained for staff use on their days off. According to Joe Kowalsi, "Just about everyone at Wilderness Tours learns to kayak. We send all interested staff to our kayak school at the beginning of the season." Staff housing and meals are provided.

TO APPLY: Applicants should send a cover letter and résumé to Rick Troutman, Operations Manager, Wilderness Tours, Box 89, Beachburg, Ontario, K0V 1C0, Canada; (613) 646-2241. The company attempts to respond to all applications within three weeks.

YOSEMITE INSTITUTE
(Yosemite National Park, California)
Year-Round

In Yosemite's rich and diverse terrain of incomparable beauty, the Yosemite Institute creates unique educational adventures. The institute offers residential educational programs that study and explore the natural and human history of the Sierra Nevadas and Yosemite National Park. Students study nature in all of its diversity, wonder, and beauty. In the spring and summer, institute groups might explore the wildflowers and waterfalls of Yosemite. In the winter, students might strap on a pair of snowshoes or cross country skis to investigate the winter adaptations of plants and animals.

SPECIFICS: The institute receives more than 100 applications each year for its few job openings. Although the institute employs more than thirty staff members, a low employee turnover rate means that only five or six new staffers are hired annually. Applications are accepted throughout the year for instructors. A bachelor's degree in the sciences or a related discipline is required along with certificates in advanced first aid and CPR. Salaries start at $60 per day, plus housing and medical benefits.

INSIDER TIPS: "Our expert faculty is here not to get rich, but for the profits of sharing and teaching about the natural environment."

PERKS: Employee perks include free housing and meals, free uniforms, and a medical and dental insurance program. The institute offers an excellent staff training program.

TO APPLY: Applicants should write for an official application from Brian Empie, Executive Director, Yosemite Institute, P.O. Box 487, Yosemite National Park, California 95389; (209) 372-9300. Management is unable to respond to all applications.

The following listings, found under the chapter headings given below, also include exciting positions of "high adventure":

RIVERS

Adrift Adventures

American River Recreation

American River Touring
  Association

Glacier Raft Company (Canada)

Sierra Whitewater Expeditions

USA Whitewater, Inc.

TROPICAL ISLANDS

Magton, Ltd.

Underwater Safaris

V.I. Divers, Ltd.

Virgin Islands Diving Schools

Mountains

~~~~~~~~

A-LINE MOTOR INN
(Queenstown, New Zealand)
Seasonal (Summer and Winter)

Named after its A-frame mountain chalet–style accommodations, this hotel is located just a short walk from the center of bustling Queenstown on a hillside overlooking a magnificent alpine lake. Queenstown is New Zealand's version of Lake Tahoe, only more beautiful and less plagued by recent overdevelopment than Tahoe. Queenstown is a year-round vacation destination famous for its superb skiing in the summer and its sailing, sunning, whitewater river rafting, hiking, and camping in the winter (remember, seasons are reversed in New Zealand).

SPECIFICS: The A-Line Motor Inn hires twenty new employees annually to fill its fifty-member staff. Positions are available for both summer and winter personnel. Note that New Zealand's summer is winter in the U.S. and Canada, therefore summer staff should be available from October through April; winter season runs from July through September. There is no application deadline and the hotel

hires as needed throughout the year. Positions are available for porters, front desk clerks (called house staff), room service attendants
(called waiting staff), and bar staff.

INSIDER TIPS: Management seeks friendly, honest employees who
are willing to work hard. Applications are welcomed from non–New
Zealand citizens with proper work permits.

PERKS: Employees are permitted to use the hotel's facilities (including the spa, pool, sauna, and gym) when not on duty.

TO APPLY: Applicants should send a cover letter, résumé, photograph, and SARP to Manager, A-Line Motor Inn, P.O. Box 149,
Queenstown, New Zealand; phone: (0294) 27700.

ALPINE LODGE
(Mammoth Lakes, California)
Year-Round

The Alpine Lodge is a scenic sixty-six-room mountain hotel with
four cottages located at Mammoth Lakes, California, a popular recreation area in California's Sierra Nevadas. Nearby activities include
skiing (snow and water), hiking, fishing, camping, and rock climbing.

SPECIFICS: The Alpine Lodge hires approximately thirty new staff
members each year. The most common employee vacancies are for
front desk clerks and housekeepers. Salaries start at $5.00 per hour
and up. Peak season runs from November 15 through April 30. Employees may use the resort's jacuzzi and sauna when off duty.

INSIDER TIPS: Management seeks energetic, honest employees with
a willingness to learn.

TO APPLY: Applicants should send a cover letter, résumé, and SARP
to Joel Otoshi, Manager, Alpine Lodge, Box 389, Mammoth Lakes,
California 93546.

ANDREW MOTOR LODGE LTD.
(Jasper National Park, Alberta, Canada)
Seasonal (Summer)

Jasper is one of the most popular resort areas in Canada. This year-round vacation spot is famous for hiking, horseback riding, fishing, cycling, swimming, boating, whitewater rafting, tennis, and golf in the summer. Favorite winter activities include Nordic skiing, downhill skiing, snowshoeing, ice climbing, ice skating, and dog sledding. The Andrew Motor Lodge is a ninety-nine-room hotel located in the heart of Jasper.

SPECIFICS: Andrew Motor Lodge hires forty new employees each year to fill its thirty-six off-season and eighty peak-season positions. Summer seasonal staff should be available to work from May 15 through October 1. There is no application deadline and staff are hired as needed throughout the year. Applications are accepted for chambermaids, waitpersons (experience required), front desk clerks (excellent cash management and organizational skills required), kitchen help, and dishwashers. Starting salaries typically begin at CAN$5.25 per hour and up depending on the position and qualifications.

INSIDER TIPS: "Andrew Motor Lodge looks for clean-cut, self-motivated, hard-working, well-mannered applicants who are good with people, neat, and physically able to handle the busy tourist season."

PERKS: Staff housing is available for female employees. All staff members receive a 30% discount on meals and are allowed to use the hotel's outdoor jacuzzi, lounge, and patio when off duty.

TO APPLY: Applicants should request an official application from Carl B. Hesse, General Manager, Andrew Motor Lodge, P.O. Box 850, Jasper, Alberta T0E 1E0 Canada; (403) 852-3394.

A.R.A. OUTDOOR WORLD: McKINLEY CHALET RESORT, DENALI PARK HOTEL, McKINLEY VILLAGE LODGE, AND LYNX CREEK CAMPGROUND (Denali National Park, Alaska)

Seasonal (Summer)

Denali is the perfect place to come face to face with nature's extremes. Its six million acres of awe-inspiring mountains, twisting glacial streams, and sweeping tundra meadows play host to some of North America's most magnificent species of wildlife, including grizzly bears, moose, caribou, fox, and wolves. It is in this setting that A.R.A. Outdoor World operates a number of national park guest facilities including the famous McKinley Chalet Resort and the Denali National Park Hotel. The McKinley resort is a beautiful, modern facility located on the east boundary of the park overlooking the Nenana River. The Denali Park Hotel is the bustling center for visitor activities in the park. The McKinley Village Lodge is a newly renovated guest facility located seven miles south of the park's entrance. Lynx Creek is a camping facility complete with a favorite local pub boasting "the best pizza in Alaska."

SPECIFICS: A.R.A. Outdoor World hires 550 seasonal employees annually to operate its four facilities in Denali National Park. Positions are available in the following areas: accounting (bookkeepers, cashiers, night auditors), bar (bartenders, cocktail servers), dining room (hosts, bus staff, waitpersons for dinner theater), front desk (cashiers, desk/reservations clerks, night security guards, locksmiths), gift shop (salesclerks), grocery store (clerks, cashiers), housekeeping (staff persons), kitchen (breakfast and line grill cooks, dishwashers), service station (attendants), snack shops, pizza parlor and deli (grill cooks, counter clerks), transportation (tour and courtesy transportation drivers, bus mechanics, bus washers, and desk staff). Experience is helpful but not required for most positions. For most positions, pay starts at $3.85 per hour for tipped employees and $4.50 for non-tipped staff members (subject to change). Most employees average $5.00 to $6.50 per hour including bonus. Tour drivers earn $9.00 per hour and department managers and a few other positions are salaried. Specific wages are discussed during job interviews. Note that all employees must be at least nineteen years or older by May 15 of the year they are hired and must be either U.S. citizens or have a valid work permit and social security card.

INSIDER TIPS: A positive attitude toward work is extremely important in landing a job here. Be prepared to enjoy the rugged beauty and *isolation* of Denali. Work here is hard, but staff members seem to love their positions and almost half return to work again the following summer. The park is spectacular but, as with most of Alaska, rain and mosquitos are a natural part of the summer. Maturity is extremely important to management and should be stressed in any application. Interviews are required for all positions. Management conducts an annual interviewing trip that begins in California in February and continues throughout the United States through the first half of March. Interviews are also held in Alaska from February through March. If there are no interviews offered within a reasonable distance from you, a phone interview can be arranged. A neat and well-kept appearance is extremely important to the company, so insiders suggest sending a photo with your application if you are unable to interview in person. All applicants must be able to stay through at least September 4 to be considered for a job. With rare exceptions, all employees must start work by June 10, although a few positions open up as late as June 30. Transportation positions are the most sought after and only a few are available each year.

PERKS: Living in America's spectacular last frontier is perhaps the ultimate perk. Employee housing is provided for $2.50 per day in rustic condos. (Generally, two staff members share a room.) Breakfast, lunch, and dinner are provided to employees for $7.50 per day.

TO APPLY: Applicants should write for an official application and information package from A.R.A. Outdoor World, Ltd., Box 87, Denali Park, Alaska 99755; (907) 279-2653.

THE ASPEN LODGE RANCH RESORT
(Estes Park, Colorado)
Seasonal (Summer and Winter) and Year-Round

The Aspen Lodge Ranch Resort is not just another Rocky Mountain dude ranch. "We are a beautiful, AAA-rated resort and conference center. Our conference center is housed in the largest log building in Colorado." On-site activities include horseback riding, racquetball, tennis, hot tubbing, a sports center, year-round swimming, hiking, cross-country skiing, snowmobiling, sleigh rides, fishing, ice skating, children's programs, and mountain bike rides. Nearby activities include downhill skiing (Eldora ski area), whitewater rafting, golf, and backpacking. Rocky Mountain National Park is nearby and offers wonderful opportunities for hiking, backpacking, and nature photography.

SPECIFICS: The Aspen Lodge employs forty year-round plus forty summer seasonal and fifteen winter seasonal employees. Applications are accepted for sports center attendants (these employees also operate the children's program and pool area), wranglers, bartenders, housekeepers, waitstaff (experience preferred), maintenance workers, prep cooks, dishwashers, and conference attendants. Salary information available upon request.

INSIDER TIPS: The ranch looks for "a willing attitude, and people who are honest, intelligent, hard-working, friendly, and team spirited. We have also employed seasonals who are studying hotel management."

PERKS: Employees are welcome to use the lodge's recreational facilities including horses, racquetball courts, swimming pool, tennis courts, and weight room. Employee dormitory housing is available for single employees.

TO APPLY: Applicants should write for an official application from Personnel Officer, The Aspen Lodge Ranch, Longs Peak Rt., Estes Park, Colorado 80517; (303) 586-8133.

BEAVER RUN RESORT
(Breckenridge, Colorado)
Seasonal (Winter and Spring) and Year-Round

Nestled in the Rocky Mountains, Breckenridge's Beaver Run Resort is a luxury year-round destination resort. When it snows this is a skier's paradise!

SPECIFICS: Beaver Run Resort has 388 staff positions. Seasonal employees must be available from December 10 through April 15. Applications are accepted for pool attendants, disk jockeys, housekeepers, snow shovel crew, grounds keepers, security officers, janitors, laundry attendants, van and shuttle drivers, switchboard operators, bell staff, auditors, reservation agents, front desk clerks, sales clerks, waitstaff, bartenders, cocktail waitstaff, cooks, doormen, kitchen staff, cafeteria staff, and all areas of management and supervision (previous experience necessary for supervisory positions).

INSIDER TIPS: Housing is a major problem during the winter season. According to Personnel Manager John Mullen, Housing shortages occur about November 1 with not too many jobs starting until December. The result is often a severe labor shortage. If you accept a winter job here, begin your housing search early.

TO APPLY: Applicants should send a cover letter, résumé, and SARP to John Mullen, Personnel Manager, Beaver Run Resort, P.O. Box 2115, Breckenridge, Colorado 80424; (303) 453-6000.

BEST WESTERN BUCK'S T-4 LODGE OF BIG SKY
(Big Sky, Montana)
Seasonal (Summer and Winter)

Buck's T-4 Lodge is the ideal base from which to explore both the summer and winter activities of Big Sky, Montana. The lodge is located in the Gallatin Canyon and rests at the base of Lone Mountain ski hill. This log cabin-style lodge is a favorite rest stop for skiers, fishermen, hikers, and nature lovers.

SPECIFICS: Buck's hires thirty new seasonal staff members each year to fill its forty positions. Applications are accepted for waitpersons, housekeepers, front desk clerks, night auditors, dishwashers, bartenders, bar managers, maintenance staff, cooks, and bus drivers. Summer staff should be available to work from June 10 through September 15. Winter staff usually work from early December through mid-April.

INSIDER TIPS: Buck's looks for articulate, friendly, and courteous applicants with professionalism, good grooming, and a "team work" attitude.

PERKS: Staff members are free to use the lodge's bar, lounge, restaurant, and hot tubs (if not busy) when off duty. Discounts on dining. Housing available.

TO APPLY: Applicants should either write for an official application or send a cover letter, résumé, and list of references to Debra Dechert, Operation Manager, Best Western Buck's T-4 Lodge of Big Sky, P.O. Box 279, Big Sky, Montana 59716; (406) 995-4111.

BLUE MOUNTAIN RESORTS
(Collingwood, Ontario, Canada)
Seasonal (Summer and Winter) and Year-Round

Blue Mountain Resorts operates the highly acclaimed five-star Blue Mountain Inn located at the base of Ontario's largest ski area, Blue Mountain. This year-round destination resort caters to families, singles, and business conference travelers. The hotel's facilities include an indoor pool, whirlpool, sauna, exercise room, squash and racquetball courts, three lounges, and a deluxe dining room. While this is a year-round resort, it enjoys particularly busy summer and winter seasons. During the winter months the main activity centers around Blue Mountain ski area's twenty-seven ski trails, including a 4,000-foot-long run.

SPECIFICS: Blue Mountain Resorts hires more than 500 new winter staff members each year (100 in summer). Jobs are available for seasonal as well as year-round personnel. Winter seasonal staff must be available from December 1 through March 31. Summer staff work from July 1 through September 1. Positions are available for housekeepers, front desk clerks, bartenders, waitpersons, cafe cleaners, grill cooks, line cooks, prep cooks, and cooks' helpers. Starting wages begin at CAN$5.50 per hour for tipped positions and CAN$6.00 per hour for non-tipped employees (subject to change). The application deadline is September 1 (winter) and March 1 (summer) and hiring is done as needed throughout the year.

INSIDER TIPS: "We are a rapidly expanding destination resort with a solid business conference clientele as well as single and family travelers. We look for employees with a high energy level and good grooming. We also like applicants who are good with people and enjoy working with the public."

PERKS: The hotel's dining room and lounges are open to staff members when not on duty. Employees are eligible for special rates on skiing and golf. Staff members are not permitted to use the hotel's indoor recreation facilities.

TO APPLY: Applicants should send a cover letter and résumé to Human Resources, Blue Mountain Resorts, RR 3, Collingwood, Ontario L94 3Z2 Canada; (705) 445-0231.

BOLTON VALLEY SKI AND SUMMER RESORT
(Bolton, Vermont)

Seasonal (Winter, Summer, and Fall) and Year-Round

High atop Vermont's scenic Green Mountains lies Bolton Valley, a year-round destination resort. Each winter this tranquil wonderland is transformed into one of Vermont's finest ski resorts, dedicated to providing a small resort atmosphere (sans lengthy lift lines) with all the features of a huge ski area. Bolton Valley enjoys an annual average snowfall of 275 inches and boasts forty ski trails. At a 2,150-foot elevation, Bolton Valley claims the highest base elevation in the East. With the spring thaw comes an entirely different lifestyle at Bolton. Summer guests keep busy with tennis, golf, swimming, boating, and other activities.

SPECIFICS: Bolton Valley hires approximately 200 new staff members annually to fill its 350 ski season employees and its 175 summer and fall positions. Jobs are available for both seasonal and long-term work. Winter seasonal employees should be available from December 15 through April 1. Summer staff must be available from May 25 through September 10. There is no application deadline and employees are hired as needed throughout the year. Positions are available for front desk clerks, housekeepers, waitstaff, hosts/hostesses, bartenders, switchboard operators, day care staff, ski instructors, lift operators, snowmakers, cafeteria line workers, cashiers, sports club recreation staff, and tennis instructors. Starting salaries for most positions range between $4.50 and $5.50 per hour.

INSIDER TIPS: Management seeks employees who are energetic, self-motivated, reliable, professional, personable, team-spirited, and able to deal with the public.

PERKS: All winter employees enjoy unlimited free skiing privileges at Bolton Valley when off duty, while summer staff members enjoy tennis and swimming. All facilities are available to staff on a free or discounted basis. Many employees earn generous tips and various discounts are available.

TO APPLY: Applicants should write for an official application or send a cover letter, résumé, and SARP to Julie Frailey, Human Resources Manager, Bolton Valley Resort, Bolton Valley, Vermont 05477; (802) 434-2131.

BOOMERANG LODGE
(Aspen, Colorado)
Seasonal (Summer and Winter) and Year-Round

The Boomerang Lodge is located just a short walk from the hustle and bustle of downtown Aspen, Colorado. Facilities include whirlpool, swimming pool, and sauna. Aspen offers skiing, skating, hiking, biking, horseback riding, and numerous cultural activities.

SPECIFICS: The Boomerang Lodge hires ten new staff members annually to fill its fifteen-person crew. The lodge requires both long-term and seasonal help. Summer help should be available June 1 through August 27; winter staff should be available November 26 through April 15. Applications are accepted for front desk staff and housekeepers. Pay ranges from $6.00 to $6.50 per hour (subject to change).

INSIDER TIPS: "We look for applicants with a willingness to work, intelligence, honesty, and enthusiasm."

PERKS: Housing is provided to employees for $90 per month (rate subject to change).

TO APPLY: Applicants should write for an official application or send a cover letter, résumé, photograph, and SARP to Charles Paterson, Owner/Manager, Boomerang Lodge, 500 W. Hopkins, Colorado 81611; (303) 925-3416.

CHATEAU LAKE LOUISE
(Lake Louise, Alberta, Canada)
Seasonal (Summer and Winter) and Year-Round

Perched high in the Canadian Rockies, Chateau Lake Louise over-looks magnificent Victoria Glacier and Lake Louise. This 515-room hotel is one of Canada's most celebrated "alpine-style" resorts. Fishing, mountain climbing, skiing, biking, ice skating, and riding the gondola to the high snow-covered peaks are favorite activities. The Chateau is part of the highly acclaimed Canadian Pacific resort chain.

SPECIFICS: Chateau Lake Louise hires approximately 300 new employees each year for its 500 winter and 625 summer positions. While seasonal jobs are available, most positions are year-round. Summer seasonal staff should be available to work from early May through late September; start and finish dates for winter positions vary depending on seasonal snowfall. Applications are accepted for house-keeping attendants, stewards, dishwashers, cooks, buspersons, wait-staff, front desk clerks, reservation clerks, secretaries, accounting clerks, bartenders, and cashiers. Starting wages range from CAN $4.50 to $5.50 per hour for most positions. Cooks earn CAN$6.00 to $12.00 per hour depending on experience.

INSIDER TIPS: Although hiring is done throughout the year, most summer jobs are filled in February. Christmas seasonal work is available for a six-week period in December and January. "We look for career-oriented applicants with a pleasant and friendly personality and a positive outlook toward their work. All staff should be highly motivated." Hotel or hospitality industry experience is an asset, although not required for many positions. An applicant's willingness to commit to a lengthy term of employment is important (minimum summer seasonal is early May through late September; minimum winter seasonal is a three-month term). Non-Canadian citizens must have a valid working visa before applying.

PERKS: Room and board are provided at the resort at subsidized rates (currently CAN$60 per month for housing; CAN$46 per month for meals). Other employee perks include a staff games room, staff pub, and free use of the resort's pool, jacuzzi, and steam room. Discounts are available for canoe rentals, horseback riding, cross-country ski lessons, and ice skating.

TO APPLY: Applicants should either write for an official application or send a cover letter, résumé, and two letters of reference from former employers to Carole Misericordia, Human Resources Manager, Chateau Lake Louise, Lake Louise, Alberta T0L 1E0 Canada; (403) 522-3635.

CHEYENNE MOUNTAIN CONFERENCE RESORT (Colorado Springs, Colorado)

Seasonal (Summer) and Year-Round

The Cheyenne Mountain Conference Resort is located adjacent to the Country Club of Colorado, which features extensive outdoor activities including fishing, boating, windsurfing, and canoeing on a private 35-acre lake.

SPECIFICS: The Cheyenne Mountain Conference Resort employs 400 staff members and hires up to 200 new employees annually. Management recruits both summer seasonal (June through August or September) and long-term employees. Entry-level positions are available in the following areas: food and beverage (food servers, cocktail servers, bartenders); rooms (desk clerks, guest services staff, transportation, switchboard, housekeeping); engineering (maintenance, grounds keepers); conference services (room set-up), kitchen (cooks, stewards); and accounting and personnel. Starting salaries range from minimum wage to more than $7.00 per hour.

INSIDER TIPS: "We look for service-oriented, dependable, flexible, career-oriented applicants with an ability to work."

TO APPLY: Applicants should write for an official application or send a cover letter, résumé, and SARP to Ms. Marcia Whittaker, Director of Human Resources, Cheyenne Mountain Conference Resort, 3225 Broadmoor Valley Road, Colorado Springs, Colorado 80906; (719) 576-4600.

LAKE TAHOE HORIZON CASINO RESORT
(Stateline, Nevada)

Seasonal (Summer) and Year-Round

Lake Tahoe Horizon Casino Resort is a huge casino hotel employing up to 1,800 staff members during peak season. Located in Stateline, Nevada, the resort sits on the southern shores of spectacular Lake Tahoe. The casino hotel is popular year-round but enjoys both summer and winter high seasons. Lake Tahoe Horizon Casino Resort is located within a few minutes drive from the Heavenly Valley ski area, the self-proclaimed highest ski area in the Sierras.

SPECIFICS: Lake Tahoe Horizon Casino Resort hires more than eight hundred new employees annually to fill its 1,800-person staff. Management recruits both year-round as well as summer seasonal staff members. Seasonal staff should be available from Memorial Day through Labor Day. Numerous college students are hired throughout the year but especially during the busy summer months and winter ski weekends. Applications are accepted for lifeguards (summer only), "21" dealer trainees (summer only), keno writers, changepersons (money-handling experience required), cashiers, waiters, waitresses, hostpersons, front desk clerks, buspersons, fry or broiler cooks (one year of experience required), snack bar attendants, valet attendants, front desk clerks, housekeepers, bellpersons, security officers, and food cashiers.

INSIDER TIPS: "We look for (applicants with) a dependable personality, good appearance, a stable work record, good communication skills, and flexibility in work schedule."

PERKS: Staff members are welcome to use restaurants, lounges, cabaret shows, and gaming facilities when not at work.

TO APPLY: Applicants should telephone for an official application and information on current openings. Personal interviews are usually required before a final hiring decision is made. Lake Tahoe Horizon Casino Resort, Personnel Office, P.O. Box C, Stateline, Nevada 89449; (702) 588-6211, ext. 2588.

THE DON-K RANCH
(Pueblo, Colorado)
Seasonal (Summer)

The Don-K is a western-style family ranch located sixty-five miles southwest of Colorado Springs, outside of Pueblo. The ranch re-creates the charm of the Wild West of yesteryear with the modern comforts of today. While horseback riding is the primary ranch activity, the Don-K also features swimming, tennis, hiking, campfires, square dancing, whitewater rafting, and nature photography. The ranch is nestled in a valley surrounded by the San Isabel National Forest.

SPECIFICS: The Don-K Ranch hires college-age youths for summer seasonal work. Applications are accepted for children's counselors, wranglers, pool/yard maintenance staff, cabin helpers, food servers, and food preparation staff.

INSIDER TIPS: "The ranch needs personable, talented, and outstanding students who enjoy working with people."

TO APPLY: Applicants should write for an official application from The Don-K Ranch, 2677 South Siloam Road, Pueblo, Colorado 81005; (303) 784-6600.

DRAKESBAD GUEST RANCH
(Lassen National Park, California)
Seasonal (Summer)

Drakesbad is a secluded guest ranch nestled in a beautiful mountain valley in the heart of Lassen Volcanic National Park. These are the only accommodations inside the national park, and they are wonderfully rustic—there are no phones or electricity here to interfere with the natural beauty. Even the swimming pool and hot spas are naturally heated by volcanic steam. Favorite ranch activities include fishing, hiking, horseback riding, and exploring the unlimited beauty of this unique national park.

SPECIFICS: The guest ranch hires twelve seasonal employees annually. Applications are accepted for wranglers (first aid and CPR certification, knowledge of horses, and trail guiding experience required), waitpersons (some food service experience desired, but not required), maids, dishwashers, cooks, and chefs. Pay ranges from minimum wage to $1,000 per month plus tips.

INSIDER TIPS: Drakesbad prefers applicants who can be available from June through September. Although hiring is done as needed, most jobs are filled by April. Management reports that they look for applicants who are outgoing, friendly, and hard working. Be warned this is not the place for diehard urbanites—the nearest town is seventeen miles away.

PERKS: The ranch provides staff members with dormitory-style housing and meals for approximately $9 per day (subject to change). Employees are welcome to use the ranch's horses, hot springs, pool, and hiking trails.

TO APPLY: Applicants should write for an official application from Ranch Manager, Drakesbad Guest Ranch, 2150 N. Main, Suite #5, Red Bluff, California 96080; (916) 529-1512. Enclose a SASE with all application requests.

THE EXPLORER HOTEL
(Yellowknife, Northwest Territory, Canada)

Year-Round

Located in the capital of the Northwest Territory, the Explorer Hotel provides an ideal spot from which to explore Canada's northern wilderness. In the summer, local activities include fishing, boating, and camping. The summer is Yellowknife's big tourist season as visitors from around the world come to take advantage of the north's long hours of daylight. Winter activities include skiing and viewing the Northern Lights.

SPECIFICS: The Explorer Hotel employs a staff of 140. Most jobs are year-round. Applications are accepted for front desk clerks, night auditors, accountants, bartenders, waitpersons, cooks, maintenance personnel, and security officers. Wages are negotiable on either a monthly or hourly basis.

INSIDER TIPS: The Explorer looks for "reliable, hard-working individuals who like to deal with people and who have experience in the hotel business." Staff members are not permitted to use any of the hotel's facilities when not on duty.

PERKS: Employee perks include guest gratuities, employee meal allowances, and a housing allowance for management personnel.

TO APPLY: Applicants should write for an official application or send a cover letter, résumé, photograph, and SARP to Harry Symington, General Manager, Postal Service 7000, Yellowknife, Northwest Territory X1A 2R3 Canada; (403) 873-3531.

FLAMING GORGE LODGE
(Dutch John, Utah)

Seasonal (Summer)

Flaming Gorge is a secluded mountain resort lodge featuring a restaurant, general store, rafting outfitter supply store, Green River guide service, and service station. The lodge is the only private enterprise operation on the mountain.

SPECIFICS: Flaming Gorge has a staff of seventy and employs more than forty new employees each year. The lodge's season runs from Memorial Day weekend through Labor Day weekend. All applications should be received by March 1. Positions are available for food service counter clerks, store clerks, waiters/waitresses, chambermaids, service station attendants, and cooks.

INSIDER TIPS: Management looks for individuals who enjoy working with the public and are willing to stay at least three months.

PERKS: The lodge provides dormitory-style employee housing at a cost of approximately $1 per day (rate subject to change).

TO APPLY: Applicants should write for an official application from Craig W. Collett, Flaming Gorge Lodge, Greendale U.S. 191, Dutch John, Utah 84023; (801) 889-3773.

GLACIER BAY COUNTRY INN
(Gustavus, Alaska)
Seasonal (Summer)

Deep in the Alaskan woods, down a narrow, twisting road, sits the charming Glacier Bay Country Inn. Situated on a 160-acre private homestead overlooking the majestic Fairweather Mountains, the Glacier Bay Country Inn offers a rare peek at true Alaskan hospitality. This small inn plays host to no more than twenty-two guests at any one time. Of course, true to its namesake, the inn is conveniently located near Glacier Bay, home of giant icebergs, countless whales, seals, bears, and sixteen active glaciers.

SPECIFICS: The Glacier Bay Country Inn hires four to six new employees each summer to fill its eight-person staff. All positions are seasonal, beginning in mid-May and lasting through mid-September. The inn has positions for two chefs, boat captain (fish cleaner, fishing guide), and four persons to serve as waitstaff/maid/dishwasher/van driver. Salaries range from $1,000 to $1,500 per month depending on the position, experience, and qualifications.

INSIDER TIPS: According to innkeepers Al and Annie Unrein, the Country Inn looks for "neat, clean, honest, hard-working, mature, tolerant, loyal, multitalented applicants with a good sense of humor, an ability to accept criticism, and an ability to cope well with stress." This is a job for someone who would rather spend an evening on the porch watching the Northern Lights than watching "Monday Night Football."

PERKS: Perks are somewhat negotiable but food and lodging are possible. Employees earn generous tips from guests.

TO APPLY: Applicants should either write for an official application or send a cover letter, résumé, and SARP to Al or Annie Unrein, Innkeepers, Glacier Bay Country Inn, Box 5, Gustavus, Alaska 99826; (907) 697-2288. If writing for an application form, please enclose a SASE. From October through April, send correspondence to: Glacier Bay Country Inn, P.O. Box 2557, St. George, UT 84771; (801) 673-8480.

GLACIER NATIONAL PARK HOTELS
(Glacier National Park, Montana)
Seasonal (Summer)

Perched just below the Canadian border, Glacier National Park is famous for its magnificent snowcapped peaks, booming waterfalls, crystal clear glacier lakes, and wide array of wildlife and flora. Glacier National Park is the fourth largest national park in the continental United States, encompassing more than two hundred lakes, fifty glaciers, and seven hundred miles of horse and hiking trails. Glacier National Park Hotels operates four hotels, three motor inns, coffee shops, camp stores, and an extensive transportation system.

SPECIFICS: Glacier National Park Hotels offers summer employment to approximately 900 individuals each year. The major tourist season extends from early June through late September, although some employees begin work as early as May 1 and a few remain as late as October 1. Applications are accepted for waitpersons, buspersons, front desk clerks, bartenders, cocktail servers, cashiers, bell porters, room attendants, housepersons, porters, line cooks, kitchen workers, gift shop and camp store clerks, reservation clerks, general office personnel, accounting clerks, gardeners, laundry workers, warehouse clerks, truck drivers, bus driver, tour guides, and country western musicians. In addition to regular jobs, all employees have opportunities to participate as singers, dancers, musicians, movie projectionists, and sound/lighting technicians in evening entertainment programs.

INSIDER TIPS: The Glacier National Park hotels are known for their evening entertainment presentations. Accordingly, music and voice majors, as well as those with special talents or skills, are given extra consideration. When applying list on a separate sheet of paper your talents or interests that might be useful in the evening entertainment program. Hotel, restaurant, accounting, and culinary arts students may also apply for special trainee positions within those divisions. Be aware that Glacier National Park is an area of vast pristine wilderness. While there are numerous opportunities for horseback riding, hiking, swimming, fishing, and other outdoor activities, city-style entertainment is not readily available—leave your bowling ball at home.

PERKS: Room and board are provided for employees for a nominal charge. Details on available positions, wages, and perks are available from the company at the address below.

TO APPLY: Applicants desiring a complete listing of available positions, salaries, and other important details should write to Ian B. Tippet, Executive Director of Personnel, Glacier National Park Hotels, Glacier Park Inc., Greyhound Tower, Mail Station 1210, 3800 North Central Avenue, Phoenix, Arizona 85077; (602) 248-2612 (mid-September through mid-May); or P.O. Box 147, East Glacier Park, Montana 59434; (406) 226-9311 (mid-May through mid-September).

HAMILTON STORES, INC.
(Yellowstone National Park, Montana/Wyoming)
Seasonal (Summer)

Hamilton Stores owns and operates fourteen general stores and photo shops in Yellowstone National Park. The stores sell a wide variety of merchandise including apparel, gifts, jewelry, fishing supplies, food, photo supplies, etc.

SPECIFICS: Hamilton Stores hires approximately 950 employees each year for its seasonal summer positions in Yellowstone. The first of the company's fourteen stores opens in April and the rest open in May and June. Stores begin to close in September and all are closed by mid-October. Applications are accepted for sales clerks, food service clerks, grill and fountain fry cooks, employee dining room cooks and assistants, fountain maintenance personnel, cashiers, grocery store clerks, distribution center workers, data entry operators, security guards, custodians, dormitory supervisors, and auditors. Starting pay ranges from a minimum of $4.25 per hour and up depending on the position. Most employees are needed from mid-May through mid-September.

INSIDER TIPS: Most positions are filled by March, although mid-season vacancies are filled during the months of April through August. The company looks for employees with "initiative, a cheerful attitude toward customers and fellow workers, dependability, and a commitment to complete their employment agreement dates." All employees must be at least nineteen years old.

PERKS: Room and board are provided for all employees at a minimal charge. Most room accommodations are two-person rooms with a shared bath. Trailer sites with full hookups are also available. Tips are available for most food service personnel. Employees are free two consecutive days each week to enjoy the park's many outdoor recreational activities. Yellowstone has a summer recreation cooperative that provides activities for all employees in the park and includes activities such as dances, whitewater rafting trips, sports leagues, etc.

TO APPLY: Applicants should write for an official application from Nina Sims, Director of Human Resources, Hamilton Stores, P.O.

Box 2700, Santa Barbara, California 93102 (November through March); or P.O. Box 250, West Yellowstone, Montana 59758; (406) 646-7325 (April through October). Send a SASE with all correspondence.

THE IMPERIAL HOTEL AND CASINO
(Cripple Creek, Colorado)
Seasonal (Summer and Fall) and Year-Round

The Imperial Hotel was built in 1896 and maintains its turn-of-the-century charm. The hotel's main attraction is a daily series of classic melodramas that have been produced at the hotel for the past forty years. The hotel itself has been completely restored to its original condition and re-creates the Gold Rush era. The Grand Opening for the Casino is scheduled for June 6, 1992. There are 200 slot machines and twelve table games. The Imperial Casino is the largest most complete facility in Cripple Creek.

SPECIFICS: The hotel employs waitrons, bus persons, host/hostess, bartenders, housekeepers, cocktail waitresses, cooks, pantry help, dishwashers, buffet runners, cafe attendants, theater bar waitresses, reservations secretaries, desk clerks and night desk clerks. The casino employs (Colorado Support License required) slot technicians, change persons, dealers, floorpersons, cashiers, soft and hard count teams, surveillance, and security personnel.

INSIDER TIPS: "We look for people who are willing to work closely with their fellow employees and show a sense of pride and commitment to their work." All applicants must be at least eighteen years of age to work in the hotel and at least twenty-one years of age to work in the Casino (plus possess a valid Colorado Support License).

PERKS: Medical and life insurance benefits, and room and board is available on a limited basis.

TO APPLY: Applicants should write for an official application by sending a SASE to The Imperial Hotel and Casino, P.O. Box 1003, Cripple Creek, Colorado 80813; (719) 689-2922.

INCLINE VILLAGE PARKS AND RECREATION DEPARTMENT
(Incline Village, Nevada)
Year-Round and Seasonal

The Incline Village Parks and Recreation Department services Incline Village and Crystal Bay, Nevada, two continuous recreation areas located on the northeastern shore of Lake Tahoe. The Incline Recreation Center opened its doors in October 1992. Features of the $6.4 million center include a 25-yard by eight-lane swimming pool with a one-meter diving board, gymnasium, dance studio, game room, sport shop, health food bar, and child care center. The department also operates two private beaches, parks facilities, and numerous recreation programs during the summer months.

SPECIFICS: Available positions include recreation/sports leaders, child care coordinators, child care leaders, recreation clerk, recreation center host, lifeguards, pool and building maintenance staff, aerobic instructors, and other activity instructors. A brochure listing temporary seasonal Parks and Recreation positions for office staff, parks staff, aquatic staff, and recreation programs is published annually in the spring.

PERKS: Free or discounted employee and family use of all recreational facilities, including pools, beaches, golf courses, tennis, ski and other recreation areas is provided for all employees. Benefits for permanent staff are extensive.

TO APPLY: Applicants should write for an application and listing of job opportunities to Incline Village Parks and Recreation Department, 980 Incline Way, Incline Village, Nevada 89451; (702) 832-1300.

INCLINE VILLAGE GOLF RESORT
(Incline Village, Nevada)
Seasonal (Spring through Fall)

The Incline Village Golf Resort consists of two picturesque golf courses on the North Shore of Lake Tahoe. The Championship Course is rated in the top seventy-five public courses in America, and the Executive Course is generally regarded as one of the finest courses of its type in the world. Both courses attract upscale clientele looking for a premier golfing experience.

SPECIFICS: The Incline Village Golf Resort hires numerous new employees to fill its seasonal staff each year. The season typically extends from mid-April through early November. Seasonal opportunities are available in the following general areas: grounds maintenance, pro shop operations, office operations, and food and beverage.

INSIDER TIPS: Incline Village Golf Resort is a progressive employer looking for employees with high standards who enjoy working with people. Applications should be submitted in early to mid-March.

PERKS: Staff members receive golfing privileges as well as other recreational privileges such as free beach and recreation center access.

TO APPLY: Résumés should be sent to: Incline Village Golf Resort, P.O. Box 7590, Incline Village, Nevada 89452.

THE INN OF THE ROCKIES/
HOLIDAY INN ESTES PARK
(Estes Park, Colorado)

Seasonal (Summer) and Year-Round

The Inn of the Rockies/Holiday Inn is a 155-room resort in Colorado's snowcapped Rocky Mountains. The resort is open year-round and features an indoor pool, whirlpool spa, restaurant, and conference center. The inn is located five miles from the entrance to Rocky Mountain National Park, sixty miles from Denver.

SPECIFICS: The inn hires up to eighty peak-season staff members. Staff are recruited for both seasonal as well as year-round help. Seasonal employees are usually needed from mid-May or early June through late September. Applications are accepted for guest services representatives to register hotel guests, book reservations, and handle telephone inquiries, waitstaff, buspersons, dining room hosts and hostesses, room attendants, and laundry personnel. Salaries for new 1993 employees started at $2.13 per hour plus tips for waitstaff and $4.50 per hour for other positions (subject to increase).

INSIDER TIPS: "We look for applicants with professional public contact skills who display a professional demeanor and appearance."

PERKS: Staff are welcome to use the inn's pool, whirlpool spa, and fitness room during the off season. Employees receive 50% discounts on meals, and 40% discounts in the gift shop. Year-round employees enjoy paid holidays, sick time, and profit sharing.

TO APPLY: Applicants should send a cover letter, résumé, photograph (optional), and SARP to Bill Lodge, Holiday Inn Resort, P.O. Box 1468, Estes Park, Colorado 80517; (303) 586-2332.

THE INN OF THE SEVENTH MOUNTAIN
(Bend, Oregon)
Seasonal (Summer and Winter) and Year-Round

The Inn of the Seventh Mountain is one of the Northwest's premier destination resorts. Open year-round, the inn attracts guests with its modern condominium and studio units overlooking the vast virgin forests of central Oregon. In the summer months, guests explore the nearby lakes, Deschutes River, and vast forest lands. The winter months bring skiing, snowmobiling, ice skating, sleigh riding, and snow shoeing.

SPECIFICS: The inn employs 220 seasonal and year-round employees. Applications are accepted throughout the year for positions as maids, housepersons, custodians, exterior and interior laborers, recreation leaders, skating attendants (winter only), front desk clerks, reservationists, switchboard operators, coffee shop bussers, coffee shop waitpersons, coffee shop hosts/hostesses, catering waitpersons, catering setup staff, catering bartenders, cooks, pantry persons, secretaries, supervisors/managers, fast food attendants, grocery store clerks, night auditors, gas station attendants, and security guards. There is also a unique recreation intern program for qualified students. Applicants should indicate the positions they are interested in and whether or not they would accept another position if offered. Salaries range from minimum wage to $4.75 per hour during the first ninety-day probationary period. A salary review and possible wage increase occurs following the probationary period.

INSIDER TIPS: "We are always willing to accept applications for employment. We only interview, however, as positions become available. At that time, we review all applications on file and will contact you for an interview should your skills and experience match our job requirements. We look for individuals who can give what we like to call 'value added' service, people who take pleasure in serving others."

PERKS: Housing is available for recreation interns only. Waitpersons receive guest gratuities. Employees are permitted to use all the resort's facilities during days and hours as specified by management.

TO APPLY: Applicants should either write for an official application or send a cover letter, résumé, and SARP to Sharon Thornton, Personnel Department, Inn of the Seventh Mountain, P.O. Box 1207, Bend, Oregon 97709; (503) 382-8711, ext. 568. Applicants for the recreation internship program should write and request the program information brochure.

INNS OF BANFF PARK
(Banff, Alberta, Canada)
Seasonal (Summer and Winter) and Year-Round

The Inns of Banff Park offer a choice of four hotels and motels from which visitors can explore the many varied attractions of Banff and Banff National Park. This region is famous for its spectacular alpine beauty, abundant wildlife, and world-class skiing.

SPECIFICS: The Inns of Banff Park hire between 80 and 120 employees for both year-round and seasonal positions. While there are some winter seasonal opportunities, most jobs are either summer seasonal (late May through September 10) or year-round. Applications are accepted for housekeepers, laundry attendants, buspersons, waitpersons, and front desk clerks. Front desk clerks must have prior experience. Starting wages range from CAN$4.50 to CAN$5.75 depending on the position and experience. All applications for summer employment must be completed by March 31.

INSIDER TIPS: The inns look for "hard-working, dedicated, enthusiastic, responsible employees who understand the important (aspects) involved with working in the hospitality industry." The only facilities that employees may use are the resorts' lounges. Non-Canadian citizens with proper work visas are welcome to apply.

PERKS: Staff accommodations are available at a minimal cost and staff meals are available at a significant discount.

TO APPLY: Applicants should write for an official application or send a cover letter, résumé, photograph, and SARP to Jean-Alfred Beland, Assistant Manager, P.O. Box 1077, Banff, Alberta T0L 0C0 Canada; (403) 762-4581.

MT. RAINIER GUEST SERVICES
(Mt. Rainier National Park, Washington)
Seasonal (Summer)

Mt. Rainier Guest Services is the official concessionaire for Mt. Rainier National Park. The centerpiece of the park is 14,410-foot Mt. Rainier. The company operates several facilities, including the Paradise Inn at the 5,400-foot level on Mt. Rainier. Activities include hiking, fishing, cross-country skiing, camping, climbing, and photography.

SPECIFICS: Mt. Rainier Guest Services hires 200 seasonal employees annually. Most employees start between mid-May and mid-June and stay through Labor Day or mid-October. Applications are accepted throughout the year including during the busy summer season. Applications are accepted for all entry-level positions including kitchen utility staff, pantry helpers/cook helpers, housekeepers, cafeterias, snack bar help, gift shop sales, front desk clerks, hosts/hostesses, cashiers, auditors, night security officers (no weapon carried), bellhops, and waitpersons.

INSIDER TIPS: Management looks for a willingness to work very hard during the incredibly busy summer season. "To increase your chances of being hired, show the exact dates you are available and be realistic about your job choices." Applicants are encouraged to call or write to update their application status. As with all national park concessionaires, Mt. Rainier Guest Services enforces a strict dress, conduct, and drug policy.

PERKS: Housing and meals are available for most employees within easy walking distance from work areas.

TO APPLY: Applicants should write for an official application from Mt. Rainier Guest Services, Personnel Director, P.O. Box 108, Ashford, Washington 98304; (206) 569-2400.

NATIONAL PARK CONCESSIONS, INC.
(Blue Ridge Parkway, North Carolina and Virginia)
Seasonal (Summer)

The Blue Ridge Parkway is a spectacular roadway administered by the National Park Service. The parkway traverses the highlands of Virginia and North Carolina from Shenandoah National Park in Virginia to Great Smokey Mountain National Park in North Carolina and Tennessee. From May 1 through October 31 National Park Concessions operates a variety of services on the roadway including Doughton Park (lodge, coffee shop, photo and crafts shop, and service station), Rocky Know (cabins), Mabry Mill (coffee shop and crafts shop), Price Park (park and boat dock), and Crabtree Meadows (coffee shop, crafts shop, and service station).

SPECIFICS: National Park Concessions hires more than 125 new employees each year to fill its staff positions on the Blue Ridge Parkway. Approximately 200 applications are received annually. Jobs are available for seasonal summer employment and applications must be completed by February 28. Applications are accepted for waitpersons, room clerks, bellhops, sales clerks, hosts/hostesses, cooks, cooks' helpers, general kitchen helpers, housemen, maids, service station attendants, and general maintenance staff. Starting salaries range from $3.65 per hour to more than $6.00 per hour depending on the position, experience, and unique qualifications. All summer seasonal staff must be available to work at least from June through Labor Day. Most positions are for May 1 through October 31.

INSIDER TIPS: According to National Park Concessions, "Working in a national park (or along the parkway) can be a rewarding experience. Besides earning money, the work offers the opportunity to gain an intimate knowledge of your park, its environment, and the unique features that earned it a place in the national park system. National Park Concessions seeks applicants who are genuinely interested in serving the national park visitor. Employees must be able to get along with fellow workers and conduct themselves, both on and off duty, in a manner that will reflect favorably upon their park and their employer." As emergency medical care is often not immediately available, individuals with conditions that require frequent or sudden medical care should not apply. Applicants should be aware that all employees will be required to work some holidays and weekends. Applicants with the longest availability dates receive first consideration for positions. Apply early for employee housing as staff accommodations on the parkway are extremely limited.

PERKS: When available, room and board are provided at a subsidized employee rate (currently $6.25 per day; subject to change). All linens and blankets are provided for employees living in company housing. Uniforms are provided for some positions.

TO APPLY: Applicants should write for an official application from G. B. Hanson, President & General Manager, National Park Concessions, General Offices, Mammoth Cave, Kentucky 42259-0027; (502) 773-2191. Management does not respond to all applications, but individuals who are selected for employment will be contacted prior to May 1. While not required, submission of a résumé and photograph with your application is helpful. Note that this company also operates concessions in Mammoth Cave, Isle Royale, Big Bend, and Olympic national parks. Only one application is required for work in any of these areas. (See separate listings herein.)

RED LION INN
(Durango, Colorado)
Seasonal (Summer and Winter) and Year-Round

The Red Lion Inn is a new 159-room hotel on the banks of the Animas River in Colorado's Rocky Mountains. Nearby attractions include skiing, horseback riding, whitewater rafting, golf, fishing, biking, and hiking.

SPECIFICS: The Red Lion Inn employs 135 people with approximately fifty new openings annually. Both long-term as well as seasonal staff are recruited. Summer seasonal workers must be available by approximately May 20. Applications are accepted for food servers, front desk clerks, bellmen, housekeepers, host/hostesses, cooks, and bartenders.

INSIDER TIPS: "We seek applicants who are well-groomed, responsible, professional, honest, dependable, and are career- or goal-oriented. Experience in the hospitality industry is helpful but not required."

PERKS: Employees receive free meals during shifts. Food and beverage staff earn generous tips and all staff are eligible for a full benefit package after ninety days.

TO APPLY: Applicants should write for an official application or send a cover letter, résumé, photograph (optional), and SARP to Patrick D. Rice, General Manager, Red Lion Inn, 501 Camino Del Rio, Durango, Colorado 81301; (303) 259-6580.

ROCKY MOUNTAIN PARK COMPANY
(Rocky Mountain National Park, Colorado)
Seasonal (Summer)

Rocky Mountain National Park was created in 1915 and contains seventy-one peaks reaching over 12,000 feet into the air. The park straddles forty miles of the Continental Divide. As a brochure proudly proclaims, "this is truly where mountains soar above the trees—where only the sturdiest of animals survive—and only the tundra can grow."

SPECIFICS: The Rocky Mountain Park Company hires fifty summer seasonal staff members to work in retail and food service positions at its Trail Ridge Store in Rocky Mountain National Park. Applicants should be available to work Memorial Day through September. The company accepts applications for gift shop sales clerks, stockroom staff, kitchen assistants, office help, and supervisory staff.

INSIDER TIPS: "Like our visitors, our employees come from all areas of the United States and the total summer experience is one of work, fellowship, and friendship. Employment here also provides an excellent opportunity to work in an area containing some of the world's most beautiful scenery. All applicants must be physically able to work at a 12,000-foot elevation. People with asthmatic, upper respiratory, or heart conditions should not apply. Staff must maintain an attractive appearance, a high level of energy, and be well-groomed."

PERKS: Staff housing is provided in modern facilities in nearby Estes Park. Employees are welcome to use the Estes Park Holiday Inn Holidome (pool, sauna, etc.) and are entitled to a 40% discount at the Trail Ridge Store and a 50% meal discount at the Holiday Inn's restaurant.

TO APPLY: Applicants should write for an official information packet and application from the Rocky Mountain Park Company, P.O. Box 2680, Estes Park, Colorado 80517; (303) 586-9319.

RUBY HOUSE RESTAURANT
(Keystone, South Dakota)

Seasonal (Summer)

Ruby House Restaurant will take you back 100 years to the home of Ruby Tucker, the local "madam" of this reconstructed Wild West mining town. The restaurant is located in Keystone, South Dakota, at the base of Mt. Rushmore.

SPECIFICS: Ruby House hires more than fifty new employees annually to fill its seasonal staff of sixty-four. Management prefers staff who can be available as soon as possible after April 15 and stay as late as possible until October 15. Applications are accepted for waiters, waitresses, concession personnel, bartenders, cocktail waitresses, cooks, prep cooks, cashiers, hosts/hostesses, office persons, dishwashers, and janitors. Salaries range from $275 to $400 per month plus free room and board or minimum wage without room/board.

INSIDER TIPS: Early applicants have the best chance of obtaining a position.

PERKS: Staff members have the option of free room and board. All employees receive a "Black Hills Badland Pass" that allows free or discounted admission to many local attractions.

TO APPLY: Applicants should write for an official application from Personnel Manager LaCinda Paxton, Ruby House Restaurant, P.O. Box 163, Keystone, South Dakota 57751; (605) 666-4404.

ST. MARY ENTERPRISES, INC.
(St. Mary, Montana)
Seasonal (Summer)

St. Mary Lodge & Resort is one of Montana's most notable full-service high country resorts. Located in the heart of St. Mary Valley at the east entrance to Glacier National Park, the resort offers hiking, horseback riding, fishing, nature and wildlife photography, and easy access to the natural wonders of Glacier National Park. The resort village, operated by St. Mary RB Inc., includes two motels, a wide variety of cabins, a supermarket, three service stations, a sporting goods store, clothing store, gift shop, dining room, beer parlor, lodge, laundromat, and post office.

SPECIFICS: St. Mary Enterprises hires approximately 140 new employees each season to fill its 200 summer positions. Hiring begins in December with advertising and interviews at many major midwestern colleges and universities. The resort is open from early May to mid-October, although most employees work approximately June 15 through September 10. Applications are accepted for bartenders, maids, cooks, cashiers, kitchen help, retail clerks, cocktail servers, desk clerks, maintenance staff, office personnel, and waitpersons.

INSIDER TIPS: Most employees are needed from June 15 through September 10; however, the longer an applicant can stay the better his or her chances of being hired. Do not accept a position unless you are certain that you can stay through the date stated in your employment contract as the resort is isolated and one former employee reported difficulties in getting home when leaving ahead of schedule.

PERKS: Room and board is provided for all employees and the company pays an end-of-season bonus to employees who fulfill their employment contracts.

TO APPLY: Applicants should write for an official application and employment information brochure from St. Mary RB, Inc., P.O. Box 1808, Sun Valley, Idaho 83353; (208) 726-7203 (winter address); or St. Mary RB, Inc., St. Mary, Montana 59417; (406) 732-4431 (summer address).

SIGNAL MOUNTAIN LODGE
(Moran, Wyoming)
Seasonal (Summer)

This exclusive mountain lodge is nestled on the shores of Jackson Lake in the heart of Grand Teton National Park between Yellowstone and Jackson. Signal Mountain Lodge operates a variety of lodging facilities, stores, marinas, and restaurants.

SPECIFICS: Signal Mountain hires 130 seasonal employees annually. The lodge employs marina workers, office staff, waitstaff, cooks, gift shop clerks, lodging staff, maintenance workers, buspersons, and dishwashers. Pay varies but many positions are eligible for end-of-season bonuses of fifty cents per hour worked. Applicants without prior experience in the hospitality industry are encouraged to apply for positions as lodging help, buspersons, and dishwashers.

INSIDER TIPS: Management seeks employees who can be available from May through September. The later an applicant is willing to stay, the better his or her chances of being hired. Most hiring decisions are made from January through March. Applications should list easy to reach references.

PERKS: Housing is available to employees for $6.50 per day (rate subject to change). The staff is welcome to use the resort's marina and recreation facilities. The lodge organizes numerous employee activities including sporting events and employee whitewater rafting trips.

TO APPLY: Applicants should write for an official application from Cindy Artist, Personnel Manager, Signal Mountain Lodge, P.O. Box 50, Moran, Wyoming 83013; (307) 543-2831 or 733-5470.

SMILE CLICK
(Queenstown, New Zealand)
Seasonal (Winter and Summer)

Smile Click is a photo company located in spectacular Queenstown, New Zealand. The company's photographers take action and staged photos of skiers at Queenstown's nearby ski resorts and action shots of participants on jet boat and whitewater rafting trips.

SPECIFICS: A limited number of positions are available for photographers, photo lab technicians, and photo shop sales staff. Positions are seasonal, with winter positions running July through September and summer positions available from December 20 through the end of March. (Remember, seasons in New Zealand are the opposite of those in the Northern hemisphere.)

INSIDER TIPS: Management considers all applicants who have proper New Zealand work permits.

PERKS: Perks vary according to the photographers' assignments.

TO APPLY: Write for an official application or send a cover letter, résumé, and photograph to Smile Click, P.O. Box 196, Queenstown, New Zealand; phone: (294) 29-249. Photographers should send samples of their work for consideration with applications. Samples will not be returned so do not send original prints or negatives.

STEIN ERIKSEN LODGE
(Park City, Utah)
Seasonal (Winter and Spring) and Year-Round

The Stein Eriksen Lodge is a ski in–ski out access lodge located mid-mountain in Utah's Deer Valley. The lodge is one of the most luxurious in Utah and caters to a demanding, high-class clientele.

SPECIFICS: The Stein Eriksen Lodge employs more than 250 staff members for the busy ski season and 150 summer season personnel. The lodge hires more than one hundred new employees annually. Most winter season hiring is done in September and October. Applications are accepted for both seasonal and long-term help. Summer staff work from approximately May 15 through September 15. Winter seasonal staff must be available to work from approximately November 15 through April 15. Applications are accepted for all typical hotel positions.

INSIDER TIPS: "We are a service-oriented hotel. We need self-starters who are well-groomed, articulate, outgoing, motivated, and friendly."

PERKS: All employees receive free ski privileges at Deer Valley.

TO APPLY: Applicants should write for an official application or send a cover letter and résumé. A personal interview is required before a final commitment to hire is made. Contact Cheryl L. DeCastro, Human Resources Administrator, Stein Eriksen Lodge, P.O. Box 3177, Park City, Utah 84060; (801) 649-3700.

SUNSHINE VILLAGE
(Banff National Park, Alberta, Canada)
Seasonal (Winter and Summer) and Year-Round

Sunshine Village is an alpine year-round destination resort located high atop the Canadian Rockies in Banff National Park. The village is nestled at an elevation of 7,200 feet and is accessible only by a scenic twenty-five-minute, 5-kilometer gondola ride. The Swiss-engineered gondola is the longest in Canada and provides unbeatable sights as it passes waterfalls, canyons, and sheer rock mountain faces.

SPECIFICS: Sunshine Village receives more than 3,000 applications each year for its 325 annual job openings. The resort employs 430 winter season staff, 130 summer season staff, and seventy year-round employees. Jobs are available for both summer and winter seasonal staff as well as year-round personnel. Summer seasonal staff should be available from June through Labor Day. Winter seasonal staff usually begin work in mid-November and stay until the snow melts in late spring. Applications are accepted for winter positions as lift operators, ski school instructors (CSIA level II, III, or IV certification required), ski patrollers (strong skiing skills and emergency medical technician certificate or equivalent required), Sunshine Ambassadors (lead mountain tours; excellent skiing ability required), gondola operators, CAT drivers (must have 2,000-plus hours experience operating heavy machinery), ticket checkers, parking attendants, village services attendants, warehouse shipping and receiving personnel, ticket sellers, and customer service staff. Winter and summer seasonal jobs are available for waitpersons, food service cashiers, cooks, bartenders, food preparation workers, dishwashers, buspersons, janitors, front desk clerks, switchboard operators, chamberpersons, house persons, reservationists, luggage attendants, night auditors, and day care attendants. Year-round jobs are available for maintenance workers, millwrights, electricians, mechanics, and clerical/secretarial staff. Applications for all positions are accepted throughout the year. Most starting salaries are between CAN$5.00 and CAN$5.50 per hour.

INSIDER TIPS: "We look for friendly, enthusiastic individuals who are self-motivated, enjoy life, and have good attitudes. If you enjoy a mixture of hard work and great skiing, you are encouraged to apply. When completing your application, be neat, accurate, and complete, and include previous employment and references. If possible, include a résumé with your application. Applications are welcomed from non-Canadian citizens with valid work permits."

PERKS: Sunshine offers a unique perk in that employees receive a free season ski pass valid at Sunshine and eight other local ski areas. Free skiing lessons, subsidized transportation, and on-site accommodations are provided for employees. Sunshine offers employee discounts on food and ski equipment.

TO APPLY: Applicants should either write for an official application (and enclose a résumé) or send a cover letter, résumé, and photograph to Sunshine Village Corporation, Employment Coordinator, Box 1510, Banff, Alberta T0L 0C0, Canada; (403) 762-6545. Management reports responding to all applications within two weeks.

TAMARRON RESORT
(Durango, Colorado)
Seasonal (Summer and Winter) and Year-Round

As Tamarron's brochure proudly proclaims, "In all the world there is no setting more exquisite than Tamarron's." While most brochures tend to exaggerate the facts just a bit, Tamarron's boast holds true. This 630-acre year-round resort offers elegance and service unmatched in the Rocky Mountains. This is truly a year-round resort. In the summer there is the challenge of the eighteen-hole golf course. In the winter guests sharpen their skiing skills at Tamarron's own ski mountain or at nearby Purgatory ski area. Tamarron is located in the heart of the San Juan National Forest, 18 miles north of Durango.

SPECIFICS: Tamarron employs an average of 375 staff members (450 during the peak summer and winter seasons). Employment opportunities are available for both summer seasonal, winter seasonal, and year-round help. Summer season is Tamarron's busiest and generally runs from May through early October. The peak winter season begins on Thanksgiving weekend and lasts through March. The months of April and early November are the only slow months and the resort lays off a portion of its staff during these brief periods. Management actively recruits food and beverage servers, buspersons, bartenders, cocktail waitpersons, golf course greens keepers, ski lift operators, janitors, maids, cooks, front desk clerks, clerical support staff, bus drivers, security officers, accounting clerks, banquet staff, purchasing agents, recreation department staff (operates all recreational programs except golf and tennis), stable wranglers, a tennis pro, and a golf pro.

INSIDER TIPS: According to Personnel Director Adelle Anderson, "Fifty percent of our hiring decision is based on attitude. Our employees must enjoy giving service to our guests. We want pleasant outgoing 'people' types." As with many resort hotels, Tamarron suffers from a shortage of qualified applicants. This past year the employee shortage was so critical that Tamarron contacted seventy-five other resorts that had laid off employees for their slow season and recruited from them. Most hiring is done during a twice yearly "job fair." If you are unable to attend the job fair (held roughly two weeks prior to the beginning of each peak season), a phone interview can be arranged.

PERKS: Winter employee perks include a free lift pass for the Tamarron Ski Hill, use of the resort's Nordic ski trails, 50% discounts on alpine and Nordic ski lessons, 50% discount on sleigh rides and snowmobiling (limited days), complimentary health spa membership during slow business times and employee days, and numerous social and recreational activities. Summer employees enjoy one complimentary whitewater rafting trip, complimentary jeep trips (space available), discounts on golf and tennis, complimentary health club membership (limited days), and numerous company-sponsored social and sporting activities. All employees receive group insurance, paid vacations, and various food, drink, and merchandise discounts. Some perks do not apply until after completion of a probationary period.

TO APPLY: Applicants should either attend one of the Tamarron job fairs (contact the employment office at the address below for dates and times) or write for an official application or send a cover letter and résumé to Adelle Anderson, Personnel Director, Tamarron Resort, P.O. Box 3131, Durango, Colorado 81301; (303) 259-2000.

TIMBERLINE LODGE
(Timberline Lodge, Oregon)
Seasonal (Summer and Winter)

For true ski enthusiasts there is no place closer to paradise than the Timberline Lodge. Timberline is one of the few resorts in the world to offer year-round skiing. In addition to excellent winter skiing, Timberline offers summer glacier skiing on beginning to intermediate terrain. The lodge itself is a deluxe fifty-seven-room hotel with two restaurants. Lest you think the lodge's address is incomplete, the hotel has the distinction of being its own postal town!

SPECIFICS: Timberline hires more than 100 new employees each year to fills its 200- to 290-person staff. Summer seasonal employees are needed from May through September. Winter staff should be available from November through May. The resort employs twenty room attendants, twenty food servers, twenty cooks and food prep staff members, twenty-five waitpersons, and thirty to seventy ski instructors and lift operators.

INSIDER TIPS: Previous experience is helpful but not essential. Management only responds to applications if a position is being offered. All applications are kept on file for one year.

PERKS: Employees receive ski passes to use when not on duty.

TO APPLY: Applicants should write for an official application from the Personnel Office, Timberline Lodge, Timberline Lodge, Oregon 97028; (503) 272-3311.

TOPNOTCH AT STOWE
(Stowe, Vermont)
Seasonal (Summer and Winter) and Year-Round

Topnotch, nestled in the heart of the Green Mountains, is situated in one of Vermont's most picturesque villages. This internationally acclaimed, 120-acre, four-star resort is one of the top fifty tennis resorts in the country and Stowe's Mt. Mansfield is consistently ranked as one of the top ten ski areas. The resort has its own equestrian center, tennis facilities, pools, cross-country ski trails, exercise room, and health spa.

SPECIFICS: Topnotch at Stowe employs more than 140 staff members. At least fifty seasonal positions are available annually. The busiest seasons are from June through October and December through March. While experience is preferred, it is not required. Positions are available for dishwashers, prep cooks, cooks, bartenders, cocktail staff, waitpersons, housekeepers, maintenance staff, reservationists, cashiers, front desk help, and bell staff. Starting pay ranges from minimum wage to $6.50 per hour.

INSIDER TIPS: Management seeks mature individuals interested in personal growth through working in a team atmosphere.

PERKS: Employees are allowed to use resort facilities on a limited basis. Employee discounts are offered at resort restaurants and lounges. There is an employee incentive program, a staff tennis program, and discounts at the equestrian and Nordic ski centers.

TO APPLY: Applicants should send a cover letter and résumé to Personnel Manager, Topnotch at Stowe, P.O. Box 1260, Stowe, Vermont 05672; (802) 253-8585.

TW RECREATIONAL SERVICES, INC.
(Bryce Canyon National Park, Utah)
Seasonal (Summer)

Bryce Canyon National Park is located in the Color Country of southern Utah. This diverse environment combines the towering Ponderosa pine and spruce forest with the mystifying freestanding spires and sculptured pinnacles of the red rock of Bryce Canyon—formations unique in all the world. TW Recreational Services operates the lodge and all concession facilities in the park. TW also operates lodges at Zion, Grand Canyon (North Rim), and Scotty's Castle national parks and monuments.

SPECIFICS: TW Recreational Services employs 400 seasonal staff members to work in its seasonal operations from mid-May through mid-October. Employment is available in the following departments: tour guides, front desk, dining room, cafeteria, snack bar, kitchen, housekeeping, service station, maintenance, cocktail lounge, accounting, and gift store. Some management positions are also available. The minimum age required for all employees is eighteen and proof of age and citizenship are required.

INSIDER TIPS: This is not a job for those who yearn for the excitement of the big city. Bryce Canyon National Park is a place of awesome beauty and peaceful isolation. As with all jobs with national park concessionaires, TW Recreational Services enforces a strict dress code and drug policy. Details of all employee rules and regulations are provided with the official application.

PERKS: Room and board are provided to all employees at a minimal cost. The company sponsors recreational and social activities throughout the season.

TO APPLY: Applicants should write for an official application from LaMar Snyder, Personnel Manager, TW Recreational Services, 451 N. Main St., P.O. Box 400, Cedar City, Utah 84720; (801) 586-9476.

TW SERVICES, INC.
(Yellowstone National Park, Wyoming)

Seasonal (Summer)

TW Services is the official National Park Service concessionaire for most guest services within Yellowstone National Park. TW's operations include hotels, lodges, dining rooms, cafeterias, gift shops, bus service, boat rentals/charters, and horse facilities. In addition to its famous geysers, hot springs, steam vents, and mud pots, the park protects large areas of pristine wilderness and a rich wildlife population.

SPECIFICS: TW Services employs more than 2,200 summer seasonal staff to operate its park activities. Seasonal staff is needed from April into November. However, many employee positions are available for those who can only work June through September. All employees must be a minimum of eighteen years of age when reporting for work. Available positions include food and beverage manager, assistant food and beverage manager, food production manager, bar manager, dining room manager, employee dining room supervisor, steward, senior cook, cook, cook's helper, kitchen help, fast food help, dining room help, bartender, pub manager, pub tender, pizza cook, storekeeper, food and beverage payroll clerk, front office manager, executive housekeeper, room clerk, room attendant, bell porter, linen coordinator, laundry help, night security, cashier, audit clerk, night auditor, location controller, carpenter, plumber, electrician, painter, maintenance personnel, boiler technician, gift shop manager, gift shop sales clerk, bus driver, tour guide, dock helper, fishing guide, excursion boat staff, wrangler, stagecoach/wagon team driver, activity sales agent, camper service supervisor, vending machine help, warehouse staff, employee activities coordinator, employee activities assistant coordinator, personnel manager, residence coordinator, dorm crew, activity control clerk, reservationist, group tour office, accounting office staff, data entry operator, seasonal clerk, and location manager. Most hiring is done between January and May. Apply early for best position availability.

INSIDER TIPS: "While we hope that you will enjoy Yellowstone on your days off, we expect that you will work hard when you're scheduled to work. We are looking for employees with previous experience in the hotel/restaurant industries or other guest services, and for employees who may have had little previous job-related experience but are willing to work hard, enjoy working with and for other people, and take pride in a job well done." Employment chances increase if you can arrive early and work through September or later. Your hiring prospects also increase if you are flexible about your job choices. All references are checked.

PERKS: The company provides lodging and meals for all employees. Most lodging is in dormitory-style rooms with some units for married couples. The national park offers a wide variety of activities plus an organized employee activities program, which includes athletics, rafting, rodeos, films, talent shows, dances, bus trips, and more.

TO APPLY: Applicants should write for an official application and information brochure from TW Services, Inc., Employment Office, Yellowstone National Park, Wyoming 82190.

THE VILLAGE AT BRECKENRIDGE RESORT
(Breckenridge, Colorado)
Seasonal (Summer and Winter) and Year-Round

The Village at Breckenridge is a 590-unit destination resort located at the famous Breckenridge ski area. Facilities include thirty-three shops, nine restaurants, and conference areas. Nearby activities include downhill and Nordic skiing, hiking, water sports, biking, horseback riding, tennis, and golf.

SPECIFICS: The resort's staff varies from 150 to 400 depending on the season. More than 200 new employees are hired annually. Management recruits both long-term and seasonal help. Seasonal staff should be available either November to April (winter season) or May to October (summer season). Applications are accepted for all typical resort hotel positions. Contact the Personnel Office for information on specific job openings. Wages are above average for the area and start significantly above minimum wage.

INSIDER TIPS: "We look for applicants who have even-tempered dispositions and who are cheerful, articulate, and confident. Career-oriented individuals are especially encouraged to apply."

PERKS: Management provides an extensive benefit package including a ski pass program, free employee meals, and limited assistance with employee housing.

TO APPLY: Applicants should send a cover letter, résumé, and SARP to Keith Schmotzer, Personnel Department, The Village at Breckenridge Resort, P.O. Box 8329, Breckenridge, Colorado 80424; (303)-453-2000, ext. 5152.

YELLOWSTONE PARK SERVICE STATIONS
(Yellowstone National Park, Montana)
Seasonal (Summer)

Yellowstone Park Service Stations (YPSS) is an official National Park Service concessionaire. YPSS operates seven service stations and four automotive repair facilities in Yellowstone National Park. Employees enjoy a full range of outdoor activities in Yellowstone and Grand Teton national parks as well as the surrounding national forests.

SPECIFICS: YPSS hires ninety-five employees each year to fill its seasonal summer positions. While management reports some flexibility in start and finish employment dates, ideal candidates are available from late May or early June through Labor Day. The maximum possible employment is from May 1 through October 31. Applications are accepted each year from January through May. The com-

pany has positions for fifty service station attendants, eighteen mechanics (ASE enrollment or certification required), two report clerks,
one dispatcher/clerk, and various office and warehouse staff. Starting
wages are generally above minimum wage and employees can enhance their wages through a commission program for driveway service station sales. All employees must be at least eighteen years of
age and have at least one year of school or other experience after high
school by the date they report for work.

INSIDER TIPS: Applicants have the best chance of being hired if applications are received during January. There is a minimal chance of
being hired if your application is received after May 1. "We look for
motivated people who enjoy hard outdoor work and public contact
and who are 'coachable.' Employees meet and greet the public forty
hours a week. Work is outdoors at elevations approaching 8,000 feet.
It is essential that you be both able and willing to be employed
continuously in Yellowstone National Park during the period June 10
(give or take a few days) through August 31. If these dates aren't
feasible, it will be difficult to give favorable consideration to your
application."

PERKS: Employees who fulfill their contracts earn an end-of-season
bonus. For information on employee housing in the national park,
contact the company at the address below. Yellowstone has a recreation cooperative that provides activities for all employees in the park
during the summer season. The Yellowstone Park Campus of Northwest Community College offers summer courses for credit that is
transferrable in most cases.

TO APPLY: Applicants should write for an official application form.
Résumés are welcome with your completed application. For an application contact Yellowstone Park Service Stations, Section R, P.O. Box
11, Gardiner, Montana 59030; (406) 848-7333.

YOSEMITE PARK AND CURRY COMPANY
(Yosemite National Park, California)

Seasonal (Summer and Winter) and Year-Round

The Yosemite Park and Curry Company operates all guest services within Yosemite National Park. Yosemite, one of the most spectacular national parks in the United States, was created when giant glaciers cut a deep canyon through the Sierra Nevadas. The resulting valley has huge sheer granite cliffs with huge waterfalls. The Yosemite Park and Curry Company operates campsites, cabins, lodges, restaurants, retail stores, recreational activities, and the luxury Awhanee Hotel.

SPECIFICS: The Yosemite Park and Curry Company receives more than 8,000 applications each year for its 1,800 peak-season positions. More than 900 new employees are hired each year. Summer is the park's busiest season; summer staff should be available to work from May through September. Applications are accepted for housekeepers, dishwashers, kitchen cleaners, buspersons, waitstaff, restaurant hosts/hostesses, retail sales clerks, hotel front desk staff, recreation attendants, and wranglers.

INSIDER TIPS: "We seek employees who enjoy guest contact and are willing to enjoy the Yosemite experience." Apply as early as possible for seasonal positions.

PERKS: Employee housing is available in the park. A staff meal plan is offered. Employees receive a discount at retail outlets, the park grocery store, and at all recreational facilities.

TO APPLY: Applicants should write or call for an official application from Dorothy Richards, Manager of Employment, Personnel Department, Yosemite Park and Curry Company, Yosemite National Park, California 95389; (209) 372-1236. Management requests applicants include a résumé with their completed application forms.

The following listings, found under the chapter headings given below, also include positions near mountainous areas:

AMUSEMENT AND THEME PARKS

Dogpatch USA

Dollywood

Ponderosa Ranch

COASTS & BEACHES

Acadia Corporation

National Park Concessions, Inc.

DESERTS

National Park Concessions, Inc.

HIGH ADVENTURE

Grizzly Ranch

McGee Creek Pack Station

Pacific Crest Outward Bound
  School

Shotover Gorge Jet Boats, Ltd.

Ski Guides Hawaii

Ski Utah

Yosemite Institute

LAKES

Callaway Gardens

Clevelands House Resort

Crater Lake Lodge Inc.

El Rancho Stevens

Fairfield Pagosa Resorts

Grand View Guest
  House

Grand View Lodge Golf &
  Tennis Club

Harrah's Tahoe

Indianhead Mountain Resort

Kettle Falls Hotel, Inc.

Lake Arrowhead Hilton Lodge

Lake Louise Inn

MISCELLANEOUS

Eldorado Hotel Resort

Hilton of Santa Fe

RIVERS

Adventure Connection

All-Outdoors Adventure Trips

American River Touring
  Association

Baker-Ewing Scenic Float Trips

Beyond Limits Adventures

Chuck Richards' Whitewater,
  Inc.

Libra Expeditions

Sierra Outfitters & Guides

Sierra Whitewater
  Expeditions

Triangle X Float Trips
Whitewater Expeditions &
  Tours

Whitewater Voyages
Wilderness Aware, Inc.

SNOW & SKIING

Alta Ski Lifts
Angel Fire Resort
Attitash Ski Resort
The Big Mountain Ski &
  Summer Resort
Big Sky of Montana
Big White Ski Resort Ltd.
Blackcomb Ski Enterprises
  Ltd.
Bogus Basin
Boyne Mountain Lodge
Brian Head Ski Resort
Copper Mountain Resort & Ski
  Area
Crested Butte Mountain Resort
Crystal Mountain Resort
  (Washington)
Crystal Mountain Resort
  (Michigan)
Diamond Peak and Ski Resort
  and Cross Country Center
Elk Mountain
Fox Peak Ski Field
Hunter Mountain Ski Bowl
Jack Frost Mountain Ski Area
Loon Mountain Ski Resort

Mt. Bachelor Ski & Summer
  Resort
Mt. Hood Meadows
Northstar-at-Tahoe
Pico Ski Resort
Purgatory (Durango Ski
  Corporation)
The Remarkables Ski Area
Seven Springs Mountain Resort
Sheraton Steamboat Resort
Skiing Louise Ltd.
Snowbasin
Snowbird Ski and Summer
  Resort
Snowmass Ski Area
Steamboat Ski Area
Sugarbush Ski Resort
Sugarloaf USA
Sunday River Ski Resort
Telluride Ski Resort, Inc.
Topnotch at Stowe
Vernon Valley Great Gorge Ski
  Area
Whiteface Mountain Ski Center
Winter Park Resort

Tropical
Islands

~~~~~~~~~

CITY AND COUNTY OF HONOLULU LIFEGUARD SERVICE
(Honolulu, Island of Oahu, Hawaii)
Year-Round

If you are looking for just a bit more adventure than handing out towels at your local YMCA pool, consider applying for a job with the Honolulu Parks and Recreation Department. The department hires a large staff of lifeguards for all public beaches on the island of Oahu, including world-famous Waikiki Beach.

SPECIFICS: The City and County of Honolulu has a staff of approximately fifty full-time and sixty part-time beach lifeguards. About twenty-five new lifeguards are hired annually. Pay starts at $1,307 per month for full-time lifeguards and about $6.00 per hour for new, part-time lifeguards. The average part-time lifeguard earns $7.10 per hour. Applicants must have a current Red Cross advanced lifesaving certificate and a valid first-aid card *before* applying.

INSIDER TIPS: The Lifeguard Service gives mandatory physical fitness tests three times each year. The top finishers from each test are then offered positions. Once hired, the county will train lifeguards who are not already certified in CPR. Most vacant positions are part-time and there is a lengthy waiting list for full-time positions.

PERKS: For those in search of the ultimate tan, what better perk could you ask for than to be paid to work outdoors on Hawaii's beautiful beaches?

TO APPLY: Applicants must be in Honolulu to take the mandatory physical fitness test. For information on the next testing, contact Buster Wallwork, Officer in Charge, Water Safety Division, City and County of Honolulu, Parks and Recreation Department, 3823 Leahi Avenue, Honolulu, Hawaii 96815; (808) 922-3888.

CLUB MED
(Worldwide opportunities)
Seasonal (All Seasons) and Year-Round

As their advertisements boast, Club Med is the perfect antidote for civilization. Club Med villages are a veritable summer camp for grown-ups. The company operates more than 110 resort villages worldwide, offering complete vacation packages with all meals and activities included. The resorts are casual with absolutely no clocks or strict schedules. With the exception of a few skiing villages, most Club Med sites are beachfront and tropical with a strong emphasis on water sports such as sailing, SCUBA diving, snorkeling, windsurfing, and volleyball. Club Med currently operates villages in Austria, Switzerland (eight villages), France (thirteen villages), Copper Mountain in the United States, the Bahamas (Paradise Island and Eleuthera), Bermuda, Mexico (five villages), Spain (four villages), French Polynesia (on Moorea and Bora Bora), the Caribbean (Turkoise, Turks and Caicos, Magic Isle, Haiti, Punta Cana, Dominican

Republic, Caravelle, Guadeloupe, Martinique, St. Lucia), Portugal, Brazil (two villages), Morocco (seven villages), Senegal (two villages), Tunisia (five villages), Ivory Coast in Africa, Reunion Island, Mauritius, Egypt (four villages), Italy (eight villages), Israel (two villages), Turkey (three villages), Maldive Islands (two villages), Indonesia, Malaysia, Thailand, New Caledonia, China, Greece (five villages), Bulgaria, Japan, Romania, and Yugoslavia (two villages).

SPECIFICS: Club Med recruits GO's (GO stands for *gentil organisateur,* French for congenial host) from around the world. GO's perform all the staff positions at the villages. They act as activities directors, entertainers, water sports instructors, hotel staff, and more. Knowledge of a foreign language is not required for clubs in the "American Zone" (South Pacific, Mexico, United States, Caribbean, Bermuda, and the Bahamas); however, French is helpful. Various foreign languages (usually French) are required for work in other zones.

INSIDER TIPS: Club Med's staff is extremely friendly and helpful. They describe their GO's as "very talented and versatile young men and women from all walks of life and all parts of the world. [GO's] are hosts, instructors, entertainers, and friends, and their goal is to help [guests] have a fabulous vacation." Specific skills and experience in one activity area is essential. Club Med employees are usually "jacks of all trades." You may find yourself teaching windsurfing during the day and singing in the staff cabaret show during the evening.

PERKS: GO's are hired for a period of six months. At the end of that period the GO's performance is evaluated and those with a good rating are offered another six-month contract at another of Club Med's worldwide locations. GO's are encouraged to mix and mingle with guests and are free to use all of the village's resort facilities. Pay is $450 per month plus free room and board at the resort village.

TO APPLY: American and Canadian applicants should call the Club Med Job Hotline at (212) 977-2382 for application information.

COUNTY OF MAUI LIFEGUARD SERVICE
(Islands of Maui, Molokai, and Lanai, Hawaii)

Seasonal (limited opportunities) and Year-Round

Perhaps the ultimate Hawaiian dream job is to work as a lifeguard on a powder-white sand beach. The County of Maui's Personnel Office hires all public lifeguards for the islands of Maui, Molokai, and Lanai.

SPECIFICS: The County of Maui has positions for eleven lifeguards (serving the county's public pools) and seventeen water safety officers (beach lifeguards). Hiring is done as needed throughout the year when positions become vacant. Starting salaries are $1,796 and $1,941 per month. Applicants must be high school graduates with a current American Red Cross first aid and personal safety certificate, water safety instructor's certificate, Lifeguard Training Certificate and a valid motor vehicle license.

INSIDER TIPS: Before applying, contact the Department of Personnel Services at the address below to determine if they are currently hiring.

TO APPLY: Lifeguards are hired through the County Department of Personnel Services. Applications are only accepted during recruitment periods. Call or write for an official application and to determine when the next recruitment period will occur. Contact Raymond Y. Kokubun, Director of Personnel Services, County of Maui, Kalana O Maui Building, Sixth Floor, 200 South High Street, Wailuku, Hawaii 96793.

FRENCHMAN'S REEF AND MORNING STAR BEACH CLUB
(St. Thomas, U.S. Virgin Islands)
Seasonal (Winter) and Year-Round

Frenchman's Reef Hotel is a landmark resort center located on a scenic cliff overlooking the harbor entrance to St. Thomas. The hotel is located at Morning Star Beach and operates the beach club.

SPECIFICS: Frenchman's Reef employs 600 staff members with a 15% to 20% annual turnover. The most common vacant positions are for food service staff, restaurant waitpersons, bar staff, and front desk clerks.

INSIDER TIPS: "We look for applicants who can speak well and have a pleasant look." Housing on the island runs from moderate to expensive.

PERKS: Employees are permitted to use the hotel's beach. Because these islands are U.S. territories, U.S. citizens do not need work permits.

TO APPLY: Frenchman's Reef has one of the most stable staffs on the island. If possible, applicants should apply in person while visiting the island. For further information contact Personnel Department, Frenchman's Reef Hotel & Morning Star Beach Club, P.O. Box 7100, St. Thomas, U.S. Virgin Islands 00801; (809) 776-8500. The general manager is Nic Pourzel.

HOTEL KING KAMEHAMEHA
(Kailua Kona, Island of Hawaii, Hawaii)
Seasonal (August only) and Year-Round

The King Kamehameha is a modestly priced 460-room hotel rich in Hawaiian history. The hotel is located in the heart of Kailua Kona. "Our hotel is very special to people who are tuned in to learning the meaning of 'Hawaiiana.' We are not, however, for people who have a teen film idea of Hawaii."

SPECIFICS: The King Kamehameha hires more than seventy-five new staff members annually to fill its 265-person employee roster. Most positions are year-round as the Kona coast tends to enjoy a twelve-month tourist season. Applications are accepted for clerks, storekeepers, night auditors, front office cashiers, PBX operators, bell clerks, bell attendants, housekeepers, room inspectors, linen room attendants, and laundry staff. Pay starts at minimum wage for tipped positions and $6.00 to $8.50 per hour for non-tipped positions. (Note that during first the ninety days, employees are paid 80% of salary.)

INSIDER TIPS: "We look for long-term employees with guest contact skills, consistency in past employment, related experience, honesty, a proven history of accuracy and dependability, and good old-fashioned manners. We employ primarily long-term employees but hire seasonal help for the busy August Billfish tournament."

TO APPLY: Applicants should write for an official application from the Personnel Office, King Kamehameha Hotel, 75-5660 Palani Road, Kailua Kona, Hawaii 96740; (808) 329-2911. Enclose a SASE.

HOTEL ON THE CAY
(Christiansted, St. Croix, U.S. Virgin Islands)
Seasonal (Winter) and Year-Round

For those who have dreamed of working on a small private island, the fifty-five-room Hotel on the Cay sits on a private 7-acre island of its own. The resort's private island is located just across the bay from Christiansted, St. Croix.

SPECIFICS: The Hotel on the Cay employs seventy-one employees and hires approximately twenty new staff members each year. Applications are accepted for department managers (experience required), maintenance crew, grounds keepers, front desk clerks, housekeepers, waitpersons, cooks, chefs, and hostesses. The resort also has positions for qualified ferryboat captains to operate a tender service between the hotel's private island and St. Croix.

INSIDER TIPS: Management prefers long-term employees, but has an occasional need for seasonal workers. High season is approximately December 15 through April 15.

PERKS: Employees may use the resort's beach, tennis courts, and water sports facilities (there is a fee for water sports equipment) while off duty.

TO APPLY: Applicants should send a cover letter, résumé, photograph, SARP, and letters of reference (if available) to Hotel on the Cay, Carole Pappas, Assistant Secretary, P.O. Box 4020, Christiansted, St. Croix, U.S. Virgin Islands 00820; (809) 773-2035.

HYATT REGENCY CERROMAR AND HYATT DORADO BEACH CLUB
(Dorado, Puerto Rico)
Year-Round

More than one thousand acres of tropical paradise on Puerto Rico are home to Hyatt's beautiful Regency Cerromar and Dorado Beach Club hotels. The resort complex includes spectacular Caribbean beaches, four golf courses, tennis courts, and one of the largest swimming pools in the world.

SPECIFICS: The two Hyatt hotels in the complex employ more than 1,700 staff members. The jobs are considered excellent and turnover is rare. Nonetheless, the resorts hire more than 100 new employees each year. The resort has positions available for management trainees, restaurant assistant managers, first line supervisors, front desk clerks, housekeepers, and cooks.

INSIDER TIPS: The Hyatt generally prefers year-round employees. Management seeks employees who "have common sense and are interested in personal growth and hard work." Fluency in both English and Spanish is required. Since Puerto Rico is a U.S. territory, no visas or work permits are required for U.S. citizens.

PERKS: Employees are permitted to use the golf course during their off hours.

TO APPLY: Applicants should send a cover letter, résumé, and SARP to David Cardona, Director of Human Resources, Hyatt Hotels of Puerto Rico, Dorado, Puerto Rico 00646; (809) 796-1010.

HYATT REGENCY MAUI
(Island of Maui, Hawaii)
Seasonal (Summer) and Year-Round

The Hyatt Regency Maui hires more staff members than almost any other employer on the world-famous Kaanapali coast. This luxury hotel fronts on the sparkling white sand of Kaanapali Beach with 815 deluxe rooms on eighteen lush acres.

SPECIFICS: The Hyatt Regency Maui has a total staff of 1,250 employees with approximately 480 new staff openings annually. Major departments with frequent openings include housekeeping, food service, and recreation. Most positions are year-round and management prefers applicants interested in long-term employment. The recreation department occasionally hires short-term staff members to help during the busy summer season.

INSIDER TIPS: Applicants who can demonstrate that they can provide service to a very discriminating clientele stand the best chance of being hired. If applicants want to stand out they should dress appropriately. Applicants have a better chance of landing a job here if they know in which department they want to work.

PERKS: Employees at the Hyatt Regency Maui can qualify for free and discounted rooms at Hyatt hotels around the world.

TO APPLY: Applicants should send a cover letter, résumé, school grades, and references to Employment Manager, Hyatt Regency Maui, 200 Nohea Kai Drive, Lahaina, Maui, Hawaii 96761-1985. A photo is not required. Applicants who can apply in person are preferred.

HYATT REGENCY WAIKIKI
(Honolulu, Island of Oahu, Hawaii)
Year-Round

The Hyatt Regency Waikiki is one of the premier resort hotels on Oahu. Fronting Waikiki Beach, this 1,200-plus-room resort boasts numerous bars and restaurants including Spats Nightclub and Trappers Jazz Club, two of the hottest night spots in the area.

SPECIFICS: The Hyatt Regency Waikiki employs 1,100 employees and hires more than 300 people each year. Applicants can apply for entry-level line positions in all departments including housekeeping, front desk, bell, room service, bars, and food and beverage. Positions are also available for applicants with clerical or accounting skills. The hotel welcomes applicants who are interested in positions as management trainees or in entry-level management.

INSIDER TIPS: Applicants who are interested in staying for an extended period of time are more likely to land jobs.

PERKS: Complimentary meals are offered in a special employee cafeteria. Uniforms are provided for managers, management trainees, and line employees.

TO APPLY: Applicants should send a cover letter, résumé, and SARP to Sharen Wago, Director of Human Resources, Hyatt Regency Waikiki, 2424 Kalakaua Avenue, Honolulu, Hawaii 96815; (808) 923-1234.

HYATT REGENCY WAIKOLOA
(Waikoloa Beach, Hawaii)
Year-Round

The Hyatt's brand new hotel at Waikoloa Beach is one of the world's first "super resorts." This huge resort complex is an all-inclusive destination attraction located on 62 acres of spectacular oceanfront property on the Big Island of Hawaii's Kohala coast. The hotel consists of more than 1,200 guest rooms located in three towers. The resort complex is so large that guests are transported between buildings by monorail trains and "Disneyesque" canal boats. The complex includes a huge man-made lagoon complete with dolphins that guests can swim with (a lottery system is used to select guest participants) and a ¾-acre swimming pool with waterfall. The resort operates a full-service children's program known as Hyatt Camp Waikoloa, which is part of the nationwide Camp Hyatt program.

SPECIFICS: The Hyatt Regency Waikoloa employs 2,100 employees to service its 1,241 guest rooms and eight restaurants and twelve bars and lounges. As the hotel is brand new, the employee turnover rate has not yet been determined. As the resort expects to operate at near capacity year-round, Hyatt seeks long-term employees. Jobs are available in sixty-one different departments. Positions are available for managers (350 positions) as well as all typical hotel front line employees including front desk staff, luggage attendants, parking valets, housekeepers, waitpersons, cooks, bartenders, cocktail servers, maintenance staff, room service staff, recreation department staff, and more. Some of the more unusual jobs at this mega-resort include musicians (koto players, accordionists, guitarists, ukulele players, pianists, cellists, and big band musicians), recreation staff (aerobics instructors, kids' camp attendants, tennis facilities staff, spa staff, personal fitness trainers, and massage and loofan therapists), wildlife staff (responsible for the care of the countless exotic birds and wild animals that live around the hotel's lagoons), and fish staff (responsible for care of the resort's large collection of tropical fish and for taking guests on night fishing tours). Red Sail Sports and Dolphin

Quest act as concessionaires operating the watersports/activities and the dolphin encounter programs. For information on jobs with Red Sail Sports write Red Sail Sports, 909 Montgomery Street, Suite 601, San Francisco, CA 94133; (415) 981-4411.

INSIDER TIPS: Hyatt, a major employer (currently employing almost 3% of the island's population), is always hiring for many different positions. A personal on-site interview is required for most jobs.

PERKS: Contact the Personnel Office for specifics on wages and perks.

TO APPLY: Applicants should apply in person at the Hyatt's Personnel Office located at One Waikoloa Beach, Waikoloa Beach, Island of Hawaii, Hawaii 96743; (808) 885-5621.

THE ILIKAI HOTEL NIKKO WAIKIKI
(Honolulu, Island of Oahu, Hawaii)
Year-Round

The Ilikai Hotel Nikko Waikiki is a 1,500-room hotel and a landmark in Waikiki. It sits on the Ewa* end of famous Waikiki Beach overlooking the Ala Wai yacht harbor. The hotel is within easy walking distance from Waikiki Beach and the huge Ala Moana shopping center.

SPECIFICS: The Ilikai hires more than 100 new employees annually to fill its 550-person staff. Hourly wage positions are available in the housekeeping, food and beverage, front desk, and maintenance departments. Jobs are also available in upper and mid-level management positions. Salaries vary by position and experience.

---

*On Oahu, directions are given by Diamond Head, Eva, Malka, and Makai rather than north, south, east, and west. Diamond Head and Eva are landmarks on opposite ends of Oahu, while Malka means "toward the mountains" and Makai means "toward the sea."

INSIDER TIPS: Flexibility in work schedule is essential for all positions. Applicants should be able to communicate well, both verbally and in writing.

PERKS: Employees enjoy complimentary meals while on duty, lucrative tips, health benefits, uniforms, paid vacations and sick leave, and complimentary hotel rooms in other Nikko Hotel properties in the continental United States.

TO APPLY: Applicants should send a cover letter and résumé to Director of Human Resources, The Ilikai Hotel, 1777 Ala Moana Boulevard, Honolulu, Hawaii 96815; (808) 949-3811.

ISLANDER ON THE BEACH
(Kapaa, Island of Kauai, Hawaii)
Year-Round

The Islander on the Beach is an older 200-room hotel that is currently undergoing major physical and interior renovations. The hotel is centrally located to both shopping and beaches.

SPECIFICS: The Islander has forty-eight employees. Applications are accepted for maids, housemen, maintenance staff, front desk cashiers, and auditors (PBX and cashier experience required). Pay ranges from $5.90 to $9.20 per hour.

INSIDER TIPS: The Islander prefers long-term employees. "We like to consider ourselves as part of a family rather than just employees. We seek aggressive, innovative, mature, flexible, and motivated applicants."

PERKS: Employee benefits include health and life insurance as well as sick leave and paid vacations.

TO APPLY: Applicants should send a cover letter, résumé, and SARP to Islander on the Beach, Noreen Woodward, Accounting & Personnel, 484 Kuhio Highway, Kapaa, Hawaii 96746; (808) 822-7417.

KAANAPALI BEACH HOTEL
(Kaanapali Beach, Island of Maui, Hawaii)
Year-Round

The Kaanapali Beach Hotel is situated on beautiful Kaanapali Beach with 431 rooms, two restaurants, one bar, and full conference facilities. "We are the most authentically Hawaiian hotel in the area."

SPECIFICS: The Kaanapali Beach Hotel hires fifty new employees annually to fill its staff of more than 280. Entry-level positions (high school graduation is the only requirement) include food and beverage servers, room attendants, and office/clerical positions. Entry-level management positions (two years of college or hotel experience required) are also available. Upper management positions require previous hotel experience (four-year college degree preferred).

INSIDER TIPS: "We look for hard-working, stable people who are enthusiastic and willing and able to learn about our industry. Also people who show commitment and sincerity to their employers."

PERKS: Employees are welcome to participate in the hotel's aerobics classes.

TO APPLY: Applicants should send a cover letter, résumé, and SARP to Beverly Balberdi, Personnel Director, 2525 Kaanapali Parkway, Kaanapali, Hawaii 96761; (808) 661-0011.

KAHALA HILTON HOTEL
(Honolulu, Island of Oahu, Hawaii)
Year-Round

The Kahala Hilton is world renowned as a destination resort located on the island of Oahu. While the hotel is only a short drive from the excitement of downtown Waikiki, it is located in the exclusive Kahala area. The resort emphasizes quiet elegance in a secluded beachfront setting.

SPECIFICS: The Kahala Hilton employs more than 550 staff members and hires 100 to 150 new employees annually. Staff positions are available for buspersons, waitpersons, hosts/hostesses, bartenders, porters, front desk clerks, front office cashiers, food and beverage cashiers, bellhops, parking valets, housekeepers, and utility stewards. Additionally, the Hilton offers entry-level management positions.

INSIDER TIPS: The Kahala Hilton looks for neat and well-groomed applicants who are committed to service excellence. Management also reports they seek applicants with "good interpersonal skills, and a positive, hard-working, willing-to-learn attitude." Applicants who can be flexible in the shifts they are willing to work stand a much better chance of being hired.

PERKS: The resort offers free employee duty meals and uniforms are supplied and maintained by the hotel.

TO APPLY: Applicants should send a cover letter and résumé to Gaylynne Sakuda, Personnel and Training Manager, Kahala Hilton Hotel, 5000 Kahala Avenue, Honolulu, Hawaii 96816; (808) 734-2211.

KONA VILLAGE RESORT
(Kaupulehu-Kona, Hawaii)
Year-Round

Paradise is the only word that aptly describes the Kona Village Resort. This exclusive south seas getaway is located on the magnificently stark and beautiful Kona coast of Hawaii's Big Island. The Village is dotted with a series of 125 grass thatched roof huts, built in the traditional South Pacific style, and spread across 82 lush acres of prime oceanfront property. Primitive luxury is the watchword here. The resort is a favorite getaway for celebrities and other prominent guests from around the world.

SPECIFICS: The Kona Village's staff is extremely loyal and many have worked at the resort for years. Guests and staff alike enjoy the camaraderie that is formed. Here in paradise, returning guests are treated more as friends than as visitors. The Village employs a total of approximately 240 staff members and hires about ten to fifteen new employees each year. Jobs at the Village are few and far between, highly coveted, and well worth seeking. Positions at the resort include all typical hotel positions including waiter, busperson, bartender, cocktail waitress, maid, grounds keeper, beach shack staff, front desk staff, and security. The resort also employs its own private fire department.

INSIDER TIPS: As noted above, jobs here are few and far between. Most of the staff have been around for years and have no plans to leave. Nonetheless, a few positions open up each year and it is well worth the effort and persistence that landing a job here takes.

PERKS: The resort hosts employee parties and events and offers employees discounted meals at the village's two highly acclaimed restaurants. Although meals are included in the daily hotel rate, restaurant staff receive generous tips.

TO APPLY: Applicants should send a cover letter, résumé, and photograph to Human Resources Manager, Kona Village Resort, P.O. Box 1299, Kailua-Kona, Hawaii 96745. A personal interview is required of all applicants. No phone calls, please.

KON TIKI PARTY RAFT OF ST. THOMAS
(St. Thomas, U.S. Virgin Islands)
Year-Round

If you hear the sound of laughter and Calypso music floating across the tropical waters of Charlotte Amalie harbor, it's a safe bet that the Kon Tiki is approaching. The Kon Tiki is a huge glass-bottomed party boat. Kon Tiki's daily trips generally run about two to three hours and involve sightseeing, dancing, and drinking (from bottomless vats of rum punch). Kon Tiki also operates on Grand Cayman Island.

SPECIFICS: Kon Tiki employs approximately thirty staff members with about ten employees working on the boat at any one time. Shipboard jobs include captain, first, second, and third mates, shipboard boutique sales staff, and bar staff. Salaries start at $25 per sailing. (Captains must have U.S. Coast Guard certificates.)

INSIDER TIPS: Kon Tiki seeks "outgoing, polite applicants with a neat appearance and cleanliness. Experience with boats and ships' lines is helpful but not required. Lifesaving certificates also helpful but not required."

PERKS: Because these islands are U.S. territories, U.S. citizens do not need work permits.

TO APPLY: Applicants should send a cover letter, résumé, and photograph to Judy Reeve, Kon Tiki, P.O. Box 8803, Charlotte Amalie, St. Thomas, U.S. Virgin Islands 00801; (809) 775-5055.

MAUNA KEA BEACH HOTEL
(South Kohala Coast, Island of Hawaii, Hawaii)
Year-Round

The Mauna Kea Beach Hotel is a landmark on the south Kohala coast of the Big Island. For more than twenty years the Mauna Kea has been one of Hawaii's top resort destinations.

SPECIFICS: The Mauna Kea annually employs 225 new employees to fill a staff of 780. Applicants are commonly recruited for positions as dishwashers, polishers, cleaners, housekeepers, room attendants, dining room waitpersons (experience required), dining room buspersons, clerical staff (experience required), grounds keepers, and engineering staff (experience required). Starting pay ranges from minimum wage to $11.00 per hour with full medical, dental, and life insurance paid for full-time employees.

INSIDER TIPS: Management looks for applicants with "strong communication skills, a neat appearance, experience in the particular job applied for, friendliness, and the unique ability to express a warm feeling of 'aloha' to guests and fellow employees."

PERKS: Employees are welcome to use the resort's tennis and golf facilities when off duty.

TO APPLY: Applicants should send a cover letter, résumé, and SARP to Director of Human Resources, Mauna Kea Beach Hotel, P.O. Box 218, Kamuela, Hawaii 96743.

RUSSELL HOUSE OF KEY WEST
(Key West, Florida)
Seasonal (Winter) and Year-Round

When Ernest Hemingway chose to move to the most perfect spot on earth, he chose the tiny island city of Key West. Key West, also known as the Conch Republic, is the last inhabited island in the Florida Keys island chain. Amid the tropical splendor of Key West, Russell House provides a spa and fitness getaway for guests from around the world. Russell House concentrates on holistic dieting and a natural way of life that befits this small island paradise.

SPECIFICS: Russell House has positions available for both winter seasonal as well as year-round staff members. The spa's thirty-two-person staff is universally dedicated to the Russell House method of holistic living. Applications are accepted for both fitness instructors and front desk clerks. College degrees are required for most fitness instructors. Seasonal employees must be available from December 15 through May 15.

INSIDER TIPS: "We look for professional, kind individuals with positive attitudes and a loyalty to the Russell House health program."

PERKS: Limited housing is available for female employees if desired.

TO APPLY: Applicants should send a cover letter, résumé, and photograph to E. Badler, Executive Director, Russell House of Key West, 611 Truman Avenue, Key West, Florida 33040; (305) 294-8787. Management responds to all applications.

SEA CLIFF BEACH RESORT
(Water Island, U.S. Virgin Islands)
Seasonal (Winter) and Year-Round

The Sea Cliff Beach Resort is a one hundred-room destination resort located on exclusive Water Island, a small island located just a few minutes off the coast of Charlotte Amalie, St. Thomas. Regular ferry service and water taxis connect Water Island to St. Thomas.

SPECIFICS: The Sea Cliff Beach Resort employs up to seventy staff members. Both long-term and winter seasonal staff are recruited. Applications are accepted for pool and beach staff, housekeepers, restaurant food servers, and front desk staff.

PERKS: Because these islands are U.S. territories, U.S. citizens do not need work permits.

TO APPLY: Each department head hires his or her own staff. Applicants should send a cover letter, résumé, and photograph (optional) to "Department Manager" of the department in which they are interested. Main departments are Food and Beverage (includes beach and pool staff), Purchasing, Front Desk, Accounting, and Management. The hotel's address is Sea Cliff Beach Resort, P.O. Box 2325, St. Thomas, U.S. Virgin Islands 00801; (809) 774-1207.

STOUFFER GRAND BEACH RESORT
(St. Thomas, U.S. Virgin Islands)
Seasonal (Winter) and Year-Round

Stouffer's Grand Beach Resort is a year-round 34-acre facility in a lush tropical setting on a 1,000-foot beach located seven miles northeast of Charlotte Amalie. The hotel's facilities include 333 luxury rooms and suites, two swimming pools, six tennis courts, beach, two restaurants, gift shop, and a water sports dock, which offers snorkeling, windsurfing, sailing, and deep-sea fishing.

SPECIFICS: Stouffer's Grand Beach Resort has a staff of more than 460 employees with approximately 100 new employees hired annually. Applications are frequently solicited for beach attendants, windsurfing instructors, bartenders, cooks, waiters/waitresses, housekeepers, food and beverage personnel, and front desk clerks. Pay ranges from minimum wage to $7.50 per hour.

INSIDER TIPS: Employees may use the hotel's beach, restaurants, and lounges during their off-duty hours. "We look for applicants with sparkle, energy, motivation, self-discipline, and flexibility. We strongly prefer long-term employees."

PERKS: Employee benefits include free shift meals and insurance for full-time staff.

TO APPLY: Applicants should send a cover letter, résumé, and photograph (optional) to Director of Personnel, Stouffer Grand Beach Resort, P.O. Box 8267, St. Thomas, U.S. Virgin Islands, 00801 (809) 775-1510. Enclose a SARP with all correspondence.

TURTLE BAY HILTON HOTEL & COUNTRY CLUB (Kahuku, Hawaii)

Year-Round

The Turtle Bay Hilton is the only major resort located on Oahu's famous North Shore. Oahu's North Shore is the site of Hawaii's world famous big waves. Along this coast, surfers battle it out for fame and fortune at Sunset and Pipeline beaches.

SPECIFICS: Turtle Bay employs more than 560 staff members including housekeepers, wait and bus help, security officers, clerical employees, bartenders, bar porters, front desk and reservations staff, maintenance personnel, and bellpersons.

INSIDER TIPS: Long-term employees are preferred as the hotel is busy throughout the year. Seasonal help is rarely needed. Management reports seeking applicants who appear willing to be trained and who are responsible, neat, clean, and have a positive attitude.

PERKS: After an initial probation period, employees receive discounts at the hotel's restaurants. Employees receive complimentary meals during their shifts, paid meal time, and furnished uniforms.

TO APPLY: Applicants should either apply in person or send a cover letter, résumé, and SARP to Employment Manager, Turtle Bay Hilton Hotel and Country Club, P.O. Box 187, Kahuku, Hawaii 96731; (808) 293-8811, ext. 558.

UNDERWATER SAFARIS
(St. Thomas, U.S. Virgin Islands)
Seasonal (Winter) and Year-Round

Underwater Safaris is a retail dive shop that operates SCUBA diving tours. The company specializes in shallow water, reef, wreck, and night water trips for certified divers as well as a half-day introductory "resort course" for individuals seeking an introduction to SCUBA diving.

JOB OPENINGS: Underwater Safaris employs twelve staff members each year. Positions are available for certified SCUBA instructors, dive masters, retail shop staff, and bookkeeper/clerical staff. Pay is $5.00 per hour for trainees and increases quickly to $5.50 per hour plus commissions. Most retail shop employees average about $1,200 per month in salary and commissions.

INSIDER TIPS: "SCUBA is an outdoor sport. We look for healthy nonsmokers, nondrinkers, and no drugs! Our staff members must have lots of energy and a pleasant personality."

PERKS: Employee benefits include free use of rental SCUBA equipment, free air tanks, free SCUBA tours (space available) and significant discounts on SCUBA certification lessons for nondivers.

TO APPLY: Applicants should send a cover letter, résumé, and photograph to Mel Luff or Ty Mayo, Underwater Safaris, P.O. Box 8469, St. Thomas, U.S. Virgin Islands 00801; (809) 774-1350. Include character and work references with easy-to-reach phone contacts.

V.I. DIVERS, LTD.
(Christiansted, St. Croix, U.S. Virgin Islands)
Seasonal (Winter) and Year-Round

For those who have always dreamed of working under the deep blue sea, this could be your ideal opportunity. V.I. Divers operates daily SCUBA diving excursions for both experienced as well as novice divers.

SPECIFICS: V.I. Divers employs dive shop sales staff, two full-time SCUBA instructors, and three part-time SCUBA instructors. There are also positions for U.S. Coast Guard licensed boat captains.

INSIDER TIPS: "Applicants stand a better chance if already on the island or willing to fly to St. Croix for an interview. U.S. Coast Guard licensed captains who are also dive masters are encouraged to apply."

PERKS: Because these islands are U.S. territories, U.S. citizens do not need work permits.

TO APPLY: Applicants should send a cover letter, résumé, and photograph to V.I. Divers Ltd., Pan Am Pavilion, Christiansted, St. Croix, U.S. Virgin Islands 00820; (809) 773-6045. The company is owned by Jimmy and Kathleen Antoine.

VIRGIN GRAND BEACH HOTEL
(Great Cruz Bay, St. John, U.S. Virgin Islands)
Year-Round

St. John's Virgin Grand is a brand-new 264-room luxury resort with two restaurants, two bars, and a complimentary water sports center. St. John is the smallest and least populated of the U.S. Virgin Islands. The majority of the island is part of the U.S. Virgin Islands National Park and is protected from development. The island is fairly quiet with little or no nightlife outside of the few hotels.

SPECIFICS: The Virgin Grand employs 175 staff members. Applicants may apply for all typical hotel positions.

INSIDER TIPS: Management prefers applicants interested in long-term employment, but hires interns for fifteen- to twenty-week placements.

TO APPLY: Applicants should send a cover letter, résumé, school transcripts, photograph, and SARP to Ms. Eucil Brown, Personnel Manager, Virgin Grand Beach Hotel, Great Cruz Bay, St. John, U.S. Virgin Islands 00830; (809) 776-7171.

VIRGIN ISLANDS DIVING SCHOOLS, INC.
(St. Thomas, U.S. Virgin Islands)
Seasonal (Winter) and Year-Round

Virgin Islands Diving Schools Inc. is the self-proclaimed largest volume SCUBA diving, snorkeling, and dive store operator in the Virgin Islands.

SPECIFICS: Virgin Islands Diving Schools employs up to twenty staff members. The company employs numerous certified divers and instructors and hires noncertified divers in its "Earn As You Learn" program, which allows noncertified employees to work at the dive shop while at the same time earning their SCUBA certification. Under the program, employees can earn divemaster or instructor certificates. Although the company operates year-round, additional help is needed for the busy November 15 through May 1 high season.

INSIDER TIPS: "For our 'Earn As You Learn' program, we seek individuals with a strong interest and desire in becoming SCUBA instructors. All employees must have a dynamic personality, good sense of humor, and be able to relate well to large numbers of tourists."

PERKS: The company's "Earn As You Learn" program offers a unique opportunity to train for a SCUBA instructor position while working in the Caribbean.

TO APPLY: Applicants should send a cover letter, résumé, and photograph to Kathleen Fleck or Manager, Virgin Islands Diving Schools Inc., P.O. Box 9707, St. Thomas, U.S. Virgin Islands 00801; (809) 774-8687. The company sends out official applications and conducts phone interviews after screening résumés.

The following listings, found in the chapter headings given below, also include positions on tropical islands:

COASTS & BEACHES

Hilton Head Inn
The Cottages Resort &
   Conference Center

Holiday Inn Oceanfront
Little St. Simons Island Resort
Wild Dunes Associates

HIGH ADVENTURE

Atlantis Submarines
Cruiser Bob's Original
   Haleakala Downhill

Looking Glass Submarines
Red Sail Sports

Snow & Skiing

ALTA SKI LIFTS
(Alta, Utah)
Seasonal (Winter and Spring)

Alta is nationally renowned for its superlative skiing, varied terrain, and challenging expert trails. Like a number of its Utah-based contemporaries, Alta boasts plentiful powder snow and a relaxed small-town atmosphere. The resort runs eight lifts: 25% beginner, 40% intermediate, and 35% advanced.

SPECIFICS: Alta hires about sixty to seventy new staff members annually to supplement a staff of 110. Each year management hires about twenty lift operators, two ticket sales personnel, five ski instructors (PSIA certification required), five ski patrol personnel (emergency medical technician certification required), two kitchen assistants, one janitor, two slope grooming personnel, and two parking assistants. Salaries start at $400 a month plus room and board. All applications are due on or before November 1.

INSIDER TIPS: The resort's motto, "Alta is for skiers," reflects their philosophy and dedication to maintaining a small-town atmosphere, according to management. Although Alta's primary application deadline is November 1, some staff turnover allows for employment opportunities during the season.

PERKS: Outstanding skiing and close proximity to Salt Lake City make Alta one of Utah's most popular ski resorts. Employees receive housing, ski passes, meals, and insurance options. For those who choose to live outside of the resort, regional rents begin at $200 a month.

TO APPLY: Applicants should write for an official application and return it (along with a résumé and cover letter) to Alta Ski Lifts, Alta, Utah 84092; (801) 742-3333.

ANGEL FIRE RESORT
(Angel Fire, New Mexico)
Seasonal (Winter or Summer)

Angel Fire Resort is a 12,000-acre year-round resort located twenty-six miles east of Taos, New Mexico. During ski season the resort operates a luxury hotel and a six-chair ski area. The ski area provides a variety of beginner, intermediate, and expert terrain.

SPECIFICS: Angel Fire Resort employs between 200 and 300 seasonal staff members. Positions are available for both winter and summer seasonal staff. Winter seasonal staff must be available to start work as early as November 1 and no later than December 1. Positions are available for all typical ski area and resort hotel line positions, including front desk staff, food and beverage service staff, housekeepers, lift operators, cashiers, ticket takers, snowmakers, ski patrol staff, ski instructors, golf course personnel, and retail shop staff.

INSIDER TIPS: The resort seeks applicants who are dependable, organized, friendly, mature, and willing to work in all weather conditions. Although no employee housing is provided, there is affordable housing available in Angel Fire.

PERKS: Employees enjoy free skiing and golfing privileges.

TO APPLY: Applicants should write for an official application or send a cover letter and résumé to Personnel, Angel Fire Resort, Drawer B, Angel Fire, New Mexico 87710; (505) 377-6401.

ATTITASH SKI RESORT
(Bartlett, New Hampshire)
Seasonal (Winter) and Year-Round

Attitash is one of New England's foremost ski resorts with a 98% snowmaking capacity on twenty-five trails served by five chairlifts, including a new 6,400-foot-long triple-chair. The resort is surrounded by 750,000 acres of the White Mountain National Forest. Attitash's aggressive snowmaking program has earned it a place as an official U.S. Ski Team training site.

SPECIFICS: Attitash hires more than 125 new seasonal employees each year to fill its 300-person winter staff and eighty-five-person summer staff. Winter seasonal staff must be available to start work by November 21. Hiring is done as needed throughout the year. Attitash hires winter seasonal cafeteria workers, ticket sales persons, lift operators, ticket checkers, maintenance staff, and snowmakers. Contact the employment office for available summer positions.

INSIDER TIPS: "We look for employees with high energy levels, pleasant personalities, and positive attitudes."

PERKS: Attitash employees receive free ski passes for use on their days off, discounts on meals, free ski lessons, and discounts on ski equipment purchases.

TO APPLY: Applicants for all positions should write for an official application from Attitash Ski Resort, Personnel Office, P.O. Box 308,

Bartlett, New Hampshire 03812; (603) 374-2368. Management reports responding to all applications within two weeks.

THE BIG MOUNTAIN SKI & SUMMER RESORT (Whitefish, Montana)

Seasonal (Winter and Spring) and Year-Round (limited positions)

For more than forty years, Montana's Big Mountain has been thrilling skiers with its high-quality skiing. Big Mountain currently uses six chairlifts, a platter lift, and a T-bar to whisk skiers to its forty-eight established runs. There are also 4,000 acres of undeveloped mountain open for "tree skiing." As of the 1987 ski season, the mountain opened a brand-new Nordic ski area with cross country ski trails for skiers of all abilities.

SPECIFICS: Big Mountain hires more than 150 new employees each year to fill its 250 winter seasonal positions. Summer jobs number approximately fifty. Additionally, the mountain hires twenty-five to thirty year-round employees. Seasonal staff should be available from approximately Thanksgiving through mid-April for the winter season and mid-May to October for the summer season. Employees may apply for either full-time or part-time positions. Each winter Big Mountain typically hires approximately forty lift operators, twenty-five ski patrol staff, fifty food service/cafeteria employees, ten cashiers, five front desk clerks, fifteen housekeepers, eight snow groomers, ten general maintenance/janitors, three switchboard operators, five reservationists, five vehicle/lift maintenance workers, and two store clerks. Other positions at the resort include accounting personnel and security staff. Starting wages range from $3.35 to $8.10 per hour depending on the position. Beginning management employees receive $1,100 per month and up. Applications are accepted throughout the year and are held on file for one season.

INSIDER TIPS: While there is no official application deadline, most hiring is completed by mid-October. According to management, "although experience is preferred, it is not essential for certain jobs. However, it is essential that you sincerely like people and that you understand the importance of positive service to our guests." As there is no employee housing available, most staff members live in either Whitefish (eight miles away), Columbia Falls (eighteen miles away) or Kalispell (twenty-seven miles away), so access to a car is a necessity.

PERKS: All full-time seasonal and year-round employees receive a free day/night season ski pass (worth more than $500). Employees also receive discounts on food purchases at several different restaurants at the resort. Part-time employees receive discounted ski lift tickets depending on the number of days they work. Full-time year-round employees are also eligible for the company's health and life insurance program, holiday/vacation pay, and profit-sharing plan.

TO APPLY: Applicants should write for an official application from Gayle A. Lawrence, Personnel Manager, The Big Mountain (Winter Sports, Inc.), P.O. Box 1400, Whitefish, Montana 59937; (406) 862-3511. Applicants are encouraged to send a résumé and/or photograph with their applications.

BIG SKY OF MONTANA
(Big Sky, Montana)
Seasonal (Winter and Summer)

Big Sky is one of Montana's premier ski and summer resorts. The resort's ski terrain includes more than fifty-five miles of skiing spread across two mountains. The resort also features the 204-room Huntley Lodge, ninety-four condominiums, a new conference center, restaurant, bar, sauna, and jacuzzi.

SPECIFICS: Big Sky of Montana hires more than 350 new employees each year to fill its 150 seasonal summer positions and 300 winter spots. All jobs are seasonal. Winter seasonal staff should be available from approximately mid-December through mid-April; summer seasonal staff should be available from mid-June through mid-September. Winter staff selection occurs during the latter part of November; summer staff selection starts in mid-May. Positions are available for reservationists (typing skills required), front desk clerks, accounting clerks, housekeepers, lift operation staff (skiing ability required), sales clerks, dining room staff, and ski instructors. The average starting wage for 1992 seasonal employees was $4.00 per hour (subject to change).

INSIDER TIPS: "We look for the ability to make a 'good first impression.' We like employees who present a friendly and helpful attitude since we are in the hospitality industry. Since Big Sky is in what is referred to as 'God's Country,' we (seek) employees who present a clean and healthy appearance."

PERKS: Benefits for seasonal staff include an employee season ski pass (with a deposit), employee housing in dormitory-style accommodations ($100/month), and a 40% discount on meals in the cafeteria.

TO APPLY: Applicants should either write for an official application or send a cover letter and résumé to Jeane Alm, Hotel Manager, P.O. Box 160001, Big Sky, Montana 59716; (406) 995-4211.

BIG WHITE SKI RESORT LTD.
(Kelowna, British Columbia, Canada)
Seasonal (Winter)

Big White is one of British Columbia's most popular ski areas. This winter resort features five chair and two surface lifts covering a wide array of ski terrain. The resort's terrain is rated easy through expert.

SPECIFICS: Big White hires more than 200 new employees each year to fill its 300 winter seasonal positions. Winter staff should be available to work from late November through late April. While most hiring occurs in late October and early November, applications are accepted throughout the season for positions that become available due to employee turnover. Applications are accepted for ski instructors (level I, II, or III certification required), ski patrol staff (first-aid training required), lift attendants, ski rental shop staff, ticket sellers, snowcat drivers, waitpersons, bartenders, and cooks.

INSIDER TIPS: Management seeks very friendly and ambitious applicants who enjoy teamwork and are inclined to participate in afterwork functions. An ability to withstand working in a cold outdoor environment is essential. While related work skills are helpful, management states that friendliness matters more than experience.

PERKS: Big White staff pay $20 per month for a mountain ski pass. The pass fee is refunded to employees who stay through the end of the season. Staff housing is available for approximately CAN$7.00 per day (rates subject to change).

TO APPLY: Applicants should send a cover letter and résumé to Personnel Manager, Big White Ski Resort, P.O. Box 2039, Station R, Kelowna, British Columbia, V1X 4K5 Canada; (604) 765-3101.

BLACKCOMB SKI ENTERPRISES LTD.
(Whistler, British Columbia, Canada)
Seasonal (Winter)

If you thought Seventh Heaven was only a state of mind, you haven't visited Blackcomb ski resort at Whistler, British Columbia. At Blackcomb, Seventh Heaven is "where snow gets to go when it's good." Seventh Heaven is a ski run at the top of Blackcomb's 5,280-foot vertical drop. A new contraption called the "Wizard" whisks skiers to the mountain top in a carbon fiber craft complete with retractable weatherproof Lexan bubble. Blackcomb offers virtually year-round skiing with summer skiing on Horstman Glacier. New for the 1992-93 ski season is Blackcomb's mountaintop restaurant, The Lodge at Sunspot, and lift accessibility to the Parsenn Bowl skiing.

SPECIFICS: Blackcomb employs more than 1,200 winter seasonal staffers and 300 summer employees. More than 500 new employees are hired each year. Winter interviews and hiring occur in early October. Employees may start work any time in November. Applications are accepted for lift hosts, food services staff, sports shops staff, guest relations personnel, snowmakers, and snow groomers. For expert skiers there are also positions as ski instructors and ski patrollers.

INSIDER TIPS: "Jobs as lift hosts, ticket sellers, and food service staff are the easiest to obtain. Our ski patrol and ski school have very little turnover."

PERKS: All Blackcomb employees receive a dual mountain ski pass and discounts on meals and retail ski equipment purchases.

TO APPLY: Applicants should send a cover letter, résumé, and photograph to Human Resources Department, Blackcomb Skiing Enterprises Ltd., P.O. Box 98, Whistler, British Columbia, V0N 1B0 Canada; (604) 932-3141, ext. 366 or 395.

BOGUS BASIN
(Boise, Idaho)

Seasonal (Winter)

Ski magazine has called Bogus Basin "one of the twelve best-kept secrets in skiing. . . . Bogus Basin has magnificent terrain, promising snow, short lift lines, and low prices." Bogus Basin features six chair lifts covering more than 1,800 vertical feet of ski terrain.

SPECIFICS: Bogus Basin hires 250 new employees each season to fill its 300 winter seasonal positions. Employees should be available to start work around mid-November. Bogus Basin accepts applications for all typical ski resort positions, including lift operators, ski patrollers, ski instructors, hotel front desk clerks, housekeepers, and maintenance staff.

INSIDER TIPS: Bogus Basin seeks dependable, service-oriented employees. "We sell service!"

PERKS: Perks vary according to position and tenure.

TO APPLY: Applicants should write for an official application or send a cover letter and résumé to Bogus Basin Recreational Association, Inc., Attention: Personnel, 2405 Bogus Basin Road, Boise, Idaho 83702; (208) 336-4500.

BOYNE MOUNTAIN LODGE
(Boyne Falls, Michigan)
Seasonal (Winter and Summer) and Year-Round

Management reports that since 1947, more than six million skiers have snowplowed, stem christied, and paralleled the slopes of Boyne. The lodge is open year-round. In the winter months, the resort draws skiers from across the Midwest attracted by Boyne's fine facilities, challenging slopes, and short lift lines. In the summer guests can enjoy golf, tennis, and hiking.

SPECIFICS: Boyne Mountain Lodge employs 247 staff each summer and 300 staff each winter. Positions are available for both year-round as well as seasonal staff. Winter seasonal staff should be available from December 15 through March 20. Summer staff should be available from May 15 through October 15. There is no application deadline. Applications are accepted for front desk clerks, waitpersons, buspersons, conference staff, and golf course staff.

INSIDER TIPS: Management seeks employees with a neat appearance, an eagerness to learn, a loyalty to the ski area, an honest background, and proper work experience. The more information sent with an application the better.

PERKS: Employees are permitted to use most of the lodge's facilities.

TO APPLY: Applicants should either write for an official application form (enclose SASE) or send a cover letter, résumé, photograph, and SARP to Scott Hall, Lodge Manager, Boyne Mountain Lodge, U.S. 131, Boyne Falls, Michigan 49713; (616) 549-2441, ext. 177.

BRIAN HEAD SKI RESORT
(Cedar City, Utah)
Seasonal (Winter)

Brian Head Ski Resort is the southernmost ski area in Utah and has a peak elevation of approximately 11,000 feet. Brian Head prides itself on being a friendly family resort with unusually short lift lines. The ski area has seven chair lifts and forty runs.

SPECIFICS: Brian Head Ski Resort hires through the Cedar City Job Service. The resort hires approximately seventy-five new employees each year to fill its 200 positions. All jobs are seasonal and employees should be available from mid-November through the end of April or early May. Brian Head will train employees without prior experience for positions as ski rental technicians (twenty positions), boot adjusters/fitters (twenty positions), cafeteria helpers (twelve), janitors (two), day care helpers (five), and lift operators (fifty). For applicants with cash handling skills there are twenty cashier positions. Strong skiers can apply for twenty ski school instructor positions. Strong skiers with a CPR and either an advanced first-aid or emergency medical training certificate may apply for jobs on the ski patrol. The resort also hires two shuttle bus drivers (chauffeur's license required). There is no application deadline.

INSIDER TIPS: Brian Head looks for dependable, outgoing, friendly, tolerant, and patient staff members who are responsive to customers' needs and questions.

PERKS: Full-time employees are given free ski passes.

TO APPLY: Applicants should either write for an official application (send a SASE with your request) or send a cover letter and résumé to Cedar City Job Service, 176 East 200 North, Cedar City, Utah 84720; (801) 586-6585.

COPPER MOUNTAIN RESORT & SKI AREA
(Copper Mountain, Colorado)
Seasonal (Winter and Spring) and Year-Round

Nestled in the Colorado Rockies, Copper Mountain is repeatedly recognized as one of the top ski and resort areas in the United States. Area activities include skiing, golfing, tennis, and horseback riding.

SPECIFICS: Copper Mountain hires more than 1,200 employees during peak season and usually hires 800 to 900 new staff each year. Both long-term and seasonal (early November through late April) workers are needed. Apply early for the best variety of available positions. Most seasonal hiring is done in early October. Applications are accepted for ski instructors, day care teachers, ski lift operators, bus drivers, ski rental fitters, lift ticket checkers, ticket sellers, parking attendants, phone operators, ski repairmen, bellmen, cooks, food and beverage staff, front desk staff, lodging staff, shop sales, and base crew. During the summer season, jobs in the various warm weather activities areas are available (golf, athletic club, horseback riding, and scenic chair lift rides). Pay ranges from $5.00 to $7.50 per hour.

INSIDER TIPS: "A job at Copper Mountain is no ordinary job. How many people do you know who ski on their lunch breaks and savor beautiful mountain views on their way to work? We want friendly people who are able to work with the public and enjoy the outdoors."

PERKS: "Employee benefits include free season ski passes, complimentary ski tickets, ski lesson discounts, lodging discounts, and ski accessory discounts."

TO APPLY: Potential applicants should write or call and request an employment opportunities brochure. To apply send a cover letter and résumé (or call to schedule an interview) to Human Resources Department, Copper Mountain Resort, P.O. Box 3001, Copper Mountain, Colorado 80443; (303) 968-2882.

CRESTED BUTTE MOUNTAIN RESORT
(Crested Butte, Colorado)
Seasonal (Winter)

Crested Butte Mountain Resort is a destination ski resort in the Colorado Rockies. The resort's facilities include thirteen ski lifts and eighty-five maintained ski trails for skiers of all levels.

SPECIFICS: Crested Butte actively recruits college-age students for its student employee program. The program is designed for students interested in taking a semester off from school and offers the opportunity for participants "to learn about resort operations, earn money, ski like crazy, and earn a scholarship for use when returning to school." Crested Butte recruits for entry-level jobs in the following departments: lift operations (lift operators, ticket checkers), base area (maintenance, parking lot attendants, janitorial), food and beverage (grill cooks, line servers, buspersons, waiters/waitresses), ski rental shop (ski and boot fitters, cashiers, sales clerks), group hosts/hostesses, Buttetopia Children's Center (day care/ABC's on skis program, children's private lesson instructors), front desk clerks, housekeepers, and general clerical positions.

INSIDER TIPS: "Our program begins in mid-November and for most positions concludes in mid-April. The pay is at least above minimum wage and benefits include prearranged housing, free season ski passes, ski trips, and parties. Those completing their contracts and finishing the season earn a $500 tuition scholarship."

TO APPLY: Applicants should write or call and request an official application from Kim Gailey, Personnel Director, Crested Butte Mountain Resort, Box A, Crested Butte, Colorado 81225; (303) 349-2333.

CRYSTAL MOUNTAIN RESORT
(Crystal Mountain, Washington)

Seasonal (Winter)

With a peak elevation of 7,000 feet, Crystal Mountain is Washington State's highest destination ski resort. The resort boasts more than 1,300 acres of skiable terrain with thirty-two runs and a 1,000-acre back-country area.

SPECIFICS: Crystal Mountain employs 500 staff members during its winter season. Approximately 300 new employees are hired each year. Positions are available for both full-time and part-time winter seasonal staff. Preseason training begins in late October and early November. The ski resort opens in mid-November. Although some hiring is done throughout the season, most hiring is done in late September and early October. Applications are accepted for lift operators, lift attendants, ski patrollers, slope groomers, child care staff, ticket sellers, parking attendants, pool attendants, shuttle drivers, road crew, janitors, shop mechanic helpers, lift maintenance helpers, ski checkers, cooks, fry cooks, prep cooks, dishwashers, hostesses, waitpersons, buspersons, bartenders, cafeteria servers, and cashiers.

INSIDER TIPS: For the best job opportunities, complete your application before mid-September as most job screening is done on the third weekend of September.

PERKS: Employees are given free ski passes to Crystal Mountain and discount weekday passes to other nearby ski areas. Additionally, employees receive free ski lessons, discounts on food, a free employee shuttle bus and various employee recreational and social activities during the season.

TO APPLY: Applicants should write for an official application from Personnel Department, Crystal Mountain Resort, One Crystal Mountain Blvd., Crystal Mountain, Washington 98022; (206) 663-2265.

CRYSTAL MOUNTAIN RESORT
(Thompsonville, Michigan)
Seasonal (Winter) and Year-Round

Crystal Mountain is a year-round destination resort with winter skiing as its number one attraction. Crystal Mountain Resort also features a 22-kilometer cross country ski area, two lounges, a dining room, a cafeteria, an outdoor heated pool, an indoor pool and fitness center, full ski rental, nursery and ski school facilities. For summer guests the resort operates a twenty-seven-hole golf course and clay-court tennis facility.

SPECIFICS: Crystal Mountain Resort hires approximately 100 new employees each year to fill its 250 to 300 staff positions. Jobs are available for both year-round as well as winter seasonal employees. Most winter seasonal jobs begin in mid-November and last through March. There is no application deadline. Crystal Mountain accepts applications for ski instructors, children's instructors, ski rental technicians, lift operators, cafeteria staff, restaurant workers, bar staff, and snowmakers.

INSIDER TIPS: Crystal Mountain seeks honest applicants "who are able to work cheerfully with the public and are able to lend a hand when they see a job that needs to be done—i.e., team players."

PERKS: Staff members receive free season ski passes.

TO APPLY: Applicants should write for an official application to Marty Beard, Personnel Director, M-115 Crystal Mountain Resort, Thompsonville, Michigan 49683; (616) 378-2000, ext. 126.

DIAMOND PEAK SKI RESORT AND CROSS COUNTRY CENTER
(Incline Village, Nevada)
Seasonal (Winter and Spring)

Lake Tahoe's premier family ski resort, Diamond Peak Ski Resort and Cross Country Center is a medium-sized resort located on the Nevada side of beautiful North Lake Tahoe. The resort is famous for consistently great snow, friendly staff, and spectacular skiing with the best views of the lake.

SPECIFICS: Diamond Peak Ski Resort and Cross Country Center hires numerous new employees each year to fill winter seasonal staff positions. The resort's ski season typically extends from November through April. Available positions include ski instructor for adults and children, ski patroller, lift operator, snow groomer/snowmaker, rental shop attendant, repair shop technician, cashier, accounting clerk, bartender, cook, food server, busperson, dishwasher, maintenance personnel, parking lot attendant, and shuttle bus driver. The pay range depends upon position and experience. The ski resort will train for many positions. Seasonal summer employment is available for those interested in working in the golf and summer beach/pool recreation industries through Diamond Peak Ski Resort's parent organization, Incline Village General Improvement District.

INSIDER TIPS: Interested applicants will receive an employment application and a description of the various job opportunities and the specific qualifications required for each position.

PERKS: Free skiing and free ski lessons are available to staff members.

TO APPLY: Applicants should write for an application for employment and listing of job opportunities to Diamond Peak Ski Resort, 1210 Ski Way, Incline Village, Nevada 89451; (702) 832-1177.

ELK MOUNTAIN
(Union Dale, Pennsylvania)
Seasonal (Winter) and Year-Round

When most nearby ski areas are forced to start closing runs due to lack of snow, Elk Mountain's vast array of snowmaking machinery keeps this resort's 1,000 vertical feet of skiable terrain open. Located in northeast Pennsylvania, Elk Mountain offers day and limited night skiing on seventeen slopes and trails.

SPECIFICS: Elk Mountain hires more than 200 new employees each year to fill its 400 peak-season staff positions. There are also approximately twenty-five year-round employee slots. The ski area hires for all typical ski resort positions. Contact the employment office for further information on available positions. Seasonal employees should be available from December 1 through March 20. Starting salaries range from minimum wage to more than $6.50 per hour depending on the position and experience.

INSIDER TIPS: Elk Mountain looks for "friendly, well-groomed individuals who are willing to learn (and perform) specific duties."

PERKS: The primary fringe benefit at Elk Mountain is the staff ski pass program.

TO APPLY: Applicants should either write for an official application or send a cover letter, résumé, and list of references (or letters of reference) to Gregg Confer, General Manager, Elk Mountain, Box 258, Union Dale, Pennsylvania 18470; (717) 679-2611.

FOX PEAK SKI FIELD
(Timaru, New Zealand)

Seasonal (Summer)

For those seeking summer skiing down under, there is no better place than New Zealand. With New Zealand's cold season running during the Northern Hemisphere's summer, excellent skiing is available from July through September. The mountain has five lifts, primitive accommodations, a canteen, and day shelter facility.

SPECIFICS: Fox Peak usually hires approximately five new employees each year. Possible positions include ski instructor, ski field manager, ski hut custodian, ski patrol staff, tow/lift operator, and canteen operator. Employees earn between NZ$150 to $360 per week. All applications must be received by early June.

INSIDER TIPS: Fox Peak employees must really enjoy skiing as there are few other activities or diversions nearby and staff are required to live on the mountain. Applications from non–New Zealand citizens with proper work permits are accepted.

PERKS: All employees enjoy free skiing and free accommodations.

TO APPLY: Applicants should send a cover letter, résumé, and SARP to Tasman Ski Club (Fox Peak), Attn: the Club President, P.O. Box 368, Timaru, New Zealand; phone: (56) 80703.

HEAVENLY SKI RESORT
(South Lake Tahoe, California)

Seasonal (Winter)

Heavenly offers more than 20 square miles of skiable terrain straddling the California/Nevada border. Located only three and a half hours from San Francisco, Lake Tahoe receives sunshine an unbeatable 80% of the time and is a place of unsurpassable natural beauty.

SPECIFICS: Heavenly hires close to 1,000 seasonal employees for the ski season. The season typically commences on Thanksgiving weekend. Applications are accepted for a wide variety of positions in lifts, mountain operations, and retail and food service. Most entry-level hiring is done through a series of hiring clinics that usually take place in late October. Contact the personnel department in late summer for more information.

INSIDER TIPS: Heavenly is a world-class resort with a focus on guest service. Employees should be enthusiastic, friendly, and work well with the public. Attending a hiring clinic is helpful in applying for a winter position.

PERKS: Employees receive a free ski pass, discounted dependent passes (if full-time), free ski rentals, free ski lessons, discounts on food and beverage, retail discounts, discounts at other local ski areas, and numerous employee social and recreational activities. Free lift tickets to Steamboat Springs, our sister resort, are also available.

TO APPLY: Applicants should write or call for an application and employment opportunities brochure to Heavenly Ski Resort, P.O. Box 2180, Stateline, Nevada 89449; (702) 586-7000, ext. 6255.

HIDDEN VALLEY RESORT
(Somerset, Pennsylvania)
Seasonal (Winter)

For those seeking an Alpine ski atmosphere in Pennsylvania, look no further than the Hidden Valley Resort. Hidden Valley includes 64 skiable acres spread over eleven ski trails. The resort also includes a 50-kilometer Nordic ski area.

SPECIFICS: Hidden Valley employs 550 staff members and hires approximately 250 new employees each winter. Positions are available for winter seasonal work from December through March. Applicants may apply for positions as snowmakers, lift operators, ski patrol staff, office staff, ticket sellers, ticket checkers, cashiers, and food and beverage help. Salaries start at minimum wage and go up depending on the position and experience.

INSIDER TIPS: Although there is some hiring done throughout the ski season, most positions are filled in November. Apply in October or early November for the best selection of jobs.

PERKS: All employees receive a free season ski pass. Staff members also receive a 20% discount on food purchased at the resort.

TO APPLY: Applicants should send a cover letter and résumé to Personnel Office, Hidden Valley Resort, 1 Gordon Craighead Drive, Somerset, Pennsylvania 15501. Phone number withheld by request.

HUNTER MOUNTAIN SKI BOWL
(Hunter, New York)
Seasonal (Winter) and Year-Round

Hunter has been dubbed the "snowmaking capital of the world." Its snowmaking capability allows it to stay open for skiing an average of 160 days a year. Hunter is the closest major ski area to New York City.

SPECIFICS: Hunter hires approximately 250 new employees each year to fill its more than 350 positions. While there are some year-round assignments, most jobs are winter seasonal beginning November 1. Applications are accepted for group sales staff, snowmakers, kitchen helpers, porters, buspersons, cashiers, ticket sellers, security officers, lift attendants, parking lot attendants, ski patrol staff, and snow groomers. Most jobs pay between $4.00 and $7.00 per hour.

INSIDER TIPS: Hunter seeks "neat, polite, honest, self-motivated applicants with an ability to follow orders and produce (results)."

PERKS: Hunter offers free skiing, free ski lessons, and overtime pay.

TO APPLY: Applicants should either write for an official application or send a cover letter, résumé, and photograph (optional) to Personnel Director, Hunter Mountain Ski Bowl, P.O. Box 295, Hunter, New York 12442; (518) 263-4223.

JACK FROST MOUNTAIN SKI AREA
(Blakeslee, Pennsylvania)
Seasonal (Winter)

Jack Frost Mountain encompasses two ski areas. Skiers have a choice of skiing either Jack Frost Mountain or nearby Big Boulder. Together these mountains are called the Big Two Resorts and offer more than thirty ski trails served by fourteen chair lifts.

SPECIFICS: Jack Frost Mountain Ski Area hires a large number of winter seasonal staff members. Winter staff should be available from December through late March. There are also a limited number of year-round positions available. Applications are accepted throughout the year for ticket sellers, guest services agents, lift attendants, snowmakers, babysitters, and ski school instructors. Instructor applicants should call (717) 443-8425 for employment information.

INSIDER TIPS: Employees must be dependable and friendly.

PERKS: The primary perk is a complimentary ski pass for employees and their immediate family.

TO APPLY: Applicants should either write for an official application or send a cover letter and résumé to Melanie Murphy, General Manager, Jack Frost Mountain Ski Area, P.O. Box 703, Blakeslee, Pennsylvania 18610; (717) 443-8425.

LOON MOUNTAIN SKI RESORT
(Lincoln, New Hampshire)
Seasonal (Winter) and Year-Round

Loon Mountain is located along the East Branch of the Pemigewasset River in Lincoln, New Hampshire. While the resort's base facilities are on private land, most of the ski terrain is part of the 750,000-acre White Mountains National Forest. Loon is New Hampshire's most popular ski area.

SPECIFICS: Loon Mountain hires 400 to 450 new employees each year to fill its 750 staff positions. Winter seasonal staff should be available to work from December 15 through April 15. Loon hires snowmakers, lift attendants, ski rental attendants, ticket sellers, cooks, ski instructors, waitpersons, day care workers, food service attendants, cashiers, parking lot attendants, and grounds keepers. Wages range from minimum wage to more than $6.00 per hour (subject to change). There is no application deadline.

INSIDER TIPS: Loon wants people-oriented applicants with "dependability, attention to detail, and an interest in the resort or ski industry."

PERKS: Employees receive free season ski passes, housing assistance, day care assistance, meal discounts, and transportation assistance. The resort offers dormitory-style staff housing.

TO APPLY: Applicants should either write for an official application form or send a cover letter and résumé to Sara Sawyer, Personnel Manager, Loon Mountain, Route 112, Lincoln, New Hampshire 03251; (603) 745-8111, ext. 576.

MAMMOTH/JUNE MOUNTAIN SKI AREA
(Mammoth Lakes, California)

Seasonal (Winter)

Mammoth/June Mountain Ski Area is Southern California's largest ski resort. With thirty-one lifts reaching over 3,000 acres of skiable terrain, Mammoth/June offers all conceivable guest services.

SPECIFICS: Mammoth/June hires over 1,400 new employees each year to fill its 1,835 seasonal ski resort positions. Applicants should be available from at least mid-November through Easter. The company's personnel office will provide a detailed list of over fifty different jobs upon request. Hiring is done as needed throughout the year.

INSIDER TIPS: Applicants must have good people skills, high energy, and be a team player.

PERKS: Employees receive a free season ski pass and discounts at the company's numerous food and retail establishments.

TO APPLY: Applicants should either phone or write for an official application from Personnel Office, Mammoth/June Mountain Ski Area, P.O. Box 24, Mammoth Lakes, California 93546; (619) 934-2571, ext. 3654.

MT. BACHELOR SKI & SUMMER RESORT
(Bend, Oregon)

Seasonal (Winter)

Mount Bachelor is one of the Pacific Northwest's premier ski areas. The ski area's base elevation is 6,000 feet and the mountaintop is at 9,000 feet. Mount Bachelor's 3,100-foot vertical drop is served by nine chair lifts including five triple chairs and three quad chairs. The mountain's 16-foot average annual snowfall allows Mt. Bachelor to operate without any snowmaking machinery.

SPECIFICS: Mt. Bachelor hires approximately 350 new employees each year to fill its 750 positions. It is open year-round as both a summer and winter resort. However, as winter ski season is the busiest quarter, most seasonal positions are from November 1 through the end of the ski season (date varies by year depending on the annual snowfall). Applications are accepted for cooks, buspersons, cashiers, ski shop staff, lift operators, parking lot attendants, cocktail servers (must be at least twenty-one years old), bartenders (previous experience required, must be at least twenty-one years old), snow groomers, snow plow operators, and ski instructors. Starting pay ranges from minimum wage to $8.60 per hour.

INSIDER TIPS: Mt. Bachelor looks for employees with good communications skills and an ability to work with the public as a team player in a high-energy environment.

PERKS: All employees receive free season ski passes. The company provides free shuttle transportation from nearby Bend, free ski lessons, and discounts on food, ski rentals, and ski equipment.

TO APPLY: Applicants should write for an official application from Personnel Office, Mt. Bachelor Ski and Summer Resort, P.O. Box 1031, Bend, Oregon 97709-1031; (503) 382-2442.

MT. HOOD MEADOWS
(Mt. Hood, Oregon)
Seasonal (Winter)

Mt. Hood Meadows is the premier ski resort on Mt. Hood featuring 2,150 acres of terrain serviced by ten chair lifts. Its vertical drop of 2,777 feet offers steep and rugged terrain complete with mogul-filled bowls, chutes, ridges, and the outback skiing experience of Heather Canyon. And with a new master plan, Meadows is working toward becoming a regional destination resort.

SPECIFICS: Mt. Hood hires approximately 300 new employees each winter to fill its 650-person staff. All jobs are winter seasonal, lasting from early November through late April. Starting wages range from minimum wage to more than $5.50 per hour. Applications are accepted for lift operators, ski patrol, cashiers, ticket checkers, bartenders, cocktail servers, buspersons, cooks, cafeteria workers, bus drivers, and snow groomers, and rental technicians.

INSIDER TIPS: Mt. Hood conducts a job fair the first week of October. Mt. Hood looks for "gregarious, neat applicants with previous service-oriented experience and the tenacity to work in a mountain environment."

PERKS: Mt. Hood staffers receive a free season ski pass, free ski lessons, free shuttle bus transportation to the ski area, and discounts on food and ski shop purchases.

TO APPLY: Applicants should write for an official application and send a letter describing their qualifications and interests to Mt. Hood Meadows, Human Resources, P.O. Box 470, Mt. Hood, Oregon 97041; (503) 337-2222.

STOWE MOUNTAIN RESORT
(Stowe, Vermont)
Seasonal (Summer and Winter)

Stowe Mountain Resort is set in the picturesque village of Stowe, one of Vermont's most charming towns. The resort is popular as both a summer and winter getaway. Summer brings horseback riding, hiking, and tennis, while winter brings sleigh rides and skiing.

SPECIFICS: Mount Mansfield hires over 400 new employees each year to fill its 600-person staff. Summer staff must be available from approximately May 30 through October 15; winter staff work from November 20 through April 15. Applications are accepted for bartenders, kitchen staff, waitpersons, cashiers, cafeteria workers, retail clerks, ski rental and ski repair technicians, ski patrol staff, ski instructors, day-care workers, ticket sellers, snow makers, trail workers, lift operators, hotel front desk clerks, and hotel reservationists.

INSIDER TIPS: Management looks for applicants "with a commitment to customer service excellence, and an interest in skiing."

PERKS: Winter employees receive free season ski passes, free ski lessons, a 45% discount on food, and a 30% discount at the ski shop. Summer employees receive free golf and tennis and use of the Alpine slide. Some employee housing is available and the company holds an annual job fair in early November.

TO APPLY: Applicants should write for an official application or send a cover letter and résumé to Personnel Dept., Stowe Mountain Resort, 5781 Mountain RD, Vermont 05672; (802) 253-7311, ext. 2239

NORTHSTAR-AT-TAHOE
(Lake Tahoe, California)
Seasonal (Summer and Winter) and Year-Round

For those who appreciate the alpine beauty of California's Sierra Nevadas, there is no better place to live and work than Lake Tahoe. Northstar-at-Tahoe is a year-round resort offering downhill and Nordic skiing, lodging, and fine dining in the winter. The summer season brings golf, horseback riding, swimming, and tennis.

SPECIFICS: While Northstar has a few year-round positions, almost all employees are hired seasonally. This resort employs between 100 to 150 summer employees and more than 800 to 900 winter employees each year. The busy summer season runs from approximately June 1 through October 1 and winter season runs from approximately November 1 to April 1. Positions are available for ski instructors, lift attendants, food and beverage service employees, bus drivers, ski rental shop staff, housekeepers, parking attendants, child care workers, etc. Northstar also offers programs where students may work during school breaks and receive daily skiing privileges.

INSIDER TIPS: This is one of the most friendly resorts in the Sierras. Employees seem to honestly enjoy working here.

PERKS: Northstar offers employees free skiing privileges, free ski lessons, medical benefits, and discounts on ski rentals, food, and gas. Employees may buy discount passes to the Northstar Homeowners Recreation Center.

TO APPLY: Applicants should send a SASE for an official application to: Northstar-at-Tahoe, Nancy Barna, Personnel Administrator, P.O. Box 129, Truckee, California 95734; (916) 562-1010.

PICO SKI RESORT
(Rutland, Vermont)
Seasonal (Winter and Summer)

Pico is a small yet well-regarded ski area perched high atop Vermont's mountains. Nine lifts, including two new detachable quads, whisk skiers to forty ski trails. Pico's ski terrain is rated 27% "most difficult," 57% "more difficult," and 16% "easiest." In the summer, Pico operates an Alpine slide.

SPECIFICS: Pico hires more than 250 new employees each year to fill its 300-plus seasonal positions. Seasonal staff should be available to work from the week before Thanksgiving through mid-April. A few summer seasonal positions are also available to work on Pico's Alpine slide. Jobs are available for lift attendants, cafeteria cashiers, cafeteria linepersons, cocktail waitstaff, snowmakers, snow tractor operators, ski shop personnel, ski rental staff, ski repair technicians, ticket sellers, ski school staff, bartenders, and office help. Starting wages range from minimum wage to more than $6.00 per hour.

INSIDER TIPS: Friendliness is the most important asset an applicant can bring to Pico. "We bill ourselves as 'The Friendly Mountain' and we really mean it. This quality is a prime consideration in employee selection."

PERKS: All employees receive a free season ski pass, a 50% discount on food purchased at the resort, and a ski shop discount.

TO APPLY: Applicants should either write for an official application or send a cover letter and résumé to Paul Denton, Personnel, Pico Ski Resort, HCR 34 Sherburne Pass, Rutland, Vermont 05701; (802) 775-4346. Management typically responds only to applicants in whom they are interested. An SARP will expedite a response.

PURGATORY (DURANGO SKI CORPORATION) (Durango, Colorado)
Seasonal (Summer and Winter) and Year-Round

For almost twenty-five years, Purgatory has been thrilling skiers on its 10,822-foot summit mountain. The resort is open year-round, with a winter season lasting from Thanksgiving through early-April and a summer season from Memorial Day through September. The ski mountain features a 2,022-foot vertical drop and approximately 600 acres of varying ski terrain.

SPECIFICS: Purgatory hires approximately 300 to 400 new staff members each year to fill its 750 positions. Jobs are available for both full-time and part-time workers as well as seasonal and year-round employees. A detailed list of available positions is mailed with all applications.

INSIDER TIPS: Purgatory looks for "neat, clean, well-groomed, outgoing, friendly, dependable, helpful applicants. Many positions require good health and endurance (to work at high altitudes)." Most winter positions are filled in September and early October. Most summer positions are filled in April and May.

PERKS: Benefits include free season ski passes, meal discounts, free uniforms, retail shop discounts, and ski rental discounts.

TO APPLY: Applicants should write for an official application (which includes an introductory letter, job fact sheet, complete winter and summer job list, and schedule of when to apply for each specific job) from Durango Ski Corporation, Attn: Halla Garrity, Personnel Administrator, P.O. Box 666, Durango, Colorado 81302; (303) 247-9000.

THE REMARKABLES AND CORONET PEAK SKI AREAS
(Queenstown, New Zealand)
Seasonal (North America's Summer)

Skiers from around the world flock here to enjoy New Zealand's summer ski season. Access from the nearby lakeside town of Queenstown is by car or regular bus service. Remember, New Zealand is below the equator, so ski season runs from June through October.

SPECIFICS: The Remarkables and Coronet Peak in Queenstown employ 340 staff members each summer. Generally about 160 new employees are hired annually and the remainder of the staff is made up of returning employees. For applicants without prior ski area experience, the resort hires fifty-five lift operators, thirty-five restaurant employees, fifteen ticketing agents, thirty ski rental shop personnel, thirty snowmaking and grooming employees, six retail shop clerks, six maintenance staff, and ten people in administration. For employees with prior ski area work experience, 135 ski school staff and fifteen ski patrol positions are available. Pay starts at about NZ$8.00 per hour for most positions. Ski instructors are paid by the lesson and top instructors can earn more than NZ$800 per week.

INSIDER TIPS: The resort attracts skiers from around the world and tries to hire an international staff. Usually, about 30% of all employees are from overseas. With the exception of ski instructors, overseas applicants must obtain their own work visas prior to starting with the company. The Remarkables and Coronet Peak advertise for employees through early-April and most positions are filled by early May. With the exception of ski instructor positions, the resort will rarely guarantee applicants a job without a personal interview.

PERKS: All employees are given free ski passes that may be used at either The Remarkables or at Coronet Peak ski area. The staff receives discounts at all ski area shops and restaurants.

TO APPLY: Applicants should send a cover letter, résumé, and photograph to Personnel, The Remarkables, P.O. Box 359, Queenstown, New Zealand; phone 64-3-442 7520.

SEVEN SPRINGS MOUNTAIN RESORT
(Champion, Pennsylvania)
Seasonal (Winter and Summer) and Year-Round

Seven Springs is a year-round destination resort, located approximately one hour by car from Pittsburgh, Pennsylvania. The resort's ski area has twenty-seven slopes and trails, including the Giant Steps Slope with a 970-foot vertical drop and mile-long run. When the snow melts, the resort transforms itself into a summer vacation and conference center with tennis and golf. There is also a huge summer slide down the ski slopes.

SPECIFICS: The resort employs a year-round staff of more than 750 that swells to more than 1,100 personnel in winter. Most winter seasonal staff are hired between October and December. A personal interview may be required. Applications are accepted for both seasonal and year-round convention sales representatives, office staff, personnel staff, food service workers, bar service staff, laborers, housekeepers, maintenance staff, activities staff, and front desk clerks. Winter seasonal applications are accepted for chair lift operators, mountain crew, ski rental shop staff, ski safety patrol staff, ski school instructors, cashiers, ticket checkers, etc. Salaries start at minimum wage and go up.

INSIDER TIPS: Management seeks applicants with a neat and clean appearance who are motivated, dependable, honest, and have a genuine interest in working for Seven Springs.

PERKS: Year-round employees are eligible for profit sharing, a pension plan, paid vacations, medical insurance, and various activity privileges. All employees are permitted to use the resort's swimming pool, golf course, racquetball facility, tennis courts, volleyball courts, ski area, spa, and windsurfing center at a reduced employee rate.

TO APPLY: Applicants should send a cover letter, résumé, and SARP to Personnel Office, Personnel Director, Seven Springs Resort, RD #1, Champion, Pennsylvania 15622; (814) 352-7777, ext. 7013.

SHERATON STEAMBOAT RESORT
(Steamboat Springs, Colorado)
Seasonal (Winter and Summer)

Steamboat is one of Colorado's best known winter ski resorts. The deep annual snowfall means the ski season usually opens November 20 and lasts through the spring thaw in early April. During the summer months, Steamboat opens about half of the resort for hiking and nature enthusiasts.

SPECIFICS: Steamboat employs 185 staff members. Approximately 100 new employees are hired annually. Almost all jobs are either winter or summer seasonal. The large winter mass hiring occurs in early November and workers usually report to work by November 20. Applications are accepted for front desk clerks, reservation agents (computer experience and accounting skills helpful), housekeepers, cashiers, hosts (cash handling experience preferred), food service workers, cocktail servers, stewards, cleaners (no experience necessary), and cooks (one year of cooking experience required). Starting wages for most positions are at least $6.00 to $5.75 per hour.

INSIDER TIPS: "We want friendly service-oriented individuals. Our staff is comprised of people who are proud of the type of job they do and who are team players."

PERKS: Ski passes can be financed through payroll deductions. Staff members are welcome to use the following facilities: winter—bars, and restaurants (reservations required); summer—bars, restaurants and golf course. Discounts in hotel outlets, gift shops, and other Sheraton hotels. Short-term insurance plan available.

TO APPLY: Applicants should send a cover letter and résumé to Ann Fitzgerald, Personnel Director, Sheraton Steamboat Resort & Conference Center, P.O. Box 774808, Steamboat Springs, Colorado 80477; (303) 879-2232.

SKI BEECH
(Banner Elk, North Carolina)
Seasonal (Winter)

Ski Beech is a premier destination resort featuring the Southeast's first and only detachable quad chair, "The Beech Mountain Express." The base complex consists of a ski school, nursery, restaurants, shops, and ice skating complex. At an elevation of 5,505 feet, Ski Beech is one of the highest ski areas east of the Rocky Mountains.

SPECIFICS: Ski Beech hires up to 150 new employees each year to fill its 300-plus total staff positions. Positions are available for seasonal winter staff who can be available from early November through late March. There is no application deadline. Applications are accepted for hosts/hostesses, ski instructors, ski patrols, lift maintenance staff, lift attendants, restaurant staff, group sales personnel, cash controllers, ticket sellers, and nursery attendants.

INSIDER TIPS: "Employees are selected based on experience and maturity as well as an ability to work with and handle people. Applicants must also demonstrate a willingness to accept authority."

PERKS: Perks vary according to position.

TO APPLY: Applicants should send a cover letter and résumé or call Ski Beech at P.O. Box 1118, Banner Elk, North Carolina 28604; (704) 387-2011.

SKIING LOUISE LTD.
(Lake Louise, Alberta, Canada)
Seasonal (Summer and Winter) and Year-Round

Skiing Louise is the largest ski area in Canada. In addition to thousands of acres of open bowls, there are forty-four named runs. The resort's facilities include eleven ski lifts, three day lodges, a hotel, a back-country hiking and ski lodge, and a summer gondola.

SPECIFICS: Skiing Louise receives more than 3,000 applications each year for its 200 annual job openings out of a staff of more than 350 employees. Jobs are available for both summer and winter staff as well as year-round personnel. Summer staff must be available from early June through September; winter staff must work November through mid-May. Winter seasonal positions include trail crew, CAT operators, ski rental shop staff, ski shop staff, ticket sellers, ticket checkers, nursery attendants, cafeteria staff, restaurant staff, bar staff, kitchen staff, ski school personnel, ski patrol, lift operators, snowmakers, Skoki lodge staff, hotel employees, and customer service attendants. Summer seasonal jobs include gondolier staff, food service workers, souvenir shop personnel, trail crew, hotel employees, maintenance crew, and Skoki lodge staff. Year-round and seasonal jobs are available for equipment operators, mechanics, maintenance staff, electricians, welders, carpenters, plumbers, pipe fitters, office staff, hotel personnel, and employee housing staff. Starting wages range from CAN$4.90 per hour to CAN$2,000 per month.

INSIDER TIPS: "Many jobs require no prior experience. Ski area work is generally not suitable for those who lack the enthusiasm or the desire to serve the public. At the same time we ask that people employed by us consider their job as a job and not as a ski vacation. While there is no application deadline, for the best opportunities apply by mid-April for summer jobs or mid-September for winter jobs."

PERKS: Subsidized employee housing and meals are available for some job categories. All staff receive a complimentary five-area ski pass for use on their days off.

TO APPLY: Applicants should write for an official application from Neil Millar, Personnel Manager, Skiing Louise, P.O. Box 555, Lake Louise, Alberta, T0L 1E0, Canada; (403) 522-3611. Management reports mailing applications within three days of any request.

SKI ROUNDTOP OPERATING CORPORATION
(Lewisberry, Pennsylvania)

Seasonal (Winter) and Year-Round

The Ski Roundtop Operating Corporation operates Ski Roundtop in south central Pennsylvania. Facilities include a ski school, ski patrol, ski shop, rental equipment office, children's learning center, cafeteria, and logo shop.

SPECIFICS: Ski Roundtop hires more than 500 new employees annually to fill its staff. While there are a few year-round positions, most jobs are seasonal, starting at Thanksgiving and lasting through the middle of March. The resort hires lift attendants (150-plus positions), ski instructors (100-plus positions), cashiers (eighty-five-plus positions), food service staff (seventy-five positions), courtesy staff, parking attendants, and snowmakers. For information on other positions, contact the employment office at the address below. Starting salaries begin at minimum wage and go up. Hiring is done throughout the year.

INSIDER TIPS: "We look for friendly applicants with honesty, enthusiasm, integrity, and wholesomeness."

PERKS: Employee perks include free skiing, free ski equipment rentals, free ski lessons, and discounts on food at the resort's outlets.

TO APPLY: Applicants should write for an official application from Personnel Director, Ski Roundtop Operating Corporation, 925 Roundtop Road, Lewisberry, Pennsylvania 17339; (717) 432-9631.

SNOWBASIN
(Huntsville, Utah)
Seasonal (Late November Through Early April)

As the largest ski recreation area in northern Utah, Snowbasin contains some of the most outstanding terrain in the area. Located in the Wasatch-Cache National Forest near Ogden, Snowbasin covers 1,800 acres with 2,400 vertical feet of slope.

SPECIFICS: Snowbasin hires seventy-five new employees annually to fill a staff of 145. The resort runs a ski patrol, ski school, ski shop and rentals, and a restaurant, so candidates can apply for a range of jobs. Each year about fifteen lift operators, eight ski patrol staff (emergency medical training certificate required), eighteen ski school instructors, sixteen food service staff, four ticket sales personnel, and six parking assistants are hired.

INSIDER TIPS: Management looks for candidates who are dependable and have a "good customer service attitude." All applications are due on or before November 1.

PERKS: Superb skiing and discounts on passes and meals are the primary benefits of working at Snowbasin. The resort's proximity to Ogden affords urban entertainment and conveniences to all employees.

TO APPLY: Candidates should write for an official application from Reeta Young, Office Manager, Snowbasin, Box 348, Huntsville, Utah 84317; (801) 399-1135.

SNOWBIRD SKI AND SUMMER RESORT
(Snowbird, Utah)
Seasonal (Winter and Summer) and Year-Round

With a mid-mountain average annual snowfall of more than 500 inches, Snowbird attracts more fresh powder snow than almost any other resort in the country. Snowbird's mountain trails cover more than 2,000 skiable acres. The ski area features a 3,100-foot vertical drop from the 11,000-foot summit of Hidden Peak. As summer hits and the sun thaws the deep snow pack, guests enjoy the resort's activities center, spa, tennis center, mountain bike tours, backpacking treks, hikes, and heli golf.

SPECIFICS: Snowbird employs more than 800 new people each year to fill its 1,600 peak season jobs. The year-round staff averages approximately 650 individuals. Management recruits both year-round as well as winter and summer seasonal staff. Due to the ski area's extended ski season, winter seasonal staff should be available from mid-November through at least late-April, business levels permitting. Snowbird accepts applications for a wide variety of jobs including buspersons, cashiers, line cooks, prep cooks, pantry cooks, child care attendants, counter food servers, dishwashers, door persons, front desk clerks, restaurant hosts/hostesses, ski hosts/hostesses, housekeepers, laundry workers, lift attendants, janitors, pantry workers, parking attendants, warehouse laborers, rental technicians, repair technicians, reservation clerks, sales clerks, ski school staff, security officers, setup crew, ski checkers, spa attendants, stockpersons, switchboard operators, tram operators, valets, and waitpersons.

INSIDER TIPS: "We feel that our employees are our most important asset. We expect the best, and in return we provide a benefits package that is outstanding in the recreation industry. Snowbird Ski and Summer Resort is committed to the employment of exceptional people and will provide a fair compensation, personal recognition, and the opportunity for career growth."

PERKS: Snowbird's employee perks feature a generous ski privilege program that includes dependent passes, group health/hospitalization, life insurance, free transportation, and discounts on food, ski lessons, and lodging.

TO APPLY: Applicants should write or call for additional application information from Snowbird Ski and Summer Resort, Human Resources Department, 7350 S. Wasatch Blvd., Salt Lake City, Utah 84121; (801) 943-2243.

SNOWMASS SKI AREA
(Aspen, Colorado)
Seasonal (Winter and Spring)

Snowmass rises up from the chic golden streets of Aspen like a mighty giant. Aspen's largest and most popular ski area is actually a conglomeration of six ski areas in one place.

SPECIFICS: Snowmass hires 300 to 400 new employees each year to fill its 1,800- to 2,000-person staff. Most positions are seasonal beginning in early November and lasting through early April. The resort accepts applications for lift operators, food service staff, snowcat drivers, maids, hotel staff, ski school personnel, ski patrol members, and more. There is no application deadline. Starting pay ranges from $7.00 to $11.50 per hour depending on the position (subject to change).

INSIDER TIPS: Snowmass prides itself on its friendly staff and looks for "outgoing, people-oriented" applicants.

PERKS: Most employees receive a free ski pass.

TO APPLY: Applicants should write for an official employment brochure and application from Aspen Skiing Company, P.O. Box 1248, Aspen, Colorado 81611; (303) 925-1220. The Aspen Skiing Company also operates nearby Aspen Mountain and Buttermilk ski areas.

SNOW SUMMIT SKI AREA
(Big Bear Lake, California)

Seasonal (Winter)

Snow Summit is one of California's southernmost ski areas. Visitors can spend the morning skiing on Snow Summit's fresh powder and bask on a California beach in the afternoon.

SPECIFICS: Snow Summit receives approximately 1,500 applications for its 1,000 winter job openings. Although applications are accepted throughout the year, hiring doesn't start until mid-October. The resort's ski season usually opens by Thanksgiving. Applications are accepted for lift attendants, ticket sellers, base hosts/hostesses and ski hosts/hostesses, parking attendants, snowmakers, mechanics, food service staff, ski rental shop staff, ski instructors, ski patrol members, and janitorial staff. Pay varies according to position but starts at $4.50 per hour (subject to change).

INSIDER TIPS: According to Personnel Director Tony Hagmann, "Working at Snow Summit provides an alternative mountain living lifestyle, clean air, a variety of co-workers, and a chance to learn to ski or to·become a better skier with free lift tickets, free ski lessons, and free ski equipment. Most of our jobs are unskilled and training is provided."

PERKS: Snow Summit offers free skiing, free ski lessons, free ski rentals, free employee uniforms, and an end-of-season bonus.

TO APPLY: Applicants should either call for employment information or apply in person to Tony Hagmann, Personnel Director, Snow Summit Resort, Box 77, Big Bear Lake, California 92315; (714) 866-5766, ext. 141.

SQUAW VALLEY SKI CORPORATION
(Olympic Valley, California)
Seasonal (Winter) and Year-Round

Squaw Valley USA is California's twenty-first century destination resort and the site of the 1960 Winter Olympics. Thirty-three lifts, including a 120-passenger cable car and a six-passenger gondola, make Squaw Valley a premier skiing experience. The High Camp Bath & Tennis Club is open year-round at Elevation 8200, and offers ice skating, tennis, a mountain bike park, volleyball, bungee jumping, hiking, and various restaurants and bars.

HIRING SPECIFICS: Squaw Valley hires more than 500 new employees each year to fill more than 900 seasonal (winter) and 100 year-round positions. The seasonal (winter) staff begin work sometime between November and mid-December and will usually stay through late spring. Applications are accepted for ski school sales persons, snow hostesses, ticket cashiers, snow school teachers, skier safety/ski patrol staff, gondola operators, competition services crew, lift operators, parking lot attendants, security guards, lift ticket checkers, ski rental/shop staff, lift maintenance staff, snow groomers, clerical staff, and race team members. Hiring clinics are held in October.

INSIDER TIPS: According to the employee handbook: "All employees must have a clean and well-groomed appearance. Each employee is expected to work the entire winter season."

PERKS: Most employees will receive a free season pass to Squaw Valley and an end-of-season bonus. Discounts are available to staff members at the resort's shops and restaurants.

TO APPLY: Applicants should write for an official application and an employment opportunities brochure. Please send application requests to Rena Sullivan, Personnel Director, Squaw Valley USA, Olympic Valley, California 96146; (916) 583-6985.

Squaw Valley also has several food concessions. For information regarding food service positions call Hagan Management at (916) 583-2555 or Olympic Plaza Food and Beverage at (916) 583-1588.

STEAMBOAT SKI AREA
(Steamboat Springs, Colorado)
Seasonal (Winter) and Year-Round

Steamboat Springs is one of the world's top ski areas, with more than 2,500 skiable acres and 101 ski trails. Perched high atop Colorado's magnificent Rocky Mountains, this resort gathers an average cumulative snowfall of more than 27 feet each season.

SPECIFICS: Steamboat Springs employs 120 year-round and 700 to 800 seasonal staff members. More than 300 new employees are hired annually. The ski area and resort hires all typical resort and ski area positions including numerous openings in lift operations, ski school, nursery ski school, ticket office, food service, and mountain maintenance departments. Pay ranges from $4.70 to $5.50 per hour for most positions. Ski season runs from November 22 through April 15 and new employees should be available in mid-November.

INSIDER TIPS: Most hiring is done the first week of November; however, there is some turnover after January 1 and hiring continues throughout the season. According to the Personnel Department, "We look for friendly, outgoing individuals who are enthusiastic about their jobs as well as their time off."

PERKS: All employees receive a season ski pass, a 30% discount at shops and restaurants, and free uniforms.

TO APPLY: Applicants should write for employment information or send a cover letter and résumé to Patti Brown, Human Resources Coordinator, Steamboat Ski Corporation, Personnel Department, 2305 Mt. Werner Circle, Steamboat Springs, Colorado 80487; (303) 879-6111.

SUGARBUSH RESORT
(Warren, Vermont)
Seasonal (Winter and Summer) and Year-Round

Sugarbush Resort is situated between two scenic mountains in the middle of Green Mountain National Forest. The resort is open year-round and features skiing in the winter and tennis, swimming, golf, and other outdoor activities during the summer.

SPECIFICS: Sugarbush employs 150 year-round and 530 peak-season employees. Ideally, winter seasonal employees should be available from November 15 through the end of April. Summer staff should be available to work from early June through late August or early September. There is no application deadline. Applications are accepted for winter seasonal snowmaking staff, mechanics, trail groomers, lift attendants, lift ticket checkers, day care staff, ticket sellers, ski school instructors and staff (experience required), ski rental shop staff, parking attendants, ski patrol members (Red Cross advanced first-aid and CPR certificates required), hotel and restaurant staff, and buildings and maintenance staff. Summer seasonal and year-round jobs are available at the sports center as front desk/pro shop staff, maintenance workers, fitness instructors, lifeguards, and camp counselors, waitstaff, bartenders, cooks, bellhops, and front desk staff. Positions are also available for part-time employees and short-term holiday season staff. Sugarbush also offers a unique college internship program for students interested in resort management careers.

INSIDER TIPS: Sugarbush looks for "energetic, creative, and fun people who are responsible and take pride in themselves and in their work." Employees value safety, service, and quality while enjoying their jobs.

PERKS: All winter employees receive a free full-season ski pass, discounts on meals and retail services, free ski lessons, health insurance, and more. Year-round employees also receive complimentary membership at the sports center complex. A limited amount of winter employee housing is available.

TO APPLY: Applicants should send a cover letter and résumé to Sugarbush Resort, Attn: Personnel Department, Access Road, Warren, Vermont 05674-9993; (802) 583-2381, ext. 400.

SUGARLOAF/USA
(Carrabasset Valley, Maine)
Seasonal (Winter) and Year-Round

Sugarloaf/USA is a true year-round destination resort. During the winter, Sugarloaf Mountain provides 40-plus miles of skiable trails with a vertical drop of more than 2,800 feet. Additionally, the resort has more than 80 kilometers of double-tracked cross country ski trails that loop their way through beautiful Carrabasset Valley. Summer activities include golf, tennis, swimming, hiking, fly fishing, and whitewater rafting.

SPECIFICS: Sugarloaf/USA employs 625 employees and annually hires 250 new staff members. Positions are available for both winter seasonal and year-round jobs as well as for both full-time and part-time employees. Most winter seasonal help must be available to start work by December 1. Hiring is done as needed throughout the year, but most hiring is done from early August through late February each year. For available positions and job information, contact the employment office at the address below.

INSIDER TIPS: Sugarloaf/USA seeks friendly, outgoing, people-oriented employees. A personal interview is required of all potential employees before a final hiring commitment is made. Limited employee housing is provided.

PERKS: Perks vary depending on an employee's status. However, most employees are eligible for various types of insurance and most employees receive courtesy lift tickets, ski shops discounts, free ski lessons, and discounted food and ski shop rentals.

TO APPLY: Applicants should write for an official application or send a cover letter and résumé to Donna L. Morey, Personnel Manager, Sugarloaf Mountain Corporation, Box 5000, Kingfield, Maine 04947; (207) 237-2000.

SUNDAY RIVER SKI RESORT
(Newry, Maine)
Seasonal (Summer and Winter) and Year-Round

Sunday River is a destination ski resort located 75 miles northwest of Portland and 180 miles from Boston. Sunday River is the fastest growing ski resort in the United States. The mountain receives an average annual snowfall of 150 inches and is committed to snowmaking. It has pumps that can send 6,000 gallons of water per minute up the hill, and the resort calculates that it made more than 4,500 acre feet of snow last year.

SPECIFICS: Sunday River Ski Resort employs nearly 1,000 staff members during the winter months and nearly 200 staff members during the summer period. Positions are available for both summer and winter help. Winter seasonal staff begin work between September and December. Summer seasonal positions start in mid-May or June. Applications for summer employment should be completed by mid-May. Applications for winter employment should be completed between September and November. Staff with a wide range of training and background in accounting, advertising, engineering, communications, development, finance control, and food/beverage, hotel, marketing, personnel, and retail management are required. Technical positions include artists, computer specialists, heavy equipment operators, lift mechanics, photographers, pump and compressor mechanics, rescue, secretarial, and ski professionals, snowmaking research personnel, vehicle mechanics, and waste water treatment operators. Sales positions include retail sales, vacation sales, and real estate sales. In addition, cashiers, carpenters, child care personnel, custodians, customer service reps, housekeepers, lift operators, ski technicians, security guards, snowmakers, telesales agents, trail groomers, and waitstaff are needed.

INSIDER TIPS: "We attempt to attract candidates who seek a challenge in their work and who are willing to contribute time and effort for career advancement and excellent opportunities. Sunday River is committed to being the best at what we do and all individuals sharing that philosophy are encouraged to apply." While Sunday River recruits both seasonal as well as year-round employees, there is a much greater demand for seasonal applicants.

PERKS: Employee benefits vary according to an employee's status. Year round employees are eligible to receive health and life insurance, profit sharing, bonuses, and vacation pay. Seasonal employees are eligible to receive child care assistance, housing referral assistance, 401(k) plan, free season passes, and cafeteria, ski lessons, ski rental, and ski shop discounts as well as many restaurant and health club discounts in the region.

TO APPLY: Applicants should write or call for an official application or send a cover letter and résumé to Sunday River Ski Resort, Jeffrey Kelcourse, Personnel Manager, P.O. Box 450, Bethel, Maine 04217; (207) 824-3000.

TELLURIDE SKI RESORT, INC.
(Telluride, Colorado)
Seasonal (Winter)

Telluride is one of the fastest-growing ski areas in the Rocky Mountain region. It is an isolated ski area located southeast of Grand Junction, Colorado. Telluride's isolation and Victorian charm has made this one of the preferred destination resorts in the Rockies.

SPECIFICS: Telluride employs 125 year-round and 525 winter seasonal staff members. The resort actively solicits applications for seasonal winter jobs from applicants who can be available from approximately November 24 through April 13. Positions are available in the following departments: lift operations (ticket checkers, lift operators, and lift supervisors), food service (waitpersons, cooks, bartenders, buspersons, and cashiers), rentals (technicians, ski mechanics, and shop supervisors), tickets (window sales), nursery (child care attendants), guest services (individual sales, group sales, and information desk attendants), ski school sales (front desk personnel and ski school window sales clerks), and ski school (ski instructors for ages three and up). Base pay begins at approximately $5.00 per hour and goes up according to experience, position, and responsibility. Most hiring is done between mid-October and mid-November.

INSIDER TIPS: Housing can be scarce and expensive in Telluride. Before accepting a job you should be sure you have a place to live at a price you can afford. Shared housing is common among seasonal employees. The company requires all employees to be neatly groomed and attired.

PERKS: All employees are eligible to receive a complimentary season ski pass (contact the personnel office for restrictions).

TO APPLY: Applicants should either write for an official application and job information letter or send a cover letter and résumé to Don Smith, Personnel Director, Telluride Ski Resort, P.O. Box 307, Telluride, Colorado 81435; (303) 728-3856. Send a SASE with all correspondence. A personal interview may be required.

TOPNOTCH AT STOWE
(Stowe, Vermont)
Seasonal (Summer and Winter) and Year-Round

Topnotch is in one of Vermont's most picturesque villages. This internationally acclaimed 120-acre, four-star, four-diamond resort is one of the top fifty tennis resorts in the country, and Mt. Mansfield in nearby Stowe is ranked as one of the top ten U.S. ski areas. The resort has its own equestrian center, tennis facilities, pools, putting green, exercise room, and health spa.

SPECIFICS: Topnotch at Stowe employs more than 140 staff members for both seasonal and year-round positions. Typically, at least fifty seasonal positions are available annually. The busiest seasons are from June through October and November through January. While experience is preferred, it is not required. Positions are available for dishwashers, prep cooks, cooks, bartenders, cocktail staff, waitpersons, housekeepers, maintenance staff, reservation clerks, cashiers, front desk help, and bell staff. Starting pay ranges from $2.10 (plus tips) for waitpersons to $5.25 for reservations and front desk staff.

INSIDER TIPS: A good sense of organization, commitment, and a positive attitude are also important and should be stressed on your application.

PERKS: Employees are allowed to use all resort facilities as long as they do so with discretion. There is an employee tennis program, and discounts are offered at the equestrian center and Nordic ski center. The spa offers an employee fitness program.

TO APPLY: Applicants should send a cover letter and résumé to Personnel Manager, Topnotch at Stowe, P.O. Box 1458, Stowe, Vermont 05672; (802) 253-8585.

VERNON VALLEY/GREAT GORGE SKI AREA
(McAfee, New Jersey)
Seasonal (Winter) and Year-Round

Vernon Valley Great Gorge Ski Area is a unique combination ski resort and amusement park located in rural Sussex County, New Jersey, just 47 miles from New York City. During the winter, Vernon Valley Great Gorge's three interconnected mountains offer more than 25 miles of skiable terrain over a 1,000-foot vertical drop. Each summer the ski resort gives way to Action Park, a huge theme park with about fifty exciting participation rides. The Ski Area and Action Park are part of the Great Gorge Resort that also features a $12 million dollar health spa, 1,400 condominiums, and the Great Gorge Village Hotel, which has a nine-hole golf course.

SPECIFICS: Each winter Vernon Valley Great Gorge hires more than 800 new staff members to fill its 750 ski resort positions. Jobs are available for both winter seasonal staff as well as year-round help. (For information on summer jobs see the "Action Park" listing in the *Theme and Amusement Parks* chapter.) Winter seasonal staff should be available from mid-December through March, if possible. However, extra help is hired for the January and February peak season. There is no application deadline. Most starting salaries range from $5.05 to $9.00 per hour, although a few skilled positions pay higher. Winter seasonal applications are accepted for ski instructors (fifty jobs available, training available), ski patrol (certification required, twenty positions available), food and beverage attendants (150 positions), cashiers (fifty positions), retail sales clerks (twenty-five positions), equipment specialists (training required, fifty positions), and slope patrollers (excellent skiing skills required, twenty-five positions). For applicants over the age of eighteen jobs are also available for lift attendants (250 positions), security guards (twenty positions), and snowmakers (seventy-five positions).

INSIDER TIPS: Apply early for the best selection of available positions. By January 1 most choice ski resort positions are filled.

PERKS: Winter staff perks include free skiing privileges, subsidized housing, 50% off all meals, retail shop discounts, discount skiing for friends and family, employee contests, and bonuses. Limited housing on premises available for those who apply early. Many winter staff members are invited back to work during the summer at Action Park.

TO APPLY: Applicants should write for an official application from the Vernon Valley Recreation Association, Beth Masters, Personnel Director, Box 848, McAfee, New Jersey 07428; (201) 827-2000. Applications should be returned with a photograph and cover letter outlining positions of interest. Management responds only to applicants who will be offered employment.

WHITEFACE MOUNTAIN SKI CENTER
(Wilmington, New York)

Seasonal (Winter) and Year-Round

Whiteface Mountain Ski Center was a host of the 1980 Winter Olympic Games. In addition to this international honor, Whiteface boasts the largest vertical drop on the East Coast—3,216 vertical feet.

SPECIFICS: Whiteface hires 100-plus new employees each season to fill its staff of 275. Long- and short-term employment is available. The resort hires about forty snowmaking personnel, fifty lift attendants, fifty ski school instructors, eighteen ski patrol members, eight custodians, six parking attendants, and nine vehicle maintenance personnel. All candidates must be available for a personal interview. Employment requirements for ski patrol and ski school personnel are given upon application. Wages are set by union agreement.

INSIDER TIPS: High school diploma preferred. Candidates who demonstrate reliability, neatness, and show up on time for their interview are favored by management.

PERKS: Employees enjoy some of the best skiing on the East Coast.

TO APPLY: Applicants should write for an official application from Teddy Blazer, Whiteface Mountain, Route 86, Wilmington, New York 12997; (518) 946-2223.

WINTER PARK RESORT
(Winter Park, Colorado)

Seasonal (Winter and Summer)

Winter Park Resort is Colorado's favorite ski resort. Located 67 miles west of Denver in Colorado's Rocky Mountains, Winter Park uses twenty lifts to carry skiers to 112 trails covering 1,301 skiable acres.

SPECIFICS: Winter Park Resort hires more than 500 new employees annually to fill its 1,100-plus-member winter staff. Most positions are seasonal, lasting from mid-November through April. There isn't a firm deadline for applications, but most hiring takes place in September and October. A high school diploma or GED is required for winter and summer jobs. For applicants with limited or no skiing ability there are positions available as food service employees, facilities crew members, snow removal crew, parking attendants, ticket sales clerks (some cashier experience required), and reservationists. For applicants with some basic skiing ability, there are numerous openings for lift attendants. Finally, advanced skiers may apply for positions as race and trail crew, ski instructors, and ski patrol members. Summer job opportunities include seasonal positions as Alpine slide, mountain bike, mini-golf attendants and food service staff. These jobs last from mid-June through Labor Day. Starting wages for most positions range from $5.50 to $6.00 per hour.

INSIDER TIPS: "Qualities our supervisors will be looking for (in screening applicants) include responsible individuals with a neat appearance, a pleasant friendly personality, and an upbeat, positive attitude. Previous experience for jobs such as lift attendants, food service employees, facilities crew members, or snow removal/parking attendants is certainly helpful, but not required. Most lift attendants will be required to ski and, therefore, should have ski equipment. Ticket sellers and cashiers need some type of experience in handling money." A personal interview is generally required before a final hiring commitment is made.

PERKS: All employees receive a free season ski pass, free ski lessons, meal discounts (complimentary meals for food service employees), and have the option of using a free shuttle to and from work. Eligible employees receive paid holidays, sick pay, the potential for an end-of-season bonus, and insurance. An employee nursery and fitness program/sports science lab are available for a fee. The company offers a limited amount of subsidized employee housing in nearby condos. Many other benefits and special programs are available for employees.

TO APPLY: Applicants should write for an official application and ski season employment brochure from the Personnel Office, Winter Park Resort, Box 36, Winter Park, Colorado 80482; (303) 726-5514. Due to the large number of applications received, management cannot guarantee a response to all unsolicited applications.

Other ski areas that recruit applicants include:

Alpental*Ski Acres*Snoqualmie
Patty Love, Base Operations
  Supervisor
3010 77th Ave.
Mercer Island, Washington
  98040
(206) 232-8182
Number of Employees: 500–600

Cardrona Ski Area
Shawn Gilbertson, Manager
P.O. Box 117
Wanaka, New Zealand
(02943) 7341
Number of Employees: 130

49° North Ski Area
P.O. Box 166
Chewelah, Washington 99109
(509) 935-6649
Number of Employees: 145
Author's Note: All hiring is done
  by the local Chamber of
  Commerce, 102 N. Park,
  Chewelah, Washington
  99109; (509) 935-8991.

Mt. Hutt Ski Area
Mr. P. Witton, Operations
  Manager
P.O. Box 14
Methven, South Island, New
  Zealand
(0053) 28-529
Number of Employees: 240
Author's Note: Management
  reports they are unable to
  confirm a job unless an
  applicant is in Methven.
  For the best chances of
  employment arrive in
  early April. "If applicants
  are here early enough, are
  prepared to wait for
  the snow, and have
  accommodation (housing),
  they will (often) get a job."

Snowshoe Mountain Resort
Human Resources Department
P.O. Box 10
Snowshoe, West Virginia 26209
(304) 572-1000
Number of Employees: 600

The following listings, found under the chapter headings given below, also include positions at snow/ski areas:

AMUSEMENT PARKS
Action Park Vernon Valley

Eye Spy Photo

HIGH ADVENTURE
Ski Guides Hawaii
Ski Utah

Yosemite Institute

LAKES
Fairfield Pagosa Resort
Harrah's Tahoe

Indianhead Mountain Resort, Inc.
Lake Louise Inn

MOUNTAINS
A-Line Motor Inn
Alpine Lodge
The Aspen Lodge Ranch Resort
Bear Trap Ranch
Beaver Run Resort
Bolton Valley Ski and Summer Resort
Boomerang Lodge
Chateau Lake Louise
Cheyenne Mountain Conference Resort
The Explorer Hotel
Fox Ridge Resort
The Inn of the Rockies/ Holiday Inn Estes Park

The Inn of the Seventh Mountain
Lake Tahoe Horizon Casino Resort
Red Lion Inn
Smile Click
Stein Ericksen Lodge
Sunshine Village
Tameron Resort
Timberline Lodge
Topnotch at Stowe
The Village at Breckenridge Resort
Yosemite Park and Curry Company

Coasts
& Beaches

~~~~~~~~~~~~~~

ACADIA CORPORATION
(Acadia National Park, Maine)

Seasonal (Summer)

Acadia Corporation is an official concessionaire for Acadia National
Park, the second most visited national park in the United States.
Acadia National Park is located on the rugged Maine coast "where
the mountains meet the sea"—an ideal spot for nature lovers. Acadia
Corporation operates several gift shops, including one on the summit
of Cadillac Mountain, another overlooking the sea at Thunder Hole,
and another on the shores of Jordan Pond. The company also operates
a large restaurant within the park at Jordan Pond and several gift
shops in the nearby town of Bar Harbor.

SPECIFICS: Acadia Corporation hires more than 125 employees annually. All jobs are seasonal. A few positions open in early April, but
most start mid- to late May and end in mid-October. "We hire
employees to work varying lengths of time, at varying start dates."
Positions are available at the Jordan Pond House Restaurant for waiters, waitresses, buspersons, dishwashers, cooks, bartenders, porters,

cashiers, and hosts. The Acadia Shops hire supervisors, shop clerks, and assistant shop managers. The company also has positions for maintenance persons, grounds keepers, parking attendants, clerks, and delivery drivers. Most employees are eligible for a bonus if they complete their work agreements. Most tipped positions pay from $2.13 to $5.00 per hour plus tips; non-tipped positions generally start at $5.00 per hour (1992 wages).

INSIDER TIPS: Apply early for the best chance at a job—by April most hiring is completed. A few jobs require prior experience but in most cases a positive attitude and willingness to work hard and learn new tasks is the basic requirement. Nature and outdoor lovers will have a summer long remembered—people who need a city environment and daily entertainment will probably not be happy here.

PERKS: Employees have the option of living in a 60-bed company-operated dormitory for $60.00 per week including meals (subject to change). The company provides dorm recreational events including cookouts, volleyball, lobster feasts, and scheduled rides into Bar Harbor for shopping and socializing.

TO APPLY: Applicants should write for an official application and enclose a stamped, self-addressed business-sized envelope. Enclosing a cover letter and résumé with your completed application will enhance your chances of being hired. For applications or information write: Acadia Corporation, Personnel Department, Box 24, Bar Harbor, Maine 04609; (207) 288-5592.

THE ALGONQUIN RESORT
(St. Andrews By-the-Sea, New Brunswick, Canada)
Seasonal (Summer)

For more than 100 years, the Algonquin has been providing a summer respite for Canadians and Americans looking for a summer vacation by the sea. This historic 200-room hotel overlooks the beautiful Bay of Fundy, just North of the Canadian/U.S. border along the Atlantic seaboard. The resort is open annually from May to October.

SPECIFICS: The Algonquin Resort hires 175-plus new employees each year to fill its 225 staff positions. As the hotel is only open from early May through mid-October, all jobs are seasonal. While the hotel prefers applicants who can be available the entire season, there are some positions that are open for shorter periods (i.e., July through mid-October or May through August). In addition to a regular recruitment program, the hotel offers a special "Summer Work Experience Program" for students studying hotel or restaurant management. The hotel hires a wide array of employees including sous-chefs, pastry chefs, cooks, stewards, waitpersons, captain waitpersons, bartenders, buspersons, telephone operators, store clerks, front desk personnel, bellpersons, convention porters, housekeeping supervisors, chambermaids, housepersons, and linen room attendants. All applications must be completed by March 1. Starting wages for non-management positions are generally the provincial minimum wage plus tips (currently CAN$5.00 per hour).

INSIDER TIPS: The Algonquin looks for "outgoing, cheerful, well-groomed individuals who are able to not only work well with others but live and get along with co-workers in the staff residences." At the end of each season, the hotel's personnel department prints up a brochure with brief résumés and photographs of all Algonquin employees looking for winter seasonal work in other Canadian Pacific hotels.

PERKS: Room and board are supplied at a nominal rate for employees. Other employee perks include an end-of-season bonus for all employees who fulfill their employment contracts.

TO APPLY: Applicants should either write for an official application or send a cover letter and résumé to Kelly Lord, Manager, Human Resources, The Algonquin Resort, St. Andrews, New Brunswick, E0G 2X0 New Brunswick, Canada; (506) 529-8823.

BEACH COVE CLARION RESORT
(North Myrtle Beach, South Carolina)
Seasonal (Spring and Summer) and Year-Round

Beach Cove Clarion Resort is located at the southern tip of North Myrtle Beach overlooking the area's celebrated white sand beach.

SPECIFICS: The Beach Cove hires 100-plus new staff members annually to fill its 170 positions. Positions are available for both year-round as well as seasonal work. Seasonal staff are hired for the peak April through September season. There is no application deadline. The resort frequently recruits waitpersons, buspersons, banquet servers, banquet setup staff, bartenders, pool bar attendants, dishwashers, front desk clerks, PBX operators, bellpersons, and children's activities leaders. Wages vary according to position.

INSIDER TIPS: The resort seeks applicants who are neat and well-mannered and have a pleasant personality.

PERKS: Employees in many departments receive tips and meals.

TO APPLY: Applicants should send a cover letter, résumé, photograph, and SARP to Betty Osborne, Personnel Manager, Beach Cove Clarion Resort, 4800 South Ocean Boulevard, North Myrtle Beach, South Carolina 29582; (803) 272-4044.

BOCA RATON HOTEL & CLUB
(Boca Raton, Florida)
Seasonal (Winter and Spring) and Year-Round

Located in world-famous Boca Raton, the Boca Raton Hotel & Club is a huge luxury resort with 1,200 guest rooms, twenty-two tennis courts, golf, a fitness club, and numerous fine lounges and restaurants.

SPECIFICS: The Boca Raton hires more than 1,000 new employees each year to fill its 2,000-person peak-season staff. Both winter seasonal and year-round positions are available. Winter seasonal staff members should be available to work from November 1 through April 30. Applications are accepted for waitpersons, dining room captains, maitre d's, cooks, buspersons, housekeepers, housekeeping supervisors, front office clerks, bellhops, and cashiers. Starting wages vary according to position and experience.

INSIDER TIPS: Management seeks service-oriented applicants who are clean-cut, responsible, alert, and professional.

TO APPLY: Applicants should either write for an official application or send a cover letter, résumé, and SARP to Barbara Tomasso, Employment Coordinator, Boca Raton Hotel & Club, 501 E. Camino Real, Boca Raton, Florida 33432; (305) 395-3000.

BOOTHBAY HARBOR YACHT CLUB
(Boothbay Harbor, Maine)
Seasonal (Summer)

The Boothbay Harbor Yacht Club is a major northeastern yacht club with approximately 150 members and an active sailing and tennis program.

SPECIFICS: The yacht club has seasonal summer positions available for sailing instructors. Instructors must be available from the last week of June through the end of August. All candidates must be at least eighteen years old and possess strong sailing skills. Salaries are negotiable up to approximately $1,400 per month.

INSIDER TIPS: Aside from a strong sailing background, applicants must demonstrate that they are able to assist in planning a creative sailing school schedule and teach seamanship, basic sailing techniques, and racing skills to students age eight and up.

PERKS: This job provides a rare opportunity to spend a summer sailing and working outdoors.

TO APPLY: Applicants should send a cover letter and résumé to Peter Edwards, 10 Cranberry Lane, Dover, Massachusetts 02030; (617) 785-1043 or to James Steane, 186 Hunter Drive, Hartford, Connecticut 06107; (203) 521-3561.

BRADLESS DEPARTMENT STORE
(Cape Cod, Massachusetts)
Seasonal (Summer) and Year-Round

Bradless is a chain of popular department stores on Cape Cod, a popular summer vacation spot for beach lovers and an excellent place to enjoy a winter of solitude along the Atlantic seacoast.

SPECIFICS: Bradless accepts applications for retail salesperson positions. Jobs are available for summer seasonal, year-round, part-time, full-time, and Sunday-only work. No experience is necessary for most positions.

INSIDER TIPS: Bradless management believes a summer job on Cape Cod should be interesting, rewarding, and fun.

PERKS: Employees receive a discount in the stores.

TO APPLY: Applicants must apply in person at each store while on Cape Cod. Drop in during normal business hours to complete an application. Bradless guarantees on-the-spot interviews. Starting dates can usually be confirmed the same day for successful applicants. Bradless stores are located in Hyannis, (617) 778-1980; Falmouth, (617) 540-7006; South Yarmouth (617) 394-2136; Dennisport (617) 398-6004; and Orleans (617) 255-5301.

CARMEL COUNTRY SPA
(Carmel Valley, California)
Seasonal (Summer) and Year-Round

Where better to rejuvenate one's soul while losing weight than Carmel Valley? Located near Clint Eastwood's home town, Carmel-by-the-Sea, this 7-acre health resort is spread across a sprawling retreat hidden by giant oak trees.

SPECIFICS: The Carmel Country Spa hires approximately five new employees each year. Jobs are available for both year-round and seasonal staff. Seasonal workers must be available from at least April through October or November. Applications are accepted for front desk clerks, office receptionists, aerobics instructors, massage therapists, cosmetologists, accountants, bookkeepers, and landscapers.

INSIDER TIPS: "We look for applicants with enthusiasm, honesty, and a go-getter, positive attitude. Dependability is essential."

PERKS: Room and board are possible for some positions. All staff may use the spa's gym, outdoor heated swimming pool, sauna, hot tub, and exercise classes during off-duty hours.

TO APPLY: Applicants should send a cover letter, résumé, photograph, and SARP to Carla Adkins, Assistant Manager, Carmel Country Spa, 10 Country Club Way, Carmel Valley, California 93924; (408) 659-3486.

CEMETERY DEPARTMENT, TOWN OF YARMOUTH
(West Yarmouth, Massachusetts)
Seasonal (Summer)

If you enjoy working in an environment where things tend to go "bump" in the night, this is the perfect job for you. West Yarmouth is a quaint town on Cape Cod. The town offers summer jobs for a small skeleton crew of laborers in its cemetery department.

SPECIFICS: The West Yarmouth Cemetery Department hires three seasonal summer laborers to work in the seven local cemeteries. All employees must be at least eighteen years of age when starting work. All positions are seasonal beginning in April and lasting through Labor Day.

INSIDER TIPS: As customer relations skills are not exactly essential for cemetery personnel, personal interviews are *not* required. Two laborer positions are also available in the town's Highway Department. For Highway Department employment information contact Town of Yarmouth, Highway Department, Buck Island Road, West Yarmouth, Massachusetts 02673; (617) 775-2516. Application deadline is June 1.

TO APPLY: Applicants interested in jobs as cemetery laborers should contact Philip Whitten, Director of Parks and Cemeteries, 74 Townbrook Road, W. Yarmouth, Massachusetts 02673; (508) 775-7910.

THE COTTAGES RESORT & CONFERENCE CENTER
(Hilton Head Island, South Carolina)
Seasonal (Fall and Summer)

The Cottages Resort & Conference Center is located in Shipyard Plantation on Hilton Head Island, South Carolina. Hilton Head Island is one of the South's prime vacation destinations.

SPECIFICS: The Cottages hires approximately ten new employees each year to fill its thirty-six staff positions. Seasonal employees should be available from approximately March through September. Positions are available for housekeepers, front desk clerks, clerical staff (excellent typing skills required), and bellpersons (valid driver's license required).

INSIDER TIPS: The Cottages looks for dependable, enthusiastic, neat employees with previous related experience.

PERKS: Staff members are allowed to use the resort's racquetball courts, exercise equipment room, saunas, and indoor/outdoor heated swimming pools on specified days.

TO APPLY: Applicants should write for an official application form or send a cover letter and résumé to Doris Penrod, Executive Assistant, The Cottages Resort & Conference Center, P.O. Box 7528, Hilton Head Island, South Carolina 29938; (803) 686-6470.

FAIRFIELD OCEAN RIDGE RESORT
(Edisto Beach, South Carolina)
Seasonal (Summer) and Year-Round

Located 45 miles south of Charleston, Fairfield Ocean Ridge provides the ideal vacation getaway. Although primarily a golf resort, Fairfield's facilities include tennis, swimming, miniature golf, and fishing.

SPECIFICS: Fairfield Ocean Ridge hires twenty new employees each year to fill its 200-person staff. Jobs are available for both summer seasonal and year-round employment. Summer staff must be available to work from at least late May through August. Applications are accepted for secretaries, switchboard operators, front desk clerks, receptionists, golf maintenance personnel, grounds keepers, housekeepers, building maintenance workers, sales people, restaurant staff, and construction workers. Salaries start at minimum wage and go up depending on the position. There is no application deadline.

INSIDER TIPS: The resort looks for hard-working applicants who are dependable, honest, and loyal.

PERKS: Limited employee housing is available for certain recreation department positions.

TO APPLY: Applicants should send a cover letter, résumé, and SARP to Personnel Director, Fairfield Ocean Ridge Resort, 1 King Cotton Road, Edisto Beach, South Carolina 29438; (803) 869-2561. Recreation staff applicants should address applications to the attention of the Recreation Director.

FITNESS ADVANTAGE AT THE PLUNGE
(San Diego, California)
Seasonal (Summer) and Year-Round

Fitness Advantage at the Plunge is a brand-new, full-service fitness center located on the sand at San Diego's Mission Beach. Fitness Advantage offers circuit weight training, free weights, aerobics, and one of the largest heated indoor swimming pools in California. The club is built on the site of historic Belmont Park, a beachfront amusement park and arcade.

SPECIFICS: Fitness Advantage hires approximately thirty new employees each year to fill its fifty to seventy seasonal and year-round positions. Summer staff should be available to work starting mid-June. Applications are accepted for weight trainers, aerobics instructors, lifeguards, aquatic instructors, front desk clerks, and child care attendants. Most summer positions are for aquatic instructors and child care attendants (work in the children's summer camp program).

INSIDER TIPS: According to management, Fitness Advantage looks for "neat, healthy, sharp dressers, with good communications skills. We are about fitness and all employees should enjoy exercise."

PERKS: Employees are given a complimentary fitness club membership and discounts on many special interest programs such as SCUBA lessons, etc.

TO APPLY: Applicants should either stop by and apply in person or send a cover letter, résumé, and photograph to the Personnel Manager, Fitness Advantage at the Plunge, 3115 Ocean Front Walk, San Diego, California 92109; (619) 488-3110.

GURNEY'S INN RESORT & SPA
(Montauk, Long Island, New York)
Seasonal (Summer) and Year-Round

Since 1926 Gurney's Inn has been one of the foremost resorts and spas at the threshold of the Hamptons.

SPECIFICS: Gurney's Inn employs over 200 seasonal and year-round staff members. Summer staff are hired to work June through Labor Day. Starting salaries range from minimum wage to $6.50 per hour depending upon position. Applications are accepted for lifeguards, front desk staff, bellhops, valets, switchboard operators, dining room waitpersons, buspersons, restaurant hostesses, housekeepers, porters, cooks, spa attendants, and receptionists.

INSIDER TIPS: According to personnel director Dorothy Bates, Gurney's looks for "reliable, trustworthy, loyal staffers with a good team spirit and an ability to pitch in no matter what the job title. (Employees must also have) an ability to provide service with a smile."

PERKS: Housing is available to some employees on a first come, first served basis. Some positions have free meals included. All staffers are permitted to use the resort's spa during off-peak hours. A separate part of the hotel's beach is reserved for staff use.

TO APPLY: Applicants should either write for an official application or send a cover letter, résumé, photograph, and SARP to Dorothy Bates, Personnel Director, Gurney's Inn, P.O. Box UUU, Montauk, New York 11954; (516) 668-2345, (516) 668-2664.

HIGHLANDS INN
(Carmel, California)
Seasonal (Summer) and Year-Round

The Highlands Inn is a luxury four-star hotel perched high atop a bluff overlooking the blue Pacific in Clint Eastwood's hometown of Carmel-by-the-Sea, California. The resort's location provides awesome views of California's rugged Big Sur coast. The Highlands Inn is one of the most exclusive resorts on the Northern California coast.

SPECIFICS: The Highlands Inn employs 250 staff members. Applications are accepted for all typical hotel and resort positions including front desk clerks and cashiers, housekeepers, waitstaff, buspersons, cooks, kitchen helpers, bellhops, and recreation staff. Both long-term and seasonal help are needed. Seasonal staff are recruited for the busy summer season.

INSIDER TIPS: Management looks for applicants with good people skills and a sharp appearance. Service-oriented individuals with an ability to work as part of a team will do well here. The resort caters to an extremely high-calibre clientele and all staff must be dedicated to providing top-notch guest service.

TO APPLY: Applicants should send a cover letter, résumé, photograph, and SARP to Mara Cantor, Human Resource Manager, Highlands Inn, P.O. Box 1700, Carmel, California 93921; (408) 624-3801.

HILTON HEAD INN
(Hilton Head Island, South Carolina)
Seasonal (Summer) and Year-Round

Exclusive Hilton Head Island is the largest island between New Jersey and Florida. Hilton Head Inn is situated on nineteen acres of prime oceanfront land along South Forest Beach Drive. The resort features 202 guest rooms, including twenty-six cottages.

SPECIFICS: A high employee turnover and seasonal demands require the Hilton Head Inn to hire approximately 250 new employees each year to fill its 175 positions. Jobs are available for both year-round and summer seasonal staff. Summer seasonal employees should be available from approximately May 20 through Labor Day. The resort often has openings for front desk clerks, housemen, bellpersons, cashiers, hosts/hostesses, waitpersons, bartenders, cooks, housekeepers, and maintenance personnel. Starting salaries range from minimum wage to $7.50 per hour depending on the position (subject to change). There is no application deadline.

INSIDER TIPS: "For most of our positions, experience is helpful but not required. We look for intelligent, energetic, prompt, and caring employees with good attitudes."

PERKS: Many employees receive generous tips.

TO APPLY: Applicants for year-round positions should send a cover letter, résumé, photograph, and SARP to Mr. Vince DiFonzo, General Manager, Hilton Head Inn, P.O. Box 7828, Hilton Head, South Carolina 29938; (803) 785-5111. Applicants for summer seasonal positions should write asking for an application (enclose SASE with request).

HOLIDAY INN OCEANFRONT
(Hilton Head Island, South Carolina)
Seasonal (Summer) and Year-Round

The Holiday Inn Oceanfront is a five-story, 201-room resort on South Carolina's plush Hilton Head Island. Hilton Head offers a wide array of water sports and beach activities.

SPECIFICS: The Holiday Inn Oceanfront's high employee turnover rate means that more than 300 new employees are hired each year to fill the 215 staff positions. Jobs are available for both year-round and summer seasonal staffers. Summer employees should be available from at least June 1 through September 1. There is no application deadline. Applications are accepted for front desk clerks, night auditors (accounting background necessary), restaurant waitpersons, bartenders, barbacks (bar assistants), housemen, housekeepers, bellmen, and maintenance personnel. Starting wages range from minimum wage plus tips to $6.00 per hour.

INSIDER TIPS: The Holiday Inn Oceanfront looks for "friendly, well-groomed employees who are willing to learn and have good attitudes and a good attendance record."

PERKS: Employee perks include health insurance, a staff credit union, tips, free meals, and limited use of the hotel's outside bar.

TO APPLY: Applicants should send a cover letter, résumé, photograph, and SARP to Kathi Hilgert, Personnel Manager, Holiday Inn Oceanfront, P.O. Box 5728, South Forest Beach Drive, Hilton Head Island, South Carolina 29938; (803) 785-5126. Be sure to include your availability dates in your cover letter.

HOLIDAY INN ON THE OCEAN
(Virginia Beach, Virginia)
Seasonal (Summer)

Holiday Inn on the Ocean is a beachfront 267-room hotel situated at the end of the boardwalk in Virginia Beach, just minutes from the famous resort strip but away from the crush of the crowds.

SPECIFICS: The Holiday Inn hires more than 100 seasonal staff members annually. At peak season the resort employs more than 200 employees. Seasonal help should be available to begin work in early May. Positions are open for swimming pool attendants, front office staff, restaurant and lounge staff, housekeepers, and grounds keepers.

INSIDER TIPS: Management reports that they are looking for outgoing, personable, career-oriented, well-groomed, reliable, and hard-working staff members. Being able to stay for the entire summer season greatly improves an applicant's chances of being hired.

TO APPLY: Applicants should send a cover letter, résumé, and SARP to Personnel Department, Holiday Inn on the Ocean, 3900 N. Atlantic Avenue, Virginia Beach, Virginia 23451; (804) 428-1711.

HONEST TO GOODNESS SALT WATER TAFFY COMPANY
(Wildwood, New Jersey)

Seasonal (Summer)

The Honest to Goodness Salt Water Taffy Company hires college students for their two candy and ice cream stores on the boardwalk along popular Wildwood beach. Wildwood is a popular resort town located on an island off the southern coast of New Jersey.

SPECIFICS: The company employs college students to work forty or more hours each week. Employees must be willing to work through Labor Day. Wages in 1989 started at $4.00 per hour (subject to change). Management encourages friends to apply together to save on housing costs by sharing accommodations in Wildwood.

INSIDER TIPS: The Honest to Goodness Salt Water Taffy Company looks for college students who are hard working, ambitious, and truly need to work to pay for their educations.

PERKS: Although housing is not provided, the company works with local realtors to help employees find housing.

TO APPLY: Applicants should either write for an official application or send a cover letter detailing the applicant's need, a résumé, and recent photograph (optional) to Honest to Goodness Salt Water Taffy Company, 5809 New Jersey Avenue, Wildwood Crest, New Jersey 08260; (609) 729-4769.

HOWARD JOHNSON'S HOLLYWOOD BEACH RESORT INN
(Hollywood Beach, Florida)
Seasonal (Winter) and Year-Round

Howard Johnson's Hollywood Beach Resort is a 242-room ocean-front hotel with swimming pool located minutes away from the excitement of Ft. Lauderdale and the wonder of Florida's Everglades.

SPECIFICS: Howard Johnson's Hollywood Beach Resort employs fourteen front office employees and hires approximately ten new staff members each year. Both year-round as well as seasonal help are needed. Seasonal employees should be available October through April. Applications are accepted for reservation assistants and front desk clerks.

INSIDER TIPS: "We look for a professional appearance and manner, previous experience, and an ability to make decisions."

PERKS: Employees are welcome to use the resort's pool, beach, restaurant, and gift shop when off duty.

TO APPLY: Applicants should write for an official application from Donna Mentrasti, Executive Assistant, Howard Johnson's Hollywood Beach Resort Inn, 2501 N. Ocean Drive, Hollywood Beach, Florida 33019. SARP requested with all correspondence. Write to determine if the resort is currently hiring before applying.

MARINER'S INN
(Hilton Head Island, South Carolina)
Seasonal (any six-month period between February and November) and Year-Round

Mariner's Inn, a Clarion Resort located on Hilton Head Island, is one of South Carolina's most acclaimed hotels. Located on thirteen prime oceanfront acres, Mariner's features 324 guest rooms, several restaurants and lounges, two oceanfront spas, an outdoor heated swimming pool, twenty-five tennis courts, and three golf courses.

SPECIFICS: Mariner's Inn hires up to 150 new employees each year to fill its 400-person staff. Jobs are available for year-round as well as seasonal help. Seasonal staff must be available to work for at least six to eight months between early February and November. Hiring is done as needed throughout the year. Applications are accepted for waitpersons, banquet staff, housekeepers, laundry workers, engineers, switchboard operators, recreation leaders, deli staff, room service attendants, landscapers, and bellmen. Starting wages range from minimum wage to $6.00 per hour depending upon position.

INSIDER TIPS: Mariner's Inn looks for "outgoing, friendly applicants with a strong desire to work in order to gain a broad scope (knowledge) of this industry." Applicants are encouraged to list both a first and second choice position in their cover letters.

PERKS: The hotel's facilities are available to supervisory and management staff only. All employees receive free shift meals.

TO APPLY: Applicants should send a cover letter and résumé to Patricia L. Sussman, Director of Personnel, Mariner's Inn, P.O. Box 6165, Hilton Head Island, South Carolina 29938; (803) 842-8028.

NATIONAL PARK CONCESSIONS, INC.
(Olympic National Park, Washington)
Seasonal (Summer)

Olympic National Park is a magnificent, unspoiled wilderness of glacier-clad peaks, alpine meadows, cascading streams, unspoiled coastline, and virgin forests. From the rugged Pacific Coast to the breathtaking panoramas of mile-high Hurricane Ridge, its spectacular beauty has earned this park a spot on the list of United Nations

World Heritage sites. National Park Concessions, Inc., operates two facilities within the park, Lake Crescent Lodge and Hurricane Ridge Lodge.

SPECIFICS: From a field of 100 applicants, approximately sixty new employees are hired each year to fill the sixty peak-season positions at the Lake Crescent and Hurricane Ridge lodges. Jobs are available primarily for seasonal summer employment. Applications for summer employment must be completed by February 28. For further information see the National Park Commissions listing in the Mountains chapter.

OCEAN DUNES/SAND DUNES RESORT
(Myrtle Beach, South Carolina)
Seasonal (Summer—limited positions) and Year-Round

Located on 700 feet of spectacular beachfront property in Myrtle Beach, South Carolina, Ocean Dunes/Sand Dunes Resort is one of the largest and most comprehensive vacation spots in South Carolina. With 630 rooms, efficiencies, suites, penthouses and villas, this AAA four-diamond resort is truly a destination in and of itself.

SPECIFICS: Ocean Dunes/Sand Dunes Resort hires more than 1,000 new employees each year. While a limited number of summer seasonal jobs are available, most positions are year-round. The resort is generally busy throughout the year with the exception of a brief four- to five-week slow season in mid-winter when the staff size is reduced. Summer seasonal jobs generally begin in May and extend through Labor Day. Applicants may apply for positions as front desk clerks, reservationists, restaurant supervisors, restaurant managers, bartenders, secretaries, bookkeepers, room inspectors, host/hostesses, cashiers, waitpersons, maintenance technicians, landscape technicians, convention service staff, housekeepers, and children's counselors (summer only). Wages vary according to position.

INSIDER TIPS: According to Personnel Director Veronica Strickland, Ocean Dunes/Sand Dunes looks for "people who are excited about the resort hospitality industry and interested in advancement."

PERKS: Employee perks include complimentary meals, paid vacations, health/life/dental insurance, free uniforms, and health club membership.

TO APPLY: Applicants should send a cover letter, résumé, three letters of recommendation, and a SARP to Veronica Strickland, Personnel Director, Ocean Dunes/Sand Dunes Resort, 74th Avenue North, Myrtle Beach, South Carolina 29577; (803) 449-7441.

OCEAN EDGE RESORT AND CONFERENCE CENTER
(Brewster, Massachusetts)
Seasonal (Summer)

The Ocean Edge Resort is one of Cape Cod's newest and most luxurious resorts. Facilities include a championship golf course, pools, health club, tennis courts, and beach.

SPECIFICS: More than 125 summer employees are hired annually. The resort has positions for twelve room attendants, four cooks, fifteen to twenty-five waitpersons, four bartenders, five front desk clerks, two reservationists, ten golf maintenance workers, four tennis shop attendants, six rangers, eight dishwashers, two mechanics, four golf setup porters, four bellmen, two PBX operators, and two hosts/hostesses.

INSIDER TIPS: Only applicants who can work through Labor Day will be considered.

TO APPLY: Applicants should send a cover letter and résumé to Laurie Ratcliffe, Personnel Administrator, Ocean Edge Resort, 1 Villages Drive, Route 6A, Brewster, Massachusetts 02631; (617) 896-2781.

PIER 66 RESORT & MARINA
(Ft. Lauderdale, Florida)
Seasonal (Winter) and Year-Round

Pier 66 Resort is a specialty luxury hotel and marina complex catering to incentive and business groups and upscale vacationers. Ft. Lauderdale affords easy access to both Miami and Everglades National Park.

SPECIFICS: Pier 66 employs more than 600 staff members and has 160 annual job openings. The hotel requires both year-round as well as seasonal employees. Seasonal help should be available December 15 through April 30. Applications are accepted for recreation attendants, dock attendants, marina clerks, front desk clerks, reservation clerks, night auditors, bellmen, accounting clerks, secretaries, receptionists, guest room attendants, concierges, housekeepers, supervisors, engineering helpers, mechanics, cashiers, gift shop attendants, PBX operators, painters, security guards, security supervisor, food and beverage servers, dining room attendants, bartenders, bar assistants, hosts/hostesses, pantry workers, cooks, room service waitpersons, room service cashiers, grounds keepers, gardeners, banquet captains, banquet waiters, and air conditioning mechanics. Salaries range from minimum wage to more than $10.50 per hour.

INSIDER TIPS: We look for "well-groomed professional applicants with a concern for work responsibilities, high moral character, congenial personalities, and high standards of performance."

PERKS: Free shift meals and a full benefit package are available for full-time employees.

TO APPLY: Applicants should send a cover letter, résumé, photograph, and SARP to Pier 66 Resort & Marina, Personnel Office, 2301 SE 17th Street, Ft. Lauderdale, Florida 33316; (305) 525-6666.

RECREATION DEPARTMENT, TOWN OF YARMOUTH
(Yarmouth, Massachusetts)
Seasonal (Summer)

This small picturesque Cape Cod town offers summer employment in its local recreation department. The recreation department operates a summer playground, instructional swimming program for children, and instructional sailing and tennis programs for people of all ages. The Recreation Department is also responsible for hiring lifeguards for fourteen beaches.

SPECIFICS: The recreation department employs eighty-five summer staff members including twenty-eight camp personnel (Red Cross first aid and CPR suggested), five swimming instructors (WSI required), forty-two lifeguards (lifesaving, CPR, and advanced first aid required) and five sailing instructors (lifesaving, CPR suggested). Employees usually work from June 23 through August 23. Applications are due March 1 and a personal interview is required.

TO APPLY: Applicants should write for an official application from the Town of Yarmouth, Recreation Department, 1146 Route 28, Yarmouth, Massachusetts 02664; (617) 398-2231, ext. 12.

ROSARIO RESORT & SPA
(Orcas Island, Washington)
Seasonal (Summer) and Year-Round

Rosario Resort and Spa attempts to take guests back in time to an era when life was slower and simpler. The resort shares the island with nearby Moran State Park and is set in the unspoiled beauty of Puget Sound, surrounded by snowcapped mountains.

SPECIFICS: The resort and spa employs a staff of more than 200 with up to 100 new workers hired annually. Seasonal help is slowly added from April through June and stays through September or October. Seasonal hiring is generally completed by the end of June. Applications are accepted for fitness instructors/spa clerks, attendants, dock attendants, grounds keepers, cooks, dishwashers, pantry cooks, pastry cooks, room attendants, laundry attendants, PBX operators, front desk clerks, bellmen, dining room waitstaff, dining room busperson, bartender, cocktail waitresses, banquet staff, and accounting clerks.

INSIDER TIPS: "Although the qualities we look for vary depending on the position, we consider an applicant's reliability, responsibility, good grooming, and willingness to learn and work."

PERKS: The resort provides limited modest shared housing for a fee to room attendants and dishwashers. Employees may use the resort's spa facilities for a modest staff membership fee.

TO APPLY: Applicants should write for an official application or send a cover letter, résumé, photograph, and SARP to Rosario Resort, S.E. Anthony, Personnel Director, Eastsound, Orcas Island, Washington 98245; (206) 376-2222.

SALISHAN LODGE
(Glenden Beach, Oregon)
Seasonal (Summer) and Year-Round

Salishan Lodge is comprised of 205 natural wood guestrooms nestled on a grand bluff overlooking the rocky Pacific Northwest coast. The resort features an eighteen-hole oceanfront golf links, tennis center with both indoor and outdoor courts, pool, fitness center, and sauna. The lodge is surrounded by a 750-acre forest preserve.

SPECIFICS: Salishan employs 325 staff members and hires at least seventy-five new employees annually. This seaside lodge hires both year-round and seasonal help. Seasonal workers should be available from early June through Labor Day. Numerous positions are available including lifeguard, hosts/hostesses, cook, waitperson, housekeeper, dishwasher, busperson, and more. Salishan is unable to provide employee housing, and rental housing is extremely difficult to find during peak season months.

INSIDER TIPS: The resort caters to an extremely sophisticated clientele and seeks applicants who are service oriented, willing to work hard, and can smile.

PERKS: Employees are welcome to use the resort's golf course, tennis courts, and restaurants. Be prepared: While Oregon summers can be beautiful, they are quite different from the Southern California summer. Wisps of fog are more common than bathers on Oregon beaches much of the year, and the weather can get quite cool.

TO APPLY: Applicants should send a cover letter, résumé, and SARP to Salishan Lodge, Inc., Sheahan Jenson, Personnel Director, P.O. Box 118, Glenden Beach, Oregon 97388; (503) 764-3669.

SANDESTIN BEACH RESORT
(Destin, Florida)
Seasonal (Summer) and Year-Round

Sandestin is a 2,600-acre planned resort/residential community nestled between the sugar-white shores of the Gulf of Mexico and the tranquil waters of Florida's Choctawhatchee Bay. Facilities at this resort include forty-five holes of golf, sixteen tennis courts, nine swimming pools, a complete harbor and marina, four restaurants, a shopping center, a convention center, and full health club.

SPECIFICS: Sandestin Beach Resort hires approximately 1,200 new employees annually to fill its 350 year-round and 900 seasonal positions. Most seasonal staff members work from May through September. There isn't any official application deadline for seasonal positions and hiring is done as needed throughout the year. Positions are available in the Food & Beverage Department for waitpersons, bus help, cashiers, host/hostesses, food and beverage supervisors, cooks, cocktail servers, bartenders, and management staff for the four restaurants and catering department. In the Accounting Department there are jobs for data processors and night auditors. Other resort positions include golf/grounds maintenance, recreation staff (golf/ tennis), courtesy corps staff, front desk clerks, bellpersons, reservationists, hotel telephone operators, guest services staff, and housekeepers.

INSIDER TIPS: Sandestin Beach Resort looks for "friendly, motivated, team players who are service-oriented, creative, and flexible."

PERKS: Employees receive free uniforms, group medical/life/dental insurance, and use of many of the resort's facilities.

TO APPLY: Applicants should send a cover letter and résumé to Sandestin Beach Resort, Highway 98 East, Destin, Florida 32541; (904) 267-8169.

SUN BEACH SERVICE
(N. Myrtle Beach, South Carolina)
Seasonal (Summer)

Sun Beach Service operates various beach concessions in Myrtle Beach, South Carolina. The company operates both a lifeguard service as well as beach concession stands.

SPECIFICS: Sun Beach Service hires approximately sixty new employees each summer to fill its seventy-five seasonal positions. All jobs are seasonal and employees should be available from approximately Memorial Day through Labor Day. Jobs are available for beach lifeguards (must have Red Cross advanced lifesaving and CPR certificates), beach vendors (must meet same requirements as above), and Hobie Cat operators (must have ocean sailing experience). There is no application deadline.

INSIDER TIPS: Applicants must be able to work through at least August 16 to be considered. Sun Beach Service looks for applicants who are "mature, honest, responsible, and enjoy meeting people."

PERKS: Beach vendors are paid commissions based on rental sales. Housing is provided for employees and an end-of-season bonus is paid to all employees who stay through Labor Day.

TO APPLY: Applicants should write and request an official application from David Hatley, Director, Sun Beach Service, Department JIP, P.O. Box 1431, North Myrtle Beach, South Carolina 29582; (803) 272-4170.

TROPICANA HOTEL & CASINO
(Atlantic City, New Jersey)
Seasonal (Summer) and Year-Round

The Tropicana Hotel & Casino is a year-round gambling casino and hotel located in Atlantic City. The Tropicana sits near the world-famous beach boardwalk. While the hotel casino is a popular gambling destination, the summer brings the annual crowd of sunseekers.

SPECIFICS: The Tropicana employs 3,700 staff members and hires more than 1,500 new employees each year. Positions are available for both year-round and seasonal summer employment. The busy summer season generally runs from mid-April through September 15. There is no application deadline. The hotel casino has a huge list of positions available, ranging from bellhop to bartender and blackjack dealer to dancer. For more information on available positions contact the hotel at the address below. According to the personnel office, "We accept applications for all positions throughout the year.

Qualifications range from being able to read, write, and understand English through a specific college degree, depending on position." Salaries start at $5.00 and up.

INSIDER TIPS: The key to landing a job here is to demonstrate that you are customer service–oriented and eager to work.

PERKS: Staff members may use the hotel's health club facilities for a discounted fee.

TO APPLY: Applicants should either send a cover letter and a résumé or write for an official application from Tropicana Hotel & Casino, Personnel Department, Attn: Employment Specialist, Iowa Avenue & the Boardwalk, Atlantic City, New Jersey 08401; (609) 340-4242.

TROPWORLD CASINO AND ENTERTAINMENT RESORT
Atlantic City, New Jersey
Seasonal (Summer) and Year-Round

TropWorld Casino and Entertainment Resort is a year-round casino, hotel, and entertainment resort establishment on the famous Atlantic City boardwalk.

SPECIFICS: TropWorld employs more than 4,000 staff members. Positions are available for both year-round and seasonal summer employment. The busy summer season generally runs from mid-April through September 15. There is no application deadline. The hotel casino has a variety of positions available in the food and beverage and hotel and casino areas. For more information on available positions and to obtain license information, contact the hotel at the address below.

INSIDER TIPS: Applicants must have these five-star qualities: bright smiles, friendly greetings, outgoing personalities, a willingness to work as a team player, and a dedication to service.

PERKS: All employees receive a complimentary meal daily. Uniforms are supplied and maintained at no cost to the employees. Additionally, TropWorld offers employee discounts throughout the hotel. Employee and supervisor of the month and year awards.

TO APPLY: Applicants should either send a cover letter and a résumé or write for an official application from TropWorld Casino and Entertainment Resort, Personnel Dept., Attn: Employment Specialist, Brighton Avenue & the Boardwalk, Atlantic City, New Jersey 08401; (609) 340-4243.

TRUMP PLAZA HOTEL & CASINO
(Atlantic City, New Jersey)
Seasonal (Summer) and Year-Round

When Donald Trump does things, he does them BIG and his Atlantic City hotel casino is no exception. Name another hotel in the world that has a $30 million parking garage! In addition to a huge casino, the complex boasts a 600-room, four-star hotel and seven restaurants.

SPECIFICS: Trump Plaza employs more than 4,000 staff members and hires between 800 and 1,000 new employees annually. Positions are available for both year-round and summer seasonal staff. Summer seasonal help should be available from May through September. There is no official application deadline. The hotel and casino accepts applications for a wide variety of positions, including front desk receptionists, reservationists, guest services coordinators, staff accountants, food and beverage accounting clerks, income control clerks, cage cashiers, slot cashiers, pit clerks, food servers, restaurant supervisors, buspersons, VIP coordinators, promotion booth clerks, secretaries, security guards, slot attendants, casino dealers, etc. Some casino positions require a gaming license. Contact the employment office for more information on available positions as well as instructions for obtaining any necessary licenses.

INSIDER TIPS: "We look for career-oriented individuals, with a stable work history, who take pride in their appearance."

PERKS: All employees are given one complimentary meal per shift and free uniforms. Additionally, Trump Plaza offers employee discounts on shows and attractions, as well as employee of the month and year awards.

TO APPLY: Applicants should write for an official application or send a cover letter and résumé to Human Resources Department, Trump Plaza Hotel & Casino, 750 West Delilah Road, Pleasantville, New Jersey 08232; (609) 484-7686 (job line).

VENTANA COUNTRY INN RESORT
(Big Sur, California)
Seasonal (Summer) and Year-Round

Ventana is a unique coastal hideaway perched atop a rugged mountain overlooking the churning Pacific Ocean. Big Sur is truly where the ocean meets the mountains. This is the ideal place for lovers, escapists, or those just looking for a break from the hustle and bustle of civilization.

SPECIFICS: Ventana hires approximately fifty employees each year to fill its 150-person staff. Management reports receiving approximately 100 applications each year. Jobs are available for both year-round as well as summer seasonal staff. Summer seasonal staff must be available to work from May 15 through Labor Day. While available positions vary, management reports frequent openings for buspersons, restaurant hostpersons, cocktail servers, bartenders, cooks, porters, front desk clerks, reservationists, bellstaff, housekeepers, PBX operators, night auditors, poolside servers, campground attendants, maintenance technicians, and landscape gardeners.

INSIDER TIPS: "We look for cheerful, cooperative employees with an attitude of professionalism and a sincere interest in guest services.

Previous experience is always helpful but we are willing to train candidates with potential." Management prefers to promote from within.

PERKS: There is limited staff housing available on the property.

TO APPLY: Applicants should write for an official application or send a cover letter and résumé to Ventana Inn, Kathy Farmer, Human Resources, Highway 1, Big Sur, California 93920; (408) 667-2331, ext. 201. Management prefers applicants to call to arrange an interview before applying.

WELLS CHAMBER OF COMMERCE
(Wells, Maine)
Seasonal (Summer)

The Wells Chamber of Commerce has set up a jobs program to recruit seasonal summer workers to fill positions in this picturesque Southern Maine town.

SPECIFICS: The Chamber of Commerce program will provide approximately 400 jobs for college students in the hospitality industry. Numerous Wells employers, including inns, motels, and restaurants, are participating in the program. A local college is also providing opportunities for continuing education. All applications must be completed by mid-April to receive consideration.

INSIDER TIPS: According to a news release from the Wells Chamber of Commerce, "Rising housing costs for temporary labor have created a crisis for the tourist industry along Maine's southern coast. Students can no longer afford seasonal housing—and each year we are seeing the available labor pool diminish further." The Wells program is designed to combat this trend.

PERKS: The Chamber of Commerce program provides applicants with jobs, subsidized housing (at a local college), and transportation.

TO APPLY: Applicants should write or call for an official application from the Wells Chamber of Commerce, P.O. Box 356, Wells, Maine 04090; (207) 646-2451.

WESTMARK INN SKAGWAY
(Skagway, Alaska)

Seasonal (Summer)

The Westmark Inn Skagway is one of the Westmark chain's fine tourist accommodations. Skagway is one of Alaska's old Gold Rush towns, located along the Southeast coast of Alaska. This is an ideal spot for nature lovers and for those who enjoy exploring the great outdoors.

SPECIFICS: The Westmark Inn Skagway hires sixty new seasonal employees each year to fill its 130-person staff. For best job opportunities applicants should be available to begin work before June 10 and stay through September 1. Applications for summer employment must be completed by March 1. Positions are available for room attendants, laundry workers, front desk clerks, maintenance staff, waitpersons, buspersons, cooks, food preparers, and dishwashers. Starting wages range from minimum wage to $9.00 per hour.

INSIDER TIPS: Westmark looks for applicants with professionalism and personality. Prior experience is required for some positions.

PERKS: Employees are permitted to use the hotel's lounge, cafe, and restaurant when not on duty. The Inn offers subsidized airfare from certain "gateway" cities.

TO APPLY: Applicants should either write for an official application packet or send a cover letter and résumé to Summer Jobs, Westmark Hotels (Skagway), 300 Elliott Avenue West, Seattle, Washington 98119; special phone jobline: (206) 281-5172.

WILD DUNES
(Isle of Palms, South Carolina)
Seasonal (Spring and Summer) and Year-Round

Wild Dunes Resort is the perfect place to catch the wild and wind-swept natural beauty of the South Carolina coast. While situated on a small island only 15 miles from Charleston, this resort offers the serene feeling of a faraway island retreat. Both the golf and tennis facilities have "Top 50" ratings from national sports magazines.

SPECIFICS: Wild Dunes hires more than 300 new employees each year to fill its 550 to 600 peak season positions. Jobs are available for both seasonal and year-round employees. Some seasonal positions start in early March and extend through November, while others begin in mid-May and last through mid-August or later. Applications are accepted for front desk agents, front desk supervisor, food and beverage department supervisor, conference coordinator, conference salesperson, special events coordinator, property manager, assistant golf pro, assistant tennis pro, staff accountant, and all typical hotel front-line positions. Salaries for most entry-level year-round positions begin at $11,500 to $14,000 per year.

INSIDER TIPS: Wild Dunes looks for applicants with "strong customer relations skills, excellent problem-solving skills, and a sincere interest in the hospitality business."

PERKS: Complimentary employee meals are given to food and beverage department staff. Housing is provided for some executives. Employees are permitted to use the lap pool during dinner hours, the golf and tennis facilities on a stand-by basis, and the resort's restaurants if they are not crowded.

TO APPLY: Applicants should send a cover letter, résumé, and SARP to Personnel Department, Wild Dunes Associates, 5757 Palm Boulevard, Isle of Palms, South Carolina 29451; (803) 886-6000.

YAKUTAT LODGE
(Yakutat, Alaska)
Seasonal (Summer)

The Yakutat Lodge is a fisherman's paradise. Located on the rugged Alaskan coastline, the lodge offers ocean, lake, and river fishing. The scenery is spectacular, featuring mountains, glaciers, bays, beaches, and wildlife. The Yakutat Glacier is the largest glacier in the world flowing into a freshwater lake.

SPECIFICS: The Lodge hires ten to fifteen new employees each year to fill its fifteen- to twenty-person staff. All jobs are summer seasonal and ideal applicants should be available from early April through late September. Applications are accepted for bartenders, cooks, waitpersons, housekeepers, fishing guides, and maintenance personnel. Salaries range from $1,000 to $2,000 per month plus room and board.

INSIDER TIPS: The lodge looks for ambitious, hard-working, personable, conscientious applicants with related job experience.

PERKS: Depending upon the length of employment requested, airfare reimbursement might be available. Staff members are permitted to use the hotel's hot tub, restaurant, lounge, pool table, and fishing boats.

TO APPLY: Applicants should send a cover letter, résumé, and SARP to Ken Fanning, Owner/Manager, Box 287, Yakutat, Alaska 99689; (907) 784-3232.

The following listings, found under the chapter headings given below, also include positions near coasts or beaches:

AMUSEMENT & THEME PARKS

Fantasy Island Amusement
  Park
Funland
Fun Time USA/Beach
  Amusements, Inc.
Raging Waters/Mariners
  Landing Amusement Pier

Rocky Point Amusements, Inc.
Santa Cruz Beach
  Boardwalk
Timber Rides
TropWorld/Tivoli Pier

HIGH ADVENTURE

Annapolis Sailing School of
  Long Island

Atlantis Submarines
Looking Glass Submarines

LAKES

Grand View Guest House

Indigo Lakes Resort

RIVERS

Fairfield Harbour, Inc.

TROPICAL ISLANDS

Annapolis Sailing School
  (Florida Keys)
City and County of Honolulu
  Lifeguard Service
Club Med
County of Maui Lifeguard
  Service
Frenchman's Reef and Morning
  Star Beach Club
Fun Water Tours

Hotel King Kamehameha
Hotel on the Cay
Hyatt Regency Cerromar and
  Hyatt Dorado Beach Club
Hyatt Regency Maui
Hyatt Regency Waikiki
Hyatt Regency Waikoloa
Ilikai Hotel Nikko Waikiki
Islander on the Beach
Kaanapali Beach Hotel

Kahala Hilton Hotel
Kona Village Resort
Kon Tiki Party Raft of St.
  Thomas
Longboat Key Club
Magton, Ltd.
Russell House of Key West
Sea Cliff Beach Resort

Stouffer Grand Beach Resort
Turtle Bay Hilton Hotel &
  Country Club
Underwater Safaris
V.I. Divers, Ltd.
Virgin Grand Beach Hotel
Virgin Islands Diving Schools
Windsong Water Tours

Rivers

~~~

ADRIFT ADVENTURES
(Moab, Utah)

Seasonal (Summer)

Adrift Adventures operates a wide variety of whitewater trips in Utah's Canyonlands National Park and Professor Valley regions of the Colorado River and the Desolation Canyon portion of the Green River. The company also operates guided mountain bike expeditions and jeep tours in both Canyonlands and Arches national parks. Adrift Adventures is affiliated with Adventure/Discovery Tours, Glacier Raft Company (Montana), and Glacier Raft Company (Canada). (See separate listings herein for information on the other companies' operations.)

SPECIFICS: Adrift Adventures and Adventure/Discovery Tours employ approximately twenty-two staff members each year during their peak summer season of May through September. Winter and year-round staff usually numbers approximately seven to eight individuals. Positions available include whitewater river guide and shuttle driver. River guides require both Red Cross advanced first aid and

CPR certificates as well as a Utah boatman's license. Shuttle drivers must have a clean driving record. Starting salaries range from $65 to $80 per day. There is no official application deadline. A whitewater guide training program is offered twice each spring. Contact Myke Hughes at the address below for further information on the training program for applicants without prior experience or a valid Utah boatman's license.

INSIDER TIPS: "No experience is necessary although multiple languages as well as camping experience would be helpful."

PERKS: Guides camp and eat free with their groups while on tour.

TO APPLY: Applicants should either write for an official application or send a cover letter, résumé, and photograph to Myke Hughes, Adrift Adventures, P.O. Box 577, Moab, Utah 84532; (801) 259-8594.

ADVENTURE CONNECTION, INC.
(Coloma, California)
Seasonal (Spring and Summer)

Adventure Connection was created by a dedicated group of river enthusiasts who had spent years working as river guides, managers, and booking agents for some of California's largest outfitters in California's Mother Lode Gold Rush area.

SPECIFICS: Adventure Connection employs forty-five staff members and usually hires about ten new employees each season. The company offers an annual whitewater river guide school each spring (generally the week before Easter) and hires new guides from among its best students. The course costs approximately $700. No figures are available on the percentage of students who are offered jobs each year, although Nate Rangel, owner of Adventure Connection, stresses that his company seeks to "hire as many of the top students as possible. We also train guides for many other outfitters." Positions are available for whitewater guides (prior experience or training required), kitchen supervisor, assistant kitchen supervisor, and shuttle drivers (Class I or II license required and must be twenty-one or older). Pay ranges from $50 to $110 per day plus tips, meals, and free campsites. Seasonal positions are available from March or April through September. All applications must be completed by April 1.

INSIDER TIPS: The company hires the top students from its annual whitewater school for guide positions. A river trip with Adventure Connection is viewed as a "cooperative adventure, where friends and strangers alike join together in a singular journey of discovery, sharing, responsibilities, resources, and one another's company."

PERKS: As with most river outfitters, trip guides receive generous tips, free meals and camping facilities, and a chance to work in the great outdoors.

TO APPLY: Applicants should write for an official application or send a cover letter and résumé to Nate Rangel, President, Adventure Connection, Inc., Box 475, Coloma, California 95613; (916) 626-7385. Applicants for guide positions with no prior experience should enroll in the company's annual river guide school.

ADVENTURE/DISCOVERY TOURS
(Flagstaff, Arizona)
Seasonal (Summer)

Adventure/Discovery Tours runs trips down the San Juan River, once called the "Mad River" by the Navajo Indians who lived on its shores. The San Juan is one of the fastest-running rivers in the United States, dropping over eight feet a mile. Special theme departures are available for those interested in geology, archaeology, photography, and chamber music.

SPECIFICS: Adventure/Discovery Tours hires one or two new staff members each summer to fill its eight-person staff. Applications are accepted for whitewater river guides and shuttle drivers. River guides require both advanced first aid and CPR certificates as well as a Utah boatman's license. Shuttle drivers must have a valid chauffeur's license and a clean driving record.

INSIDER TIPS: "Every member of our team is an expert guide, trained in both first aid and CPR. That's just the start of their qualifications." In evaluating applications, Adventure/Discovery Tours looks at each applicant's energy level, honesty, ability to care for people, and interpretive and cooking skills.

TO APPLY: Applicants should write for an official application or send a cover letter and résumé to Jene Kenneth Vredevoogd, President, Adventure/Discovery Tours, 319 N. Humphreys, Flagstaff, Arizona 86001; (602) 774-1926.

ALL-OUTDOORS ADVENTURE TRIPS
(Walnut Creek, California)
Seasonal (Summer and Fall)

All-Outdoors Adventure Trips offers travel through a comprehensive network of rivers in Northern and Central California. The company offers trips down the Merced, Tuolumne, Stanislaus, American, Klamath, and Scott rivers.

SPECIFICS: Twenty new employees are hired each season to complete a staff of seventy-five part-time personnel. The company offers a seven-day river guide school for $450. According to management, about half of the guide school graduates are hired by All-Outdoors and others go on to work for other rafting companies.

INSIDER TIPS: According to All-Outdoors staffer Scott Armstrong, ideal applicants are "personable, outgoing, dependable, eager to learn, and good team members."

TO APPLY: Applicants should write for an official application and return it with a résumé, cover letter, and photograph (optional) to Scott Armstrong, Personnel Department, 2151 San Miguel Drive, Walnut Creek, California 94596; (415) 932-8993.

AMERICAN RIVER RECREATION
(Rancho Cordova, California)
Seasonal (Spring and Summer)

Started in 1974 as a small raft rental service on the lower American River, American River Recreation (ARR) has become the largest raft rental center in California. ARR specializes in guided whitewater trips on the Stanislaus, American, Merced, Klamath, Salmon, and Carson rivers in the Sierra Nevadas.

SPECIFICS: ARR offers seasonal positions for whitewater river guides and shuttle bus drivers (Class II driver's license required). The company declines to reveal the number of new employees hired each year, but reports that most new river guides are hired through their annual April whitewater school. The whitewater school currently costs approximately $350 per participant. Management reports hiring 50% of the course graduates. Applications for spring and/or summer seasonal positions are due in April.

INSIDER TIPS: All whitewater guides must have current CPR and first aid cards. Graduation from ARR's (or equivalent) swiftwater rescue course is mandatory for guides on rivers with whitewater over Class III. Salaries vary from $50 to $100 per day depending on experience.

PERKS: Free meals are provided for employees while leading trips.

TO APPLY: Applicants should send a cover letter and résumé or enroll in ARR's river rafting guide school at American River Recreation, 11257 South Bridge Street, Rancho Cordova, California 95670; (916) 635-4516.

AMERICAN RIVER TOURING ASSOCIATION
(Groveland, California)

Seasonal (Spring and Summer)

The American River Touring Association (ARTA) is a non-profit corporation offering whitewater river trips down many of the West's wildest and most scenic rivers. Founded more than twenty-five years ago, ARTA operates under a philosophy that making a profit from rivers located on public lands is inconsistent.

SPECIFICS: ARTA hires approximately ten new employees each year to fill its thirty-five to fifty river guide positions. Most job vacancies are seasonal, lasting from approximately May 1 through September 1. All applications must be completed by March 1 for consideration. The company offers several whitewater guide schools in California, Oregon, and Idaho each season. According to management, while only 20% of the course participants are offered positions with ARTA, more than 80% of those who are interested in working for the company are hired (many people take the courses merely for the experience). Whitewater courses vary from seven to sixteen days and cost approximately $430 to $880, depending on the length.

INSIDER TIPS: A description of one of the managers in an ARTA brochure reads, "Eric's only claim to fame, so far, involves the first inflatable alligator descent of the Class IV Slam Dunk rapid on the Middle Fork of the American River. While that fact probably will not appear on his résumé, his imminent degree in physiology from U.C. Berkeley and his four years on the school's ski team most likely will. Although he is a native Coloradan, he is living the ultimate California lifestyle; skiing in the winter, studying in the spring and fall, rafting and kayaking in the summer. Oh, to be twenty-two again!"

In evaluating river guide applicants, ARTA's primary considerations are the ability to handle whitewater rafts safely, to entertain passengers, and to be part of the company team. Management takes great pride in the company's river guides.

TO APPLY: Applicants with experience should write for an official application from Stephen Welch, Operations Manager, ARTA, Star

Route 73, Groveland, California 95321; (209) 962-7873. Applicants without experience are encouraged to enroll in one of the company's whitewater schools.

BARKER-EWING SCENIC FLOAT TRIPS
(Moose, Wyoming)

Seasonal (Summer)

Barker-Ewing is an authorized concessionaire at Grand Teton National Park and a licensed outfitter under the Wyoming Game and Fish Commission. The company operates 5- and 10-mile scenic float trips on the Snake River through some of Grand Teton National Park's timeless beauty. These trips afford an opportunity to see diverse and exotic wildlife.

SPECIFICS: Barker-Ewing hires approximately ten to twelve new employees each year to fill its staff of twenty-four. All jobs are summer seasonal. Jobs are available for river guides, van drivers, cooks, and office personnel.

INSIDER TIPS: "Boatmen must also have some background in the natural history of Jackson Hole and a willingness to expand that knowledge." Barker-Ewing river guides (boatmen) come from a wide range of backgrounds. Head Boatman Al Klagge studied forestry before coming to Jackson Hole. At the other extreme, boatman "Sandy Z" Zvegintozov spent fifteen years as an attorney before handing in his law books for boat oars.

TO APPLY: Applicants should contact Richard C. Barker, President, Barker-Ewing Scenic Float Trips, Box 100, Moose, Wyoming 83012; (307) 733-1800. A personal interview is required of all applicants.

BILL DVORAK'S KAYAK & RAFTING EXPEDITIONS
(Nathrop, Colorado)

Seasonal (Summer)

Bill Dvorak's Kayak & Rafting Expeditions are half-day to twelve-day trips on the Arkansas, Colorado, Dolores, Gunnison, Salt, Rio Grande, Rio Chama, and North Platte rivers.

SPECIFICS: Dvorak's hires between six and eight new employees each year to fill its twenty-four-person staff. All jobs are seasonal beginning in April or May and lasting through August or September. For river guide applicants without prior experience, the company operates two river guide courses each year. The two-week-long courses occur in mid-April and late May. The course costs $300 (subject to change) and $100 is refunded to participants who are offered employment and stay through August. Management reports hiring 60% to 75% of the course graduates. First-year guides are paid $300 per month plus room and board. Applications are due on or before April 15th.

INSIDER TIPS: "As a Dvorak staffer you will be asked to work hard and long hours with free room and board plus a salary. The situation we work under is 'river time' and mother nature sets the schedule. We require a commitment of three to six months. It is a seasonal position and we favor applicants who can return for the following season. River guides are required to have a current standard first aid and CPR certification."

PERKS: Employee perks include free room and board, workman's compensation insurance, and swiftwater rescue training.

TO APPLY: Applicants should write for an official application or enroll in the company's whitewater guide school. For further information contact Bill or Jaci Dvorak, Dvorak Expeditions, 17921 U.S. Hwy 285, Nathrop, Colorado 81236; (719) 539-6851.

BLAZING PADDLES/SNOWMASS WHITEWATER, INC.
(Snowmass Village and Aspen, Colorado)

Seasonal (Summer)

For more than twenty years Blazing Paddles/Snowmass Whitewater has been specializing in family whitewater trips. The company currently runs trips on the Colorado, Arkansas, Gunnison, and Dolores rivers.

SPECIFICS: Blazing Paddles/Snowmass Whitewater hires approximately ten new employees each year to fill its forty-person staff. All positions are summer seasonal and applications should be submitted before the end of April. Most new employees are hired as either raft guides or reservationist agents. The company offers a short two-day whitewater school for approximately $60. According to management, approximately 40% of the course participants are offered employment with the company.

INSIDER TIPS: According to Bob Harris, applicants should be "friendly, outgoing, outdoorsy, flexible, and fun."

TO APPLY: Applicants should either enroll in the company's whitewater school or send a cover letter, résumé, photograph, and SARP to Bob Harris, Blazing Paddles/Snowmass Whitewater Inc., Box 5929, Snowmass Village, Colorado 81615; (303) 923-4544.

CANYONEERS, INC.
(Flagstaff, Arizona)

Seasonal (Spring and Summer; limited opportunities late Fall and Winter)

Experience the awe-inspiring scenery of the Grand Canyon from the vantage point of the Colorado River. The expansive Colorado River provides plenty of on-the-water excitement and the world-famous Grand Canyon is an outstanding spot for camping and sightseeing.

SPECIFICS: Approximately six new employees are hired each year to complete Canyoneers' staff of twenty-five. Canyoneers does not offer a training program and candidates are expected to have extensive rafting experience before applying. At management's request, salary rates are not published.

INSIDER TIPS: Applicants who can work the entire season and remain with the company for a few years are preferred.

TO APPLY: Applicants should send a cover letter, résumé, and photograph to Canyoneers, Inc., P.O. Box 2997, Flagstaff, Arizona 86003; (602) 526-0924.

CHUCK RICHARDS' WHITEWATER, INC.
(Lake Isabella, California)
Seasonal (Summer)

"WANTED: Young, skinny, wiry fellows. Must be expert riders willing to risk daily death. Orphans preferred." It is with this quote from an old Pony Express "help wanted" ad that Chuck Richards begins his recruitment letter for prospective employees. Chuck Richards operates whitewater rafting trips on California's Kern River as well as sea kayaking and sailboarding programs on Lake Isabella. Mountain bike expeditions are also a specialty of this wilderness company.

SPECIFICS: River guides as well as kayak instructors are hired each summer. Employees should be available early May through September. Weekend-only employment is available in May.

INSIDER TIPS: While experienced applicants are not required to take the company's whitewater guide school, most employees are hired from the class. Valid Red Cross CPR and first aid certificates are required; advanced first aid and emergency medical training certification are optional.

PERKS: The company provides inexpensive lodging in its bunkroom for all employees.

TO APPLY: Applicants should write or call Chuck Richards for application information and his "Prospective Guides Information Letter" at Chuck Richards' Whitewater, Inc., Box W.W. Whitewater, Lake Isabella, California 93240; (619) 379-4444 or 379-4685.

COSTA RICA EXPEDITIONS
(San Jose, Costa Rica)
Seasonal (All Seasons) and Year-Round

South America's Costa Rica is home to some of the world's most spectacular flora and fauna. Amidst the beauty and lushness of Costa Rica's rain forests, Costa Rica Expeditions operates whitewater rafting trips on the Pacuare, Chirripo, Reventazon, Guayabo, and Sarapiqui rivers. Whitewater ranges from Class II through Class V. Trips operate year-round according to demand. However, high season mirrors Costa Rica's dry season from December 15 through June 15.

SPECIFICS: Costa Rica Expeditions hires approximately five new employees each year to fill its forty-person staff. Jobs are available for both year-round as well as seasonal employees as river guides and natural history guides. Natural history guides are naturalists with extensive experience in Costa Rica's flora and fauna. All natural history guides and most river guides are bilingual in English and Spanish. A Costa Rican work permit and visa are required for non–Costa Rican citizens. The company will obtain permits for employees once they arrive.

INSIDER TIPS: "We look for outgoing, friendly, responsible applicants with leadership ability. Bilingual (English and Spanish) skills are extremely helpful."

PERKS: Guides are paid $40 per day. Housing is sometimes provided for employees; meals are not included.

TO APPLY: Applicants should send a cover letter, résumé, and SARP to Costa Rica Expeditions, P.O. Box 145450, Coral Gables, Florida 33114. The address and phone for the company's office in Costa Rica is Apartado 6941, San Jose, Costa Rica, C.A.; (506) 22-0333.

ECHO CANYON RIVER EXPEDITIONS, INC.
(Canon City, Royal Gorge, Colorado)
Seasonal (Summer)

Be prepared to "Eat Water" is the warning given to travelers on Echo Canyon River Expeditions' trips down the mighty Arkansas River.

SPECIFICS: Echo Canyon River Expeditions hires approximately fifteen new employees each year to fill its staff of forty. All jobs are summer seasonal, with employees starting work between mid-April and mid-May and working through mid-August or September. Mid-June through mid-August is Echo's busiest season. The company hires whitewater river guides, kayak support boaters, kayak videographers, shuttle bus drivers, and reservationists. Starting salaries range from $40 to $70 per day depending on experience. For applicants without prior river experience, Echo offers a two-week on-river whitewater guide school that includes training with both oar and paddle rafts. The course also includes seminars on boat repair and swiftwater rescue and exceeds Colorado state guide training requirements. The cost of the course is approximately $400 and management reports hiring 100% of the course graduates.

INSIDER TIPS: "We are looking for guides who'll be with us for several summers and who wish to continue to promote our professional quality trips. Applicants are evaluated on their intellect, whitewater experience and skill, ambition, ability to work closely with others, and willingness to go the extra mile to show people a good time on the river." Applicants must have First Aid and CPR certificates (Advanced First Aid and EMT preferred).

PERKS: Echo offers bunkhouse accommodations for most staff members.

TO APPLY: Applicants should either enroll in Echo's river guide school (if inexperienced) or send a cover letter, résumé, photograph, and SARP to David and Kim Burch, Owners, Echo Canyon River Expeditions, Inc., P.O. Box 1002, Colorado Springs, Colorado 80901; (719) 576-1234 (November–April); (719) 275-3154 (May–September). Resumes should be received by January or February.

EPLEY'S WHITEWATER ADVENTURES
(McCall, Idaho)
Seasonal (Summer for rafting and horseback riding; June through November for fishing expeditions)

The southern section of the Salmon River is the setting for Epley's Whitewater Adventures. Guests can choose from half-day to five-day expeditions, with whitewater rafting, horseback riding, or both! Anglers can cast for trout and bass during the fishing season of June through November.

SPECIFICS: Six to eight new employees are hired every year for Epley's fourteen-person staff. Applications are accepted for river guides and maintenance personnel. Due to the diversity of the company's programs, candidates familiar with rafting, horseback riding, fishing, and camping are preferred. A two-week training program for guide certification is available. Salaries begin at $100 a week, with room and board included.

INSIDER TIPS: Application requirements are stringent. Candidates must be single, non-smokers, and non-drinkers. Applications for summer employment are due in February.

PERKS: Room and board are provided for all employees. Bonuses are given for outstanding performance to staff who stay through the season.

TO APPLY: Applicants should either write for an official application or send a cover letter, résumé, SARP, and photograph to Ted Epley, Epley's Whitewater Adventures, P.O. Box 987, McCall, Idaho 83638; (208) 634-5173.

FAR FLUNG ADVENTURES
(Terlingua, Texas)
Seasonal (Summer)

Far Flung Adventures operates one- to fourteen-day river trips ranging from Class I to IV on the Rio Grande in Texas, the Rio Grande and Rio Chama in New Mexico, the Salt River in Arizona, the Arkansas and Gunnison in Colorado, and the Rio Antigua and Rio Usumacinta in Mexico.

SPECIFICS: Far Flung Adventures employs an average of thirty guides year-round and hires as many as sixty seasonal employees. Generally less than ten new guides are hired each year due to a large percentage of returning staff members. Far Flung does not hire employees directly from its own Whitewater School. The company operates an annual training trip on the Rio Grande in Texas in February; on the Salt River in Arizona in March; on the Upper Rio Grande in Taos, New Mexico, in early May; and in Mexico during September. These annual training trips are for its present employees and a few hopefuls and are free to selected applicants. The company also runs an ongoing apprentice program, which involves four months of intensive training and results in approximately six apprentices hired each year.

INSIDER TIPS: Applicants who are bilingual (Spanish, German, French, Japanese) have an advantage. All employees must have a current CPR certificate and Advanced First Aid Training (ECA or

EMT preferred). Camping, cooking, and naturalist interpretive skills are essential.

PERKS: All guides are provided with free meals while on trips. Training discounts are offered to employees on their Whitewater Schools, Swiftwater Rescue Courses, and advanced first aid training. Certified EMTs are given trip bonuses.

TO APPLY: Send a cover letter, résumé, photograph, and SARP to "Catfish," Director of Training, Far Flung Adventures, P.O. Box 377, Terlingua, Texas 79852.

FOUR CORNERS EXPEDITIONS, INC.
(Buena Vista, Colorado)
Seasonal (Spring & Summer)

Four Corners Expeditions runs half-day, full-day, and overnight whitewater trips on Colorado's Arkansas River.

SPECIFICS: Four Corners Expeditions hires between five and eight new employees each season to fill its staff of twenty-five. The summer season runs from May through August with peak season beginning in mid-June. Jobs are available for whitewater river guides and float fishing guides. All river guides must be at least eighteen years old, have current Red Cross CPR and first aid cards, and either attend or plan to attend college. Applications must be submitted by April 1.

INSIDER TIPS: The goal of Four Corners employees should be to have an enjoyable and challenging summer—not to get rich. Apply by April 1 for the best opportunities. "We pride ourselves on the kind of people we hire as guides—they must either be college students or graduates or have post-secondary training plans; be personable, clean-cut, intelligent, well-rounded, athletic, well-spoken, and react well in emergencies."

PERKS: Company equipment is available for personal river trips.

TO APPLY: Applicants should either enroll in the company's whitewater guide school or send a cover letter, résumé, and photograph (optional) to Karen & Reed Dils, Four Corners Expeditions, Box 1032, Buena Vista, Colorado 81211; (719) 395-8949 (year-round); (800) 332-7238 (May–August).

GLACIER RAFT COMPANY (CANADA)
(Banff, Alberta, Canada)
Seasonal (Summer)

Glacier Raft Company (Canada) operates whitewater and fishing expeditions in Canada's spectacular Banff/Yoho National Park and Top of the World Provincial Park. Trips cover some of the wildest whitewater in the Canadian Rockies on the Kicking Horse River. For the ultimate in awe-inspiring beauty, Glacier offers ten-day Arctic tours on the Nahanni and Coppermine rivers.

SPECIFICS: Glacier Raft Company (Canada) employs approximately twenty staff members each year during its peak summer season. Positions available include whitewater river guide and shuttle driver. River guides require both first aid and CPR certificates. There is no official application deadline.

INSIDER TIPS: "No experience is necessary although multiple languages as well as camping experience would be helpful."

TO APPLY: Applicants should send a cover letter, résumé, and photocopy of first-aid and CPR certificates to Geoff Freer, Glacier Raft Company (Canada), P.O. Box 2319A, Banff, Alberta, T0L 0C0 Canada; (403) 762-4347.

GRAND CANYON EXPEDITION COMPANY
(Kanab, Utah)
Seasonal (Summer)

The Grand Canyon Expedition Company operates all-inclusive eight-day whitewater trips through the Grand Canyon on the Colorado River.

SPECIFICS: The Grand Canyon Expedition Company hires approximately ten seasonal employees each summer to assist in its whitewater river operations. As the company does not offer a whitewater guide school, all applicants must be experienced.

INSIDER TIPS: "We look for nice people with exceptional boating experience and a genuine love of the outdoors."

TO APPLY: Applicants should send a cover letter and résumé to Marc Smith, Vice President of Operations, Grand Canyon Expedition Company, P.O. Box O, Kanab, Utah 84741; (801) 644-2691.

HERMAN & HELEN'S MARINA
(Venice Island Ferry, Stockton, California)
Seasonal (Summer) and Year-Round

California's delta is a unique and beautiful system of waterways, created by the building of levees 50 to 100 years ago to reclaim farmland. The delta is a seemingly endless waterway system beginning in the San Francisco Bay. Herman & Helen's Marina is a full-service marina located on the delta at Venice Island Ferry.

SPECIFICS: Herman & Helen's receives approximately twenty applications each year for their four or five annual job openings. The marina's staff totals nineteen to twenty-nine employees. Jobs are available for both year-round as well as summer seasonal staff. Summer staff should be available to start work sometime during May or June. Applications are accepted for store clerks, cooks, waitpersons, office staff, mechanics, and dock hands. Salaries start at $4.25 per hour and up. There is no application deadline.

INSIDER TIPS: Herman & Helen's Marina looks for "self-starters" who are "honest and intelligent."

TO APPLY: Applicants should send a cover letter, résumé, photograph, and anything else they think will help their application to Herman & Helen's Marina, Venice Island Ferry, Stockton, California 95209; (209) 951-4634.

HOLIDAY RIVER EXPEDITIONS
(Salt Lake City, Utah)
Seasonal (Summer)

Holiday River Expeditions runs river trips on twelve different sections of seven rivers in Utah, Colorado, and Idaho. Trips range from one to five days and operate on the Yampa, Green, San Juan, Colorado, Lower Salmon, Main Salmon, Snake, and Lochsa rivers. Oar and paddle boats are used; no motor-powered vessels.

SPECIFICS: Holiday River Expeditions employs approximately forty people and hires approximately fifteen new river guides each year. Positions are available for river guides, drivers, and warehouse personnel. River guides must be at least eighteen years old, have Red Cross advanced first aid and CPR certificates (or equivalent), and have a keen ability to learn. Drivers must be twenty-five years old or older, have a clean driver's record, and a valid chauffeur's license. Warehouse workers must be at least sixteen years old. Guide applicants without prior experience with a reputable river company must complete Holiday River Expedition's river guide workshop. The five-day workshop costs approximately $200. Holiday River Expeditions reports offering positions to 30% to 50% of the students from its river guide school.

INSIDER TIPS: Applicants who can be available from May to September have the best employment chances. Although there is no application deadline, apply early for the best positions. The company places emphasis on low-impact camping and wilderness values. Write the company and request their applicant information letter. Read it carefully for full details on employment terms and conditions before applying.

TO APPLY: Applicants should write for an official application and employment information letter from Personnel Manager, Holiday River Expeditions, 544 East 3900 South, Salt Lake City, Utah 84107; (801) 266-2087. A SASE is appreciated with all application requests.

KERN RIVER TOURS
(Lake Isabella, California)
Seasonal (Summer)

California's Kern River is the home of this family-owned whitewater rafting and kayaking company. Trips cover whitewater ranging from "easy moving water with a few ripples and small waves" through Class V water with "long, violent rapids that must be scouted from shore, dangerous drops, unstable eddies, and irregular currents."

SPECIFICS: Kern River Tours hires ten to fifteen new staff members annually to fill its forty-plus seasonal positions. Staff should be available from approximately May through September, although the season varies according to weather and water conditions each year. Most positions are for river guides. However, the company also hires shuttle bus drivers, photographers, retail shop staff, reservationists, and youth counselors. Salary depends on the position and experience. Like many other companies, Kern River Tours offers a guide school.

However, this is one of the few companies that conducts a preschool applicant screening and offers a substantial discount on the school's tuition to those applicants it is most interested in hiring.

INSIDER TIPS: "We are looking for mature, responsible, outdoor-loving men and women who enjoy being around people and aren't afraid of hard work. The job of a river guide is a very exciting, rewarding, and challenging experience. Applicants must be chefs, certified in first aid and CPR, good public relations people, entertainers, and interpreters of the river's natural surroundings."

PERKS: Subsidized housing is provided in a guide house for nights that are spent off the river. All guides receive free food while on trips.

TO APPLY: Applicants should send a cover letter, résumé, and photograph (optional) to Ken Roberts, Kern River Tours, P.O. Box 3444, Lake Isabella, California 93240; (619) 374-4616.

LIBRA EXPEDITIONS
(Sunland, California)
Seasonal (Summer, rafting; Spring and Fall, canoeing)

Whether racing in a raft down the whitewater of the American River or canoeing down the calm surfaces of the Colorado River, Libra Expeditions offers a variety of waterway excursions.

SPECIFICS: To supplement a staff of fifty, Libra Expeditions hires five to fifteen new employees each year. Candidates can apply for positions in cooking, raft guidance, and raft and vehicle repair. Salaries range from $5 to $7 per hour for repair workers and $65 to $75 per day for river guides and cooks (subject to change). Management requests that inexperienced applicants enroll in the company's rafting school. Management reports hiring 60% to 80% percent of the class.

INSIDER TIPS: Management looks for individuals with common sense and the ability to relate to different types of people, "from macho to meek." Employees should be able "to read whitewater rather than just know a route down a river."

TO APPLY: Applicants are asked to send in a résumé and cover letter and enroll in Libra Expeditions' rafting school. For more information contact Libra Expeditions, P.O. Box 4280, Sunland, California 91040; (818) 352-3205. There is no application deadline.

MOKI MAC RIVER EXPEDITIONS, INC.
(Salt Lake City, Utah)
Seasonal (Summer and Fall)

View the rugged beauty of the American West while rafting through some of the region's most breathtaking water routes in Utah and Grand Canyon National Park. The company is run by three brothers: Bob, Clair, and Richard Quist, whose father ran trips down local rivers thirty years ago.

SPECIFICS: Applications are accepted for positions as trainee boatmen, boatmen, and trip leaders. All positions are summer and fall seasonal.

INSIDER TIPS: Candidates should have some knowledge of river rafting since Moki Mac does not offer any training programs.

TO APPLY: For information or an official application contact Moki Mac River Expeditions, Inc., P.O. Box 21242, Salt Lake City, Utah 84121; (801) 268-6667.

NOAH'S ARK WHITEWATER RAFTING
(Buena Vista, Colorado)
Seasonal (Summer)

Noah's Ark Whitewater Rafting operates trips lasting from one to seven days on the Delores and Arkansas rivers. The company operates seasonally from May 1 through August 31 each year.

SPECIFICS: Noah's Ark hires approximately fifteen new employees each season to fill its fifty positions. All jobs are seasonal and run from approximately May 1 through the end of August. Applications are accepted for boatmen, cooks, office staff, and shuttle drivers. Pay is approximately $1,000 per month. All applications must be received by February 1.

INSIDER TIPS: Noah's Ark looks for hard-working, dependable, even-tempered employees with integrity.

PERKS: River trip staff receive free food while on the river.

TO APPLY: Applicants should write for an official application or send a cover letter and résumé to Noah's Ark Whitewater Rafting, Box 850, Buena Vista, Colorado 81211.

NORTH COUNTRY RIVER TRIPS
(Berens River, Manitoba, Canada)
Seasonal (Summer)

North Country River Trips is one of Canada's leading whitewater rafting outfits in Manitoba province. The company specializes in both wilderness raft and canoe trips.

SPECIFICS: North Country River Trips hires six to eight new whitewater guides each year to fill its ten- to fifteen-person staff. The company receives approximately twenty to thirty applications each year. All whitewater guide jobs are summer seasonal, running from June 1 through September 1. All applications are due by May 1. Starting salaries range from CAN$1,000 to CAN$1,500.

INSIDER TIPS: North Country hires only experienced whitewater guides.

PERKS: Staffers are provided with free housing and meals.

TO APPLY: Applicants should send a cover letter, résumé, and photograph to North Country River Trips, Berens River, Manitoba R0B 0A0, Canada; (204) 382-2284.

NORTH STAR LIVERY
(Balloch's Crossing, Cornish, New Hampshire)
Seasonal (Summer and Winter) and Year-Round

North Star specializes in summer canoe and bicycle rentals and winter draft horse sleigh rides. North Star also operates a working farm and forge. North Star's canoes make it possible for visitors to discover Vermont and New Hampshire's beautiful Connecticut River.

SPECIFICS: North Star hires staff for both summer and winter seasonal work as well as year-round employment. Summer staff should be available for the beginning of canoe season starting June 1. Applications are accepted for canoe and bike rental managers, hired hands, and shuttle drivers.

INSIDER TIPS: North Star seeks self-motivated applicants who enjoy the outdoors, dealing with people, and working with mountain bikes. All employees must be able to handle seventy-pound canoes. After applying, follow up with a phone call.

PERKS: Staff housing is possible.

TO APPLY: Applicants should send a cover letter, résumé, and photograph to John S. Hammond, North Star Livery, Box 894, Cornish, New Hampshire 03746; (603) 542-5802.

RAFTMEISTER
(Vail, Colorado)
Seasonal (Summer)

Raftmeister specializes in whitewater rafting trips down the Eagle, Colorado, and Arkansas. Mountain bike tours are also offered.

SPECIFICS: Raftmeister hires approximately eight new river guides and four new mountain bike guides each year to fill its twenty seasonal positions. Summer staff should be available to start work in late April to help set up for the season. Applications are accepted for river guides, kitchen help, mountain bike guides, and retail sales personnel. For applicants without experience the company offers a whitewater guide school. The two-week school costs $225 (subject to change). Management reports offering jobs to 85% of the course graduates.

INSIDER TIPS: According to owner Debbie Marquez, "Safety is the most important quality we look for in applicants."

TO APPLY: Applicants should either write for an official application or enroll in the company's rafting guide school. For further information contact Debbie Marquez, Owner, P.O. Box 1805, Vail, Colorado 81658; (303) 476-RAFT.

RIVER ODYSSEYS WEST
(Coeur d'Alene, Idaho)

Seasonal (Summer)

River Odysseys West, called "ROW" for short, operates one- to eight-day whitewater rafting and "daring duckie inflatable kayak" trips on the Salmon, Moyie, Lochsa, Grand Ronde, Snake, and Owyhee (pronounced "Hawaii") rivers in Idaho and Oregon. Additionally, ROW operates motor/sail yacht trips to Turkey, Greece, and Yugoslavia.

SPECIFICS: ROW employs twelve seasonal staff members and generally hires four new river guides each year. Part-time positions are available from April through July. Full-time seasonal employees are needed from April through September. Although there is no official application deadline, most seasonal hiring is completed by March 1. Employees earn from $50 to $95 per day plus tips. Positions are available for bus drivers (chauffeur's license and experience required), river guides (current first aid card required, experience or training necessary), office secretaries (clerical skills required), and area or river managers (considerable rafting experience required). ROW is willing to train qualified applicants.

INSIDER TIPS: ROW looks for applicants with positive, outgoing personalities, responsibility, flexibility, and interests other than rafting. Applicants with interests in archaeology, biology, botany, geology, or ornithology (scientific study of birds) are especially encouraged to apply. ROW river guides attempt to preserve and protect America's wild areas by educating passengers on intelligent and nondegrading uses of the wilderness.

PERKS: Employees are provided with many free meals. Some housing is available and generous tips supplement most river guides' earnings.

TO APPLY: Write for an official application or send a cover letter, résumé, and photograph to Peter Grubb or Betsy Bowen, Owners, River Odysseys West, P.O. Box 579JB, Coeur d'Alene, Idaho 83814; (208) 765-0841.

ROCKY MOUNTAIN OUTDOOR CENTER
(Howard, Colorado)
Seasonal (Summer)

Rocky Mountain Outdoor Center operates Class II to V paddle raft, canoe, and kayak day trips on Colorado's Arkansas River.

SPECIFICS: The company employs thirty staff and hires up to five new staff members each year. Applications are welcome from those seeking positions as either river guides or kayak instructors. Pay ranges from $35 to $60 per day. Employees must be available June 1 through August 15. Hiring is completed by early spring.

INSIDER TIPS: For the best job opportunities, applications should be received in late winter. As the company does not offer a formal river guide school, guides are usually trained at no cost to the applicant after hiring. Kayakers are preferred.

PERKS: Employees may purchase an optional housing plan for $30 and an optional meal plan.

TO APPLY: Interested applicants should send a cover letter and résumé to Dick Eustis, President, Rocky Mountain Outdoor Center, 10281 Highway 50, Howard, Colorado 81233; (719) 942-3214.

SHENANDOAH RIVER OUTFITTERS
(Luray, Virginia)
Seasonal (Summer)

Shenandoah River Outfitters specializes in canoe and inner-tube trips down the Shenandoah River between Massanutten Mountain and Appalachian trails in George Washington National Forest. The company also operates hamburger and steak cookouts along the river bank.

SPECIFICS: Shenandoah River Outfitters hires four new employees each year to fill its sixteen-person staff. Summer seasonal employees should be available to work from May through August. Applications are accepted for cooks, canoe builders, and bus drivers. Bus drivers are responsible for transporting passengers to and from the river and for loading and unloading canoes. Starting salaries range from $5.00 to $6.00 per hour depending on skills.

INSIDER TIPS: "We look for applicants who are strong enough to load canoe trailers and who have a knowledge of canoeing and a love of outdoor work. Applicants should not use drugs or alcohol."

PERKS: Staff members are allowed free use of the company's canoe equipment, free T-shirts, and free steak dinners.

TO APPLY: Applicants should send a cover letter and résumé to Shenandoah River Outfitters, RFD #3, Luray, Virginia 22835; (703) 743-4159.

SIERRA OUTFITTERS & GUIDES
(Taos, New Mexico)
Seasonal (Summer)

Sierra Outfitters & Guides operates whitewater rafting trips down Arizona's Salt River, Colorado's Arkansas River, and New Mexico's Rio Chama and Rio Grande. While the water on the Rio Chama is rated an easy Class II, all other rivers have whitewater ranging from a moderate Class III to hellraising Class V.

SPECIFICS: Sierra Outfitters & Guides hires up to three new employees each year to fill its fifteen-person staff. Applications are accepted for bus drivers (Class VI license, clean driving record, and experience required) and river guides. All Sierra Outfitters river guides must have both CPR and American Red Cross first aid certificates. Frequently newly hired river guides are offered a combination of training and work during their first season. All seasonal employees must be available from at least May through August. New employees should be available in mid-April for preseason training. Applications for summer employment must be received by early April.

INSIDER TIPS: According to Denise Corriveau, "Experience is preferred but a good learner often fits in better. The big qualities we look for in applicants are a willingness to learn, a pleasant disposition, and a commitment to safety. Common sense is a must. We want someone who can go from plan A to plan B immediately, if not sooner, when the situation changes. We're a good, safe, solid company." The company offers a river rafting guide school but only applicants that Sierra thinks it can use as future employees are accepted. The class costs approximately $15 per day and lasts until the company can certify the applicant as a qualified whitewater guide.

PERKS: Pay is per trip and varies depending on the number of passengers.

TO APPLY: Applicants should write for an official application and enroll in the company's whitewater course from Sierra Outfitters & Guides, Attn: Peter Hanson, Hiring/Training Manager, Box 2756, Taos, New Mexico 87571; (505) 758-1247. A cover letter and résumé are also helpful. Enclose a SASE with all correspondence.

SIERRA SOUTH, INC.
(Kernville, California)
Seasonal (Spring and Summer)

Teaching the rigorous and rewarding sports of kayaking and whitewater rafting is the focus at Sierra South. Located on the upper section of the Kern River, this outdoor classroom is designed to be fun and safe, with an emphasis on the latter.

SPECIFICS: Sierra South hires five new employees each year for its seasonal staff of twelve to fifteen workers. Applications are accepted for kayak instructors, raft guides, and rental store personnel. Guides are paid a minimum of $40 a day and retail staff make $4.50 an hour (subject to change). Applications for summer employment are due in February.

INSIDER TIPS: Management looks for candidates who are "outgoing, articulate, hard-working, self-directed, prompt, and adaptable."

PERKS: Sierra South provides a free two-day training course to successful applicants.

TO APPLY: Applicants should send a résumé, cover letter, and photograph to Tom Moore, Sierra South, Box Y, Kernville, California 93238.

SIERRA WHITEWATER EXPEDITIONS
(Springfield, Oregon)
Seasonal (primarily Spring and Summer) and Year-Round

Sierra Whitewater Expeditions is Oregon's largest river outfitter, running one- to five-day trips on the Owyhee, Grande Ronde, Deschutes, Santium, McKenzie, Rogue, Minam, Crooked, John Day, Umpqua, Salmon, and Klamath rivers in Oregon and Northern California. Sierra Whitewater also offers the only public Class V river guide school in the United States. This adventurous river course is open only to persons with prior river experience (either as a guide or participant).

SPECIFICS: The company employs twenty staff members and usually hires eight to twelve new employees each year. Whitewater river positions are available during the spring and summer season from April through September, although the bulk of the company's trips start after Memorial Day. Year-round commissioned sales positions are available off-site. For on-river personnel, the company has positions for river guides and shuttle bus drivers. The company operates a large number of whitewater guide schools and encourages all applicants without prior river experience to enroll. While Sierra Whitewater Expeditions declined to specify what percentage of its river course graduates it hires, it claims to have a 100% placement record in helping guides find positions. The river guide school costs $395 for a five- to six-day course.

INSIDER TIPS: The river guide courses in March are designed primarily for interested applicants. The remainder of the school courses are for those interested in learning safe boating techniques rather than those seeking employment.

TO APPLY: Applicants should write for an official application and employee information from Tom Foster, Owner, Sierra Whitewater Expeditions, Box 1330, Springfield, Oregon 97477; (800) 937-7300.

TEX'S RIVER EXPEDITIONS
(Moab, Utah)

Seasonal (Summer)

With Tex's River Expeditions you can travel the calm waters of the Green River in canoes or the roaring rapids of the Colorado River in rafts or jet boats. The spectacular scenery affords numerous outdoor opportunities, from camping to kayaking.

SPECIFICS: Applicants must be eighteen or older with state licenses and Red Cross first aid certification. Four to eight river guide positions are available each year. Salaries range between $40 to $50 for daily trips, plus $5 to $40 in gratuities. River guide applications are due June 1.

INSIDER TIPS: Management looks for "ambitious candidates with dependability and an outgoing, friendly personality." Prospective candidates for Tex's River Expeditions can enroll in an area guide school in May.

TO APPLY: Applicants should send a résumé, cover letter, and SARP to Renee Parish, Manager, P.O. Box 67, Moab, Utah 84532.

TONGARIRO LODGE
(Turangi, New Zealand)
Seasonal (December through March)

The Tongariro Lodge is a small trout-fishing lodge on the shores of the Tongariro River. This exclusive fishing retreat has played host to such notable guests as President Jimmy Carter, Larry Hagman, and Robert Mitchum.

SPECIFICS: This small resort lodge employs between four and eight staff members for its December through March season. The lodge employs a cook, kitchen hand, waitperson, barhand, and cleaner.

INSIDER TIPS: Ideal applicants are both experts in fishing and knowledgeable in the Turangi area of New Zealand. Applicants with a clean-cut appearance, pleasant, open personality, and an ability to talk to guests freely are encouraged to apply. Non–New Zealand citizens with proper work permits are welcome to apply.

TO APPLY: Applicants should send a cover letter, résumé, and photograph to Margaret Coutts or Tony Hayes, Tongariro Lodge, P.O. Box 278, Turangi, New Zealand; phone (0746) 7946.

TRIANGLE X FLOAT TRIPS
(Moose, Wyoming)

Seasonal (Summer)

Triangle X specializes in scenic float trips down the Snake River through Grand Teton National Park. The water on this portion of the Snake is not classified as whitewater, but does include several segments of fast water with dangerous obstacles.

SPECIFICS: Triangle X hires ten to fifteen new employees each year to fill its staff of twenty-five. All positions are seasonal, lasting from June through September. Applications are accepted for river guides, van/bus drivers, and outdoor cooks. Applications for summer employment should be submitted in March or April. Wages for river guides range from $900 to $1,600 per month depending on experience. Drivers and cooks earn approximately $600 per month. While not offering a whitewater school, Triangle X puts its new employees through a two- to three-week training program involving interpretive training and fifteen to twenty apprentice river trips.

INSIDER TIPS: For the best employment opportunities, apply as early as possible. "All employees must be physically strong, in excellent health, and at least twenty years of age."

PERKS: Employees receive free room and board.

TO APPLY: Applicants should send a cover letter, résumé, photograph, and SARP to John F. Turner, Float Trip Manager, Triangle X Float Trips, Moose, Wyoming 83012; (307) 733-5500.

TURTLE RIVER RAFTING CO.
(Mt. Shasta, California)
Seasonal (Summer) and Year-Round

Turtle River Rafting Company operates one- to five-day whitewater rafting and kayak trips on the Eel, Salmon, Scott, Sacramento, Owyhee, Smith, Klamath, American, and Trinity rivers. As their brochure warns guests, "you can expect to paddle, get wet, laugh, play in kayaks, relax by the river, share in the preparation of meals, and become knowledgeable about the river and its ways."

SPECIFICS: Turtle River employs fifteen river guides and hires approximately three new employees each season. The company generally hires employees out of its guide school program. The program costs approximately $450 for the five-day course. The guide school is offered in April and June of each year and approximately 50% of the course graduates are offered jobs with the company. Pay for guides ranges from $60 to $80 per day plus tips.

INSIDER TIPS: The company looks for employees who are mature, educationally oriented, good with people, willing to learn, confident, and safety oriented. Musical talent is also helpful.

PERKS: Meals are provided free while leading trips.

TO APPLY: Applicants should enroll in the company's river guide program or call for information and an interview from David Wikander, Turtle River Rafting Company, P.O. Box 313, Mt. Shasta, California 96067; (916) 926-3223.

USA WHITEWATER, INC.
(Rowlesburg, West Virginia)
Seasonal (Spring and Summer) and Year-Round

USA Whitewater is a reservation company for four whitewater outfitters: Appalachian Wildwaters, Expeditions, American Whitewater Tours, and Rough Run Expeditions. The company specializes in whitewater paddle boat treks down twelve rivers in West Virginia, Tennessee, Kentucky, North Carolina, Maryland, and Texas.

SPECIFICS: USA Whitewater hires up to twenty-five new employees each year to fill its 100-plus-member peak season staff. Each year the company receives more than fifty employment applications. Jobs are available for both year-round as well as spring and summer seasonal staff. Spring staff should be available to start work by April 1. Summer staff begins work in early June. Applications are accepted throughout the year. Positions are available for whitewater guides, reservationists, retail sales staff, and support personnel (kitchen crew, drivers, and maintenance people). Salaries range from minimum wage to $8.00 per hour.

INSIDER TIPS: "We look for outstanding individuals who can work well with a wide spectrum of personality types in an outdoor environment—i.e., 'people people'."

PERKS: Unlike many companies, USA Whitewater provides training to new employees at no cost. Employees also receive discounts on retail rafting merchandise and free housing during guide training.

TO APPLY: Applicants should write for an official application from USA Whitewater, P.O. Box 277, Rowlesburg, West Virginia 26425; (304) 454-2475.

WESTERN RIVER EXPEDITIONS
(Salt Lake City, Utah)
Seasonal (Summer) and Year-Round

Western River Expeditions advertises its trips as "the best rafting vacations in the West." Expeditions are operated in Grand Canyon National Park, Canyonlands National Park, and the Westwater and Green River wilderness areas.

SPECIFICS: Western River Expeditions employs eighty-five boatpeople each summer. The company hires approximately seventy new employees each year. While fifteen employees work for the company on a year-round basis, the majority of positions are summer seasonal. All employees must be at least twenty-one years old. Applications for summer seasonal work must be received in December or January. Summer staff work from May through August. Although the company does not offer a formal river guide school, all potential employees must attend a "training trip" in April after which final job offers are made. Pay starts at $45 per day plus housing and tips.

INSIDER TIPS: Only non-drinkers and non-smokers are considered for employment. Red Cross advanced first aid with a CPR certificate or EMT certification is required. The company has a strict appearance code and all male employees must have short hair and be clean shaven. As a lengthy multi-stage interview is required, Utah residents generally have a better chance of being hired. Attendance on the April "training trip" is mandatory. "Our river guides must be walking encyclopedias of facts and figures, stories, tall tales, and historical vignettes pertaining to the expedition features and attractions. You should be a good storyteller or willing to practice becoming one."

PERKS: Boatpersons receive free housing and free meals while on trips. All river personnel earn generous tips.

TO APPLY: Applicants should send a cover letter, résumé, photograph, and SARP to Bill George, Western River Expeditions, 7258 Racquet Club Drive, Salt Lake City, Utah 84121; (801) 942-6669. Before applying write and request the company's informative applicant "Questions & Answers" brochure for details on the application process, employment criteria, and conditions of employment.

W.E.T. (WHITEWATER EXPEDITIONS & TOURS) (Sacramento, California)

Seasonal (Spring, Summer, and Fall)

"I don't blame you for being scared—not one little bit. Nobody with good sense ain't scared of whitewater"—Humphrey Bogart. W.E.T. begins its brochure with this memorable quote from Bogart in the film *The African Queen.* W.E.T. operates whitewater trips on the south, middle, and north forks of the American River, the upper and lower branches of the Klamath, and the Scott, Calif., Salmon, East Carson, Merced, Tuolumne, and Colorado rivers.

SPECIFICS: W.E.T. hires between two and four new employees each year to fill its twenty staff positions. W.E.T.'s staff includes boatpersons, shuttle drivers, office/clerical staff, sales representatives, and a river manager. Salaries range from $400 to $2,000 per month. While exact starting dates vary, most employees work from April through October.

INSIDER TIPS: "Most of our guides stay with us for a long time. We are like an extended family. Therefore, we are careful with who comes aboard. We want applicants who are hard working, flexible, knowledgeable about many diverse subjects, good food preparers or cooks, and—of course—excellent boat handlers."

TO APPLY: Applicants should send a cover letter and résumé to Stephen Liles, Owner, W.E.T. (Whitewater Expeditions & Tours), P.O. Box 160024, Sacramento, California 95816; (916) 451-3241.

WHITEWATER VOYAGES
(El Sobrante, California)
Seasonal (Summer) and Year-Round

William McGinnis' Whitewater Voyages are one- to seven-days on twenty-plus different river runs in California and Oregon. Difficulty of these runs range from Class II to V and include the Kern, Merced, Tuolumne, Upper Tuolumne, North Fork Stanislaus, Carson, American, Giant Gap, North Fork Yuba, Cache Creek, Colorado, Burnt Ranch Gorge, Salmon, Klamath, Scott, and Rogue rivers. In addition to typical river rafting/camping expeditions, Whitewater Voyages offers such unique trips as watercolor painting wilderness excursions, yoga trips, and special half-price family and clean-up trips.

SPECIFICS: Whitewater Voyages has an excellent reputation among its employees and enjoys a relatively low turnover. Nonetheless, approximately twenty new river guides are hired each year to fill the 120-plus guide positions. Seasonal employees may start in either April, May, or June and should be able to work through August or September. There is no application deadline and river guides earn from $48 to $110 per day depending on experience and position. The company runs its own whitewater guide school and hires most of its new employees from the class. According to management, approximately 30% to 70% of the members of each guide school class are offered employment upon graduation. Whitewater Voyages' guide school is taught by William McGinnis, author of *Whitewater Rafting, The Guide's Guide,* and *The Class V Briefing.* The course costs approximately $630.

INSIDER TIPS: "We seek warm, caring, intelligent, able people who, above all else, care about creating good, safe, enjoyable river trips."

TO APPLY: Applicants should write for an official application, enroll in the company's river rafting guide school, or send a cover letter, résumé, photograph, and SARP to William McGinnis, President, Whitewater Voyages, P.O. Box 20400, El Sobrante, California 94820-0400; (510) 222-5994.

ZEPHYR RIVER EXPEDITIONS, INC.
(Columbia, California)

Seasonal (Summer)

Zephyr River Expeditions runs the Tuolumne, Kings, East Carson, American, Merced, and Stanislaus rivers. Each trip uses one to ten rafts, depending on the river. Courses range from Class II to V.

SPECIFICS: Zephyr River Expeditions hires three to six new employees each year for a total staff of twenty-five. A personal interview is a prerequisite to employment. Prospective employees must be available from May through August, but the season's schedule is flexible. River guide candidates must have current Red Cross first aid and CPR certification, as well as guide experience and related skills. Salaries range from $70 to $100 a day. Applications for summer employment are due by March 15.

INSIDER TIPS: "Our hiring process is very informal," says management. Much of the hiring takes place during the rafting school in March, where management claims between 33% to 50% of the students are hired as Zephyr river guides. First-year guides get mostly weekend work, but in a good season full-time employment is possible.

TO APPLY: For more information on Zephyr's whitewater river guide school, contact Bob Ferguson, P.O. Box 510, Columbia, California 95310. A résumé and cover letter are optional. Applicants should include a SARP with their applications.

For a list of over 125 whitewater rafting outfits in the western United States, write the Western River Guides Association, 7600 East Arapahoe Road, Englewood, Colorado 80112; (303) 771-0389.

The following listings, found under the chapter headings given below, also include positions near rivers:

DESERT

Rio Grande Rapid
   Transit/Desert Voyagers

LAKES

Houseboat Holidays   Kettle Falls Hotel, Inc.

MOUNTAINS

Red Lion Inn

HIGH ADVENTURE

Ghost Town Scenic Jeep   Pacific Crest Outward Bound
   Tours/River Runners Ltd.   School
Hells Canyon Adventures   Wilderness Tours

Lakes

ARA LEISURE SERVICES/LAKE POWELL
RESORTS & MARINAS
(Page, Arizona)

Seasonal (Spring and Summer) and Year-Round

ARA Leisure Services is considered by many to be the leading owner/ operator of water-based resort recreation facilities in Arizona and Utah. The company operates five marinas on spectacular Lake Powell. The marina operations include Wahweap, near Page, Arizona; Bullfrog and Hall's Crossing at mid-lake; and Hite at the north end of the 186-mile-long lake. For those truly in search of isolation, the company's fifth marina, Dangling Rope Marina, can be reached only by boat and is a floating service center anchored about forty miles uplake from Wahweap Marina and about seven miles from Rainbow Bridge, one of the seven natural wonders of the world. The company also operates Wilderness River Adventures, Inc., a large whitewater rafting company operating on the Colorado River through the Grand and Glen canyons.

SPECIFICS: The company hires more than 700 new seasonal and year-round staff members annually to fill its 1,200 positions. Positions are available for both long-term and seasonal work. Seasonal staff should be available from April through November. There is no application deadline. Applications are accepted for a wide variety of full-time and seasonal positions including sales clerks, dockhands, fuel dock attendants, service station attendants, van/truck drivers, food and cocktail servers, maintenance persons, housekeepers, boat cleaners, houseboat instructors, small boat instructors, stock persons, boat rental agents, front desk clerks, bellhops, buspersons, cooks, dishwashers, and marine mechanics. River rafting personnel include van/bus drivers, lead river pilots, river pilots, and river crew.

INSIDER TIPS: "The work can often be demanding during the peak season; however, it is exciting and rewarding. Our employees must meet high standards. A clean, neat appearance, pleasant personality, cheerful smile, and positive attitude are musts."

PERKS: Low-cost company housing and meals are available at Wahweap Bullfrog, Hall's Crossing, Dangling Rope, and Hite marinas. Rafting company employees camp out along with the river trip participants and find their own housing in the town of Page when not on the river. Qualified employees are eligible for credit union services, discounts on company merchandise and food, health and dental insurance, sick pay, vacation pay, and employee cafeterias. Employees are permitted to use many of the company's facilities, including air shuttles, boats, tours, and river trips, when off duty.

TO APPLY: Seasonal employees who complete their season satisfactorily earn a free houseboat vacation of seven days in the off season, paying only the cost of gas and insurance. Applicants should write for an official application or send a cover letter, résumé, and SARP to ARA Leisure Services, Human Resources, P.O. Box 1926, Page, Arizona 86040. Follow-up to application is recommended.

BAREFOOT BAY RESORT
(Elkhart Lake, Wisconsin)
Seasonal (Summer)

Barefoot Bay Resort is a unique hideaway that combines the beauty and accessibility of Wisconsin's Elkhart Lake with the pace and flavor of a tropical island retreat. Favorite Barefoot Bay activities include swimming in the two large pools (one indoor and one outdoor), sailing, waterskiing, jet skiing, fishing on Elkhart Lake, volleyball, softball, and miniature golf.

SPECIFICS: Barefoot Bay employs a summer seasonal staff of 140 people. Applications are accepted for front desk clerks, reservation clerks, sales clerks, bellpersons, bartenders, waiters/waitresses, cocktail servers, busboys, youth activities counselors, and beach/boat attendants. Salaries and hours vary according to the position held.

INSIDER TIPS: Apply early for best position selection. A special attempt is made to give applicants their first or second job choices.

PERKS: Optional employee housing is available. Resort employee housing includes all meals and linen service.

TO APPLY: Interested applicants should write or call for further employment information from Personnel Director, Barefoot Bay Resort, Elkhart Lake, Wisconsin 53020; (312) 272-9300 or (414) 876-3323 or toll-free from outside Illinois (800) 345-7784.

BEAR TRACK OUTFITTING CO.
(Grand Marais, Minnesota, and Quetico Provincial Park, Canada)
Seasonal (Summer) and Year-Round

The Bear Track Outfitting Co. is the only year-round outfitter in the self-proclaimed "world's greatest canoe country," the Boundary Waters Canoe Area. The region is dotted with hundreds of lakes surrounded by endless vistas of uninhabited native forest land. Bear Track Outfitting specializes in guiding and outfitting canoeists, fishermen, backpackers, cross-country skiers, and winter ice campers.

SPECIFICS: Bear Track Outfitting Co. receives approximately fifteen applications for its two or three annual job openings. All jobs are seasonal, running from May through September. There is no application deadline. Staff members perform a wide variety of tasks and must work as delivery drivers, retail sporting goods store clerks, tow boat drivers, guides, canoe instructors, and farm workers.

INSIDER TIPS: According to staffer David Williams, Bear Track Outfitting Co. looks for honest, loyal, hard-working, considerate, nonsmokers who have some knowledge of the outdoors, canoeing, and fishing.

PERKS: The company provides room and board for employees. Staff members are free to use the company's outdoor equipment on their days off.

TO APPLY: Applicants should send a cover letter, résumé, and photograph to David Williams, Bear Track Outfitting Co., Box 937, Grand Marais, Minnesota 55604; (218) 387-1162.

CALLAWAY GARDENS
(Pine Mountain, Georgia)
Seasonal (Spring and Summer) and Year-Round

Callaway Gardens is one of the world's largest, most diverse, and unique resorts. Located in Georgia's beautiful Pine Mountain area, Callaway's 12,000 acres offer everything one could dream of for an active vacation getaway. Guests enjoy golf on four separate courses staffed with PGA and LPGA pros, seventeen lighted soft and hard tennis courts, racquetball, trap and skeet shooting, horseback riding, quail hunting, sailing, bass and bream fishing, swimming, and assorted lake water sports. Callaway Gardens is set on 175-acre Mountain Creek Lake.

SPECIFICS: Callaway Gardens hires up to 500 new employees each year to fill its 1,500-person peak season staff. Positions are available for both year-round as well as spring/summer seasonal employees. Callaway prefers seasonal staff who can be available from March 15 through Labor Day. The resort hires a wide variety of staff including food servers, reservation clerks, front desk clerks, gate attendants, golf course attendants, hostesses, cashiers, salespersons, greenhouse attendants, grounds keepers, housekeepers, cooks, stewards, clerical staff, and maintenance help. For information on other positions, contact the employment office. There is no application deadline.

INSIDER TIPS: According to management, applicants "must have a good work record, be able to pass a preemployment physical and drug-screening test, and be willing to work in any area assigned."

PERKS: Limited housing is provided to some employees. One complimentary meal per day is provided to all food service employees. All of the resort's facilities are open to staff members on a space-available basis.

TO APPLY: Applicants should either write for an official application or send a cover letter, résumé, and SARP to Carol Price, Employment Manager, Callaway Gardens, Pine Mountain, Georgia 31822; (404) 663-5170.

CLEVELANDS HOUSE RESORT
(Minett, Muskoka, Ontario, Canada)
Seasonal (Summer)

For more than 120 years Clevelands House has been accommodating guests at its spectacular lakefront property on Lake Rosseau, one of

Ontario's top tourist destinations. The Clevelands estate is nested on a hillside overlooking Lake Rosseau and its myriad of small lake islands. Organized activities include waterskiing, sailing, fishing, canoeing, shuffleboard, golf, and badminton. Clevelands House boasts a private 1,750-yard, nine-hole golf course plus sixteen modern tennis courts.

SPECIFICS: Clevelands House Resort hires approximately 180 new employees each year to fill its 200 seasonal staff positions. All jobs are seasonal, running from May through September or mid-October. Positions are available for dining room waitstaff, housekeepers, cooks, dishwashers, front desk staff, and children's counselors. All applications must be received by March 1. Starting salaries range from CAN$6.00/hour to CAN$6.50/hour.

INSIDER TIPS: Most staff members range in age from eighteen to twenty-two years old. The single most important characteristic that management looks for in screening applicants is enthusiasm. According to management, the resort wants employees with "outgoing personalities—someone who smiles and is willing to work long hours."

PERKS: Housing is provided for employees at the resort. Bonuses are paid to employees who fulfill their contracts by staying through the entire season. Staff members are free to use the resort's tennis, waterskiing, windsurfing, boating, golf, and nightclub facilities.

TO APPLY: Applicants should write for an official application or send a cover letter, résumé, photograph (optional), and SARP to Personnel Director, Clevelands House Resort, P.O. Box 60, Minett, Ontario, P0B 1G0 Canada; (705) 765-3171.

CRATER LAKE LODGE INC.
(Crater Lake National Park, Oregon)
Seasonal (Summer and Winter)

The magnificent Crater Lake Lodge provides lodging and other guest services at Oregon's only national park, Crater Lake. Located at the park's Rim Village, the lodge is designed to blend into its natural environment and offers unspoiled views of the lake and surrounding wilderness areas.

SPECIFICS: The Crater Lake Lodge receives 500 applications for its 120 annual job openings among its 150-person staff. Jobs are available for both summer and winter seasonal work. Summer seasonal positions begin in early June and last through mid-September; winter positions begin in October and end in May. Applications are accepted for boat operators, front desk clerks, housekeepers, laundry attendants, night watchpersons, maintenance staff, food preparation personnel, food servers, bartenders, campground maintenance staff, and grocery store clerks. Most summer hiring is done in February and March.

INSIDER TIPS: Apply as early as possible for best chances of selection. The Crater Lake Lodge looks for "outdoor-oriented applicants who enjoy isolation, hard work, working with the public, and working closely with fellow employees."

PERKS: Room and board are provided at a moderate cost to employees (currently $7.50 per day, subject to change). Discounts on food and other guest services are available.

TO APPLY: Applicants should write for an official application from Personnel, Crater Lake Lodge Inc., P.O. Box 128, Crater Lake, Oregon 97604; (503) 594-2511.

EL RANCHO STEVENS
(Gaylord, Michigan)

Seasonal (Summer)

El Rancho Stevens has been providing fun-packed Western-style vacations to couples, families, and singles for years. This western resort is located on a 1,000-acre lakefront ranch in northern Michigan. The resort is very casual, with such activities as rodeos, hay rides, nature hikes, canoeing, horseback riding, sailing, tennis, archery, swimming, and river trips. Nightly campfire entertainment is a favorite El Rancho Stevens activity.

SPECIFICS: This Western-style resort hires approximately twenty-five new seasonal summer staff members each year to fill its thirty positions. Most summer seasonal staff work from mid-June through Labor Day. Hiring is done in March and April. Positions are available for waitpersons, cooks, buspersons, kitchen helpers, maids, waterski instructors, horseback riding instructors/trail guides (must be at least twenty years old), lifeguards, children's counselors, recreation directors, guitar and banjo players, musicians, bartenders, and clerical/office workers (must have typing skills).

INSIDER TIPS: El Rancho Stevens is a family-oriented resort ranch providing a wide array of outdoor activities. However, there is no swinging nightlife here.

PERKS: Management reports that room and board may be available for some employees. Staffers are permitted to use most of the facilities when off duty, subject to certain restrictions.

TO APPLY: Applicants should either write for an official application (enclose a SASE with any application request) or send a cover letter, résumé, photograph, and SARP to Mr. Stevens, El Rancho Stevens, Dept. JIP, P.O. Box 366, Gaylord, Michigan 49735; (517) 732-5090.

GRAND VIEW GUEST HOUSE
(Manapouri, Fiordland National Park, New Zealand)
Seasonal (New Zealand Summer [winter in USA and Canada])

This family guest house on the shores of Lake Manapouri has been providing hospitality since 1889. The hotel is located in a small scenic village on the fringe of Fiordland National Park, a large pristine World Heritage Park of unsurpassed beauty.

SPECIFICS: Four seasonal employees are hired each year to fill the six-person guest house staff. Seasonal staff must be available from either February through March or for October and November. There is no application deadline. Available positions include housekeeper/waitperson, kitchen assistant, groundsperson, and general staffperson (who does a bit of all of the above).

INSIDER TIPS: Although applications are considered for seasonal staff at both of the above listed times, most employees work from February through March. Applications are welcomed from non–New Zealand citizens provided the applicant has a valid New Zealand work permit.

PERKS: All employees are provided with full accommodations.

TO APPLY: Send a brief cover letter, résumé, photograph, and SARP (complete with two international return postage certificates) to Jack Murrell, Grand View Guest House, Manapouri, New Zealand; phone: (02296) 642 or 619.

GRAND VIEW LODGE, GOLF & TENNIS CLUB
(Gull Lake, Minnesota)
Seasonal (Summer) and Year-Round

Between the scenic shores of Roy and Gull lakes lies this full-service family and conference resort that hosts up to 350 guests. Grand View Lodge boasts modern luxury facilities including eleven tennis courts, two golf courses, pool, and jacuzzi. Favorite guest and staff activities include fishing, sailing, waterskiing, and canoeing on the two lakes.

SPECIFICS: Grand View Lodge hires 120 new staff members to fill its staff of 200 annually. Some positions are year-round while others are seasonal. Jobs available include pro shop staff, beach attendants, golf course staff, front desk clerks, waiters/waitresses, cooks, dishwashers, housekeeping staff, maintenance and grounds staff, and many more.

INSIDER TIPS: Grand View Lodge prefers those who are available from early April through late October. Employees pay $150 per month for room and board. Although late applications will be considered, you should apply by March 1 for the best opportunities. The management is seeking a staff that is customer oriented, service conscious, conscientious, reliable, hard working, and energetic.

PERKS: Staff members are welcome to use golf, tennis, beach, pool, whirlpool, recreation room, shuffleboard, gardens, and almost all other resort facilities. Room and board is available.

TO APPLY: Applicants should write for an official application form or send a cover letter, résumé, and photograph to Paul E. Welch, Operations Manager, Grandview Lodge Golf & Tennis Club, South 134 Nokomis, Nisswa, Minnesota 56468; (218) 963-2234.

GRENELEFE RESORT & CONFERENCE CENTER
(Grenelefe, Florida)
Seasonal (limited opportunities) and Year-Round

This huge wooded resort complex embraces 1,000 lush acres on the shores of Lake Marion, one of central Florida's largest lakes. The resort features four championship golf courses, thirteen tennis courts, four pools, a fire station, post office, three restaurants, and lounges. Water sports, beaches, and fishing are all available on the resort's 6,400-acre lake.

SPECIFICS: Grenelefe hires 550 new employees annually and employs a total of 700 staff members. Applications are accepted for golf department staff, recreation crew, tennis department personnel, front office positions, grounds workers, real estate sales staff, convention sales and services, housekeepers, food and beverage employees, cooks, chefs, clerical help, audiovisual technicians, data processing staff, and management personnel. Salaries range from $10,000 to $30,000 per year.

INSIDER TIPS: In evaluating applicants, management looks for "professionalism, experience, and good communication skills."

PERKS: Employees are welcome to use the golf and tennis facilities when off duty. New employees are provided housing for thirty days while they seek accommodations.

TO APPLY: Applicants should write for an official application or send a cover letter, résumé, photograph (if available, but not necessary), and SARP to Karen Stephens, Director of Personnel, Grenelefe Resort & Conference Center, 3200 State Road 546, Grenelefe, Florida 33844; (813) 422-7511.

GUNFLINT LODGE & OUTFITTERS
(Grand Marais, Minnesota)
Seasonal (Summer) and Year-Round

Gunflint Lodge is a family fishing resort located on Gunflint Lake in Minnesota's northeastern wilderness. The lodge combines a quiet and personalized wilderness experience with a variety of activities ranging from fishing, hiking, mountain biking, naturalist activities, canoeing, camping, cross-country skiing, and dogsled rides. The lodge boasts a professional fishing pro and staff of eight fishing guides.

SPECIFICS: Gunflint employs six year-round and fifty seasonal summer staff. The summer season runs from late April to late October. Applications are accepted for the following positions: dishwasher, waitstaff/housekeeper, baker, prep cook, assistant cook, breakfast cook, dinner cook, bartender, hostess, front desk staff, store clerk, dock staff, maintenance, grounds keeper, naturalist, fishing guides, general outfitting staff, canoe guides, and assistant outfitting manager. Salaries start at $865 per month plus bonus. Room and some meals available at minimal cost.

INSIDER TIPS: Management seeks applicants with both initiative and a positive attitude. Special interest is in employees available for either spring and/or fall season in addition to the summer season. While there is no official application deadline most hiring is done between January and March of each year.

PERKS: Access to the BWCA Wilderness area. All staff members may use the resort's boats, canoes, and camping gear during their off hours.

TO APPLY: Contact Shari Baker for application and job descriptions. Call (800) 328-3325 or fax (218) 388-9429. Or write to Shari Baker, Gunflint Lodge, 750 Gunflint Trail, Grand Marais, Minnesota 55604.

HARRAH'S TAHOE
(Stateline, Nevada)
Seasonal (Summer) and Year-Round

The combination of a spectacular alpine lake and the constant sound of quarters hitting hundreds of slot machine buckets is irresistible for tens of thousands of annual Harrah's visitors.

SPECIFICS: Harrah's hires approximately 500 new employees annually to fill its 3,500 staff positions. Jobs are available for both year-round and summer employment. Seasonal summer jobs extend from approximately May 15 through Labor Day. Available jobs in the casino include change/jackpot payoff staff, keno writers, cashiers, and dealers. In the food and beverage department, there are positions for cocktail servers, food servers, and bar attendants. All casino and beverage staff must be a minimum of twenty-one years of age. The hotel department hires housekeepers, cleaners, room clerks, front desk cashiers, reservationists, and all other typical front-line hotel positions. Harrah's will train applicants without experience for most positions. Starting wages range from minimum wage to $5.50 per hour plus tips.

INSIDER TIPS: "We look for applicants with excellent communication skills who are guest-oriented and possess a record of stability and reliability shown by previous employment or academic history." Most summer seasonal staff members are college students.

PERKS: All food employees receive complimentary meals while on duty. The company offers a 401k retirement plan, credit union, insurance programs, discounted health club memberships, discounts in Harrah's gift shops, an annual employee picnic, on-site medical facilities, company-sponsored sports teams, and an employee training program. Employees are permitted to use many of the resort's facilities when off duty.

TO APPLY: For application information write or call Harrah's Tahoe, Personnel Office, P.O. Box 8, Stateline, Nevada 89449; (702) 588-6611, ext. 2126 or 2121.

INDIANHEAD MOUNTAIN RESORT, INC.
(Wakefield, Michigan)
Seasonal (Winter and Summer)

Indianhead is perhaps one of the Great Lakes' best kept vacation secrets. Located atop Indianhead Mountain in the far western corner of Michigan's Upper Peninsula, this resort offers year-round activities. During the winter, Indianhead is home to one of the newest ski resorts in the Midwest, Bear Creek. The mountaintop setting overlooking Lake Superior and the largest national forest in Michigan is ideal for summer hiking, biking, fishing, canoeing, and simply enjoying nature at its best.

SPECIFICS: Indianhead Mountain Resort hires approximately 75 to 100 new employees each year to fill its 310 peak season staff positions. Summer seasonal staff should be available to work from June 15 through October 12; winter staff should be available from November 14 through April 3. Applications are accepted throughout the year. Jobs are available for cooks, prep cooks, dishwashers, dining room servers, dining room buspersons, dining room hosts/hostesses, janitors, housekeepers, laundry attendants, front desk clerks, night auditors, and reservationists. During the winter season there are also positions for ski rental shop staff, lift operators, lift attendants, snowmakers, ski instructors, ski school desk secretaries, and "kindershole" (children's) aides.

INSIDER TIPS: Indianhead looks for service- and hospitality-minded individuals who are flexible and willing to work shift work. Employees should also have outgoing personalities and be able to cope well when working under pressure. Most employees find housing within three to ten miles of the resort. Shared housing ranges from $150 to $250 per month per person.

PERKS: All winter employees receive a midweek ski pass.

TO APPLY: Applicants should send a cover letter and résumé to Mary Jo Valesano, Personnel Director, Indianhead Mountain Resort, Wakefield, Michigan 49968; (906) 229-5181.

INDIGO LAKES RESORT
(Daytona Beach, Florida)
Year-Round

Indigo Lakes Resort sits on a portion of the former 20,000-acre Mount Oswald plantation in Daytona Beach, Florida. Today, the former plantation has been transformed into a 212-room luxury resort hotel and conference center. Famous Indigo Lakes visitors have included former president Reagan, Paul Newman, Burt Reynolds, Reggie Jackson, and astronaut John Glenn. The grounds of the resort are noted for hosting a wide array of wildlife including eagles, foxes, raccoons, alligators, and deer.

SPECIFICS: Indigo Lakes hires more than 200 new employees each year to fill its 370-plus staff positions. The resort hires all typical hotel employees including front desk clerks, food and beverage servers, bartenders, cooks, cashiers, hosts/hostesses, buspersons, housekeepers, bartenders, and maintenance staff. All positions are year-round. There is no application deadline.

INSIDER TIPS: The resort looks for "honest, motivated, career-oriented applicants with good working skills."

PERKS: During off-duty hours, employees are permitted to use the resort's golf and tennis facilities, spa, and pool. Other staff perks include free shift meals, free uniforms, paid vacation, and a comprehensive insurance program.

TO APPLY: Applicants should send a cover letter, résumé, photograph, and SARP to Sue Wylan, Personnel Manager, Indigo Lakes Resort, P.O. Box 10809, Daytona Beach, Florida 32020; (904) 254-3658.

KETTLE FALLS HOTEL, INC.
(Voyageurs National Park, Minnesota)
Seasonal (Summer)

Step back in time to an era when fur traders, gold miners, and explorers paddled their canoes through the waters of what is known today as Voyageurs National Park. This vast wilderness area looks much as it did in the seventeen and eighteen hundreds, when rival fur traders navigated this region of bogs, marshes, beaver ponds, and lakes. In the midst of this spectacular national park, the Kettle Falls Hotel has been offering guests a base from which to explore the park for more than eighty years. This summer resort hotel is accessible only by boat. The historic hotel dates back to 1913 and was first turned into a tourist spot by Bob and Lill Williams, who purchased the hotel for four barrels of whiskey and $1,000 in 1918.

SPECIFICS: The Kettle Falls Hotel receives approximately forty applications each year for its twenty annual job openings. The hotel's staff totals twenty-two summer workers. Although some hiring continues after the summer season begins, most jobs begin May 15 and last through the end of October. Apply before May 1 to be considered for main summer hiring. A few late summer positions are also available for summer school students. Applications are accepted for dock staff, cooks, bartenders, waitpersons, dishwashers, and cleaning personnel. Most summer hiring is completed by mid-May.

INSIDER TIPS: "Our hotel is located in Voyageurs National Park in Minnesota and is on the National Register of Historic Sights. We are located seventeen miles by boat from the nearest road access. Be aware that due to the hotel's isolation, phone service can occasionally be erratic and unreliable."

PERKS: Free room and board are provided for all hotel staff. A 25 cent per hour bonus is paid at the end of the season to all staff members who fulfill their employment contracts.

TO APPLY: Applicants should either write for an official application or send a cover letter and photograph to Rebecca Williams, Vice President & Personnel Manager, Kettle Falls Hotel, Inc., P.O. Box

1272, International Falls, Minnesota 56649; (218) 374-3511 (summer) or (218) 286-5685 (winter).

LAKE ARROWHEAD HILTON RESORT
(Lake Arrowhead, California)
Seasonal (Summer) and Year-Round

The Lake Arrowhead Hilton Resort is a beautiful 261-room lodge on the shores of Lake Arrowhead in the San Bernardino Mountains. Lake Arrowhead is renowned for waterskiing, swimming, boating, and fishing.

SPECIFICS: Hilton's Lake Arrowhead Resort employs up to 390 staff members and hires 150 new employees each year. Both long-term as well as seasonal employees are recruited. Seasonal help should be available from Memorial Day through Labor Day. Positions are available for pool attendants, food and beverage waitpersons, buspersons, cooks, cocktail servers, pantry/food prep persons, bartenders, bell persons, valet attendants, and interns from college hospitality degree programs.

INSIDER TIPS: Some experience in hospitality or service industry (restaurant or hotel) work is preferred. Management searches for people-oriented candidates with an interest in the hotel and lodging industry. Applicants should be able to work a flexible schedule with full-time hours from at least Memorial Day through Labor Day.

PERKS: Employee benefits include free use of the resort's pool and health club (Monday–Thursday), tips, and free meals.

TO APPLY: Applicants should send a cover letter, résumé, and SARP to Lake Arrowhead Hilton Resort, Janie Kirk, Human Resources Director, Box 1699, Lake Arrowhead, California 92352; (714) 336-1511, ext. 652.

LAKE LOUISE INN
(Lake Louise, Alberta, Canada)
Seasonal (Summer and Winter/Spring) and Year-Round

The Lake Louise Inn is a year-round resort hotel in the Canadian Rockies. The hotel is located just off the Trans Canada highway in Lake Louise village.

SPECIFICS: The Lake Louise Inn hires approximately sixty new employees each year to fill its 125 staff positions. Positions are available for both year-round and seasonal staff. Summer staff should be available to work from late May through late September. Winter jobs begin in late November and extend into late April. Winter seasonal applications should be tendered by November 1 and summer applications must be complete by early February. Applications are accepted for chambermaids, laundry workers, food servers (experience preferred but not required), front desk clerks, and management personnel (year-round positions only, experience required).

INSIDER TIPS: Management seeks "well-groomed, personable, enthusiastic, intelligent applicants with experience where necessary." Foreign applicants must have a valid Canadian work visa.

PERKS: Shared housing is provided for staff members at the rate of CAN $2.00 to CAN $4.00 per day (rate subject to change). All housing units are coed and generally house a maximum of six staffers.

TO APPLY: Applicants should send a cover letter, résumé, photograph, and SARP to Personnel Department, Lake Louise Inn, P.O. Box 209, Lake Louise, Alberta, T0L 1E0 Canada; (403) 522-3791.

MISSION POINT RESORT
(Mackinac Island, Michigan)

Seasonal (Summer)

The Mission Point Resort is sprawled over 18-plus acres of land on Michigan's popular vacation spot, Mackinac Island. This 245-room resort serves as both a tourist destination as well as a full-facility conference center.

SPECIFICS: The Mission Point Resort hires more than 325 new employees each year to fill its 250-person staff. The resort's season runs from May 1 through October 31. Jobs are available for waitpersons, hosts/hostesses, buspersons, cooks, food prep staff, bakery employees, dishwashers, kitchen sanitation specialists, maintenance staff, grounds keepers, bellmen, dock porters, convention set-up staff, reservations staff, switchboard operators, clerical personnel, front desk clerks, accounting clerks, night auditors, bike rental clerks, housekeepers, laundry workers, bartenders, cocktail servers, bar porters, security guards, and storeroom clerks. In 1989 wages began at $2.25 per hour plus tips for waiters and waitresses; $4.00 to $5.50 for most other positions (subject to change). All applications must be submitted prior to April 15.

INSIDER TIPS: Most hiring is done in February and March and all successful applicants are notified by April 15. While experience is preferred for skilled positions, the resort will train unskilled employees for a variety of posts.

PERKS: Employees are provided dormitory-style room and board at a nominal weekly rate. Management sponsors numerous staff recreational programs.

TO APPLY: Applicants should either write for an official application or send a cover letter, résumé, photograph, and SARP to Human Resources Manager, Mission Point Hotel, P.O. Box 430, Mackinac Island, Michigan 49757; (906) 847-3312.

NATIONAL PARK CONCESSIONS, INC.
(Isle Royale National Park, Michigan)
Seasonal (Summer)

Located on a small island in northwestern Lake Superior, Isle Royale National Park is set on a beautiful natural wilderness island. The island houses the Rock Harbor Lodge but is otherwise undisturbed by mankind. Trails offer visitors access to many parts of the island; there are no roads or vehicles on Isle Royale. National Park Concessions operates both the lodge and various other guest services including a store, boat rentals, boat tours, and marina.

SPECIFICS: National Park Concessions hires sixty-five new employees each year to fill its staff positions in Isle Royale National Park. Approximately 100 applications are received annually for positions at Isle Royale. Jobs are available for seasonal summer employment. Applications for summer employment must be completed by February 28. For further application information see the National Park Concessions listing in the Mountain chapter.

WHITE OAKS INN & RACQUET CLUB
(Niagara-on-the-Lake, Ontario, Canada)
Seasonal (Summer) and Year-Round

The White Oaks Inn & Racquet Club is a top-rated hotel and sports center offering indoor and outdoor tennis courts, squash and racquetball courts, nautilus, aerobics, and swimming. The resort is located on the beautiful Niagara peninsula, close to the Niagara Falls.

SPECIFICS: The White Oaks employs 130 summer seasonal and year-round staff. Summer seasonal staff should be available from May through September. Applications are accepted for waitpersons, banquet servers (experience required), kitchen staff, dishwashers, and porters. Wages for food servers start at CAN$5.50 per hour; porters start at CAN$6.00.

INSIDER TIPS: The resort looks for "honest, competent, well-groomed staff with an eagerness to learn."

PERKS: Off-duty staff are permitted to use the resort's recreational facilities during off-peak hours.

TO APPLY: Applicants should either write for an official application or send a cover letter, résumé, and SARP to Personnel Department, White Oaks Inn & Racquet Club, R.R. 4 Taylor Road, Niagara-on-the-Lake, Ontario L0S 1J0, Canada; (416) 688-2550, ext. 146.

The following listings, found under the chapter headings given below, also include positions near lakes:

AMUSEMENT & THEME PARKS
Cedar Point   Ontario Place Corporation

COASTS & BEACHES
National Park Concessions, Inc.

HIGH ADVENTURE
Tonquin Valley Pack Trips

MISCELLANEOUS
Holiday Inn   Marriott's Orlando World
  Maingate West   Center Hotel

MOUNTAINS
Chateau Lake Louise   Lake Tahoe Horizon Casino
Cheyenne Mountain   Resort
  Conference Resort   Signal Mountain Lodge
Glacier National Park
  Hotels

RIVERS
Herman & Helen's Marina

SNOW & SKIING
Seven Springs Mountain Resort

Deserts

ADVENTURE DISCOVERY TOURS
(Moab, Utah)

Seasonal (Summer)

Adventure Discovery Tours operates guided mountain bike expeditions in both Canyonlands and Arches national parks. Mountain bike treks range from half-day easy rides to three-day challenging rides over the White Rim Trail. Although summer is the company's high season, trips are operated in the spring as well with a Spring Ski/River trip special.

SPECIFICS: Adventure Discovery Tours and Adrift Adventures employ approximately twenty-two staff members each year during the peak summer season of May through September. Winter and year-round staff usually numbers approximately seven to eight individuals. Applications are accepted for mountain bike guide positions. Mountain bike guides must have both Red Cross advanced first aid and CPR certificates. Starting salaries range from $65 to $80 per day. There is no official application deadline.

INSIDER TIPS: "No experience is necessary although multiple languages as well as camping experience would be helpful."

PERKS: Guides camp and eat free with their groups while on tour.

TO APPLY: Applicants should either write for an official application form or send a cover letter, résumé, and photograph to Myke Hughes, Adventure Discovery Tours, P.O. Box 577, Moab, Utah 84532; (801) 259-8594.

DESERT INN HOTEL & CASINO
(Las Vegas, Nevada)
Seasonal (limited opportunities all seasons) and Year-Round

The Desert Inn is an 830-room hotel complete with a health spa, eighteen-hole golf course, restaurants, lounges, and casino. Located on the world famous Las Vegas casino strip, the Desert Inn is a landmark in Las Vegas.

SPECIFICS: The Desert Inn employs 1,800 staff members and expects to hire approximately 800 new employees per year. Applications are accepted for a wide variety of positions in all departments including specialty shops, spa, accounting, human resources, purchasing, marketing, sales, food and beverage, hotel, housekeeping, and casino.

INSIDER TIPS: "We look for friendly, courteous, and outgoing people for our staffing needs—individuals who truly enjoy their work and make our guests feel welcome.

PERKS: The Desert Inn hosts special employee events such as golf tournaments, parties, and promotions. All employees are entitled to free shift meals, subsidized insurance, vacations, and holidays.

TO APPLY: Applicants should send a cover letter, résumé, and SARP to Douglas McCombs, Director of Human Resources, Desert Inn & Country Club, Box 93598, Las Vegas, Nevada 89193; (702) 733-4444.

GRAND CANYON NATIONAL PARK LODGES
(Grand Canyon National Park, South Rim Village, Arizona)
Seasonal (Summer) and Year-Round

Grand Canyon National Park Lodges is an official National Park concessionaire, providing food, lodging, retail outlets, and transportation services to the more than three million visitors who arrive at the canyon's south rim each year.

SPECIFICS: Grand Canyon National Park Lodges employs 1,100 employees during its peak summer season and 650 employees in the winter. The company hires approximately 1,000 staffers each year. The most common available positions are for kitchen utility staff, guest room attendants, retail clerks, food and beverage cashiers, buspersons, hosts, and cooks. While applications are accepted throughout the year, the busy season at the Grand Canyon is Easter through Labor Day. Initial work agreements are written for three, four, five, or six months, with cash bonuses paid upon completion of the work agreement. Wages for entry-level positions begin above minimum wage.

INSIDER TIPS: Grand Canyon National Park Lodges looks for applicants who are nineteen years of age or older. They seek a good employment record and a willingness to accept an entry-level position. A professional appearance and the ability to work with the public is essential. This is hard work in a beautiful location.

PERKS: Dormitory-style housing is available and housing costs are deducted from wages. Meals are available in employee cafeterias at reduced rates. Comprehensive medical, dental, and vision insurance are available. Employees are eligible for ten days paid vacation after one year of employment. All staff may ride free on Canyon tours on a space-available basis. A recreation center, organized recreational activities, well-equipped weight training facility, and reduced rate employee trips are available. For days off, Grand Canyon is a hiker's paradise.

TO APPLY: To receive information and an application form write or call: Grand Canyon National Park Lodges, Recruiting Coordinator, P.O. Box 699, Personnel Department, Grand Canyon, Arizona 86023; (602) 638-2343, Monday through Friday (8:00 A.M. to noon or 1:00 P.M. to 5:00 P.M. Mountain Standard Time).

MARRIOTT'S MOUNTAIN SHADOWS
(Scottsdale, Arizona)
Seasonal (limited to on-call banquet employees) and Year-Round

Marriott's Mountain Shadows resort is located between the exclusive desert resort areas of Scottsdale and Paradise Valley, Arizona. Mountain Shadows is nestled at the foot of Camelback Mountain with the broad blue Arizona skies and the rugged beauty of the desert for its backdrop.

SPECIFICS: Marriott's Mountain Shadows hires approximately 400 new staff members each year to fill its 450 to 480 employee positions. While most positions are year-round, there are a limited number of seasonal positions for "on-call" banquet personnel. For applicants without prior experience, the resort will train employees for positions as front desk clerks, reservationists, and housekeepers. For those with typing experience, positions are available as sales secretaries and catering secretary. For those with prior restaurant experience, jobs are available as food servers, hosts/hostesses, and buspersons. Applications are also accepted from individuals with experience in accounting, cooking, and engineering. Starting pay ranges from minimum wage to $6.30 per hour depending on the position and experience (subject to change). There is no application deadline.

INSIDER TIPS: We look for applicants with a "positive attitude, flexible work schedule, potential, and applicable experience."

PERKS: Employees are eligible for complimentary meals, insurance, uniforms, tips, profit sharing, and paid vacation and holidays.

TO APPLY: Although the company will accept résumés (send with a cover letter) sent through the mail, management requests applicants apply in person. For further information contact Ilona Hargitay, Human Resources Recruiter, Marriott's Mountain Shadows, 5641 E. Lincoln Drive, Scottsdale, Arizona 85253; (602) 948-7111, ext. 1450.

NATIONAL PARK CONCESSIONS, INC.
(Big Bend National Park, Texas)
Seasonal (Summer and Winter) and Year-Round

Big Bend National Park is located in the center of the "Big Bend Country" of west Texas. Big Bend is one of the United States' most diverse national parks. The park's grounds include the vast lowlands of the Rio Grande floodplain, the high country of the Chisos Mountains, and the dry seabed of the Chihuahuan Desert. National Park Concessions operates the Chisos Mountains Lodge and a nearby service station at an elevation of 5,400 feet. The park is open year-round.

SPECIFICS: National Park Concessions hires approximately thirty new employees each year from a field of 200 applicants to work in Big Bend National Park. The company has a total of sixty employees working in the park during peak season. Jobs are available for both year-round and summer and winter seasonal employment. For further information see the National Park Concessions listing in the Mountains chapter.

PACK CREEK RANCH
(Moab, Utah)

Seasonal (Summer and Winter) and Year-Round

Pack Creek is a country inn in the finest tradition. Located in the foothills of the LaSal Mountains, the ranch affords a cool retreat from the sizzling desert sun of southeastern Utah. Horseback riding is the main ranch activity.

SPECIFICS: Pack Creek Ranch receives fifteen to twenty applications each year for its ten annual job openings. The ranch's peak season staff totals seventeen. All employees rotate duties between housekeeping, grounds keeping, kitchen work, food serving, and wrangling. Starting salaries are minimum wage plus tips. Summer seasonal applicants are given priority if they can work from May 1 through October 30. However, applicants who can only work June through August are often hired.

INSIDER TIPS: Jobs here fill early. Your application should be completed before mid-February. Tips are split between all employees and management reports that gratuities average about $1.00 per hour worked.

PERKS: "We run the ranch in a family atmosphere. Employees may go on free horse rides anytime they are off duty on a space-available basis. We can often arrange for staff to go on river trips at a free or discounted rate."

TO APPLY: Applicants should send a cover letter, résumé, and photograph to Jane Sleight, Pack Creek Ranch, P.O. Box 1270, Moab, Utah 84532; (801) 259-5505.

RIO GRANDE RAPID TRANSIT/DESERT VOYAGERS
(Pilar, New Mexico)
Seasonal (Summer) and Year-Round

Rio Grande Rapid Transit offers half-day, one-day, and multi-day float trips on New Mexico's Rio Grande and Rio Chama and on Arizona's Salt River and Rio Verde.

SPECIFICS: Rio Grande Rapid Transit and Desert Voyagers hires approximately four new employees each year to compliment its fifteen-person staff. Jobs are available for both seasonal as well as year-round river guides, shuttle drivers, and shore duty staff.

INSIDER TIPS: Employees must have advanced first aid and CPR certificates as well as a Class VI or VIII driver's license.

TO APPLY: Applicants should send a cover letter, résumé, and SARP to Operations Manager, Rio Grande Rapid Transit, Box A, Pilar, New Mexico 87571; (505) 758-9700.

SCOTTY'S CASTLE NATIONAL MONUMENT, OPERATED BY TW RECREATIONAL SERVICES, INC.
(Death Valley, California)
Seasonal and Year-Round

Often cited as the hottest spot in the United States on the morning network news, Death Valley provides a beautiful slice of the stark desert ecosystem. Imagine spending your winter working in a place where the daily temperature can soar to over 100 degrees!

SPECIFICS: TW Recreational Services employs 400 seasonal staff members to work in its various park operations from mid-May through mid-October. Employment is available in the following departments: tour guides, front desk, dining room, cafeteria, snack bar, kitchen, housekeeping, service station, maintenance, cocktail lounge, accounting, and gift store. Some management positions are also available. The minimum age required for all positions is eighteen and proof of age and citizenship are required before starting work.

INSIDER TIPS: As with all national park concessionaire jobs, TW Recreational Services enforces a strict dress code and drug policy. Details of employee rules and regulations are provided with the official application.

PERKS: What other job absolutely guarantees that you'll never have to shovel snow? Full room and board in the national park are provided at minimal cost to all employees. The company also organizes numerous recreational and social activities for its employees.

TO APPLY: Applicants should write for an official application from LaMar Snyder, Personnel Manager, TW Recreational Services, P.O. Box 400, 451 N. Main Street, Cedar City, Utah 84720; (801) 586-9476.

TW RECREATIONAL SERVICES, INC.
(Grand Canyon National Park, Utah)
Seasonal (Summer)

TW operates the lodge at the North Rim of the Grand Canyon. The lodge commands one of the most magnificent views in the world. Situated in the desert at an altitude of 8,000 feet, the air is crisp, pine and aspen trees abound, and the awesome Grand Canyon National Park is your backyard.

SPECIFICS: See Scotty's Castle listing above.

TW RECREATIONAL SERVICES, INC.
(Zion National Park, Utah)
Seasonal (Summer)

Awesome is the only description for the monumental rock formations in Zion National Park. Zion is situated midway between Bryce
Canyon National Park and the Grand Canyon's North Rim. The cliffs
of Lady Mountain, Temple Somawava, and Angel's Landing face the
scenic Virgin River and look down onto the canyon floor where TW
Recreational Services operates the lodge. TW is the exclusive National Park Service concessionaire for Zion. It also operates lodges at
Bryce Canyon, Grand Canyon, and Scotty's Castle national parks and
monuments. (See separate listings herein.)

SPECIFICS: See Scotty's Castle listing above.

WATERWORLD USA
(Phoenix, Arizona)
Seasonal (Summer)

Cool water comes to the hot Arizona desert with the annual opening
of Arizona's Waterworld USA, a family fun water park featuring
wave pools, water slides, children's areas, and numerous other activities centered around fun in the sun.

SPECIFICS: Waterworld USA hires more than 300 new applicants
each summer to fill its 200 regular staff positions. Approximately 500
applications are received annually. The park gives preference to applicants who can work weekends in the spring and fall and daily in
the summer. However, many employees who can only work during
the summer are also hired. Jobs are available for ride operators, lifeguards (must have current CPR and first aid certificates), managers,
security officers, park ambassadors, clerical staff, emergency medical

technicians (EMT certificate or qualifications in emergency medical care required), accounting/marketing interns, food service staff, grounds keepers, landscape staff, and ticket salespersons. Staff members earn from minimum wage to $5.00 per hour.

INSIDER TIPS: Applicants must be enthusiastic, reliable, and have high grooming standards. The most important qualification is a genuine desire to please the public. The park calls its employees ambassadors.

PERKS: Employees are permitted unlimited use of the park's facilities when not on duty. Additionally, Waterworld USA gives employees free passport park admission tickets and sponsors numerous employee parties and events as well as an employee benefit and incentive program.

TO APPLY: Applicants should send a cover letter and résumé to Personnel Office, Waterworld USA, 4243 W. Pinnacle Peak Road, Phoenix, Arizona 85310; (602) 266-5299.

The following listings, found under the chapter headings given below, also include positions in desert areas:

LAKES

ARA Leisure Services/Lake
  Powell Resorts & Marinas

MOUNTAINS

TW Recreational Services

RIVERS

Adrift Adventures
Adventure/Discovery
  Tours
Canyoneers, Inc.

Grand Canyon Expedition
  Company
Libra Expeditions
Wild & Scenic, Inc.

Tour Escorts

Traveling for Free as a Tour Escort

Pursuing the Dream Job, the Fantasy Career: The Companies that Hire, the People They Hire

Chapter Introduction by Arthur Frommer

A "tour escort": The words imply a dream job, the fantasy career. In blue blazer and natty scarf (one typical vision), you stroll through life with well-mannered groups of sensitive adults as they view the storied sites of antiquity.

Just think: you are traveling for free, and getting paid to boot!

The reality can be jarringly different. As a paid travel professional, on call around the clock, your phone rings at all hours of the night with unreasonable demands: change my room, get me more blankets or towels. You learn the awful truth: that of every forty persons on earth, thirty-eight are gentle, caring souls and two are monsters. In my own past life as a tour operator, I sent an escort to China with twenty auto dealers and their spouses, of whom two refused to eat Chinese food after the first day. The poor tour escort, in addition to her other tasks, labored in a hot hotel kitchen at mealtimes to prepare hamburgers or spaghetti for the obstinate duo. Still another member of the group was a surly drunk who slipped pitchers of Mai Tais onto the bus, creating scandal and problems in a dozen Chinese towns.

Want an additional whiff of reality? Well, people get sick while on tour, and you, the tour escort, rush them to the hospital at 3 A.M. and pace the waiting room. People occasionally die while on tour—that being a tiring activity—and you, the tour escort, trudge to a grisly foreign morgue to ship the body home.

Yet for all the horrors, thousands of Americans—in love with travel, in love with people—are joyfully at work as tour escorts, either part-time or full-time; and many thousands more would kill to land a like position. In this essay I appraise that dream vocation, and provide pointers—based on interviews with personnel directors of nearly a dozen tour operators—on how to be hired.

THE COMPANIES THAT HIRE

As travel becomes increasingly group-oriented (economies of scale bring the lower prices to groups), creating an obvious need for one escort per group, more than 450 tour companies are now making use of tour escorts—some hiring fewer than ten a year, others as many as 200. (Author's Note: The *Jobs in Paradise* listings that follow detail job opportunities with many of the larger tour operators.)

To obtain a more comprehensive list of every such potential employer, including escort-using companies in your own immediate vicinity, I'd go to a local retail travel agency and ask (politely and shyly) to look at their current copy of one of the "travel trade personnel directories." These yearly publications, some the size of a small telephone book, are issued by the three major trade periodicals: *Travel Weekly, Travel Agent,* and *Travel Trade.* Each lists all the major companies of the travel industry. By scanning the sections called "tour operators," and reading the descriptions of each, you can usually spot the many firms that hire tour escorts.

THE PEOPLE THEY HIRE

The activity is largely a woman's profession—to such an extent that some personnel managers say they now give preference to men to redress the balance!

THE PLACES TO WHICH YOU GO

By a three-to-one ratio (and probably higher than that), domestic tours outnumber international ones as opportunities for escorting; you are far more likely to crisscross New England than New Zealand. And this numerical imbalance has an important part in determining the duties you'll perform.

On an international tour you'll seldom be asked to deliver the lectured commentary on what the group is seeing. That's done by local art historians or other specialists picked up along the way (who accompany the group, say, to the Uffizzi Galleries in Florence) or by full-time, highly paid British tour guides assigned to the bus for the entire tour. The tour escort from the United States, if there is one, performs the homelier tasks: dealing with mishaps and travel emergencies, overseeing transfers of baggage, watching the air connections, acting as liaison between the group and their hotels, or between the group and the tour operator's head office. Ironically, the foreign tour is thus the easiest to escort.

In the United States, by contrast, both practice and tradition cast the tour escort, in most cases, as the commentator: you provide a running lecture on all that passes by.

Accordingly, virtually all tour companies cite "a knowledge of the place," "experience in the area," as one of the prime requisites for a majority of their escort positions. That's not to say that you must memorize scores of facts about various destinations to get the job; no escort is made to "solo" on a particular tour until he or she has first accompanied a trained escort on at least two departures of the same tour. But to the extent that you are already heavily traveled, or know particular areas well, you become a prime prospect for domestic escorting.

Therefore, if you know New England like the palm of your hand, if you grew up on the coast of California, if Alaska was your kindergarten or Florida your life-long home, say so. Lead off your résumé with travel experience and half the job is done.

THE CRITERIA THEY USE

With ten applications for every opening, tour escorting rivals the theater world in the brutal competitiveness of its job-seeking process. The analogy is apt. "We're looking for stars," says Nancy Jepson of Globus Gateway/Cosmos Tours. "You have to be a bit egotistical to be a tour director, which is why unemployed actresses are often our best prospects."

To find out the criteria leading tour companies use for choosing escorts, I interviewed (by phone) the personnel managers for a dozen large tour companies. Apart from a knowledge of the destinations to which the tours go—a talent heavily stressed by most—what other attributes cause ten résumés to be plucked from a stack of a hundred?

"Let me tell you first what we're not seeking," says John Stachnik of Mayflower Tours, Downers Grove, Illinois. "We're not impressed by people in a mid-life crisis seeking a 'cure' through travel or escaping from reality—and we can read those aims in a great many of the applications we receive."

"We're looking for people who like being leaders, responsible for the welfare of a group," says Bruce Beckham of Beckham Travel, Canton, Massachusetts. "I scan the résumés mainly for organizational background, prior experience as the head of a group or effort, however small. . . ."

"The underlying quality," says Rohan Wanigatunga, director of tour managers for Olson/Travelworld, "is that they be caring; they must enhance the tour on a personal level, go all out. In the very first interview with them, perhaps by phone, we are looking for that caring quality."

"Too often," says John Stachnik of Mayflower Tours, "we hear applicants stressing how much they love to travel. We would rather hear them say, 'I love to be with people.'"

The subsidiary qualities for success in the field? "The strength of Superman and the patience of God" (says Joan Dunne of Pacific Delight Tours, New York City); "good grooming, we stress appearance very, very strongly" (Bill Strickland, American Express, New York City); "high energy level, liking to have fun" (Kathy Ackers, Rural Route Tours); "incredible patience, mature judgment, and the vigor to bear up under a physically demanding job: the end of the day is not the end of their day; that's when problems start" (Dick Sundby, tour escort supervisor for Tauck Tours).

Possessed of such qualities, how do you bring them to the fore and snare the job? Through persistence, answer all my interviewees. The mailing of a résumé to multiple tour operators is only the first step in a protracted campaign. You follow up by phone, perhaps two or three times in a season. You regard turndowns as mere temporary setbacks—the simple lack of an opening in an industry whose needs are notoriously volatile, fluid. You shrug off rejection, press on in requesting interviews, submit updated résumés. One reason why some companies prefer graduates of the two major schools of "tour management" is because attendance at such a school evidences a profound determination to enter the field.

If some companies demand prior experience of their potential escorts (as American Express, for one, does), you obtain that experience by leading a small, local tour for one of your own local tour companies or travel agencies, even for free. And then you headline your résumé with that event. Either way—with or without experience, with or without tour-school training, but through persistence—you obtain an interview and presumably obtain the job.

THE JOB ITSELF

Once employed, do you work full time or part time? In most instances you work seasonally, say all my informants; at least 70% of all tour escorts do it on a part-time basis, and only 10% to 20% of the 450 companies hiring tour escorts are able to employ people year-round. Even the giant Tauck Tours employs the great bulk of its escorts during the May through October season only (but operates every day of the week throughout that season). Actually, according to Tauck's supervisor, Dick Sundby, that intense seasonality is well suited to the type of escort Tauck seeks to hire. "We like people who have other things in their lives. We look for escorts willing to work their heads off May through October and use the other months to pursue life goals."

How much do escorts earn? While the arrangements vary broadly from firm to firm, most companies report an average of $80 to $100 a day while on tour (and tours can extend for as many as fourteen or twenty-one days), much of it from tips that escorts traditionally receive from their passengers. And since escorts are usually housed and fed at the tour company's expense, most of that income can be retained as savings. "You live a rather high life when you're a tour director," says Nancy Jepson of Globus Gateway/Cosmos Tours. "If you're doing it full time, you often don't pay rent, because the company will put you up when you're between tours. If you're away seven months, you make a lot of money."

But: "It's a 24-hour job," Ms. Jepson continues. "You have to be a little crazy to do it, and you have no social life. At the same time, it's the most rewarding job you'll ever have."

Which is why those résumés keep arriving in an endless stream, seeking the dream job, the fantasy career.

PROFILE OF TAMI TIMMER
TOUR ESCORT, GRAMERCY TRAVEL SYSTEM

"Tour escorting is more about people than travel."

HOMETOWN: Chicago, Illinois
SCHOOL: Texas Christian University (2 years)
JOBS: Tour Director (Gramercy Travel System, tour escort to Alaska, Mexico, and the Caribbean)

"Three years ago I was fortunate enough to land a job as a tour escort for Singleworld Cruises & Tours *(operated by the Gramercy Travel System, see listing herein)*. What I learned almost instantly is that tour escorting is more about people than travel."

Tami's experience is similar to that of most tour escorts. As Tami explains, "If you escort enough tours you can see quite a bit of the world. However, if you don't love working with people you will hate your job. Like most tour escorts, I find myself leading the same tour time and time again. If you don't thrive off working closely with people you get bored quickly. After all, how exciting can the same port be when you are visiting it for the three-hundredth time!

"To land a tour escort job you have to convince the employer that you are good at and love working with people. As a tour escort your phone will ring in the middle of the night several times each week with minor emergencies. Whether it's a group member who is locked out of their room or a major medical emergency, you have to be able to handle the situation professionally and with a smile. I think that one of the main skills necessary to do this job is the ability to think clearly and effectively in an emergency."

Tour escorting is a job that Tami loves. "I wouldn't trade my job for any other in the world. Sure I have traveled to some exotic places, but what really stands out in my mind are the hundreds of great people I have met from all across the country."

ALLIED TOURS AND TRAVEL
(Sioux City, Iowa)
Seasonal (Summer)

Allied Tours and Travel operates escorted tours for senior citizens throughout the United States and Canada. More than seventy tour departures are offered annually.

SPECIFICS: Allied employs approximately twelve tour escorts each year.

INSIDER TIPS: While most of Allied's tour escorts are senior citizens themselves, some younger escorts are hired. Applicants must be able to handle effectively a group of approximately forty elderly people and know how to handle emergency situations. Working with the elderly requires a special sensitivity for seniors.

PERKS: As with almost all tour operators, Allied pays most travel, meal, and lodging expenses for leaders.

TO APPLY: Send a cover letter and résumé to Lucille Gilbert, Allied Tour and Travel, P.O. Box 568, Sioux City, Iowa 51102; (800) 228-8002 or (712) 255-0141.

AMERICAN EXPRESS
(New York, New York, and London, England)
Seasonal (All Seasons) and Year-Round

American Express, one of the largest tour operators in the world, operates numerous escorted tours throughout the world.

SPECIFICS: American Express employs approximately 500 tour escorts each year. Approximately half of all positions are in Europe while the remainder are in the United States and Canada.

INSIDER TIPS: American Express calls their escorts "tour managers." Tour managers for American Express are among the best-qualified and most experienced in the world. Prior experience is required.

PERKS: As with almost all tour operators, American Express pays most travel, meal, and lodging expenses for leaders.

TO APPLY: For tours throughout Europe, applicants should send a cover letter and résumé to Mr. Angelo Pozzi, Tour Manager Department, American Express, 19–20 Berners Street, London, England W1P 3DD; phone 637-8600. For tour manager positions for U.S. and Canadian tours, apply to American Express, Destination Services, 65 Broadway, New York, New York 10006; (212) 493-6500.

CASSER TOURS
(New York, New York)
Seasonal (All Seasons) and Year-Round

Casser Tours operates escorted tours throughout Canada and the United States (occasional departures to other countries).

SPECIFICS: Casser employs approximately fifty tour escorts each year.

INSIDER TIPS: "Personality and people skills are the key to getting a job. We prefer some knowledge of the tour region, but don't require experts. We train all escorts before their departures."

PERKS: As with almost all tour operators, Casser pays a meal allowance and lodging expenses for leaders.

TO APPLY: Applicants should send a cover letter, résumé, and photograph (optional) to Mike Azzolino, Casser Tours, 46 W. 43rd Street, New York, New York 10036; (212) 840-6500 or (800) 251-1411.

CONTIKI
(New Zealand, Australia, England, and USA)
Year-Round

Contiki is one of the world's largest tour operators specializing in escorted trips for eighteen- to thirty-five-year-olds. Company trips include whitewater rafting, jet boating, hiking, and ski vacations.

SPECIFICS: Contiki's worldwide operations employ numerous tour escorts (called "tour managers" at Contiki). Employees for each country are hired by the local offices.

INSIDER TIPS: According to management, Contiki looks for outgoing, confident people aged approximately twenty-three through thirty-five. All employees must be clean-cut and good working with people. Long-term employees with an interest in a travel industry career are preferred. Personal interviews are preferred to phone interviews.

PERKS: Contiki pays all travel, meal, and lodging expenses for its tour managers.

TO APPLY: Applicants should write for an official application. For positions leading trips in New Zealand write Operations Manager, Contiki Travel Ltd., 100 Anzac Road, P.O. Box 6774, Wellesley, St. Auckland, Auckland 1, New Zealand; phone: (09) 398-824. For jobs working in Australia write Operations Manager, Contiki Australia Pty. Ltd., 100 Clarence Street, Sydney, NSW 2000, Australia; phone: Sydney 290-3977. For trips to England, Ireland, Scotland, and Europe, apply to Operations Manager, Contiki Travel Agency, 7 Rathbone Place, London, W1P IDE, England; phone: (01) 637-121. For positions leading trips through the United States, Asia, and Africa write to Operations Manager, Contiki Travel America Ltd., 1432 East Katella Avenue, Anaheim, California 92805; (714) 937-0611.

COSMOS TOURS/GLOBUS GATEWAY TOURS
(Los Angeles, California, and Rego Park, New York)
Seasonal (All Seasons) and Year-Round

Cosmos operates budget escorted motorcoach tours throughout Canada and the United States. Most tours last ten days.

SPECIFICS: Cosmos employs approximately ninety full-time tour escorts per year, plus numerous temporary tour leaders.

INSIDER TIPS: "Convince us that you *love* people and that you are dying to do this type of work. The job has nothing to do with a love of travel and has everything to do with a love of people." Cosmos will sometimes hire on the basis of a phone interview, but prefers personal interviews. Most summer season hiring is completed by the end of April.

PERKS: As with almost all tour operators, Cosmos pays most travel, meal, and lodging expenses for leaders.

TO APPLY: Applicants should send a cover letter, résumé, and photograph (optional) to Nancy Jepson, Manager, Cosmos Tours, 95-25 Queens Boulevard, Rego Park, New York 11374-4511; (718) 268-1700. For tours departing from the West Coast apply to Kate Robinson, Cosmos Tours, 727 W. 7th Street, Los Angeles, California 90017; (213) 621-3196.

GRAMERCY TRAVEL SYSTEM
(operating Singleworld Cruises & Tours)
(Rye, New York)
Seasonal (Summer) and Year-Round and Part-Time

Gramercy operates Singleworld Cruises & Tours, the nation's largest wholesaler of trips for singles. Known for its individualized service and attention to detail, Singleworld has been the leader in cruises and tours for singles for more than thirty years. Their Singleworld division has thousands of tour and cruise departures annually. Some trips are exclusively for eighteen- to thirty-five-year-olds, while others are open to passengers of all ages. The company's land tour division offers tours throughout Europe. The company's cruise division offers exciting three-, four-, and seven-day cruises to Alaska, the Bahamas, Bermuda, Mexico, and the Caribbean aboard Carnival Cruises, Norwegian Cruise Lines, Royal Caribbean Cruise Lines, Pearl Cruises, Regency Cruises, and Bermuda Star Line.

SPECIFICS: Gramercy employs approximately fifteen tour escorts per year, with a few additional escorts hired exclusively for the summer season. Most cruise ship tour escort positions are year-round (Bermuda and Alaska voyages are summer only). Cruise tour escorts organize special group activities on board the ship and lead exclusive shore excursions such as sailing and snorkeling trips on the islands. Gramercy does not hire escorts for their European tours.

INSIDER TIPS: The company only considers applications from persons with prior tour escort or cruise ship employment experience. Gramercy prides itself on finding tour escorts who are creative, energetic, and responsible. Once hired, group leaders are generally free to design their own activity schedules emphasizing their own particular skills and interests. Management requests that applicants *not* phone for employment information. According to former staffer Jon Lese, "the work is hard and the hours long but if you truly love working with people there is no better job on earth."

PERKS: Gramercy pays meal and lodging expenses for leaders while aboard ship. Tour escorts are responsible for their own transportation costs to the point of departure.

TO APPLY: Applicants should send a cover letter, résumé, photograph, and SARP to Wendy Lowenstein, Operations Manager, Gramercy Travel System, Dept. JIP, P.O. Box 1999, Rye, New York 10580. No phone inquiries, please.

JOHANSEN ROYAL TOURS
(Seattle, Washington)
Seasonal (Summer)

Johansen Royal Tours operates escorted motorcoach excursions to the Canadian Rockies from late May through early October. The company offers sixteen different itineraries.

SPECIFICS: Johansen Royal Tours employs approximately thirty-five to forty tour escorts each year.

INSIDER TIPS: Leadership experience, organizational skills, and the ability to speak before groups are important.

PERKS: As with almost all tour operators, Johansen pays most travel, meal, and lodging expenses for leaders.

TO APPLY: Applicants should write for an official application from Mike Gowan, Director of Escorts, Johansen Royal Tours, 2185 2nd Avenue, Suite 400, Seattle, Washington 98121-1299; (206) 728-4207 or (800) 426-0442.

PARAGON TOURS
(New Bedford, Massachusetts)
Seasonal (Summer) and Year-Round

Paragon Tours operates escorted motorcoach tours to California, Canada, Hawaii, and the northeastern United States.

SPECIFICS: Paragon Tours employs approximately sixty tour escorts each year. About twenty-five of the company's escorts work year-round while the other thirty-five are summer seasonal. Management reports hiring lots of college students and most of the hiring occurs in March, June, and September (limited September hiring).

INSIDER TIPS: "We want escorts who love people, love travel, and can adapt to any situation that may arise. People who have trouble handling pressure should not apply."

PERKS: As with almost all tour operators, Paragon pays all travel, meal, and lodging expenses for escorts.

TO APPLY: Applicants should send a cover letter, résumé, and photograph (optional) to Cheryl A. Hudson, Director of Escort Services, Paragon Tours, 680 Purchase Street, P.O. Box B-977, New Bedford, Massachusetts 02741; (508) 996-8276 or (800) 999-5050.

PARKER TOURS, INC.
(Rego Park, New York)
Seasonal (April through January)

Each year Parker Tours operates more than 1,000 escorted tours to Canada and the United States. Most Parker tours depart between April and January.

SPECIFICS: Parker Tours employs approximately forty-five tour escorts each year with all hiring occurring in February and March. New employees are trained on a simulated tour.

INSIDER TIPS: "Personality, personality, personality!!! We want staff who love people and get along well with everyone."

PERKS: As with almost all tour operators, Parker pays most travel, meal, and lodging expenses for leaders.

TO APPLY: Applicants should send a cover letter and résumé to Bill Passeggio, General Manager, Parker Tours, Inc., 98-12 Queens Boulevard, Rego Park, New York 11374; (718) 459-6585.

PERILLO TOURS
(Woodcliff Lake, New Jersey)
Year-Round

Perillo Tours/Club Perillo operates escorted all-inclusive air/land tours to Italy, the Bahamas, St. Maarten, Caribbean cruises, and Hawaii.

SPECIFICS: Perillo hires one to three tour escorts per year in the Caribbean and Hawaii. Escorts sign one-year contracts and live on-site. Escorts in Italy are hired in that country in keeping with governmental and union regulations.

PERKS: As with almost all tour operators, Perillo Tours pays all travel, meal, and lodging expenses for leaders.

TO APPLY: Applicants should write to determine if the company is hiring by contacting Perillo Tours, Perillo Tours Plaza, Woodcliff Lake, New Jersey 07675; phone number withheld by request.

PRINCESS TOURS
(Seattle, Washington)
Seasonal (Summer)

Princess Tours operates escorted cruise/tour packages to Alaska during the summer season. Company employees work both in Alaska and aboard Princess Cruises ships.

SPECIFICS: Princess Tours employs approximately thirty-five to forty tour escorts each year. All jobs are summer seasonal. Applicants should be available from late May through early October.

INSIDER TIPS: Leadership experience, organizational skills, and the ability to speak before groups are important. Strong personal and work references are very helpful.

PERKS: As with almost all tour operators, Princess Tours pays most travel, meal, and lodging expenses for leaders.

TO APPLY: Applicants should write for an official application from Princess Tours, 2185 2nd Avenue, Suite 400, Seattle, Washington 98121-1299; (206) 728-4207 or (800) 426-0442. Mike Gowan is the company's director of escorts.

PUTNEY STUDENT TRAVEL, INC.
(Putney, Vermont)
Seasonal (Summer)

Putney Student Travel operates escorted travel programs for high school groups to China and Europe as well as camping trips to Canada, Australia, New Zealand, and the United States. Trips are "nontouristy, educational travel programs."

SPECIFICS: Putney employs trip leaders for its numerous summer departures. Employees must be willing to work in a scholastic travel environment. Group leaders are responsible for student discipline and safety as well as all typical tour escort duties.

INSIDER TIPS: Candidates for Europe and China programs should speak French, Spanish, Russian, German, Italian, or Chinese fluently. There is no language requirement for camping trips to Canada, Australia, New Zealand, and the United States. The company is especially interested in recruiting graduate students, teachers, and graduating college seniors, ages twenty-two to thirty-five, who have lived or traveled extensively abroad.

PERKS: Putney Student Travel pays all travel, meal, and lodging expenses for leaders plus $400.

TO APPLY: Applicants should send a cover letter and résumé to Lead Students, Putney Student Travel, Paradise Road, Putney, Vermont

05346; (802) 387-5885. The company's program directors are Jeffrey and Peter Shumlin.

STUDENT HOSTELING PROGRAM
(Conway, Massachusetts)
Seasonal (All Seasons) and Year-Round

The Student Hosteling Program operates escorted cycling and camping excursions throughout Europe and the United States for thirteen to seventeen year olds.

SPECIFICS: The Student Hosteling Program employs numerous senior trip leaders (who must be at least twenty-one years old at time of trip departure) and assistant trip leaders (who must be at least eighteen years old at time of trip departure) each year. The company actively recruits college students during an annual interviewing trip through the Northeast.

INSIDER TIPS: While experience with thirteen to seventeen year olds in classroom or camp situations is helpful, the key to this company's leaders is their personality, vitality, and love for kids. "If your prime concern is to get an all-expense-paid trip to some exotic place, to get a paid relaxing vacation, or even to do some serious cycle touring, please don't apply." All trip leaders must have at least a current standard Red Cross first aid course certificate (advanced training in first aid or medicine is, of course, that much better).

TO APPLY: Applicants should write or call for the official "leadership information and application form" from Student Hosteling Program, Ashfield Road, Conway, Massachusetts 01341; (413) 369-4633.

WESTOURS
(Seattle, Washington)
Seasonal (Summer) and Year-Round

Westours operates numerous escorted motorcoach and cruise tours to Alaska, the Canadian Rockies, and the Canadian Yukon. Holland America Line Westours also operates the shore excursion program aboard Holland-America ships.

SPECIFICS: Westours employs tour escorts to lead motorcoach trips. Shipboard personnel are also responsible for running the shipboard excursion sales/information desks aboard Holland America Line ships. Alaska tours are exclusively summer departures, while Caribbean regions operate during the winter.

INSIDER TIPS: Shipboard personnel are treated as staff members. As such, they are entitled to eat in the staff dining room and generally enjoy most passenger privileges.

PERKS: As with almost all tour operators, Westours pays all travel, meal, and lodging expenses for leaders.

TO APPLY: Apply to Human Resources Department, Holland-America Westours, 300 Elliott Avenue West, Seattle, Washington 98119; (206) 281-3535.

In addition to the detailed company profiles given above, the following are major operators of escorted tours. These companies all hire tour escorts and can be contacted at the addresses listed.

Beckham Reception
  Services
587 Washington Street
Canton, Massachusetts
02021
(617) 828-6700
Debbie Clark, Director of
Operations

California Holidays
P.O. Box 92734
Los Angeles, California
90009
(213) 337-2344
America's West

California Yosemite Tours
P.O. Box 2188
Merced, California 95344
(209) 383-1563
Yosemite National Park

Carton Tours
12755 State Highway 55
Minneapolis, Minnesota
55441
(612) 640-8989

Contiki Holidays
1432 Katela Avenue
Anaheim, California
92805
(714) 937-0611
*Worldwide tours for eighteen to
thirty-five-year-olds*

Flair Tours
6922 Hollywood Blvd.,

Suite 421
Hollywood, California
90028
(800) 223-5247 USA
(800) 433-5247 CA
*Alaska, West Coast, Florida,
and New York*

Four Winds Travel, Ltd.
175 Fifth Avenue
New York, New York
10010
(212) 505-0901
Lynn Healy Toy, Director
of Operations
*Western USA, Southern USA,
New England, East Canada,
and Canadian Rockies*

Jefferson Tours & Travel
1206 Currie Avenue
Minneapolis, Minnesota
55403
(612) 332-8745
Martin Lipshutz, General
Manager
*New England, Florida,
Southern USA,
Hawaii, and Eastern Canada.*

Maineline Tours
184 Main Street
S. Portland, Maine 04106
(207) 799-8527.
Marilyn Rowe, Tour
Director

Midnight Sun Tours
P.O. Box 103355
Anchorage, Alaska 99510
(907) 276-TOUR
Operates custom escorted tours

Mountain Travel
1398 Solano Avenue
Albany, California 94706
(415) 527-8100
*Cross country ski tours, ski
mountaineering, and
randonee tours through Europe,
China, Alaska, Russia,
the Andes, and Lappland
(Arctic Circle)*
(Author's Note: Company
calls escorts "tour
leaders." Most
downhill ski trips are not
escorted.)

North American Tours
P.O. Box 94819
Lincoln, Nebraska 68500
(402) 474-4111
*Western USA, Great Lakes,
and Eastern Canada*

Olson Travelworld
3333 Kirby Trees Place
Memphis, Tennessee
38115
(800) 422-2255
June Arra, Manager

Omni Tours
309 The Lincoln Blvd.
E. Sixth and St. Clair
Cleveland, Ohio 44114
(216) 781-6664

On The Road Tours
P.O. Box 183
Downers Grove, Illinois
60515
(312) 852-8666
USA (excluding Hawaii) and
Canada

Pacific Delight Tours, Inc.
132 Madison Avenue
New York, New York
10016
(212) 684-7707
Contact: Joan Dunn

Peter Pan Tours
P.O. Box 1776
Springfield, Massachusetts
01102-1776
(413) 781-2900
Alaska, Hawaii, Canada, and
mainland USA

Presley Tours, Inc.
R.R. #1
Makanda, Illinois 62958
(618) 549-0704
Alaska, Western USA, Great
Lakes, Florida, Southern
USA, Eastern Canada, and
Canadian Rockies

Robert's Hawaii Tours
444 Hobron Lane, 5th
Floor
Honolulu, Hawaii 96815
(808) 947-3939
Mostly day tours throughout
the Hawaiian Islands

Rocky Mountain Cycle
  Tours
P.O. Box 1978
Canmore, Alta
T0L 0M0
Canada
(403) 678-6770
Cycle trips through Canadian
Rockies

Starr Tours
1700 Nottingham Way
Trenton, New Jersey
08619
(609) 586-6080
Alaska, West, New England,
and Canada

Talmage Tours, Inc.
1223 Walnut Street
Philadelphia,
Pennsylvania 19107
(215) 923-7100
Enid Kaplan, Operations
Dept. Manager
American West, Great
Lakes, New England, and
Hawaii

Tauck Tours
P.O. Box 5027
11 Wilton Road
Westport, Connecticut
06880
(203) 226-6911
Dick Sundby, Escort
Supervisor
USA and Canada

Tours of Distinction
141 E. 44th Street
New York, New York
10017
(212) 661-4680

Tour of the
  Month/Hosted
  Holidays
1126 W. Baden Court
Milwaukee, Wisconsin
53221
(414) 271-0673
Robert Smithson, Director
of Operations
Alaska, Mainland USA, and
Canada

Vista Tours
1923 N. Carson Street,
Suite 105
Carson City, Nevada
89710
(702) 882-2100
Western USA, New England,
and Canada

The following listings, found under the chapter heading listed, also include positions for tour or excursion leaders:

HIGH ADVENTURE

Backroads Bicycle Touring
Country Cycling Tours
Cruiser Bob's Original
   Haleakala Downhill
Four Seasons Cycling
Ghost Town Scenic Jeep
   Tours/River Runners Ltd.
Hurricane Creek Llamas

Nature Expeditions
   International
Oregon Trail Wagon Train
Ski Guides Hawaii
Ski Utah
Sobek Expeditions, Inc.
Wagons West

Amusement & Theme Parks

ACTION PARK
(McAfee, New Jersey)

Seasonal (Summer and Winter) and Year-Round

Vernon Valley's Great Gorge Ski Area/Action Park is a unique combination of a ski resort and amusement park located in rural Sussex County, New Jersey, just forty-seven miles from New York City. During the winter, Vernon Valley Great Gorge becomes one of the most popular ski resorts in New England. Each summer the ski resort gives way to Action Park, a huge theme park with more than fifty exciting participation rides.

SPECIFICS: Action Park hires approximately 1,000 new employees each summer. Jobs are available for both summer seasonal staff as well as year-round help. Summer staff should be available from early June through September. There is no official application deadline. Most starting salaries range from $5.05 to $7.00 per hour, although supervisory and some skilled positions pay higher. Summer seasonal applications are accepted for certified lifeguards, retail clerks, ride attendants, cashiers, security guards, cooks, waitpersons, bartenders, first aiders, information services agents, switchboard operators, maintenance personnel, and mechanics. The park encourages college interns studying Recreation and Leisure Management. (For information on winter seasonal jobs, see the "Vernon Valley/Great Gorge Ski Area" listing in the Snow & Skiing chapter).

INSIDER TIPS: Apply early for the best selection of available positions. Successful applicants demonstrate "an ability to adapt to a changing environment, honesty, personality, and excellent people skills."

PERKS: See the Vernon Valley listing in the Snow & Skiing chapter.

TO APPLY: See the Vernon Valley listing in the Snow & Skiing chapter.

ADVENTURELAND PARK
(Des Moines, Iowa)
Seasonal (Summer)

Adventureland Park is one of the largest theme parks in the farm belt. The park combines eighteen major mechanical rides, five kiddie rides, costumed characters, a crafts area, an arcade, and a campground and hotel complex. The park is open summers only.

SPECIFICS: Adventureland Park hires approximately 600 workers each summer. All positions are seasonal beginning in early May and lasting through September 1. Contact the Adventureland Personnel Office for a complete listing of available positions.

TO APPLY: Applicants should either write for an official application or send a cover letter and résumé to Personnel Department, Adventureland Park, P.O. Box 3355, Des Moines, Iowa 50316; (515) 266-2121.

AFRICAN LION SAFARI
(Cambridge, Ontario, Canada)

Seasonal (Summer) and Year-Round

African Lion Safari is a drive-through wildlife park displaying North American, Asian, and African mammals in their natural setting.

SPECIFICS: African Lion Safari employs 250 staff members and hires approximately 220 new employees each year. The park receives approximately 300 applications each year. Positions are available for both year-round and summer seasonal work. Ideally, summer staff should be available starting in early May; however, applications are accepted for employment throughout the season. Applications are accepted for animal attendants, tour guides, gift shop staff, maintenance staff, and ticket booth personnel. Salaries start at CAN$4.00 per hour for employees under eighteen years old and CAN$5.00 per hour for employees over eighteen.

INSIDER TIPS: Management seeks employees with an educational background or work experience in the area of wildlife and fauna. However, inexperienced personnel are hired if they can show a willingness to learn and develop an interest in wildlife.

PERKS: Employees enjoy a meal discount program, free park passes for family members, uniform discounts, and a liberal incentive program that pays employees who stay through the entire season a bonus based on the number of hours worked. After signing in at the main office, all employees may enter the park free when off duty.

TO APPLY: Applicants should send a cover letter and résumé to Don Dailley, Jr., President/General Manager, African Lion Safari, RR #1, Cambridge, Ontario, N1R 5S2 Canada; (519) 623-2620.

AQUASPLASH & MARINELAND
(Antibes, France)
Seasonal (Summer)

Aquasplash and Marineland are located on the exotic, romantic French Riviera on France's Mediterranean coast. The park's complex combines Marineland, a marine zoo featuring live animal shows, and Aquasplash, a modern exciting water park.

SPECIFICS: Aquasplash and Marineland employ a total of 130 employees each summer. Approximately eighty new positions are available each year and the park typically receives 500 applications annually. Positions are available for lifeguards and fast food personnel.

INSIDER TIPS: Only applicants who speak French and hold a valid French work permit will be considered.

TO APPLY: Applicants should send a cover letter, résumé, and photograph to Personnel Manager, Marineland, 306 Avenue Mozart, 06600 Antibes, France; phone: (93) 470673.

ASTROWORLD/WATERWORLD
(Houston, Texas)
Seasonal (Summer)

AstroWorld and WaterWorld comprise the largest entertainment complex in the Southwestern United States. AstroWorld, one of the Six Flags parks, offers more than 100 rides, shows, and attractions. WaterWorld is a large water park complete with waterslides, pools, and volleyball.

SPECIFICS: This huge entertainment complex hires up to 3,000 new employees annually to fill the 1,700 AstroWorld and 300 Water-World jobs. The parks are open weekends during the spring and fall and daily during the summer. Salaries start at $3.50 per hour and go up depending on the position and experience. Positions are available for ride operators, games attendants, merchandise shop attendants, food service hosts and hostesses, parking lot attendants, cash controllers, and warehouse personnel. Applicants must be at least fifteen years of age.

INSIDER TIPS: AstroWorld and WaterWorld look for friendly, enthusiastic, smiling people who want to work in a fun environment.

PERKS: When off duty, employees are allowed to use all of the park's facilities, except the skill games. AstroWorld and WaterWorld provide free uniforms and cleaning and each host or hostess (the park's name for its staff) receives eight complimentary passes. Finally, the parks sponsor numerous special employee events.

TO APPLY: Applicants must apply in person to AstroWorld/WaterWorld Personnel Office, 9001 Kirby Drive, Houston, Texas 77054; (713) 794-3217. The personnel office is open Monday through Saturday 9:00 A.M. to noon and 1:00 P.M. to 5:00 P.M.

BUSCH GARDENS/THE OLD COUNTRY
(Williamsburg, Virginia)
Seasonal (Spring, Summer, Fall and limited Winter) and Year-Round

This world-renowned park is divided into English, French, French Canadian, German, and Italian theme sections. All areas feature rides, shows, shops, and restaurants reflecting the ethnic themes of the park. Busch Gardens is acclaimed for its live stage shows, animal shows, big-name concerts, and outrageous roller coasters.

SPECIFICS: Busch Gardens has a full-time staff of 140 and a seasonal staff of up to 2,500 at any one time. More than 3,500 new applicants are hired each year from an annual applicant pool of 5,800. Most seasonal help is hired for various periods between mid-March and the end of October. Positions are available for singers, dancers, actors, hosts/hostesses, musicians, stage technicians, nurses/emergency medical technicians, warehouse persons, grounds keepers, security personnel, cash controllers, clerical staff, accounting clerks, ride operators, games operators, merchandise sales staff, food service staff, theater hosts, and area hosts. All employees of the park are referred to as hosts or hostesses. Various internships are available for recreation majors.

INSIDER TIPS: The park screens applicants for an ability to communicate effectively with guests and other hosts/hostesses, availability and flexibility, neat and clean grooming standards, and overall enthusiasm. The employment office places a great deal of emphasis on personal interviews, which are mandatory for all positions.

PERKS: Busch Gardens pays a 25 cent per hour bonus to qualifying hosts/hostesses, offers free uniforms, complimentary tickets, and discount passes for family, merchandise and food discounts in the park, and assorted employee parties and sports events. Hosts/hostesses may use all of the park's facilities when off duty.

TO APPLY: Applicants should write for an official application from Busch Gardens, Employment Office, P.O. Drawer F. C., Williamsburg, Virginia 23187; (804) 253-3020.

CALAWAY PARK
(Calgary, Alberta, Canada)
Seasonal (Summer)

Calaway Park is a family-oriented theme park featuring a wide variety of rides, games, shows, and special events.

SPECIFICS: Calaway Park hires approximately 350 new employees each summer to fill its 320 staff positions. Employees are selected from an applicant pool of approximately 700. Applications for each summer's employment season are accepted beginning in mid-February. Employees should be available from the end of April through mid-October, although applicants who cannot be available for the entire season are still considered. Positions are available for ride operators, games operators, concession clerks, merchandise clerks, admissions clerks, janitors, landscapers, and guest relations hosts and hostesses. Starting pay ranges from CAN$4.50 to CAN$7.00 per hour depending on the position and experience.

INSIDER TIPS: Calaway Park seeks "positive, hard-working individuals who are friendly, enthusiastic, and enjoy working with the public." A personal interview is required before a final hiring commitment is made. Apply as early as possible after mid-February for the best employment opportunities.

PERKS: Employees may use all of the park's facilities except the games when off duty. Employees are also given free park passes, free admission to special employee social events, and have a number of employee recognition programs.

TO APPLY: Applicants should send a cover letter, résumé, and photograph to Employee Relations, Calaway Park, RR 2, Site 25, Comp. 20, Calgary, Alberta, T2P 2G5 Canada; (403) 240-3822. Management responds to all applications. Applicants who apply during the main hiring season (mid-February through early May) should expect a response by mid-May.

CANOBIE LAKE PARK
(Salem, New Hampshire)

Seasonal (Summer)

For almost ninety years Canobie Lake Park has been providing visitors with both the thrills and chills of an all-American amusement park as well as the tranquility and beauty of a charming lakefront parkland. The park features more than sixty rides, games, attractions, and live shows.

SPECIFICS: Canobie Lake Park hires between 150 and 200 new employees each year to fill its 300-person summer staff. Employees should be available from late May or early June through Labor Day. Positions are available for ride operators, game attendants, cashiers, gate attendants, lifeguards (must have either WSI or ALS certificates), boat pilots, and landscape assistants. Most starting salaries range from $4.75 to $5.00 per hour, plus an end-of-season bonus.

INSIDER TIPS: "Our jobs involve pleasant, outdoor work and provide a great opportunity to meet people. Applicants should enjoy working with people. Nonsmokers are preferred."

PERKS: All employees who fulfill their seasonal obligations are eligible for an end-of-season bonus. Additional perks include performance awards, meal discounts, free passes to the park, social activities, dances, and possible employee housing. Staff members are free to use the park on their days off and the park's swimming pool is available to employees daily during their break periods.

TO APPLY: Applicants should send a cover letter, résumé, and photograph to Carl Berni, Personnel Director, P.O. Box 190, Policy Street, Salem, New Hampshire 03079; (603) 893-3506.

CAROWINDS
(Charlotte, North Carolina)
Seasonal (Summer)

Carowinds is an 83-acre entertainment park located on the North Carolina–South Carolina border, ten miles south of Charlotte.

SPECIFICS: Carowinds hires up to 3,000 new employees annually to fill its 1,200 to 1,500 seasonal positions. The park receives approximately 5,000 applications each year. Generally, summer help should be available from March through October. Available positions include ride operators (must be at least eighteen years old), merchandise sales associates, food service staff, games personnel, and admissions staff. Salaries start at $4.25 per hour and higher.

INSIDER TIPS: Carowinds looks for "enthusiastic, energetic applicants." An ability to work with large groups of people is essential.

PERKS: Employees receive free uniforms, free park passes, local discount coupons, and park merchandise discounts. Carowinds also sponsors an employee car-pooling program, an employee softball league, and staff parties throughout the season. All employees are permitted to use all of Carowinds' facilities when off duty. Bonuses are paid to employees who stay through the end of the season.

TO APPLY: Only applicants who can apply in person are considered. For more information contact Carowinds, Employment Office, P.O. Box 410289, Carowinds Boulevard, Charlotte, North Carolina 28241-0289; (704) 588-2606.

CEDAR POINT
(Sandusky, Ohio)
Seasonal (Summer)

With their brand-new Magnum XL 200 roller coaster, Cedar Point claims boasting rights to the highest and fastest coaster in the world. This park has taken giant leaps forward in both popularity and technology since its first roller coaster made its debut in 1892. The 1892 coaster reached a top speed of six miles per hour; the Magnum will achieve speeds topping seventy miles per hour. Today, Cedar Point is a huge 364-acre amusement/theme park located on the shores of Lake Erie. The park combines fifty-four rides (including nine roller coasters), a new $3.5 million dollar waterslide complex, a 113,000-gallon performing marine tank for live sea lion and dolphin shows, a live jungle animal safari, live stage shows, costumed characters, a campground and recreational vehicle park, a 400-room historic hotel, one of Lake Erie's largest marinas, and a mile-long sand beach.

SPECIFICS: Cedar Point receives approximately 10,000 applications for its 3,200 annual openings. Prior experience is not required for most positions. While employee working dates are somewhat flexible, the park is open from early May through late September and preference is given to applicants who can work the longest. The park hires accounting clerks, admission cashiers, air brush artists, arcade hosts/hostesses, barkeepers, camper village attendants, cash control tellers, cooks, craftsmen, housing supervisors, firefighters, emergency medical technicians, food hosts/hostesses, games hosts/hostesses, glass blowers, group sales staff, group utility crews, hotel desk clerks, hotel reservationists, internal auditors, landscape gardeners, lifeguards, musicians, merchandise cashiers, nurses, restroom stewards, ride hosts/hostesses, singers, animal handlers, office cleaners, security patrol officers, telephone operators, traffic/tram operators, waitpersons, and warehouse persons. There is no application deadline although the bulk of hiring is completed by mid-April. Starting wages are generally about $3.70 per hour (subject to change).

INSIDER TIPS: According to former Cedar Point sweeper Dawn Balmforth, "the company looks for all-American clean-cut college students. My job was ideal . . . while sweeping my way around the park I got to meet all our visitors while getting both exercise and a great tan." Interviews are not required although they greatly increase an applicant's chances. Between January and March interviews are held at Cedar Point and at thirty-eight colleges and universities across the country. An interview schedule is attached to the official application form/summer jobs brochure. Positions as performers and musicians are filled through auditions held in January. For audition information contact the Live Shows Department at (419) 626-0830, ext. 2388.

PERKS: Low-cost housing in either dormitory or apartment rooms is available for employees who come from more than twenty-five miles away from the park. More than 2,000 housing slots are available. Other perks include a generous end-of-season bonus to employees who fulfill their contracts, free rides/attractions/beach privileges, four free Cedar Point guest tickets, free employee picnics/dances, movies, and a complete employee recreation program. Free ferryboat transportation to downtown Sandusky is also available for employees. Employees are welcome to use the park's beach and rides without charge. Special employee "soak city" nights are offered at the water park.

TO APPLY: Applicants should write for an official application from David Hensley, Employment Manager, Cedar Point, P.O. Box 5006, Sandusky, Ohio 44871-8006; (419) 627-2243.

CLEMENTON AMUSEMENT PARK
(Clementon, New Jersey)
Seasonal (Summer)

Clementon Amusement Park features twenty-five rides, five snack stands, ten game booths, and entertainment. A newly added high-dive show is one of the park's principal attractions.

SPECIFICS: About 175 employees are hired each summer. Applications are accepted for ride operators, games operators, food concession staff, maintenance crew, clean-up staff, cashiers, and stock workers. Salaries start at minimum wage and go up depending on the position and experience. There is no application deadline.

INSIDER TIPS: Management looks for "responsible, clean, friendly, and outgoing individuals."

PERKS: The company offers a bonus program for staffers who fulfill their contracts. Employees are permitted to use the park during their off hours.

TO APPLY: Applicants should either write and request an application or send a cover letter and résumé to Sarah Meyers, Office Manager, Clementon Park, P.O. Box 125, Clementon, New Jersey 08021; (609) 783-0263.

DISNEYLAND
(Anaheim, California)
Seasonal (All Seasons) and Year-Round

There is only one thing Mickey Mouse about Disney's western entertainment mecca, Disneyland, and that's Mickey himself. Disneyland is the original American theme park. *Time* magazine once described Disney's parks as a kind of mid-size Anytown USA with no crime, no trash, and no frowns. Disney's thirty-five-year-old western park is looked at as one huge show where visitors are "the audience," the park is "a stage," and employees are "cast members." Fanatical attention to detail and just a dab of pixie dust keeps Disneyland zip-a-dee-doo-dahing into the hearts of visitors from around the world. Although Disneyland is probably most famous for its awe-inspiring adventures (Disneyland has adventures—never rides), guests consistently rate the park's cleanliness and friendly employees as its major attractions. The combined effort of the park's cast members and creative imagineers (the designers who create Disney's adventures), along with the infectious spirit of Mickey worship (which, as one travel writer put it, permeates every twist and turn of the attraction lines), helps assure Disneyland's spot as the "Happiest Place on Earth."

SPECIFICS: Disneyland's casting office (employment office) receives 14,000 to 15,000 applications each year for its 9,000 to 10,000-plus peak season positions. To fill these numerous positions, Disneyland hires almost 5,000 new cast members each year. While Disneyland's complete list of positions would fill an entire book, the park is almost always hiring parking lot hosts/hostesses, ticket sellers, ticket takers, merchandise hosts/hostesses (operators of the plethora of souvenir shops, crafts outlets, and ever-present mouse ear shops), custodial hosts/hostesses, culinary hosts/hostesses (operators of the numerous restaurants, snack bars, and buffeterias), attractions hosts/hostesses (ride operators), shipping and receiving staff, entertainment hosts/ hostesses (costumed characters, parade actors, singers, dancers, and musicians), and costuming hosts/hostesses (wardrobe attendants). However, the park also has such diverse positions as pony farm breeders, kennel operators, lost children attendants, firefighters, nurses, and craftsmen. Disneyland hires cast members for seasonal (all seasons), year-round, full-time, and part-time employment. Beginning in 1989, the park introduced a college recruitment program called "college relations." The program is designed to give students who otherwise live too far away an opportunity to spend a summer working at Disneyland. The college relations program provides subsidized housing and an opportunity for college credit through an evening seminar program. The program travels around the western United States offering interviews at numerous colleges and universities. A similar program is offered by Disney World.

INSIDER TIPS: "Disneyland cast members are people experts. Working with people on a personal basis can be fun and fulfilling, but it can also be tiring and frustrating. Our roles are for extroverts who enjoy helping others. In a sense, we work while others play. When your family and friends are enjoying their leisure time on weekends and holidays, you may be scheduled to work. This is an important commitment you should seriously consider. People the world over have come to expect our cast to have the 'Disney Look,' a neat, trim appearance—with no extremes to distract from the show. Each applicant is evaluated during an interview on the following factors: attitude, availability, education, enthusiasm, friendliness, neatness, personality, poise, politeness, skills and talents, communication skills, and access to reliable transportation." Richard Ramsey, head of the park's college relations program, offers this advice to applicants: "Apply early and be willing to accept any position in the park. Any position at Disneyland is going to be a rewarding one. It requires all of our 10,000 cast members and 300 job classifications to put on our show. If you enjoy contact with the public, consider applying for our custodial department. Our custodial cast members probably enjoy the most extensive contact with our guests."

PERKS: Disneyland offers its cast members a wide array of perks. Seasonal employee perks include a free subscription to Disneyland Line (an exclusive employee publication), flexible scheduling, parking shuttle, co-op education credits, discounted employee cafeteria meals, free costumes and costume laundering, free employee lockers, and subsidized housing for college relations program participants. All employees are admitted to Disneyland free on their days off and may purchase guest admissions at a significant discount. The park offers membership in an employee credit union and a wide array of social activities for cast members. Returning cast members are offered first choice for scheduling and all employees can participate in the park's job transfer policy, which allows cast members to switch jobs if they are unhappy. Other perks are available to year-round cast members.

TO APPLY: Applicants should write, call, or drop by in person to request an official application. A personal interview is required for all cast members. The park's casting office is open Monday through Saturday from 8:30 A.M. to 5:00 P.M. Applicants for positions as singers, dancers, musicians, or entertainers should call for audition information.

DISNEY WORLD/EPCOT CENTER/ DISNEY-MGM STUDIOS/TYPHOON LAGOON/ PLEASURE ISLAND (Lake Buena Vista, Florida)

Seasonal (All Seasons) and Year-Round

Disney's mega attraction center in Lake Buena Vista, Florida, defies description. Walt Disney World Resort, including the Magic Kingdom and its accompanying EPCOT Center, Disney-MGM Studios theme park, and the newly added Pleasure Island and Typhoon Lagoon water park, are the accumulation of all of Walt Disney's pixie dust dreams multiplied to the nth degree. Fanatical attention to detail and almost unlimited space to grow is allowing Disney's imagineers to outdo themselves. The new Disney-MGM Studios theme park, Typhoon Lagoon, and a nocturnal hot spot called Pleasure Island will allow Disney's Florida mecca to supplant P. T. Barnum's circus as "The Greatest Show on Earth."

SPECIFICS: Disney's seven Florida resorts and five parks employ a total of more than 30,000 staffers (called "cast members" in "Disneyspeak"). All employees for all Disney properties are hired from one central casting office. Jobs are available for seasonal (any season), year-round, full-time, and part-time employment. While Disney's complete list of positions would fill an entire book, the parks are almost always hiring parking lot hosts/hostesses, ticket sellers, ticket takers, merchandise hosts/hostesses (operators of the plethora of souvenir shops, crafts outlets, and ever-present mouse ear shops), custodial hosts/hostesses, culinary hosts/hostesses (operators of the numerous restaurants, snack bars, and buffeterias), attractions hosts/ hostesses (ride operators), shipping and receiving staff, entertainment hosts/hostesses (costumed characters, parade actors, singers, dancers, and musicians), and costuming hosts/hostesses (wardrobe attendants). However, the parks also have such diverse positions as pony farm breeders, kennel operators, lost children attendants, fire fighters, nurses, and craftsmen. Walt Disney World has a well-established college recruitment program called "college relations." The program is designed to assist students who otherwise live too far away an opportunity to spend a season working for Disney. The college relations program provides subsidized housing and an opportunity for college credit through an evening seminar program. The program travels around the midwestern, southern, and eastern United States offering interviews at numerous colleges and universities. A similar program is offered by Disneyland. The Florida college relations program employs at least 2,100 cast members annually. The program operates year-round, accepting students for summer, fall, or spring semesters. Through another unique program called international relations, Disney's EPCOT Center recruits citizens of other countries to work in its park pavilions. Disney takes care of obtaining most visas and work permits for foreign applicants hired through the international relations program.

INSIDER TIPS: According to college relations representative Katheryn Kirk, "Disney looks for enthusiastic, clean-cut, college students with a high energy level and good attitude. Most of our employees are college sophomores or juniors majoring in business, public relations, communications, journalism, drama, travel/hospitality, or broadcasting. However, we consider all college students." Kent Phillips, head of Walt Disney World's college relations program, explained, "We want students interested in studying people skills. The kind of students who are majoring in recreation, communications, or hotel management. We hire animators, illustrators, and even engineers for the program. College relations offers a unique educational opportunity to learn, work, and grow interpersonally while learning about the exciting leisure industry." Walt Disney summed up his parks' policies best when he said, "You can dream, create, design, and build the most wonderful and exciting place on earth, but it takes people to make the dream a reality."

PERKS: See Disneyland listing above.

TO APPLY: Applicants should write, call, or drop by in person to request an official application. A personal interview is required for all cast members. The park's casting office is open Sunday through Saturday from 9:00 A.M. to 4:00 P.M. and is located at 1155 Buena Vista Boulevard, Lake Buena Vista, Florida 32830; (407) 828-3088. Applicants for positions as singers, dancers, musicians, or entertainers should call the above number for audition information. Applicants interested in the college relations program should call or write for a program information letter and interview schedule from Walt Disney World College Relations Department, P.O. Box 10090, Lake Buena Vista, Florida 32830-0090; (407) 828-3091. Foreign applicants interested in positions at Epcot Center should write for employment information from Disney World/Epcot International Relations Department, P.O. Box 10090, Lake Buena Vista, Florida 32830-0090.

DOGPATCH USA
(Dogpatch, Arkansas)
Seasonal (Summer)

For fans of the "Li'l Abner" comic strip, Dogpatch is pure heaven. Located nine miles south of Harrison in the Ozark Mountains, this theme park is based on the Al Capp comic strip "Li'l Abner." Dogpatch USA is a family theme park with ten major rides.

SPECIFICS: Dogpatch USA employs more than 250 seasonal summer employees. A wide variety of positions are available including musician, performer, ride operator, ticket seller, ticket taker, maintenance staff, cook, waitperson, cashier, and food stand operator.

TO APPLY: Applicants should send a cover letter and résumé to Personnel Manager, Dogpatch USA, P.O. Box 20, Dogpatch, Arkansas 72648; (501) 743-1111.

DOLLYWOOD
(Pigeon Forge, Tennessee)
Seasonal (Summer) and Year-Round

Popular country-western singer Dolly Parton says it best: "Take pride in being an employee of the friendliest, safest, cleanest town in America." Dollywood is the result of a marriage between Dolly Parton's dream of becoming the next Walt Disney and the popular Silver Dollar City theme park built in 1959. The 1880s style theme park features Dolly's Smokey Mountain heritage of mountain music, crafts, and rides. Dollywood is located in the Great Smokey Mountains, only five miles from the entrance to Smokey Mountain National Park.

SPECIFICS: Dollywood receives more than 3,500 applications a year and selects 600 new employees and rehires 800 for the operating season of April 30 through October 29. Host and hostess positions are available for work in food service, on rides and attractions, or as admission gate attendants, parking attendants, clerks, or grounds keepers. Entry-level salaries for 1989 began at $4.00 per hour with ongoing opportunities for raises and performance evaluations.

INSIDER TIPS: Employees are expected to adhere to Dolly's creed of excellence and strict standard of conduct and appearance. Management looks for "very friendly applicants with bright smiles who are mature, responsible, enjoy working with people, and are able to withstand working outdoors."

PERKS: All rides, music shows, and craft demonstrations are available to employees during their off hours. Staff members are eligible for meal and merchandise discounts, exchange privileges at other theme parks, and discounts at Dollywood concerts. Most importantly, employees can take advantage of being situated in the heart of the Great Smokey Mountains.

TO APPLY: Applicants should send a cover letter and résumé to Dollywood Personnel Office, 700 Dollywood Lane, Pigeon Forge, Tennessee 37863; (615) 428-9417. Dollywood attempts to respond to all applicants within two weeks.

DORNEY PARK & WILDWATER KINGDOM
(Allentown, Pennsylvania)
Seasonal (Summer)

From the thrills and chills of the hair-raising Thunderhawk to the twists and turns of the Torpedo Tubes and the park's wild and winding waterslide, Dorney Park & Wildwater Kingdom offers it all. This is the nation's oldest family-owned and -operated amusement center. The neighboring water kingdom boasts thirty-eight acres of splashy attractions including a football-field size wave pool.

SPECIFICS: Dorney Park & Wildwater Kingdom hires 2,000 to 2,300 seasonal summer employees each year. Most employees are hired to work from the end of their school terms through Labor Day. The park employs cashiers, ride operators, sales clerks, game operators, cooks, caterers, lifeguards, and ticket takers. Cashiers and game operators must be at least sixteen years old; ride operators must be at least eighteen years of age.

INSIDER TIPS: This place is as friendly as it sounds. This is an ideal summer job for anyone looking for a simpler lifestyle working in a clean entertainment environment.

PERKS: Dorney Park assists employees in finding housing. Management offers an end-of-season bonus and incentive program for summer staffers. Staff members receive an allotment of free passes.

TO APPLY: Applicants should write for an official application from Eileen Minninger or Leslie Kutz, Personnel Managers, Dorney Park & Wildwater Kingdom, 3830 Dorney Park Road, Allentown, Pennsylvania 18104; (215) 395-9140.

ELITCH GARDENS AMUSEMENT PARK
(Denver, Colorado)
Seasonal (Summer)

In 1989 Elitch Gardens celebrated its 100th birthday of providing fun, games, entertainment, food, and laughs to the Denver area. The park's grand opening was attended by world-renowned showman P. T. Barnum and General Tom Thumb, star of Barnum's circus.

SPECIFICS: Elitch Gardens receives approximately 2,000 applications each year and hires almost 1,600 new staff members annually. The park employs approximately 900 employees at any given time. Positions are available for summer seasonal staff between April and September. Hiring is done as needed throughout the season. Most employees are high school or college students, over age sixteen. According to management, for applicants who like the color green and have strong math skills, the cashier department has a variety of positions. For those who have the munchies, positions are available in the foods department. For aspiring entertainers, the entertainment department has just the position for you: either singing, juggling, dancing, or just acting NUTS! Aspiring physics students will learn that what goes up must come down with a job in the rides department, which turns guests upside down, inside out, and every other which way. For applicants who want to work and play the day away with some of the park's smaller and younger visitors, the Kiddieland department is perfect for you. Other departments include games, grounds, guest services, park office, retail, personnel, picnic, and warehouse. Positions are also available for supervisors, crew leaders, stand managers, assistant stand managers, and breakers (responsible for giving breaks to employees and training new employees). Most crew positions start at minimum wage. Supervisor positions start at $5.00 per hour.

INSIDER TIPS: "We especially look for employees who smile and like to make others smile. We're not just a summer employer—we're a teacher, social director, entertainer, counselor, and friend! We provide an atmosphere that is conducive to both learning and having fun. If an applicant is interested in coming to Colorado, there's no better place to spend a summer!"

PERKS: Employees are allowed to use the park's facilities when off duty, with the exception of prize winning games (employees may purchase the prizes at a discount). Other employee perks include four ride passes a month, an employee commissary, five employee dances each season, putt-putt golf tournaments, a breakfast club, a happy hour, employee dinners, employee contests, discounts on merchandise, and an employee continuing education program.

TO APPLY: Applicants should send a cover letter and résumé to Patty Slattery, Personnel Manager, Elitch Gardens Company, 4620 W. 38th Avenue, Denver, Colorado 80212; (303) 455-4771.

EYE SPY PHOTO
(Aptos, California)

Seasonal (Summer and Winter) and Year-Round

Can you say "smile" and take a photograph? If so, this may be just the job for you. Eye Spy operates photography concessions in major theme parks and ski resorts around the United States.

SPECIFICS: Eye Spy hires approximately 500 photographers each year. The company's staff shoots upwards of 15,000 pictures each day! Photographers are paid based on how many pictures they take and how well everyone's photographs sell (a percentage of the day's sales). Most employees average between $5.00 to $6.00 per hour. However, the company reports that highly motivated photographers can earn upwards of $8.00 per hour. Summer seasonal photographers should be available to start work between mid-May and mid-June. Ideally, summer staffers stay through Labor Day. Winter seasonal dates vary according to the ski season at the specific location to which an employee is assigned.

INSIDER TIPS: The key to landing a position with Eye Spy is the dates you can commit to work. The longer you can stay, the better the chances of your being hired. "We use idiot cameras. Anyone can learn to take our photographs. There really aren't too many people we wouldn't give an opportunity to if they are highly motivated." When selecting photographs to send as samples, choose people pictures.

PERKS: Employee housing is provided at a moderate cost at most work locations. A bonus, usually averaging $200 to $300, is paid to employees who fulfill their contracts and stay through the end of the season.

TO APPLY: Applicants should send a cover letter, résumé, and sample photographs to Eye Spy Photo, Personnel, Attn: Sandy Gelfand, 7221 Viewpoint, Aptos, California 95003; (408) 662-3337 or 3338. Outside of California call toll-free (800) 237-4164.

FANTASY ISLAND AMUSEMENT PARK
(Beach Haven, Long Beach Island, New Jersey)
Seasonal (Summer) and Year-Round

Contrary to the image created in the popular television show of the same name, you won't find any dwarves in white suits shouting "THE PLANE . . . THE PLANE" here. Rather, Fantasy Island is a family-style amusement park located six miles south of Surf City.

SPECIFICS: Fantasy Island receives more than 300 applications each year and hires approximately 250 new employees. During the peak summer season, 175-plus staff members work for the company at any one time. The park's year-round staff numbers approximately thirty. Summer seasonal positions begin on Memorial Day and last through Labor Day. There is no application deadline. Fantasy Island employs food handlers, game operators, ride operators, golf attendants, arcade attendants, ice cream attendants, maintenance staff, and mechanics.

INSIDER TIPS: Fantasy Island looks for "outgoing, personable, clean-cut, friendly, hard-working applicants." The park is located in a beach resort town and is within walking distance of the ocean.

PERKS: Employees receive meal discounts, free park guest passes, free uniforms, and participation in an employee bonus program. Fantasy Island employees are allowed unlimited access to the park when not on duty. Some housing is available for management employees.

TO APPLY: Applicants should write for an official application from the Personnel Department, Fantasy Island Amusement Park, 320 W. 7th Street, Beach Haven, New Jersey 08008; (609) 492-4000.

FRONTIER CITY THEME PARK
(Oklahoma City, Oklahoma)

Seasonal (Summer)

Frontier City Theme Park is modeled after a Wild West motif and is located in Oklahoma City, home of the Cowboy Hall of Fame. The park features a wide variety of rides, including several waterslides. Entertainment at Frontier City centers around the Old West theme, with gunfight demonstrations and multimedia shows depicting Oklahoma's history and heritage.

SPECIFICS: The park is an extremely popular employer with local students. Frontier City generally receives 1,200 applications for its 320 positions. However, due to a relatively high turnover, Frontier City usually hires about 600 new employees each year. Applicants must be available from about March through September. Positions include: food service attendant, ride operator, retail clerk, grounds attendant, games operator, and cash control attendant. Cash control attendants must be at least eighteen years old and games operators must have an extremely outgoing personality. Pay ranges from minimum wage to more than $7.00 per hour.

INSIDER TIPS: The park hires outgoing, intelligent, hard-working individuals who have big smiles.

PERKS: All of the park's facilities are available to employees while not on duty.

TO APPLY: Applicants should write for an official application from Tamorah Wright, 11501 NE Expressway, Oklahoma City, Oklahoma 73131; (405) 478-2140.

FUNLAND
(Rehoboth Beach, Delaware)
Seasonal (Summer)

For those seeking a summer working in a lively beach environment, Delaware's Funland is the perfect employer. Funland is a family-owned and -operated amusement center on the boardwalk in Rehoboth Beach, the self-proclaimed "Nation's Summer Capital."

SPECIFICS: Funland hires sixty-five seasonal staff members each summer to run its beachfront operations. The park's season runs daily from early June through early September. Available positions include ride operators, cashiers, games operators, and maintenance staff.

PERKS: Funland offers employee housing.

TO APPLY: Applicants should either write for an official application or send a cover letter and résumé to Funland/Seaside Amusements Inc., 6 Delaware Avenue, Rehoboth Beach, Delaware 19971; (302) 227-2785.

FUN TIME USA/BEACH AMUSEMENTS, INC.
(Long Beach, Mississippi)
Seasonal (Summer) and Year-Round

If you thought the only Long Beach was in Southern California, think again. Long Beach, Mississippi, is home to Fun Time USA beach amusement park.

SPECIFICS: Fun Time USA employs thirty-five to forty seasonal and year-round employees. The park is open daily year-round and hires both year-round and summer seasonal staff. Contact the Fun Time USA personnel office for information on specific positions available.

TO APPLY: For employment information contact Ken Davis, General Manager, Fun Time USA, 216 Trautman Avenue, Long Beach, Mississippi 39560; (601) 896-7315 or 863-0800.

HERSHEYPARK
(Hershey, Pennsylvania)
Seasonal (Summer)

Located in what is often referred to as Chocolate Town USA, Hersheypark is one of the twenty most popular amusement parks in America. This theme park lies on the original site of Mr. Hershey's "community park," which was founded in 1907.

SPECIFICS: Hersheypark typically receives 2,900 applications annually and employs 2,500-plus employees each year. The park is open each summer and applicants should ideally be available from Memorial Day through Labor Day. There is no application deadline. The park's employment office can provide applicants with a detailed list of positions and, when specified, applicable age requirements. Starting salaries in 1992 ranged from $4.50 per hour and higher.

INSIDER TIPS: Hersheypark seeks friendly, energetic employees who will maintain the company's reputation for excellent hospitality and quality. Like most large employers, Hersheypark has a detailed employee handbook, which enumerates the company's numerous rules and policies.

PERKS: Employees receive free or discounted admission to numerous other theme parks, discounts from many local merchants (with their Hersheypark employee ID), invitations to numerous Hersheypark activities, prizes via interdepartmental contests, and discounts at all park shops.

TO APPLY: Applicants should write or call for an official application and a copy of the Hersheypark Summer Employment Listings & Job

Descriptions brochure from Employment Manager, Hersheypark Employment Office, 100 West Hersheypark Drive, Hershey, Pennsylvania 17033; (717) 534-3326.

HOLIDAY WORLD
(Santa Claus, Indiana)
Seasonal (Summer)

Have you always dreamed of visiting Santa's workshop at the North Pole? Well, Holiday World may not be located in the arctic, but Santa Claus, Indiana, is about as close as most of us will ever get. Holiday World is a theme park featuring twenty-one rides, three gift shops, a museum, and a glassblower. And, new in 1992, a water park.

SPECIFICS: Holiday World hires 300 new employees annually to fill its 335 staff positions. The park receives approximately 700 applications annually. Wages range from minimum wage to approximately 50 cents per hour over minimum wage. Many employees are eligible for an end-of-season bonus of up to 12 cents per hour worked. Ideally, employees should be available from Memorial Day through Labor Day. The park has no application deadline. Positions are available for singers, dancers, games attendants, ride operators, food servers, sweepers, gift shop clerks, ticket takers, costume characters, cleaning personnel, warehouse persons, security officers, and gardeners. A marketing internship is also offered.

INSIDER TIPS: Applicants are screened on the basis of school grades, community and school activities, a neat and clean appearance, and positive personalities.

PERKS: Holiday World offers its employees free passes for family members, a 40% discount on food, 20% discount on souvenirs, free admission to the park when off duty, a 50% subsidy on mandatory uniforms, and several "Holiparties" throughout the summer.

TO APPLY: Applicants may either send a cover letter and résumé or write for an official application from Holiday World, Attn: Steve Hauser, Director of Personnel, Box 179, Santa Claus, Indiana 47579-0179; (812) 937-4401.

THE HUNTSVILLE DEPOT MUSEUM
(Huntsville, Alabama)
Seasonal (Summer) and Year-Round

For those who crave the nostalgic sound of the old steam engine, the Huntsville Depot Museum is the perfect spot. This attraction features both a railway museum and streetcar tours of Huntsville.

SPECIFICS: The Huntsville Depot Museum & Railroad Company employs five full-time plus twenty-five summer seasonal employees. Positions include ride operator, train engineer, ticket seller, maintenance staff, and food sales person.

TO APPLY: For application information write or call Personnel Director, Huntsville Depot Museum & Railroad Company, 320 Church Street, Huntsville, Alabama 35801; (205) 539-1860 or 532-7500.

HYLAND HILLS WATER WORLD
(Denver, Colorado)
Seasonal (Summer)

Located just fifteen minutes from downtown Denver, Hyland Hills' twenty acres provides gallons of summer aquatic enjoyment.

SPECIFICS: Hyland Hills Water World hires more than 400 new applicants each summer to fill its 575 staff positions. Each year the park receives approximately 1,000 applications. Employees must be available to work from Memorial Day weekend through Labor Day. All applications must be received by March 15. Positions are available for shallow water lifeguards (fifteen years old and older required), Ellis & Assoc. certified deep water lifeguards (sixteen and older), certified concessions attendants (sixteen and older; concessions experience preferred), cashiers (sixteen and older; cash register experience preferred), maintenance workers (sixteen and older), and grounds keepers (fourteen and older; will train). For information on Ellis & Assoc. training and certification programs, contact the employment office at the address below.

INSIDER TIPS: Hyland Hills seeks honest and reliable employees. Deep water lifeguards must have or obtain Ellis & Assoc. training and certification.

PERKS: Employees are permitted free use of the entire water park when off duty. Management provides merit incentives, discounts on meals, and free passes as a reward for good work.

TO APPLY: Applicants should write for an official application from Steve Loose, General Manager, Hyland Hills Water World, 1800 W. 89th Avenue, Denver, Colorado 80221; (303) 650-7516.

IDLEWILD PARK
(Ligonier, Pennsylvania)
Seasonal (Summer)

Pennsylvania's Idlewild Park is home of the "H$_2$Ooooh Zone," a thrilling area with a huge swimming pool and seven water slides. The park is set in 400 wooden acres including picnic areas, pavilions, fifteen major rides, ten kiddie rides, a Western town, and, new in 1989, "Mr. Rogers' Land of Make Believe." As Mr. Rogers would say, "Can you say, 'Summer Job?' I knew you could."

SPECIFICS: Idlewild Park receives approximately 600 applications each year for its 400 annual summer position openings. The park's staff totals 425. All jobs are summer seasonal, starting approximately mid-May and lasting through Labor Day. There is no application deadline. Jobs are available as hosts and hostesses for the following departments: rides, food service, games, cashiering, merchandising, sweeping, parking, certified lifeguards, grounds and ride maintenance, and entertainment. Wages start at minimum wage for first-year employees.

INSIDER TIPS: According to Personnel Director Joanne Gibas, "Idlewild Park is looking for bright, enthusiastic personalities to provide the best in family fun and entertainment. Hard work, a positive and safe attitude, doing whatever it takes to meet our guests' needs, and your SMILE will be the key to job success."

PERKS: Employees are allowed to use all of the park's facilities when not on duty. Additionally, staff members have free access to Kennywood, Idlewild Park's sister theme park. Employees who stay through Labor Day or until school starts are eligible for a bonus.

TO APPLY: Applicants must apply in person and interview at the time their application is filed. For more information contact Idlewild Park, Personnel Department, P.O. Box C, Ligonier, Pennsylvania 15658; (412) 238-3666.

JOYLAND AMUSEMENT COMPANY
(Wichita, Kansas)

Seasonal (Summer)

If Dorothy of the "Wizard of Oz" wanted to go for a modern-day spin, she would be better off visiting Joyland than getting caught up in a Kansas tornado. Joyland is one of the state's largest summer employers.

SPECIFICS: Joyland hires more than 150 seasonal summer employees. The park is open daily from early June through late August. Applications are accepted for ticket takers, ticket sellers, food vendors, ride operators, security officers, and maintenance personnel.

TO APPLY: Applicants should either write for an official application or send a cover letter and résumé to Personnel Office, Joyland Amusement Company, 2801 S. Hillside, Wichita, Kansas 67216; (316) 684-0179.

KENNYWOOD PARK
(West Mifflin, Pennsylvania)
Seasonal (Summer)

For more than ninety-five years Kennywood Park has been a favorite local getaway for Pittsburghers tired of big city life. The park is the self-proclaimed "roller coaster capital of the world."

SPECIFICS: Kennywood Park receives approximately 1,500 applications annually for its 1,000 seasonal summer positions. Since a large percentage of employees return year after year, approximately 400 new employees are hired annually. All jobs are summer seasonal beginning May 15. There is no application deadline. Applications are accepted for ride operators, game operators, food stand attendants, parking lot attendants, secretaries, security guards, gate cashiers, and lifeguards. Management refers to employees as "team members." Wages for first-year team members are generally minimum wage.

INSIDER TIPS: "We look for guys and gals who like to smile and have fun. If you want a season of fun that you will not soon forget, apply to be a Kennywood team member."

PERKS: Team members (employees) are eligible for a 30 cent per hour bonus for all hours worked if they stay through Labor Day. A discount employee cafeteria is available for staff members and employees receive free passes to Idlewild Park. Employees are encouraged to enjoy the rides when not at work.

TO APPLY: Applicants should either write for an official application or send a cover letter and résumé to Joseph J. Barron, Personnel Director, 4800 Kennywood Boulevard, West Mifflin, Pennsylvania 15122; (412) 461-0500.

KENTUCKY KINGDOM
(Louisville, Kentucky)

Seasonal (Summer)

Kentucky Kingdom is the Blue Grass State's answer to the Magic Kingdom. This new theme park opened in May 1987, making it one of the newest and most modern theme parks in the United States.

SPECIFICS: Kentucky Kingdom hires more than 350 seasonal summer employees each year. The park is open daily from May 23 through the end of August and weekends during September, October, and November. Applications are accepted for musicians, entertainers, costumed characters, ride operators, ticket sellers, ticket takers, maintenance personnel, food stand sales clerks, and parking control staff.

TO APPLY: Applicants should either write for an official application or send a cover letter and résumé to Personnel Office, Kentucky Kingdom, 730 Market Street West #110, Louisville, Kentucky 40202.

KINGS ISLAND
(Kings Island, Ohio)
Seasonal (Summer)

Have you always wanted to turn yourself over six times aboard the Vortex, thrill to the world famous Beast, or dare to stand up to the mighty King Cobra? If your answer to any of the above questions was "yes," you'll find nirvana at Ohio's Kings Island theme park.

SPECIFICS: Kings Island hires more than 3,500 seasonal employees. The park's summer season begins in April and runs through mid-October. Applications are accepted for both seasonal as well as full-time employment. Positions are available for ride operators, sales clerks, food and beverage staff, security officers, ticket sellers, ticket takers, costumed characters, musicians, entertainers, parking personnel, game operators, and more.

TO APPLY: Applicants should either apply in person at the personnel office or send a cover letter and résumé to Personnel Department, Kings Island, 6300 Kings Island Drive, Kings Island, Ohio 45034; (513) 398-5600.

MAGIC SPRINGS
(Hot Springs National Park, Arkansas)
Seasonal (Summer)

Magic Springs is a family-oriented theme park spanning more than forty acres and featuring twenty-three rides, and seven live shows.

SPECIFICS: Magic Springs has a high employee turnover rate and hires more than 500 new staffers each year to fill its 350-plus positions. Approximately 1,000 applications are received annually. Positions are available for ride operators, game operators, food servers, merchandise clerks, ticket sellers, and grounds keepers. There is no specific application deadline, but all employees must be available from Memorial Day through Labor Day. Pay ranges from minimum wage to $5.00 per hour (subject to change).

INSIDER TIPS: According to Ray Bragg, assistant general manager, "The park looks for applicants who are friendly, able to communicate with the public, and willing to work different shifts and days."

PERKS: All employees are permitted to use the park's facilities on their days off. Employees receive food discounts of up to 50% at selected outlets and free passes to the park. Magic Springs sponsors social events for the staff throughout the season.

TO APPLY: Applicants should write for an official application from Magic Springs Personnel Director, 2001 Highway 20 East, Hot Springs, Arkansas 71901; (501) 624-5411.

WORLDS OF FUN/OCEANS OF FUN
(Kansas City, Missouri)
Seasonal (Summer)

This is a complex of two theme attractions. Worlds of Fun packs more than 140 rides, shows, and attractions into its 170 acres. Oceans of Fun is the Midwest's tribute to a tropical water paradise featuring more than thirty-five wet 'n' wild adventures plus the Surf City Wave Pool.

SPECIFICS: These two parks hire from a combined employment office, which receives 4,500 applications each year to fill the 2,300 new positions available annually. The park is open daily during the summer and on weekends during the spring and fall. Available shifts include morning, midday, evening, and midnight. Applications are accepted through October 1 for each year's hiring season. Jobs are available in the following departments: food service, merchandising, park operations, warehouse, maintenance, costumes, cash control, security, water safety, and show productions. Employees must be at least sixteen years old. In the security department, tram drivers must be at least eighteen years of age and have a valid driver's license. College internships are also possible.

INSIDER TIPS: Worlds of Fun/Oceans of Fun seeks outgoing, enthusiastic, hard-working, responsible individuals who enjoy working with the public. A personal interview is required for all positions.

PERKS: Employees receive discounted meals, free uniforms, free parking, discounted passports (park admission tickets), free family passports, a bonus incentive program, complimentary passes to other theme parks and attractions, and invitations to numerous employee sport and social events. Moreover, all employees are permitted free admission to both parks when off duty.

TO APPLY: Applicants must apply in person at the Worlds of Fun personnel office, 4545 Worlds of Fun Avenue, Kansas City, Missouri 64161; (816) 454-4545, ext. 1010.

ONTARIO PLACE CORPORATION
(Toronto, Ontario, Canada)
Seasonal (Summer)

Ontario Place is a family-oriented attraction showcasing the province's recreational, cultural, and entertainment industries. The park is located on a group of man-made islands covering ninety-six acres on Lake Ontario.

SPECIFICS: Ontario Place Corporation hires 600 new staff members annually to fill its 800 positions. The company receives approximately 2,000 applications each year. Employees must be available from mid-April to mid-September. All applications must be received by February 17. Available positions include marine staff (water safety, CPR, and harbor license required), marketing and public relations officers, security personnel, first-aid attendants, office staff, hosts, guest services staff, maintenance personnel, programming, admissions and parking workers, and attractions staff. Salaries start at CAN$6.50 to CAN$7.50 depending on the position.

INSIDER TIPS: This is an ideal job for highly motivated, enthusiastic individuals who enjoy working with the public and like working outdoors in both rain and shine. Successful applicants must be available to work irregular hours throughout the summer, including days and evenings and some weekends.

PERKS: Employees receive free access to all of the park's attractions and rides when off duty. Staff receive a discount on food, free uniforms, end-of-season bonus on completion of contract, a guest pass to the park, and free access to a special employee lounge complete with lockers, showers, and lunchroom.

TO APPLY: Applicants should write for an official application or send a cover letter and résumé to Staff Coordinator, Ontario Place, 955 Lakeshore Boulevard West, Toronto, Ontario, M6K 3B9 Canada; (416) 965-7739.

OPRYLAND USA
(Nashville, Tennessee)
Seasonal (Summer)

Opryland USA is an umbrella term that describes a collection of entertainment, broadcasting, and hospitality businesses. The major components of Opryland USA are Opryland, a musical theme park featuring twenty-one rides and adventures and up to a dozen simultaneous stage shows; the Grand Ol' Opry, the longest-running live country music radio show in the world; the Nashville Network, a cable television network available across the United States and Canada; the Opryland Hotel; the General Jackson historic river showboat; WSM AM and FM radio stations; Gaylord Syndicom, a television program syndication concern; and the Opryland Music Group, a division dedicated to songwriting, music publishing, and recording.

SPECIFICS: Opryland Park receives more than 6,000 applications annually and hires 2,200-plus new employees each year to fill its 3,000 staff positions at Opryland, the Grand Ol' Opry, and aboard the General Jackson. Opryland offers a huge variety of positions in each of its ten major departments. The cash control department functions as the bank of the park, preparing the tills for all park operations and controlling all aspects of cash control and payroll. The customer service department operates the ticket sales offices and staffs the phone reservations center. The food service department is one of the largest departments at Opryland USA. This department operates all concession stands. For those wishing to work as deck hands, deck hostesses, or guest hostesses, the General Jackson showboat department is ideal. Deckhands must be at least eighteen years old and all other employees on the showboat must be at least seventeen years old. The hospitality department is responsible for the overall operations at the park, including taking tickets, staffing information booths, and operating all of the rides and attractions. The maintenance department is responsible for the general upkeep of the park. In addition, maintenance workers care for the exotic animals in the petting zoo. The merchandise department operates all games and gift shops throughout the complex. The wardrobe department is responsible for the care and distribution of the costumes that all Opryland USA employees wear. Other departments include security, Grand Ol' Opry (tours and ticket clerks), and accounting. Pay starts at minimum wage and goes up according to the position and experience.

INSIDER TIPS: Opryland seeks responsible, mature, outgoing employees who are dependable and hard-working. A neat and clean "all-American" appearance is extremely important. Many positions are available without prior experience. There is no application deadline. Opryland provides internships for qualified candidates. The park endeavors to accommodate special needs such as scheduling, carpooling, and physical handicaps.

PERKS: After the fifth paycheck all employees receive five free passes to the park. Employee parties are held regularly both in the park, aboard the General Jackson, and throughout Nashville. Opryland offers a bonus program and has several scholarships available. All employees are allowed full access to the park during the hours they are not working.

TO APPLY: Applicants should write for an official application from Laura Cary, Employment Coordinator, 2802 Opryland Drive, Nashville, Tennessee 37214; (615) 871-6621. All applicants are required to undergo a personal interview before final hiring. For information on where and when the employment representative nearest you will be visiting, contact the office at the phone number above.

PEONY PARK
(Omaha, Nebraska)
Seasonal (Summer)

If you thought Nebraska was entirely flat, you haven't seen the steep slopes of Peony Park's twenty major rides. This large amusement park features a wide variety of both adult and children's rides.

SPECIFICS: Peony Park hires a large number of seasonal summer employees each year. Employees should be available to work from at least Memorial Day through Labor Day. Applications are accepted for ride operators, ticket sellers, ticket takers, picnic area staff, lifeguards, maintenance personnel, games operators, retail sales staff, entertainers, food servers, cooks, and hotel staff.

TO APPLY: Applicants should either write for an official application or send a cover letter and résumé to Jim Hronek, Personnel Office, Peony Park, 8100 Cass Street, Omaha, Nebraska 68144; (402) 391-6253.

PLAZA ACUATICA
(Hato Ray, Puerto Rico)
Seasonal (Summer and Winter) and Year-Round

Plaza Acuatica is one of Puerto Rico's premier theme attractions.

SPECIFICS: Plaza Acuatica hires 450 new employees each year from an annual application pool of 2,500. Positions are available for both summer and winter seasonal staff as well as year-round employees. Employees may work either full or part time. Applicants for summer positions must apply by May of each year, although some hiring is done throughout the year as positions become available. Applications are accepted for food attendants, park services staff, merchandise attendants, ticket sellers, ticket takers, parking lot attendants, cashiers, ride operators, first-aid attendants (emergency medical technicians, paramedics, nurses, or doctors), lifeguards (Red Cross lifesaving and CPR certificates required plus must pass a screening swim test), secretaries (must be bilingual in English and Spanish), guest relations operators, department supervisors (experience required), and department foremen (experience required). Pay starts at minimum wage and goes up according to the position and experience.

INSIDER TIPS: Plaza Acuatica primarily employs college students who are seventeen years of age or older. Applicants are screened on the basis of their school and social activities, club or sports involvement, appearance, and attitude. Fluency in Spanish is essential.

PERKS: All employees are permitted unlimited free access to the park when not at work.

TO APPLY: Applicants should write for an official application or send a cover letter, résumé, and photograph to Plaza Acuatica, P.O. Box 1994, Hato Rey, Puerto Rico 00919-1994; (809) 754-9800.

PLEASUREWOOD HILLS AMERICAN THEME PARK
(Suffolk, England)
Seasonal (Summer and Winter) and Year-Round

Pleasurewood is one of the few "American-style" theme parks in Europe. This park is modeled after a typical American amusement park, complete with thrill rides, water rides, costumed cartoon characters, roller coasters, and, of course, hot dogs.

SPECIFICS: Pleasurewood seeks both seasonal (summer and winter) and long-term employees. The park receives approximately 400 applications annually for its 250 staff positions. Approximately 275 new employees are hired annually. Seasonal help must be available from April 29 through late September. Applications for summer help are accepted through March. Starting wages range from approximately £115 to £118 per week. Positions are available for security guards, cashiers, attraction attendants, grounds workers, maintenance workers, train drivers, train guards, cleaners, costumed characters, catering assistants, shop assistants, and performers.

INSIDER TIPS: Management seeks honest, reliable, pleasant applicants with an ability to communicate well with members of the public. All foreign applicants must have, or be able to obtain, a valid work permit.

PERKS: Employees are allowed unlimited free access to the park when off duty. They are provided with a monthly bonus for uniforms, free staff pass, and complimentary tickets to the park for family members.

TO APPLY: Applicants should write for an official application from J. R. Packer, General Manager, Pleasurewood Hills American Theme Park, Dark. Corton, Lowestoft, England; phone: 0502-513626 or 513627. A photograph is requested with all applications.

PONDEROSA RANCH
(Incline Village, Nevada)
Seasonal (Summer)

If you've ever wished you could venture back to the wonderful days of yesteryear, here is your chance. The shores of Lake Tahoe at Incline Village are home to the famous Ponderosa Ranch of television's "Bonanza" fame. The park features the Cartwright ranch house, a replica of an old Western town, hay wagon breakfast rides, and several food and beverage outlets. The most popular menu item at the Ponderosa is, of course, the HossBurger.

SPECIFICS: The Ponderosa Ranch receives approximately 300 applications each year and hires seventy new staff members to fill its eighty positions. Seasonal summer help should be available, if possible, from Memorial Day through the Labor Day weekend. Positions are available for tour guides, sales clerks, saloon workers, photographers, tram drivers, and ranch hands. Pay ranges from $4.50 to $5.00 per hour with a bonus for employees who stay through the Labor Day weekend. The ranch responds to all applications within a month.

INSIDER TIPS: The ranch looks for "friendly, hard-working people pleasers."

PERKS: Employees are provided with free uniforms and are allowed free access to the park while off duty.

TO APPLY: Applicants should write for an official application or send a cover letter, résumé, and photograph to David Geddes, P.O. Box A.P., Incline Village, Nevada 89450; (702) 831-0691.

QUEEN MARY/SPRUCE GOOSE ENTERTAINMENT CENTER
(Long Beach, California)
Seasonal (Summer) and Year-Round

This popular Southern California attraction offers visitors both the *Queen Mary,* the world's largest ocean liner, and the Spruce Goose, the world's largest airplane. The *Queen Mary* operates as both a floating hotel and tourist attraction. The huge Spruce Goose, built by Howard Hughes, is housed on the pier adjacent to the ship under the world's largest aluminum dome.

SPECIFICS: The Queen Mary/Spruce Goose employs 1,100 personnel plus 400 additional summer staff each year. Approximately 600 new employees are hired annually from a pool of 3,300 applications. Summer staff must be available from June through Labor Day. All applications for summer employment must be received by May 15. Positions are available for attraction attendants, tour guides, food service staff, entertainers, merchandise sales staff, hotel front desk clerks, hotel housekeepers, bellhops, and all other typical hotel staff positions.

INSIDER TIPS: Management looks for clean-cut applicants who— even when dealing with large groups—demonstrate pleasant personalities, intelligence, and enthusiasm.

PERKS: All employees receive complimentary coupons to the *Queen Mary* and Spruce Goose attractions as well as discount passes to other nearby attractions such as Disneyland. Occasional discounts are also offered to the entertainment center's special events.

TO APPLY: Applicants should either write or call for an official application or send a cover letter and résumé to Human Resources Department, Queen Mary/Spruce Goose, P.O. Box 8, Long Beach, California 90801; (213) 435-3511. Management is unable to respond to all applications.

RAGING WATERS/MARINERS LANDING AMUSEMENT PIER
(Wildwood, New Jersey)

Seasonal (Summer)

Situated on the southern shore of New Jersey, these family-style amusement parks feature a variety of rides that treat guests to everything from waterslides to screaming airborne rollercoasters.

SPECIFICS: Mariner's Landing Amusement Pier hires 250 to 300 employees each summer to fill its 200 jobs. Applications are accepted for retail sales clerks, ride operators, ticket sellers, and lifeguards. For those applying for lifeguarding positions, safety certification is a must. Management can arrange accommodations for out-of-town staff but must know well ahead of time in order to make arrangements.

INSIDER TIPS: Customer safety is foremost and management looks for applicants with "honesty, a pleasant attitude and appearance, and a good attitude toward children."

PERKS: In addition to ride and water park privileges, staff members receive VIP passes, family discount tickets, and seasonal bonus plans.

TO APPLY: Applicants should write for an official application or send a résumé, cover letter, and photograph to Rom Nardi, Manager, Raging Waters/Mariner's Landing, P.O. Box 269, Wildwood, New Jersey 08260; (609) 729-0586.

ROCKY POINT AMUSEMENTS, INC.
(Narragansett Bay, Rhode Island)
Seasonal (Summer)

Situated on the shores of Narragansett Bay, Rocky Point offers more than thirty rides and daily variety shows.

SPECIFICS: Management receives about 2,000 applicants for 600 annual job openings. The park's staff totals 700. Applications are accepted for ride operators, cashiers, ticket salespersons and collectors, food servers, sanitation workers, and mechanics. Salaries range from minimum wage to $6.50 an hour (subject to change).

INSIDER TIPS: Candidates with maturity, dependability, a neat appearance, and a concern for general safety and courtesy receive top priority during the selection process.

PERKS: Employees enjoy free park passes, an end-of-season bonus program, overtime pay, and free or discounted admission to concerts and entertainment events. Staff members may use all of the facilities free of charge during their days off.

TO APPLY: For application information contact Operations Director, Rocky Point Park, One Rocky Point Avenue, Warwick Neck, Rhode Island 02889; (401) 737-8000.

SANTA CRUZ BEACH BOARDWALK
(Santa Cruz, California)
Seasonal (Summer) and Year-Round

The Santa Cruz Beach Boardwalk is a historic theme park located right on the beach. Santa Cruz is located less than an hour from both scenic Monterey and California's famous Silicon Valley. The park includes two rides that have been named U.S. historic landmarks: the 1911 Looff carousel and the popular 1924 Giant Dipper roller coaster.

SPECIFICS: The Santa Cruz Beach Boardwalk has a total staff of 1,200 employees and hires more than 1,000 new employees annually. The park receives approximately 4,000 applications annually. Seasonal staff must be available from approximately June 15 through September 4. Wages vary by position from approximately $4.50 to $6.50 per hour. Applications are accepted for arcade operators, buildings/grounds crew, cashiers, costumed characters, food service operators, ride operators, and security officers. Food service operators, arcade operators, and buildings/grounds crew must be at least eighteen years old and security officers must be more than twenty-one years old. All other employees must be sixteen years of age or older. Positions are also available in the conference and banquet facility.

INSIDER TIPS: According to management, successful employees are interested in people and have friendly, outgoing, warm personalities. Santa Cruz Beach Boardwalk requires neat grooming and appearance. All applicants should have an enthusiasm for serving others and a desire to spend a summer of work and play in beautiful beachfront Santa Cruz. Availability to work through the end of the season (Labor Day) is a major factor in the hiring decision.

PERKS: Benefits include an extensive employee activity program (highlighted by a private cruise on a San Francisco Bay party boat at the end of the season). All staff receive free uniforms and laundry, reduced meal prices, free passes to the boardwalk, discounts at other nearby attractions, and an employee housing program. Employee housing is limited and available on a first come, first served basis.

TO APPLY: Applicants should write for an official application or send a cover letter and résumé to Employment Office, Santa Cruz Beach Boardwalk, 400 Beach Street, Santa Cruz, California 90560; (408) 423-5590, ext. 2318. Foreign applicants must provide a current work visa.

SEA WORLD OF CALIFORNIA
(San Diego, California; Orlando, Florida)
Seasonal (Summer and Winter) and Year-Round

As a child, was "Flipper" your favorite television show? Have you ever longed to kiss a walrus in front of a crowd of thousands? How about babysitting for several hundred baby penguins? Sea World of California is part of Sea World's chain of premier marine-life parks.

SPECIFICS: Sea World's California operation employs between 2,500 and 3,000 staff members. Sea World of Florida employs 2,700 new staff members annually from a field of over 11,000 applicants. Full- or part-time employment is available for both summer and winter seasonal help as well as year-round employees. Summer help must be available from May 30 through September 6. Winter seasonal help is generally hired for the busy Christmas (December 18–January 2) and Easter (week before and week after Easter) seasons. Positions are available for tour guides, operations hosts/hostesses, ticket sales staff, food service employees, landscapers, payroll clerks, data entry clerks, vault case control clerks, animal care specialists, lab technicians, medical technologists, aquarium staff, aviculture staff (responsible for care of penguins), science writers, education specialists, show announcers, scenic arts craftsmen, entertainers, electronic show technicians, graphic artists, pressmen, sign makers, merchandise sales clerks, car washers, dock hands, and entertainment characters and performers. Starting wages range from $4.75 to $5.25 per hour for most positions.

INSIDER TIPS: Positions performing with live marine animals are the most popular and difficult to obtain. Sea World seeks applicants who can approach their jobs with enthusiasm and a willingness to work full time at peak efficiency.

PERKS: Seasonal employees receive park uniforms and an ID card that entitles them to a 30% discount on all food and merchandise in the park. Employees also receive several complimentary passes to the park and discount coupons for other surrounding attractions.

TO APPLY: Applicants for California should apply in person to Sea World, Personnel Office, 1720 S. Shores Road, San Diego, California 92109; (619) 222-6363. Florida applicants should either apply in person or send a cover letter and résumé to Terri Robertson, Personnel Specialist, Sea World Personnel Office, 7007 Sea World Drive, Orlando, Florida 32821; (407) 351-3600. Applications are considered active for only thirty days. If you have not been offered a position within that time and still wish to be considered, you should reapply.

SIX FLAGS GREAT AMERICA
(Gurnee, Illinois)
Seasonal (Summer) and Year-Round

Six Flags Great America is a huge 325-acre theme park and entertainment center.

SPECIFICS: Six Flags Great America employs up to 3,000 new staff members each year to fill its 190 year-round and 3,000 to 5,000 summer seasonal jobs. Employees are selected from an annual application pool of 6,000 applicants. Although there are no set dates for summer help, ideal applicants need to have flexible schedules from April through September. There is no official application deadline for summer staff positions. Jobs are available in all of Great America's five divisions: Marketing, Finance and Administration, Park Operations, Retail, and Maintenance.

INSIDER TIPS: Ideally applicants should be available from April through September; however, the park is flexible and attempts to work around candidates' schedules. "We want our employees to enjoy variety in their work and have fun, but also to keep in mind that fun is a serious business."

PERKS: Employees are permitted unlimited free access to all of Great America's facilities when off duty. Employees also receive free costumes and uniforms, free park passes and tickets, admission to numerous free employee social functions, and special discounts on park merchandise.

TO APPLY: Applicants should write for an official application or send a cover letter and résumé to Jim Franz or Jewell Bailey, P.O. Box 1776, Gurnee, Illinois 60031; (312) 249-2045.

SIX FLAGS MAGIC MOUNTAIN
(Valencia, California)
Seasonal (Summer and Winter) and Year-Round

If you've always enjoyed a little ride in the park, then you'll love the rides at Six Flags Magic Mountain. In the highly competitive Southern California theme park market, Six Flags Magic Mountain is the uncontested king of the mountain when it comes to high thrill rides.

SPECIFICS: Six Flags Magic Mountain receives more than 7,500 annual applications and hires 5,000 new staff members annually to fill its 3,500 jobs. While the park hires both year-round as well as winter and summer seasonal staff, its busiest season is from May through September. Starting wages in 1992 began at $4.25 per hour. For those applicants sixteen years old or older, positions are available in the following departments: admissions, animal farm, food service, games, merchandise, park service attendant, ride operations, traffic control, and entertainment. The following departments are also available for applicants over the age of eighteen: cash control, clerical/secretarial, crafts, guest relations, security, stage technicians, warehouse, wardrobe, and animal chatter (handles and performs with live animals during shows).

INSIDER TIPS: The park seeks applicants with a neat, clean, well-groomed look. Safety and guest-friendly hospitality are the park's primary concerns.

PERKS: All employees are allowed unlimited use of the park during their time off. Six flags offers employees free parking, free uniforms, flexible hours, free park passes for friends and family, employee parties, an employee discount cafeteria, carpool assistance, honesty award programs, safety awards, and more.

TO APPLY: Applicants should write for an official application from Patti Madsen, Six Flags Magic Mountain, P.O. Box 5500, Valencia, California 91385; (805) 255-4801.

SIX FLAGS OVER GEORGIA
(Atlanta, Georgia)
Seasonal (Summer)

Six Flags Over Georgia is one of the southeastern United States' most popular theme parks. This member of the Six Flags chain attracts nearly two and a half million visitors annually.

SPECIFICS: Six Flags Over Georgia hires 2,500-plus seasonal summer staff members each year. The park's seasonal staff should be available to work from approximately late May or early June through late August or early September. The park hires ride operators, sales clerks, food and beverage staff, parking attendants, maintenance staff, security officers, entertainers, and musicians.

INSIDER TIPS: Six Flags prides itself on its friendly, well-groomed staff. A clean-cut appearance is extremely important to management.

PERKS: Specific perks vary by position but generally include complimentary admission to the park for off-duty staff.

TO APPLY: Applicants should write for an official application from Personnel Department, Six Flags Over Georgia, P.O. Box 43187, Atlanta, Georgia 30378; (404) 948-9290 or 948-4378.

SIX FLAGS OVER TEXAS
(Arlington, Texas)
Seasonal (Summer and Winter) and Year-Round

Six Flags Over Texas opened in 1961 as the first regional theme park in the United States. The park is spread over 206 acres and features more than 100 rides, shows, and other attractions. Six Flags is Texas's top tourist attraction and plays host to more than two and a half million visitors each year.

SPECIFICS: Six Flags Over Texas hires 3,500-plus new employees each year to fill its 2,666 regular positions. The Park receives in excess of 9,000 employment applications annually. Employees are hired for both year-round work as well as either summer or winter seasonal staffing needs. The park also hires part-time staff for weekends in the spring and fall. The park has no application deadline. Applications are encouraged for those seeking positions in the following departments: host/hostess, gifts, foods, rides, traffic, games and attractions, security, park services, and shows.

INSIDER TIPS: Six Flags Over Texas looks for employees who are self-motivated, friendly, outgoing, and service-oriented. The park is anxious to hire students and attempts to work around school schedules when selecting employment dates.

PERKS: After an initial thirty-day probation period the park gives all employees five free passes. The park also has an excellent employee activity program including dances, pool parties, sporting leagues, and an employee "Olympics." Free uniforms are supplied to all employees. Employees enjoy a 400-person staff canteen, employee swimming pool, and an employee store.

TO APPLY: For employment information contact the Employment Office at Six Flags Over Texas, P.O. Box 191, Arlington, Texas 76004; (817) 640-8900. A personal interview is required.

TAMAN IMPIAN JAYA ANCOL (JAYA ANCOL DREAMLAND)
(Jakarta, Indonesia)
Seasonal (Summer) and Year-Round

Jaya Ancol Dreamland is one of the largest theme parks in Indonesia. The park is located on the beach in Jakarta.

SPECIFICS: Dreamland employs more than 2,000 staff members to run its many operations. Of these, approximately 315 new employees are hired each year out of 2,400 applicants. Thus, competition for jobs here is keen. The park hires both long- and short-term employees. Seasonal help is also hired for major Indonesian and Moslem holidays as well as Christmas and New Year. Positions are available for ticket takers, cleaners and gardeners, parking attendants, ride operators, and security and safety personnel. Naturally, all foreign applicants must have applicable work permits.

INSIDER TIPS: All employees must be under twenty-seven years old and have a high school diploma. Beware: Wages in Indonesia are extremely low by Western standards. Employees earn what is considered a typical wage for a high school graduate, RP3,500 per day (approximately US$2.00 per day).

PERKS: Employees are provided with free meals, uniforms, and park passes. Also, all employees are eligible for periodic bonuses.

TO APPLY: Applicants should send a cover letter and résumé to Pt. Pembangunan Jaya, Jalan Lodan Timur No. 7, Ancol, Jakarta, Utara, Indonesia; phone: 681511 or 681512. The park does not respond to all applications.

THUMB FUN PARK
(Fish Creek, Wisconsin)
Seasonal (Summer)

Thumb Fun Park is an amusement/theme park located in the heart of Wisconsin's self-proclaimed vacationland, Door County.

SPECIFICS: Positions are available for both full-time as well as part-time seasonal summer employment. Applications are accepted for ride hosts/hostesses, cashiers, food service staff, actors, games attendants, food service supervisors, grounds keepers, office personnel, housing supervisor, and entertainment supervisor.

INSIDER TIPS: "A fun job with fun people in a fun vacation spot."

PERKS: Perks vary according to position and are discussed at the time employment is offered.

TO APPLY: Applicants should write for an official application from Personnel Department, Thumb Fun Park, P.O. Box 128, Highway 42, Fish Creek, Wisconsin 54121; (414) 868-3418.

TIMBER RIDES
(Ocean City, Maryland)
Seasonal (Winter and Summer)

Situated on the Maryland coast, Timber Rides of Ocean City boasts a glittering array of more than 100 rides and recreational activities for the whole family. A highlight of the park is one of the world's oldest operating carousels, complete with handcrafted wooden animals.

SPECIFICS: Timber Rides of Ocean City hires 250 new staff members each season. Applications are accepted as ride operators, cashiers, game supervisors, retail clerks, flume attendants, lifeguards, and housekeepers. Most salaries for the 1989 season were set at $4.25 per hour, with a 20 cents per hour worked bonus for staff members who work through Labor Day (subject to change). Applicants must be at least eighteen years old and available to work from Memorial Day through Labor Day.

INSIDER TIPS: Management describes their ideal candidates as "trustworthy and very safety-conscious."

PERKS: Housing is available for full-time staff members. Employees can ride any of the attractions on their days off.

TO APPLY: Applicants should send a cover letter, résumé, and photograph to Linda T. Holloway, Office Manager, P.O. Box 1577, Ocean City, Maryland 21842; (301) 289-8617.

UNIVERSAL STUDIOS TOUR
(Universal City, California)
Seasonal (Summer and Winter) and Year-Round and Evening (Part-time)

Universal Studios, founded in 1915, is one of Southern California's most famous motion picture studios. With more than 420 acres, Universal Studios is the largest studio in California and produces more than twenty feature films each year. For those who want a behind-the-scenes look at Hollywood, the Universal Studios Tour explores the studio's huge lot and includes a look at many aspects of modern film making.

SPECIFICS: Employment opportunities with Universal Studios, like the studio itself, are unique. The studio employs 2,500 people during peak season and hires 1,600-plus new employees annually, for which the studio receives more than 9,000 applications each year. Between 300 and 800 additional employees are added during the busy peak seasons including summer and the Christmas and Easter holidays. Most employment opportunities are featured in and around the studio's Entertainment Center. Only the highly coveted tour guide positions allow access to the entire Universal Studios lot. Tour guide positions are especially beneficial for aspiring actors/actresses, future movie directors/producers, and special effects technicians. Since tours are given in over a dozen different languages, bilingual persons are especially encouraged to apply for tour guide positions. Tour guides must be at least seventeen years old and pass a nine-day training program prior to being accepted for employment. Tour guides must have an outgoing personality and excellent vocal skills.

Although tour guide positions are the most glamorous, all employment opportunities at Universal are exciting. Universal Studios hires numerous applicants to work in and around the Entertainment Center, the heart of the tour. At the center, employees are surrounded by visitors from around the world. Applications are accepted for Entertainment Center positions as merchandise and sales clerks, ticket sellers, patio hosts/hostesses, parking lot tollbooth attendants, food service personnel (math skill test may be required), park attendants (responsible for keeping the park clean), strollers (perform non-vocal character roles for guests—must meet certain height requirements and be able to wear heavy masks and costumes), and crowd and show control staff.

Additionally, the Universal Amphitheater hires part-time staff members for its regular evening performances. Applications are accepted for amphitheater jobs as ushers, stand attendants, house attendants (responsible for keeping the amphitheater clean), ticket takers, merchandise sales staff, and parking lot tollbooth attendants. Since shows don't happen every night, these positions are especially suited for students who need time for classes and study.

INSIDER TIPS: The studio seeks outgoing and enthusiastic employees who enjoy working outdoors. All employees must enjoy meeting and greeting people.

PERKS: Employees are given complimentary tour tickets, free uniforms, free parking, discounts on food and merchandise (food service employees are entitled to free food), and medical and dental insurance. Employees are invited to regular free preview screenings of major motion picture releases and the studio hosts a huge annual party as a "thank you" to its employees.

TO APPLY: Applicants should send a cover letter and résumé to Universal Studios Tour, Employee Selection, P.O. Box 8620, Universal City, California 91608; (818) 777-3863. A personal interview is required of all applicants.

WATER TOWN, INC.
(Shreveport, Louisiana)
Seasonal (Summer)

There is no better place to beat the heat and humidity of Louisiana's Cajun summers than Water Town in Shreveport.

SPECIFICS: Water Town hires more than 100 seasonal summer employees each year. Employees should be available from approximately May through August. Applications are accepted for ride operators, ticket sellers, lifeguards, ticket takers, maintenance staff, gift shop sales clerks, food and beverage staff, costumed characters, and arcade workers.

TO APPLY: Applicants should either write for an official application or send a cover letter and résumé to Personnel Manager, Water Town, P.O. Box 29009, Shreveport, Louisiana 71149-9009; (318) 938-5475.

WATERWORLD USA
(Sacramento, California)
Seasonal (Summer)

The ocean has come to California's capital with the 1988 opening of Breaker Beach at Sacramento's Waterworld USA. Waterworld USA is a family fun water park located on the grounds of the Cal Expo.

SPECIFICS: Waterworld USA hires more than 300 new applicants each summer to fill its 200 regular staff positions. Approximately 500 applications are received annually. The park gives preference to applicants who can work weekends in the spring and fall and daily in the summer. However, many employees who can only work during the summer are also hired. Jobs are available for ride operators, lifeguards (must have current Red Cross CPR, first aid, and lifesaving certificates), managers, security officers, park ambassadors, clerical staff, emergency medical technicians (EMT certificate or qualifications in emergency medical care required), accounting/marketing interns, food service staff, grounds keepers, landscape staff, and ticket salespersons.

INSIDER TIPS: Applicants must be enthusiastic, reliable, and have high grooming standards. The most important qualification is a genuine desire to please the public. The park calls its employees "ambassadors."

PERKS: Employees are permitted unlimited use of the park's facilities when off duty.

TO APPLY: Applicants should send a cover letter and résumé to Personnel Office, Waterworld USA, 1600 Exposition Boulevard, Sacramento, California 95815; (916) 924-0556. Waterworld also has a park in Phoenix, Arizona (see listing in Deserts chapter).

WHITEWATER WATERPARK
(Niagara Falls, Ontario, Canada)
Seasonal (Summer)

If you thought the only whitewater on the Canadian–U.S. border was at the bottom of Niagara Falls, you've never been to Whitewater Waterpark. Located just on the Canadian side of the border, this park thrills summer visitors with five giant waterslides, a huge 10,000-square-foot wave pool, hot tubs, and kiddie pools.

SPECIFICS: Whitewater Waterpark receives approximately 100 applications for its twenty annual job openings. The park's summer seasonal staff totals sixty employees. All jobs are summer seasonal, with some positions beginning as early as mid-March. There is no application deadline. Applications are accepted for lifeguards (must have CPR certificate and either Canadian National Lifesaving certificate or Bronze Cross Medallion), cashiers, park monitors, landscapers, janitors, and maintenance staff.

INSIDER TIPS: "We give a preference to those applicants with a swimming background or anyone with bilingual skills."

PERKS: Each year a CAN$250 scholarship is given to the park's best employee.

TO APPLY: Applicants should send a cover letter and résumé to Mrs. Louise Lewis, Whitewater Waterpark, 7430 Lundy's Lane, Niagara Falls, Ontario, L2H 1G8 Canada; (416) 357-3380.

OTHER EMPLOYERS

According to the International Association of Amusement Parks and Attractions (IAAPA), the following parks also recruit seasonal staff members. The IAAPA's membership includes hundreds of theme parks and attractions from around the world. The association sells a complete list of its members for approximately $65. To obtain a complete list of members contact the IAAPA and request their current *International Directory and Buyer's Guide.* The IAAPA can be reached at 4230 King Street, Alexandria, Virginia 22302-1507; (703) 671-5800.

Other parks that recruit seasonal summer employees include:

Canada's Wonderland
9580 Jane Street
Maple, ON, L0J 1E0
Canada
(416) 832-7000
Employees: 2,500 seasonal
(Summer)
Amusement Park/
Marine-Life Shows/
Stage Shows/Arcade

Edmonton Northlands
Box 1480
Edmonton, AB T5J 2N5
Canada
(403) 471-7210
Employees: 200
year-round; 1,400
seasonal (Summer); 2,500
during annual summer
fair (Klondike Days)
Ice Rink/Horse
Racing/Concert Arena

Enchanted Village
36201 Kit Corner Road S.
Federal Way, Washington
98003
(206) 838-8676; 927-9335.
Employees: 425 seasonal
(Summer)
Theme Park

**Fame City & Fame City
Waterworks**
13700 Beechnut
Houston, Texas 77083
(713) 530-7777

Employees: 250 seasonal
(Summer)
Amusement Park/Water
Park

Fantasy Island
2400 Grand Island Blvd.
Grand Island, New York
14072
(716) 773-7591
Employees: 500 seasonal
(Summer)
Theme Park/Petting
Zoo/Marine Shows

Funtown USA
774 Portland Road
Saco, Maine 04072
(207) 284-5139; 284-7113
Employees: 264 seasonal
(Summer)
Amusement Park/Arcade

Ghost Town in the Sky
P.O. Box 368, U.S. 19
Maggie Valley, North
Carolina 28751
(704) 926-1140; 926-1159
Employees: 200 seasonal
(Summer)
Old West Theme Park on
Ghost Mountain

Graceland
3797 Elvis Presley Blvd.
Memphis, Tennessee
38116
(901) 332-3322

Employees: number
unavailable
Historic Home of Elvis
Presley

**Grand Strand
Amusement Park**
P.O. Box 975
Myrtle Beach, South
Carolina 29578
(803) 448-3516; 448-6115
Employees: 100 seasonal
(Summer)
Amusement Park/
Beach/Arcade

**Grundy Entertainment
Pty. Ltd.**
P.O. Box 371
Surfers Paradise,
Queensland 4217
Australia
(075) 389011
Employees: 160
year-round; 50 seasonal
Amusement Park/
Arcade/Concert Arena

**Harbourside Amusement
Park**
P.O. Box 160
1 Olympic Drive
Milsons Point, N.S.W.
2061 Australia
(02) 922-6644
Employees: 600
year-round

Amusement Park/Arcade
on Scenic Sydney
Harbour

Heritage USA
Route 21 (Business)
Fort Mill, South Carolina
29715
(704) 542-6000
Employees: number
unavailable
Christian Amusement
Park/Home of P.T.L.
Cable TV Network

Knott's Berry Farm
8039 Beach Boulevard
Buena Park, California
90620
(714) 827-1776
Employees: 1,986
year-round; 1,615
seasonal (Summer); and
1,186 part-time
Amusement Park/Stage
Shows/Marine-Life
Shows/Concert Arena

**La Ronde Amusement
Park**
Canada Pavilion,
Montreal, PQ, H3C 1A9,
Canada
(514) 872-6120; 872-5574
Employees: 750 seasonal
(Summer)
Amusement
Park/Arcade/Concert
Arena/Owned by City of
Montreal

Lake Raystown Resort
Entriken, Pennsylvania
16638
(814) 658-3500
Employees: 275-plus
seasonal (Summer)
Water Park/Marina/Lake

**Lakewood Camping
Resort**
5901 Highway 17 S.
Myrtle Beach, South
Carolina 29577
(803) 238-5161
Employees: 180 seasonal
(Summer)
Beach/Campground/
Shows/Amusement Park

Magic Harbor
2901 S. Kings Highway
Myrtle Beach, South
Carolina 29577
(803) 238-0717; 238-5105
Employees: 400 seasonal
(Summer)
Amusement Park/Beach/
Arcade/Concert Arena

**Myrtle Beach Pavilion &
Amusement Park**
P.O. Drawer 2095
Myrtle Beach, South
Carolina 29578
(803) 448-6456
Employees: 400 seasonal
(Summer)
Amusement Park

Odyssey Land
1511 Roundhill Road

Oak Hill, West Virginia
25901
(304) 469-6841
Employees: number
unavailable
Theme Park

Riverside Park
P.O. Box 307
1623 Main Street
Agawam, Massachusetts
01001
(413) 786-9300
Employees: 2,000 seasonal
(Summer)
Amusement Park/
Speedway/Petting Zoo/
Concert Arena

Sea World of Texas
P.O. Box 686050
6854 Alamo Downs
Pkwy.
San Antonio, Texas
78268-6050
(512) 523-3000
Employees: number
unavailable; park
opening May 1988.
Marine/Aquatic Park

Seabreeze Park
4600 Culver Road
Rochester, New York
14622
(716) 323-1900
Employees: 450 seasonal
(Summer)
Amusement Park/
Arcade/Carousel Museum

Six Flags Atlantis
P.O. Box 2128
2700 Stirling Road
Hollywood, Florida 33022
(305) 926-1001; 920-9079
Employees: 400 seasonal
(Summer)
Water Park/Marina/
Arcade/Concert Arena

**Six Flags over
Mid-America**
P.O. Box 60
Eureka, Montana 63025
(314) 938-5300
Employees: 2,000 seasonal
(Summer)
Amusement Park/Beach/
Arcade/Concert Arena/
Stage Shows

Valleyfair
One Valleyfair Drive
Shakopee, Minnesota
55379
(612) 445-7600
Employees: 1,100 seasonal
(Summer)
Amusement Park/
Petting Zoo/
Arcade

**Six Flags Great
Adventure**
Route 537
P.O. Box 120
Jackson, New Jersey
08527
(201) 928-2000; 928-2775
Employees: 3,000 seasonal
(Summer)
Amusement Park/Stage
Shows/Drive-Thru Safari

**Station Touristique
Bromont**
P.O. Box 29
Bromont, PQ, J0E 1L0,
Canada
(514) 534-2200
Employees: 190 full-time;
400 seasonal (Winter);
250 seasonal (Summer)
Water Park/Ice Rink/
Golf Course

Worlds of Fun
4545 Worlds of Fun
Avenue
Kansas City, Missouri
64161
(816) 454-4545
Employees: 2,200 seasonal
(Summer)
Amusement Park/
Arcade/Concert Arena/
Aquatic Shows

The following listings, found under the chapter headings given below, also include positions at amusement or theme parks:

LAKES
Days Inn Lake Buena Vista
  Resort
Grosvenor Resort Hotel

Howard Johnson Resort Hotel
Circus Circus Hotel & Casino

MISCELLANEOUS
Holiday Inn Maingate West
Marriott's Orlando World
  Center Hotel

Cruise
Ships

~~~~~~

Sail Away to Your Dream Job

Introduction by George Foster and Tony Benade

ABOUT THE AUTHORS: George Foster is President of the Cruise Career Training Institute (CCTI), 729 S.E. 17th Street, Ft. Lauderdale, Florida 33316; (305) 561-7327 or 522-SHIP. Tony Benade is Vice President of CCTI. The institute provides training for aspiring cruise ship staff members. Both Mr. Foster and Mr. Benade are former cruise directors with Royal Caribbean Cruise Lines.

What's the first thing that comes to your mind when someone mentions "cruise ship"? If you answered "Love Boat," you share the common perception of many who find the prospect of visiting exotic ports of call, meeting that special someone, and living happily ever after an exciting fantasy.

THE FANTASY VERSUS THE REALITY

This fantasy has been stimulated by some very creative TV writers as well as the marketing directors of the cruise industry. A captain socializing throughout the ship in shorts, a clipboard-carrying cruise director "fixing up" all the singles, a bartender who knows everyone's business, and a doctor who does most of his operating in the disco instead of in the ship's hospital have little to do with the reality of cruise ship life.

In reality, a cruise ship is a hotel that floats. The operation and management principles are basically the same as at any major resort hotel. The biggest difference lies in not having to drive home in the evening after completing an eight-hour shift. Today, the average cruise ship carries about 1,500 passengers plus 500 officers, staff, and crew. The cruise industry is in a great boom, and every major cruise line is continually building newer and bigger ships to meet the growing demand for the "fantasy vacation" of everyone's dreams. All these new ships are creating new jobs and the demand for trained and skilled personnel is constantly increasing.

WHAT JOBS ARE AVAILABLE?

"How can I get a job in the cruise industry?" Answering this question effectively requires an understanding of the type of jobs available and the skills, background, and procedures necessary to procure employment aboard ship. First, let's look at the operation of a typical vessel.

The captain, officers, and crew run the ship. Maintenance, security, safety, and all maritime requirements are handled by this department. The officers and crew are usually hired in the country of the ship's registry, which is almost always *not* the United States. This is usually required by both the ships' owners and the country of registry, the laws of which often favor local nationals. The opportunities here for U.S. and Canadian citizens are almost nonexistent. (Author's Note: American-registered ships, by contrast, are required by law to use U.S. citizens for all shipboard jobs. The company listings in this chapter include numerous American-flagged ships with all-American crews.)

The greatest opportunities on foreign-flagged vessels lie in the hotel department of the ship. Most, if not all, cruise ships have five department divisions, headed and staffed as follows:The food and beverage and the two steward divisions usually hire their personnel through offices in various Third World countries where low wages prevail. While there are occasional North Americans working in these departments, the long hours and low wages make U.S. and Canadian citizens few and far between. The best opportunities for employment for U.S. and Canadian nationals lie in the cruise director and chief purser divisions.

The purser division requires personnel with strong clerical abilities coupled with good people skills. A background in business administration could also be helpful and should be stressed.

The cruise director/social staff is the most diversified and requires personnel with many talents. An example of the job descriptions in this division are: social host or hostess, assistant cruise director, disc jockey, dance instructor, fitness instructor, shore excursion sales personnel, shore excursion tour leaders, snorkeling and SCUBA instructors, children's counselors, teen activities leaders, and entertainers. Personnel directors favor applicants with sales, public relations, fitness, dance, teaching, or entertainment experience for these positions.

LANDING YOUR DREAM JOB

A well-prepared résumé stating your background in any of the above along with a good, clear 8 × 10 photograph is a must. If you have developed talent as a singer, magician, comedian, etc., a videotape of your presentation would be a great asset. The primary qualification, however, is that you must be a real "people person." If you achieve a personal interview with the cruise line, remember to be well-groomed, friendly, and stress both your amicable personality and your love of working with large groups of people.

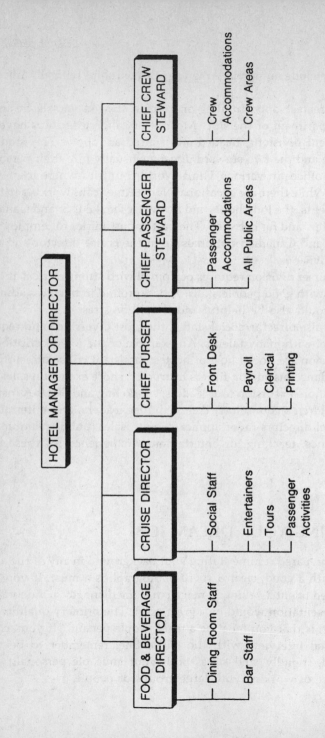

```
                        HOTEL MANAGER OR DIRECTOR
    ┌──────────────┬──────────────┼──────────────┬──────────────┐

 FOOD &        CRUISE          CHIEF          CHIEF          CHIEF CREW
 BEVERAGE      DIRECTOR        PURSER         PASSENGER      STEWARD
 DIRECTOR                                     STEWARD

 ─ Dining      ─ Social        ─ Front Desk   ─ Passenger    ─ Crew
   Room Staff    Staff                          Accommodations  Accommodations
                                ─ Payroll
 ─ Bar Staff   ─ Entertainers                 ─ All Public   ─ Crew Areas
                                ─ Clerical      Areas
               ─ Tours
                                ─ Printing
               ─ Passenger
                 Activities
```

BON VOYAGE, YOU GOT THE JOB!

If you are hired, be prepared to sever most of your responsibilities and ties to home and friends for an extended period of time. It's a good bet that once you sign onto your ship, you won't spend a night in a shoreside bed for at least three to seven months. As mail and regular communications with shore are slow, difficult, and expensive, plan on leaving your affairs in order. Make sure there is someone to pay your bills when they come in. Find a friend or family member to watch your possessions.

Before you report to your ship, get a passport or update your current one. Many cruise lines will also require you to undergo a very thorough medical examination. As major medical care can be several days away, you should be in good health before considering this type of employment.

Once on board the vessel, be prepared to work a seven-day week. The forty-hour week and time and a half overtime are unknown at sea. You will be on call at any time, whether scheduled for duty or not. This is not a nine-to-five job and your hours will vary on a daily basis. You will work hard and long, but there are rewards and benefits to this unique lifestyle. Typically, you will have time to see the ports of call, as you will probably be on a rotation schedule that allows you at least some free time in port each week. You will experience a carefree lifestyle that cannot be achieved on land. Since almost all of your living expenses are provided by the cruise line, it is possible to save money despite fairly low salaries. Think of all the money you can save with no rent, no utilities, no car, no gas, no restaurants, no insurance, etc. Additionally, you will meet new people on each and every voyage and establish some strong relationships with many of your co-workers.

A job on a cruise ship is one that requires a very strong and positive attitude, a great amount of dedication, and, last but not least, an awareness of everything around you at any given moment. The demands of life at sea are great, but most find the rewards even greater.

Good luck and bon voyage!

PROFILE OF MICHELLE SKLAR
CHILDREN'S LEADER, SITMAR CRUISES

"Volunteer if you have to"

HOMETOWN: Carlsbad, California
SCHOOL: Cal Poly San Luis Obispo (B.A. in Recreation Administration)
JOBS: Swimming instructor
Lifeguard
Gymnastics coach
Camp counselor
Shipboard volunteer children's counselor (Sitmar Cruises)
Shipboard children's program director (Carnival Cruises)

"I had wanted to work on a cruise ship since the first time I watched 'Love Boat' on television. It was when I was eighteen and in high school that I first applied. At age twenty I was finally hired by Sitmar as a volunteer children's counselor. To land that job I must have sent out at least seventy-five letters and followed up with both letters and phone calls."

Although volunteering is a unique way to get a cruise ship job, it paid off for Michelle. "After volunteering for Sitmar, I called Carnival Cruise Lines. They needed someone to work on the *Tropicale* in Alaska. I gave notice to Sitmar and Carnival flew me to Alaska the next day. I worked as a children's counselor and eventually as Carnival's children's program director every summer and school vacation while I was in college and full time after I graduated."

According to Michelle, the key to landing that shipboard job is persistence. "If you want the job, you have to either be a little better than the next applicant or a little more persistent.

"And keep calling and writing—it will pay off."

PROFILE OF DOREEN MINGOIA
AEROBICS INSTRUCTOR, MV *Homeric*

"Research your dream job to avoid disappointment"

HOMETOWN: Brooklyn, New York
SCHOOL: St. Francis College (New York)
JOBS: Flight attendant (People's Express)
High school teacher
Fitness instructor/cruise staff (MV *Homeric*)

"It is the constant meeting of new faces, learning about new people's backgrounds, and assisting them to enjoy their vacation that makes my cruise ship job everything I dreamed it would be. Of course, travel is also a major attraction of my job. The tropical islands we visit play a central part in making this job the perfect escape to Fantasy Island."

Doreen's job aboard ship is to run all the fitness programs and develop programs for the ship's children. As a staff member for Home Lines, she is allowed to partake in all passenger activities. "I am treated like any paying passenger. I am allowed to dine in the dining room, sunbathe on deck, and partake in the buffets. Best of all, I am allowed to dance the night away in the ship's disco. I am certain that cruise ships are looking for the 'All-American Person.' They want people whose speech is proper, appearance is wholesome, and manners are evident twenty-four hours a day."

According to Doreen the key to finding a shipboard job that you will enjoy is to research the ship carefully and the job for which you are applying. "It is fairly easy to have your résumé updated, take a professional picture to send with it, and follow up with a few phone calls. However, researching which ship most appeals to you is far more difficult. Remember, once you are on the ship, it's a long swim home if you are unhappy at sea!"

THE CRUISE LINE LISTINGS

The shipboard jobs listed in this book are presented in a slightly different format than the other chapter listings in *Jobs in Paradise*. As ships are in essence small floating cities, they employ a variety of positions too vast to repeat in each listing.

Before accepting a cruise ship job you should be aware that there are generally three categories of personnel at sea: the crew, the staff, and the officers. Which category your job falls in will determine what privileges and rights you will enjoy on the ship. Contrary to what you may have seen on "The Love Boat," it isn't very often that the crew dances with the passengers.

THE CREW

Among crew positions there are waitpersons, buspersons, cooks, cleaners, dishwashers, room stewards (housekeepers), bartenders, deck stewards, painters, electricians, carpenters, carpet layers, deck hands, able-bodied seamen (called A.B.'s), firefighters, printers, and a myriad of other personnel. Crew members usually live in small multi-person cabins on the lower decks of the ship. They eat different food than the ship's passengers and eat in a separate cafeteria. On most ships, crew members are barred from all passenger areas when off duty and are universally prohibited from mingling with the passengers. While there is typically a crew bar for nightly crew entertainment, it usually has all the ambiance of a seedy waterfront longshoreman's bar. On most ships, the crew members will come from various countries including Mexico, El Salvador, Indonesia, Jamaica, the Bahamas, Italy, Greece, Spain, etc. Except as otherwise noted in the listings below, very few U.S. or Canadian citizens work as crew members. While most cruise lines are willing to hire North Americans for these crew jobs, not many North Americans are willing to accept the low wages, long hours, and hard living conditions.

THE STAFF

The second category of shipboard personnel is the staff. Among most ship's staff you will typically find cruise staff (activities directors), children's counselors, singers, dancers, magicians, jugglers, musicians, casino personnel, shore excursion staff, photographers, diving instructors, fitness directors, masseuses, hairdressers, and gift shop sales staff. Staff members enjoy many of the benefits of passengers. They are usually free to bask in the sun along with the paying passengers. Staff members often eat in a separate dining room but enjoy passenger food (served by trainee waiters). Staff members either live in passenger cabins or upgraded crew cabins. Most often, staff are free to enjoy the ship's lounges at night but may be restricted from dancing or sitting at bar stools in certain rooms. Most staff members are British, Canadian, U.S., Australian, or New Zealand citizens.

THE OFFICERS

Officers make up the last category of seagoing employees. Officers are responsible for navigating the ship, running the ship's hospital (doctors and nurses are usually considered officers), and running the purser's office. Officers eat in a separate dining room and enjoy passenger food and privileges. The ship's officers are generally hired overseas, typically in Italy, Greece, or Norway.

A SHIP IS A SMALL FLOATING CITY

While small ships will, of course, have fewer crew members, most medium to large ships have a crew of more than 500 souls (souls being a nautical term for persons). A ship is a small floating city. It has many of the same jobs you might find ashore. There is a bank (the purser's office), a fire department, a hospital, a recreation center, a shopping area, and on some ships even an ice cream parlor.

ADMIRAL CRUISE LINES
(Miami, Florida)
Year-Round

Admiral Cruise Lines owns three popular ships specializing in inexpensive party-style cruises. The ships, the *Emerald Seas, Azure Seas,* and *Stardancer,* include a wide range of itineraries. The *Azure Seas* sails from San Pedro, California, on three- and four-day cruises to Mexico and San Diego. The *Emerald Seas* does similar short cruises out of Florida.

SPECIFICS: The company's three ships employ 1,225 crew members.

INSIDER TIPS: The crew comes from a wide variety of nations from around the world. Most of the cruise staff comes from the United States, Canada, and England.

TO APPLY: Applicants should send a cover letter, résumé, and photograph to Admiral Cruise Lines, Shipboard Personnel, 1220 Biscayne Boulevard, Miami, Florida 33101.

ALLDERS INTERNATIONAL (SHIPS) LTD.
(Ft. Lauderdale, Florida)
Year-Round

Allders is the official gift shop concessionaire for a large number of cruise lines. Allders operates and staffs the gift shops of Carnival, Holland America, Cunard, and P&O cruises. A separate division of Allders operates shops in airports around the world.

SPECIFICS: Allders hires managers, assistant managers, salespersons, and stock persons for ships around the world.

INSIDER TIPS: Allders has offices in both the United States and England. Most of the company's employees are American, Canadian, or British citizens. All applicants must be at least twenty-three years old with three years retail experience.

TO APPLY: Applicants should send a cover letter, résumé, and photograph to Personnel Officer, Allders International (Ships) Ltd., 1510 SE 17th Street, Ft. Lauderdale, Florida 33316.

AMERICAN CANADIAN CARIBBEAN LINE (Warren, Rhode Island)

Year-Round

For those searching for a unique cruise environment, American Canadian Caribbean Line offers the perfect solution. The company's two small yacht-like vessels offer unusual and interesting itineraries. The *New Shoreham II* carries seventy-two fortunate passengers to the Bahamas, the Virgin Islands, New England, and Canada's inland waterway. The *Caribbean Prince* is usually based in Belize and Guatemala and carries eighty lucky souls on well-planned twelve-day Caribbean voyages. Both ships are fairly informal and cater to an older, sophisticated crowd.

SPECIFICS: The company's two vessels are among the few ships registered in the United States. Each ship carries a fifteen-person all-American crew.

INSIDER TIPS: The small size of these ships means that crew members must be very well-rounded and ready to accept a wide variety of tasks.

TO APPLY: Applicants should send a cover letter, résumé, and photograph to Nancy Blount Palumbo, American Canadian Caribbean Lines, 461 Water Street, Warren, Rhode Island 02885; (401) 247-0955.

AMERICAN HAWAII CRUISES
(San Francisco, California, and Honolulu, Hawaii)
Year-Round

American Hawaii is the largest American cruise line. The company's two large cruise ships ply the beautiful Hawaiian islands on week-long voyages out of Honolulu. The SS *Constitution* (formerly *Oceanic Constitution*) and SS *Independence* (formerly *Oceanic Independence*) are the two largest U.S. flag cruise ships still in service.

SPECIFICS: American Hawaii's two vessels employ 640 crew members. All officers, staff, and crew are required by law to be U.S. citizens. Although the company is based in San Francisco, most hiring is done through a union hiring hall in Honolulu. Photographers are hired by Trans-Ocean Photos (see separate listing in this chapter). Beauty salon staff are hired by The Stylist at the Hyatt Regency Waikiki Resort, 2424 Kalakaua Avenue, Honolulu, Hawaii 96813. Gift shop staff are hired by the W. H. Smith company (phone 808-842-7100 for information on the W. H. Smith company).

INSIDER TIPS: All officers, staff, and crew are U.S. citizens. According to Assistant Personnel Director Noreen Sullivan, "We get lots of résumés every day. People who come into the office in person have a MUCH better chance of employment." Most employees are required to be members of the Seafarer's Union. Musicians are also required to be members of the American Federation of Musicians.

PERKS: Shoreside personnel receive free cruises. Shipboard personnel are required to work on a rotation basis.

TO APPLY: Applicants should send a cover letter and résumé to Seafarer's International Union, 636 Cook Street, Honolulu, Hawaii 96813; (808) 523-7516. All applicants must obtain a U.S. Coast Guard certification (Z-Card), which costs approximately $100. After reviewing and approving your résumé, an application will be sent. Persons who apply in person and are willing to wait in Hawaii will have a much higher chance of being hired. Rick Massey is the company's director of personnel.

ATLANTIC ASSOCIATES
(Springfield, Massachusetts)
Year-Round

Atlantic Associates is the official casino concessionaire for a wide variety of cruise lines including Scandinavian World, Paquet, Royal, Holland America, Sitmar, Pearl, and some Costa vessels.

SPECIFICS: The company hires card dealers, casino managers, and cashiers for casino operations.

INSIDER TIPS: While most employees are British, citizens of other nations are also hired. Most hiring is done in England.

TO APPLY: Applicants should send a cover letter, résumé, and photograph to Atlantic Associates, c/o Atlantic Maritime Services, 55 State Street, Springfield, Massachusetts 01103.

BERMUDA STAR LINE
(Teaneck, New Jersey)
Year-Round

Bermuda Star Line has expanded from a one-ship line specializing in New England/Canada cruises to a major player in the U.S. cruise market. The company currently operates three vessels: the 761-passenger *Veracruz* (formerly the *Theodor Herzl* and *Freeport*), the 783-passenger *Queen of Bermuda* (formerly the *Volendam, Canada Star, Liberte, Brazil,* and *Monarch Sun*), and the 738-passenger *Bermuda Star* (formerly the *Veendam, Monarch Star,* and *Argentina*).

SPECIFICS: Bermuda Star Line's three vessels employ a total of 935 crew members. The crew represents over thirty nationalities with most staff members originating from Canada, Europe, and the U.S.

TO APPLY: Applicants should send a cover letter, résumé, and optional photograph to B.S.L. Cruises, Inc., Shipboard Personnel, 1086 Teaneck Road, Teaneck, New Jersey 07666. Applicants are requested not to call.

BRAMSON ENTERTAINMENT
(New York, New York)
Year-Round

Bramson Entertainment engages show acts, pianist/vocalists, and cruise staff for the ships of Holland America, Norwegian America, Cunard, Linblad, Ocean Cruises, Premier, Princess, Regency, Royal Cruise, SeaEscape, Society Expeditions, and Royal, cruises. Unlike a talent agent, entertainers do not usually pay a fee to Bramson.

SPECIFICS: Cabaret artists need two totally different self-contained shows that are orchestrated for up to ten musicians. All shows must be for a family-oriented audience. Acts needed include comics, comedy magicians, female vocalists/social directresses, international vocalists (male and female), instrumentalists, and novelty acts. Pianist/vocalists are hired for piano bars and lounges. Cruise staff positions include assistant cruise directors, disc jockeys, sound and light technicians, stage managers, and youth counselors.

TO APPLY: Applicants should send a promotional package containing a cover letter, resume, 8" × 10" photograph, and video/audiotape to Bramson Entertainment, 1440 Broadway, Suite 2500, New York, New York 10018; (212) 354-9575.

CARNIVAL CRUISE LINES
(Miami, Florida)
Year-Round

From its meager beginning in 1972 with one aging ship, Carnival Cruise Lines has today become the self-proclaimed "Most Popular Cruise Line in the World." Today, Carnival operates seven vessels in the Caribbean and Mexico, including four huge superliners. These superliners, the *Tropicale, Holiday, Jubilee,* and *Celebration,* are all approximately 48,000 tons and carry well over 2,500 passengers and crew. Other Carnival ships include the *Mardi Gras* (formerly *Empress of Canada*), *Festivale* (formerly *Transval Castle* and *S.A. Vaal*), and *Carnivale* (formerly *Empress of Britain* and *Queen Anna Maria*). Construction is currently under way for three titanic 70,000-ton "megaliners." Carnival's "Fun Ships" specialize in moderately priced cruises that are marketed to the young, active set.

SPECIFICS: Carnival's ships employ a crew of more than 4,200 men and women, making it one of the largest employers in the cruise industry. When the *Fantasy* and the other Carnival megaliners arrive, Carnival's staff size should exceed 6,000 persons. Most officers (except pursers) are Italian, while the crew is of mixed nationality. All staff positions are filled with American, Canadian, and British citizens. Unlike many companies, Carnival has been known to give Americans and Canadians jobs in crew positions such as dining room waiter, bar waiter, etc. Beauty salon and massage staff are hired by Steiners, an official concessionaire (see listing in this chapter). Gift shop personnel are hired by Allders International (see listing in this chapter). Some food and beverage department staff are hired by SeaChest, a subsidiary of Carnival (see SeaChest address below).

INSIDER TIPS: Carnival tends to do its hiring at the last moment. Thus, applicants who keep their applications current and express a continuing interest in the company are the most likely to be offered positions.

TO APPLY: For non-concession positions, applicants should send a cover letter, résumé, and photograph to Shipboard Personnel, Carnival Cruise Lines, 3655 N.W. 87th Avenue, Miami, Florida 33178-2428. Food and beverage department crew should apply to SeaChest Associates, 154 N.E. 9th Street, Miami, Florida 33132.

CHANDRIS FANTASY CRUISES/CELEBRITY CRUISES
(Miami, Florida)
Year-Round

Chandris owns a large number of vessels throughout the world. Many of these vessels are leased to other cruise lines and operate under those lines' names. Chandris Fantasy Cruises is a division of the larger Chandris company and operates the *Britanis* (formerly *Monterey, Lurline,* and the World War II troop ship *Matsonia*), *Amerikanis,* and *Victoria.* The ships specialize in inexpensive cruises. The company also offers luxury cruises on the *Zenith*, *Horizon*, and *Meridian.*

SPECIFICS: The three ships that Chandris operates under its Fantasy Cruises division employ 1,390 officers, staff, and crew. Beauty salon and massage staff are hired by Steiners, an official concessionaire (see listing in this chapter).

INSIDER TIPS: While most crew members and officers are Greek, the staff tends to be mostly from Britain, Canada, the United States, Australia, and New Zealand.

TO APPLY: Applicants should send a cover letter, résumé, and photograph to Shipboard Personnel, Chandris Fantasy Cruises, 5200 Blue Lagoon Drive, Penthouse, Miami, Florida 33126.

CLIPPER CRUISE LINE
(St. Louis, Missouri)
Year-Round

Clipper is one of the premier enterprises in the fast-growing yacht-cruise industry. The company's three sleek 100- to 110-passenger ships ply the shallow waterways of New England, the Southeast, and Florida. The company currently operates the *Newport Clipper, Nantucket Clipper,* and *Yorktown Clipper.*

SPECIFICS: Clipper's three ships employ a crew of approximately ninety U.S. citizens. In a typical year, about thirty-five new crew members are hired. Since the ships are all U.S. registered, all crew, staff, and officers are required to be U.S. citizens. Positions are available for stewardesses, deck hands, bartenders, lounge attendants, chefs, cruise directors, and hotel service coordinators. Most employees perform a wide variety of tasks from waiting on tables in the dining room to cleaning cabins.

INSIDER TIPS: All personnel are U.S. citizens. Employment contracts are for one year; maximum time on board is one contract. "Since we are such a small ship, it is imperative that our crew respond with perfect manners to all customer needs. We look for applicants with an excellent positive attitude."

PERKS: Company employees are eligible for reduced-rate cruises for family and friends. Clipper also has a medical coverage program.

TO APPLY: Applicants should send a cover letter, résumé, and photograph to Personnel Department, Clipper Cruise Line, 7711 Bonhomme Avenue, St. Louis, Missouri 63105; (314) 727-2929.

COMMODORE CRUISE LINE
(Miami, Florida)
Year-Round

Commodore Cruise Line operates only one vessel, the *Caribe 1*. The *Caribe* is the former *Olympia* and was built in 1953. This ship holds 900 passengers and has been refurbished several times.

SPECIFICS: Commodore Cruise Line employs 330 officers, staff, and crew. The crew is from a wide variety of nations.

TO APPLY: Applicants should send a cover letter, résumé, and photograph to Shipboard Personnel, Commodore Cruise Line, 1007 North America Way, Miami, Florida 33131; (305) 358-2622.

COSTA CRUISES
(Miami, Florida)
Year-Round

Costa specializes in high-caliber cruises with a unique Italian flair. Costa, one of the oldest private maritime firms in Italy, operates a wide variety of ships throughout the world.

SPECIFICS: Costa employs more than 2,085 officers, staff, and crew aboard its ships. The company owns and operates the *Enrico Costa, Carla Costa, Costa Riviera,* and *Eugenio Costa* and operates the *Daphne* and *Danae* under a lease agreement. Beauty salon and massage staff are hired by Steiners, an official concessionaire (see listing in this chapter). Casino personnel are hired through Atlantic Associates (see listing in this chapter). Shipboard photographers are hired by Neptune Photographic, 202 Fulham Road, Chelsea, London, SW10 9NB, England.

INSIDER TIPS: The Costa-owned ships are staffed almost entirely by Italians in keeping with the company's Italian theme. While there are positions for U.S. and Canadian citizens, Americans will find jobs with Costa tougher to land than with most other cruise lines.

TO APPLY: Marine and Mercantile Enterprises hires most of the staff and crew for Costa's Caribbean fleet. Applicants should send a cover letter, résumé, and photograph to Costa Shipboard Personnel, Marine and Mercantile Enterprises, 6925 Biscayne Boulevard, Miami, Florida 33138. Costa's main office is located at One Biscayne Boulevard, Miami, Florida 33131.

THE CRUISESHIP PICTURE COMPANY, LTD.
(Esher, Surrey, England)
Year-Round

The Cruiseship Picture Company hires photographers under a concession agreement for numerous cruise lines including Norwegian Cruises Lines (NCL).

SPECIFICS: Photographers work taking and processing photographs and staffing the photography gallery.

INSIDER TIPS: While most Cruiseship Picture Company staff members are British citizens, persons of other nationalities are considered. An interview in England or the U.S. will be required. Photo processing experience and either three years college course experience or two years professional work experience are required.

TO APPLY: Applicants should send a cover letter, résumé, and 2" × 2" photograph to the Personnel Manager, Dawson Forwarding, Agents for The Cruiseship Picture Co. Ltd., 132 High Street, Esher, Surrey, KT10 9QB, England.

DELTA QUEEN STEAMBOAT COMPANY
(New Orleans, Louisiana)

Year-Round

No one can read the literary masterpiece *Tom Sawyer* without picturing lively steamboats paddling their way up the mighty Mississippi River. Delta Queen Steamboat Company keeps these romantic images alive. The company operates two paddleboats, the 420-passenger *Mississippi Queen* and the 180-passenger *Delta Queen*.

SPECIFICS: Delta Queen's two vessels employ a total of 300 crew members. As the ships are registered in the United States, all officers, staff, and crew are required by law to be U.S. citizens.

INSIDER TIPS: This company strives to help passengers re-create a riverboat journey up the Mississippi circa 1850. You should work here for love of the river and paddleboats. As the ships have no casinos, riverboat gamblers need not apply.

TO APPLY: Applicants should send a cover letter, résumé, and photograph to Director of Personnel, Delta Queen Steamboat Company, 30 Robin St. Wharf, New Orleans, Louisiana 70130; (504) 586-0631.

INTERNATIONAL CRUISE SHOPS
(Miami, Florida)

Year-Round

ICS is a concessionaire hiring gift shop staff for cruise lines.

SPECIFICS: The company has positions for gift shop salespersons.

INSIDER TIPS: Gift shop, employees are hired from a wide variety of nations.

TO APPLY: Applicants should send a cover letter, résumé, and photograph to ICS, 8052 N.W. 14th Street, Miami, Florida 33126.

HOLLAND AMERICA CRUISES
(Seattle, Washington)
Year-Round

Holland America is one of the world's top quality cruise lines, known for its fine service and immaculate ships. Holland America owns the *Rotterdam, Nieuw Amsterdam, Noordam,* and *Westerdam.* Former ships have included the *Volendam, Veendam, Statendam,* and *Princendam* (sank off the coast of Alaska).

SPECIFICS: Holland America employs more than 2,150 officers, staff, and crew for its four vessels. Gift shop personnel are hired by Allders International (see listing in this chapter). Casino personnel are hired through Atlantic Associates (see listing in this chapter). Beauty salon staff are hired through Ocean Trading (see listing in this chapter).

INSIDER TIPS: Almost all officers aboard Holland America ships are Dutch and most crew members are Indonesian. As hiring for these jobs is done in Holland and Indonesia respectively, only staff positions such as cruise staff, gift shop, casino, photo, and beauty salon department positions are open for U.S. and Canadian applications.

TO APPLY: Applicants should send a cover letter, résumé, and photograph to Shipboard Personnel, Holland America Lines, 300 Elliot Avenue West, Seattle, Washington 98119.

JALCRUISE (C.I.) LTD.
(Channel Islands, United Kingdom)
Year-Round

Jalcruise hires photographers for Royal Viking Line, Canberra Cruises, Princess Cruises, Olsen, and Seabourn Cruises.

SPECIFICS: While non-British citizens are considered, the company primarily hires British men and women for its shipboard positions.

INSIDER TIPS: A background in photography is essential and experience in a one-hour–type photo lab is helpful.

TO APPLY: Applicants should send a cover letter, résumé, and photograph to Jalcruise (C.I.) Ltd., P.O. Box 316, Compendium House, 1 Wesley Street, St. Helier, Jersey, Channel Islands, U.K.

NORWEGIAN CRUISE LINES (NCL)
(Miami, Florida)
Year-Round

Norwegian Cruise Lines (formerly Norwegian Caribbean Lines) is one of the most successful cruise lines in the industry. The company's six sleek vessels specialize in moderately priced, high-quality voyages to the Caribbean and Mexico. The pride of the NCL fleet is the 2,000-plus passenger 1,035-foot long SS *Norway* (formerly *France*). The *Norway* is the longest ship in the world and one of the most impressive when seen at sea. However, NCL is not standing on its laurels. In 1989 the company took delivery of the brand new *Seaward,* a 1,500-plus passenger vessel. NCL's smaller ships (called "the white ships" by crew members in honor of their sleek white hulls) include the *Southward, Starward, Skyward,* and *Sunward II.*

SPECIFICS: NCL employs 2,704 officers, staff, and crew for its six ships. The *Norway* alone employs almost 800 personnel. Photographers are hired through the Cruiseship Picture Company, and bar, beauty salon, massage, and gift shop staff are hired through Florida Export Company (see separate listings for Cruiseship Picture Company and Florida Export in this chapter). NCL's "Dive In" program hires snorkeling instructors through Shallow Water Development, P.O. Box 013353, Miami, Florida 33101. Casino cashiers and croupiers should apply through the casino concessionaire Tiber Trading, 1027 Adams St., Hollywood, Florida 33019.

INSIDER TIPS: NCL's officers are all Norwegian (except the Medical Department). The crew is of mixed nationalities. Almost all staff members are American, Canadian, or British.

TO APPLY: Applicants should send a cover letter, résumé, and photograph to Shipboard Personnel, Norwegian Cruise Lines, One Biscayne Tower, Miami, Florida 33131. Mike Ronan is responsible for hiring shore excursion staff; Armando Martinez hires the other members of the cruise staff.

OCEAN CRUISE LINES
(Ft. Lauderdale, Florida)
Year-Round

Ocean Cruise Lines is a division of Travellers, one of Europe's largest and most successful tour operators. Ocean currently operates two ships, the *Ocean Princess* (formerly *Italia*) and *Ocean Islander* (formerly *City of Andros*).

SPECIFICS: Ocean Cruise Lines employs 390 officers, staff, and crew to man its two ships. The small *Ocean Islander* is almost yacht-like with only 250 passengers and 150 crew.

INSIDER TIPS: Both Ocean Cruise Lines vessels are staffed with Greek officers and Italian dining room staff. American, British, and Canadian citizens are most likely to find positions in staff departments.

TO APPLY: Applicants should send a cover letter, résumé, and photograph to Shipboard Personnel, Ocean Cruise Lines, 1510 Southeast 17th Street, Ft. Lauderdale, Florida 33316.

ALLDERS GROUP EMPLOYMENT SERVICES LTD. (Southampton, England)

Year-Round

Allders Group Employment Services Ltd. provides gift shop, hair salon, beautician and masseuse services to a wide variety of cruise lines under concession agreements. The company currently has employees aboard the ships of the Cunard, Holland America, Sitmar, P&O lines, and Windstar.

SPECIFICS: Allders Group Employment Services Ltd. hires gift shop sales personnel, shop managers, beauticians, hairdressers, and a few masseuses. Both men and women are hired for all positions.

INSIDER TIPS: While most of the company's employees are British, a few American and Canadian citizens are hired.

TO APPLY: Applicants should send a cover letter, résumé, and photograph to Allders Group Employment Services Ltd., 84-98 Southampton Road, Eastleigh Southampton, Hampshire, 5053AB; (703) 644-599.

PREMIER CRUISE LINES (Cape Canaveral, Florida)

Year-Round

Despite the fact that the company is "the official cruise line of Walt Disney World," there is nothing Mickey Mouse about Premier Cruise Lines. The company operates the *Star/Ship Atlantic, Star/Ship Majestic,* and *Star/Ship Oceanic.* All ships are fitted with special children's play rooms and cater to families.

SPECIFICS: Premier's three ships employ 1,500-plus officers, staff, and crew. The ships offer full passenger amenities.

INSIDER TIPS: While most of the officers are Greek and the crew is international, there are many positions for Americans and Canadians on the ship's staff.

TO APPLY: Applicants should send a cover letter, résumé, and photograph to Shipboard Personnel, Premier Cruise Lines, 400 Challenger Blvd., Cape Canaveral, Florida 32920; (407) 799-1538

PRINCESS CRUISES/P&O
(Los Angeles, California)
Year-Round

Princess Cruises' *Pacific Princess* is probably responsible for making cruising the travel trend of the 1980s. The company's *Pacific Princess* has been seen by millions of Americans who watched Doc, Julie, Gopher, and Captain Stubing cavort on TV's "Love Boat" each week. The company's current four-ship fleet includes the *Pacific Princess* (formerly *Sea Venture*), *Sun Princess* (formerly *Spirit of London*), and *Island Princess* (formerly *Island Venture*). New in 1984, the company's flagship is the *Royal Princess,* a huge 1,200-passenger luxury liner.

SPECIFICS: The four Princess ships employ more than 1,550 officers, staff, and crew. Additionally, the P&O ships add another 1,650 jobs to the fleet. Gift shop personnel are hired by Allders International (see listing in this chapter). Some of P&O's other staff are hired by Ocean Trading (see listing in this chapter).

INSIDER TIPS: Both the P&O and the Princess ships use British officers and deck crews and Italian service crews. Most staff positions are British, although a few Americans and Canadians are found aboard.

TO APPLY: Applicants should send a cover letter, résumé, and photograph to Shipboard Personnel, Princess Cruises/P&O, 2029 Century Boulevard, Los Angeles, California 90067.

REGENCY CRUISES
(New York, New York)
Year-Round

Although Regency is relatively new in the passenger cruise industry, the company has established a fine reputation for moderately priced, high-quality voyages with unusual Caribbean and Alaskan itineraries. The fleet sails out of Montego Bay, Jamaica, and Vancouver, Canada (summers).

SPECIFICS: The company's fleet employs more than 1,100 officers, staff, and crew.

INSIDER TIPS: Regency Cruises mans its ships with Greek officers and a crew of mixed nationality. While there may be some crew positions for North Americans, the best job opportunities are on the ship's staff. All cruise staff members must also be professional entertainers.

TO APPLY: Applicants should send a cover letter, résumé, and photograph to Shipboard Personnel, Regency Cruises, 260 Madison Avenue, New York, New York 10016.

ROYAL CARIBBEAN CRUISE LINE
(Miami, Florida)
Year-Round

Royal Caribbean Cruise Line (RCCL) is world-famous for its custom-designed ships, specially built for Caribbean cruising. The company traces its roots back to Harry Larsen, a Norwegian who escaped the invading Nazis by sailing to the United States in a 15-foot dinghy. Today RCCL sets a standard for luxury cruising that Larsen couldn't have dreamed possible. RCCL owns and operates the *Song of Norway, Nordic Prince, Sun Viking, Song of America,* and its new flagship, the *Sovereign of the Seas,* the world's largest cruise ship.

SPECIFICS: RCCL's five Caribbean-based ships employ a total of more than 2,400 officers, staff, and crew. RCCL's food and beverage staff are hired by Royal Caribbean Food & Beverage Department, 1007 North America Way, Miami, Florida 33132 (Royal Caribbean Food & Beverage does most of its hiring abroad and does not typically hire U.S. citizens for its shipboard positions). Gift shop staff are hired through Greyhound Leisure, Attention Shipboard Employment, 8052 NW 14th Street, Miami, Florida 33126. Beauty salon personnel are hired through Coiffeur Transocean, 1101 North America Way, Suite 206, Miami, Florida 33132.

INSIDER TIPS: RCCL's officers are Norwegian; the staff and crew are international.

TO APPLY: Applicants for all other positions should send a cover letter, résumé, and photograph to Royal Caribbean Cruise Line, Human Resources Department, 906 South America Way, Miami, Florida 33132. Entertainer applicants should also send a demo tape.

ROYAL VIKING LINE
(Coral Gables, Florida)
Year-Round

Royal Viking Line is the premier line in the ultra-luxury cruise market. All operational, marketing, and financial activities are centralized at the Kloster headquarters in Coral Gables, Florida. The line owns four ships, the *Royal Viking Sky, Royal Viking Star, Royal Viking Sea,* and the new *Royal Viking Sun.* The Royal Viking Line ships ply exotic waters around the globe.

SPECIFICS: Royal Viking employs 1,700-plus crew members on its four ships. Photographers are hired through Jalcruise (see listing in this chapter).

INSIDER TIPS: Royal Viking Line (RVL) caters to a highly sophisticated clientele. All employees must be able to handle themselves with the utmost in grace and decorum and have a genuine willingness to serve passengers. Officers (including most pursers) are Norwegian and crews are European. The cruise staff, casino personnel, and entertainers are mostly U.S. and Canadian citizens.

TO APPLY: Applicants should send a cover letter, résumé, and photograph to Shipboard Personnel, Royal Viking Line, 95 Merrick Way, Coral Gables, Florida 33134. Entertainer applicants should also send a videotape of their act. A personal interview is required.

SEA GODDESS CRUISES
(New York, New York)
Year-Round

Sea Goddess Cruises' two 100-passenger vessels are unique in their style and flair. The *Sea Goddess I* and *II* are for upscale passengers who want the amenities of a private yacht without having to concern themselves with scraping the barnacles off their boat's bottom.

SPECIFICS: The company's two identical ships employ a total of seventy-one crew members. The ships offer live entertainment, a health spa, watersports from an aft sport deck, and a beauty/barber shop.

INSIDER TIPS: Sea Goddess ships employ mostly Norwegian and European crews. The few positions for North American citizens are mostly in the staff entertainment department.

TO APPLY: Applicants should send a cover letter, résumé, and photograph to Sea Goddess Cruises, Shipboard Personnel, 555 Fifth Avenue, New York, New York 10017.

SITMAR CRUISES
(Los Angeles, California)
Year-Round

Sitmar traces its maritime roots back to the Societa Italiana Transporti Marittimi of Genoa, Italy. Today the company's vessels maintain a unique Italian flair. Sitmar currently has four vessels in passenger service with a huge 60,000-ton liner currently under construction.

SPECIFICS: Sitmar's ships employ almost 2,000 officers, staff, and crew. Casino personnel are hired through Atlantic Associates (see listing in this chapter). Entertainers are hired through Bramson Entertainment (see listing in this chapter). Gift shop and beauty salon staff are hired through Ocean Trading (see listing in this chapter).

INSIDER TIPS: In keeping with the line's Italian style, all officers are Italian. Most crew members are either Italian or Portuguese. The ships are staffed with U.S., British, Canadian, Australian, and New Zealand citizens.

TO APPLY: Applicants should send a cover letter, résumé, and photograph to Shipboard Personnel, Sitmar Cruises, 10100 Santa Monica Boulevard, Los Angeles, California 90067.

STEINER PRODUCTS LTD.
(Stanmore, Middlesex, England)
Year-Round

Steiner hires all barber shop, beauty salon, and massage personnel on Carnival, Costa, Cunard, Chandris, P&O, and Ocean cruises.

SPECIFICS: Steiner hires more than 100 hair stylists, barbers, salon receptionists, make-up artists, beauty therapists, fitness instructors, and masseuses for almost twenty different cruise ships.

INSIDER TIPS: While most of Steiner's employees are from England, several U.S. and Canadian citizens also work for the company.

TO APPLY: Applicants should send a cover letter, résumé, photocopy of relevant licenses or certificates, and photograph to Maritime Personnel, Steiner Products Ltd., 57–65 The Broadway, Stanmore, Middlesex, HA7 4D6, England. Personal interviews are required.

TRANS-OCEAN PHOTOS, INC. & TRANS-OCEAN VIDEO, INC.
(New York, New York)
Year-Round

Trans-Ocean Photos has been supplying photographers for cruise ships around the world since 1946. The company's president, Bob Harrow, is a widely acclaimed photographer who has been selected as an official photographer for such notables as Ronald Reagan, Ernest Hemingway, and Harry Truman. The company has recently begun a program of hiring video photographers for various cruise ships.

SPECIFICS: Trans-Ocean hires photo technicians and video technicians for cruise ships and resorts around the world. Photo technicians take, process, print, and sell photographs of resort guests and cruise ship passengers. Photo technicians must have basic photographic skills. Applications are also accepted for video technicians. Video staff must be able to operate video equipment and must be familiar with techniques for converting still photos to video. All positions are year-round.

INSIDER TIPS: Trans-Ocean hires mostly American citizens. "The job you do for us on board is serious. If applicants appear to have other intentions, they won't pass our muster! We want applicants to understand that this is a job and not a vacation." There are no seasonal positions and a college degree (not necessarily in photography) is required.

TO APPLY: Applicants should send a "well-written" cover letter and résumé to Personnel Department, Trans-Ocean Photos, New York Passenger Ship Terminal, West 54th Street & 12th Avenue, New York, New York 10019; (212) 757-2707. An interview is usually required. Do not submit color printwork with your résumé.

WINDJAMMER BAREFOOT CRUISES
(Miami, Florida)
Year-Round

Windjammer Barefoot Cruises is one of the last companies in the world to offer passenger cruises aboard tall sailing ships. The company uses vessels with a long and colorful history. Its flagship, the 282-foot barkentine *Fantome,* was originally built for the Duke of Westminster as his private yacht. The *Fantome* was later purchased by the Onassis family. The ships cater to a young, active set who enjoy helping hoist the old canvas sails.

SPECIFICS: Crew members are expected to help out with a wide array of tasks. Be prepared to clean cabins, serve meals, tend bar, sand, paint, varnish, polish, swab the decks, work hard, and have a great time!

TO APPLY: For employment information contact Windjammer Barefoot Cruises, P.O. Box 120, Miami Beach, Florida 33119-9983.

WINDSTAR SAIL CRUISES
(Miami, Florida)

Year-Round

Windstar is a completely new concept in passenger cruising. The company operates three sleek four-masted sailing ships that are fully computerized. These are not the old wooden sailing ships of yore. Rather, the *Wind Star, Wind Song,* and *Wind Spirit* look like ultra-modern yachts from the twenty-first century. They cater to a young upscale crowd of adventurous travelers.

SPECIFICS: Each of Windstar's ships employ eighty crew members. Thus, with the expected delivery of the *Windsurf,* the company will employ a total of 320 crew. While the ships do not employ the traditional shipboard entertainers, there is a piano bar on each vessel. Despite the ships' small sizes, each has a small casino. Watersports are a big part of a Windstar voyage and each ship offers a wide array of activities.

INSIDER TIPS: Although the ships' crews are mostly European, there are positions for North Americans aboard. While the small size of this line makes jobs tougher to obtain, Windstar's unique vessels and itineraries make this company well worth pursuing.

TO APPLY: Applicants should send a cover letter, résumé, and photograph to Shipboard Personnel, Windstar Sail Cruises, 7415 N.W. 19th Street, Miami, Florida 33126.

Miscellaneous Jobs in Paradise

~~~~~~

CLARION OLD STONE INN
(Niagara Falls, Ontario, Canada)

Seasonal (Summer)

Clarion's Old Stone Inn is a country inn tucked away from the hustle and bustle, yet conveniently located only a five-minute walk from Niagara Falls. The hotel is set on the Canadian side of the falls in the honeymoon capital of the world, Niagara Falls.

SPECIFICS: The Old Stone Inn hires approximately twenty new employees each year to fill its fifty-person staff. The hotel seeks summer seasonal staff to work from early May through Labor Day. Applications are accepted for front desk clerks, dining room waitpersons, and housekeeping attendants.

INSIDER TIPS: "We look for energetic, keen employees with a willingness to learn. Experience is helpful as it reduces the necessary training time."

PERKS: Employees are allowed to use the hotel's pool, bar, and recreational facilities when not on duty.

TO APPLY: Applicants should either write for an official application or send a cover letter, résumé, and SARP to Timothy Beatrand, Executive Assistant Manager, Clarion Old Stone Inn, 5425 Robinson S., Niagara Falls, Ontario, L2G 7L6 Canada; (416) 357-1234.

KING KO INN
(King Salmon, Alaska)
Seasonal (Summer)

If you believe in the age-old adage that a bad day of fishing is better than the best day of anything else, King Salmon, Alaska, is your Eden. The King Ko Inn is not an exclusive lodge or fancy hotel, but rather a friendly place where folks gather to set off on a day's fishing expedition or a trip to nearby Katmai National Park and the "Valley of 1,000 Smokes." The hotel is located in the center of the small town of King Salmon, situated on the Naknek River. The Naknek feeds into the Bering Sea.

SPECIFICS: The King Ko hires twenty-five new employees each summer to fill its staff of thirty. All jobs are seasonal and employees should be available to work from April through September. However, a few positions are available for applicants who cannot be available until June. There is no application deadline. The King Ko Inn frequently hires cooks, housekeepers, waitpersons, bartenders, cocktail servers, dishwashers, front desk clerks, auditor/accounting clerks, and managers. Starting wages range form $5.00 per hour to $3,000 per month, depending on the position.

INSIDER TIPS: Although King Salmon is in a rather isolated part of the forty-ninth state, local attractions include excellent trout and salmon fishing, sightseeing, nature photography, hiking, whitewater rafting, and bush flying.

PERKS: The inn provides room and board for employees as well as free airfare from Anchorage to King Salmon at the time an employee begins work.

TO APPLY: Applicants should send a cover letter, résumé, and SARP to Jim Kubitz, Owner, King Ko Inn, 1407 W. 31st, Suite 302, Anchorage, Alaska 99503; (907) 277-7633. The hotel's direct address is P.O. Box 346, King Salmon, Alaska 99613; (907) 246-3377.

MOUNT HOPE ESTATE & WINERY
(Cornwell, Pennsylvania)
Seasonal (Summer) and Year-Round

Mount Hope is living proof that the fine art of winemaking in the United States is not restricted to California's Napa Valley. Mount Hope is an 87-acre Victorian estate on which wine-producing vineyards have been planted. The estate operates daily winery tours and wine tastings.

SPECIFICS: Mount Hope employs twenty full-time and fifty summer seasonal employees. Positions are available for winery tour guides, wine tasting servers, vineyard workers, winery workers, and cashiers.

INSIDER TIPS: Applicants should be at least twenty-one years old for jobs involving the production or serving of wine.

TO APPLY: Applicants should contact Barbara Lacck, General Manager, Mount Hope Estate & Winery, P.O. Box 685, Cornwall, Pennsylvania 17016; (717) 665-7021.

NATIONAL PARK CONCESSIONS, INC.
(Mammoth Cave National Park, Kentucky)
Seasonal (Summer or Winter) and Year-Round

Mammoth Cave National Park, a UNESCO World Heritage Site, is home to the world's longest network of cavern corridors. In total, the park's maze of caves covers more than 300 miles. These famous caves offer a wide array of natural spectacles including stalactite and stalagmite formations, huge cavern rooms, and spectacular pits and domes. The highlight of this park is the huge Snowball Room restaurant, located 267 feet underground. National Park Concessionarires operates the Mammoth Cave Hotel, the Sunset Point Motor Lodge, a variety of cottages, several gift and craft shops, restaurants, and a service center.

SPECIFICS: From a field of 200 applicants, approximately seventy-five new employees are hired each year to fill the 125 peak season positions at Mammoth Cave National Park. Jobs are available for both year-round and seasonal (summer and winter) employment. Applications for summer employment must be completed by February 28. For other employment information see the National Park Concessions listing in the Mountains chapter.

SILVERADO COUNTRY CLUB & RESORT
(Napa, California)
Seasonal (Spring and Summer) and Year-Round

Tucked away adjacent to its own private golf course, the Silverado Country Club & Resort is the perfect place from which to explore California's famous Napa Valley. The Napa Valley is home to California's premier wine growing region. Silverado's 1,200 acres include golf, swimming, tennis, three restaurants, and a huge conference center.

SPECIFICS: Silverado hires over 220 new employees each year to fill its 525 peak season staff positions. While the resort does not hire "summer help" per se, there are both year-round and seasonal jobs. Peak season positions usually begin in February or March and last through October or November. Applications are accepted for front office clerks, front office cashiers, secretaries, buspersons, cooks (all levels), night auditors, food servers, and banquet setup staff. Starting wages for most positions are significantly above minimum wage and range from $7.50 to $15.00 per hour (subject to change).

INSIDER TIPS: Silverado is one of the Napa Valley's premier resorts. The company is especially interested in persons serious about a career in the hospitality industry. Individuals looking for a one-time summer job will not find employment here.

PERKS: Silverado is an Amfac Resort. Employee perks include discounted room accommodations at other Amfac Resorts, a free meal for each shift worked, two weeks of paid vacation per year, sick pay, medical/dental/vision insurance, and free golf and tennis. Aside from the resort's golf and tennis facilities, employees are not permitted to use the hotel facilities without permission from management.

TO APPLY: Applicants should either write for an official application or send a cover letter, résumé, and SARP Personnel Department, Silverado Country Club & Resort, 1600 Atlas Peak Road, Napa, California 94558; (707) 257-0200.

WALL DRUG
(Wall, South Dakota)
Seasonal (Summer)

If you have ever driven anywhere within 200 miles of South Dakota, you have probably seen the hundreds of highway billboards reminding you to stop at Wall Drug. For no apparent reason except that it is there (and there is absolutely nothing else anywhere in the near vicinity), this tourist mecca pulls in thousands of visitors each day. The store is located in the thriving metropolis of Wall, South Dakota (population 800).

SPECIFICS: Despite its remote location, Wall Drug is one of South Dakota's largest seasonal student employers. The store hires approximately 120 to 200 seasonal summer staff each year. All employees must have completed at least one year of college. Positions are assigned after an applicant is hired. Employees live in twenty-seven employee dormitories owned and operated by the store. Wall Drug has positions available in its three cafeterias, numerous souvenir shops, large shopping mall, and emporium.

INSIDER TIPS: Applicants who are working their own way through college are given priority. Also, applicants who can stay through Labor Day or later are given preference. The dormitories operated by the store are run fairly strictly, with rules and regulations reminiscent of a small midwestern religious college, circa 1950. Anyone needing regular medical attention should not work here as the town has no regular doctor (a traveling physician visits Wall once each week). All applications should be completed no later than May 1.

PERKS: A job and one day off each week. Subsidized employee housing is provided and employees who successfully fulfill their contracts are refunded a large portion of their rent. Paychecks are issued every other week. The Wall Drug swimming pool and weight room provide daily recreation for employees.

TO APPLY: Applicants should write for an official application from Wall Drug Store, Personnel Director, 510 Main Street, P.O. Box 401, Wall, South Dakota 57790; (605) 279-2175.

WINDMILL'S ASHLAND HILLS INN
(Ashland, Oregon)
Seasonal (Spring and Summer) and Year-Round

To be or not to be. If you enjoy such profound Shakespearean questions, then Ashland is your nirvana. Windhill's Ashland Hills Inn is located in Ashland, home of the world-famous Oregon Summer Shakespearean Festival.

SPECIFICS: Windmill's Ashland Hills Inn employs approximately 130 summer seasonal and year-round staff members. Although hiring is done throughout the year, summer seasonal hiring occurs in two stages: first in March–April and then again in May–June. Although not required, management prefers staff members who can remain through September. Windmill's hires a wide variety of employees in the hotel/rooms, food/beverage, sales, and catering areas. "We are a growing company looking for quality-minded staff members. While experience is desired, an individual who is self-motivated and whose past job performance record is above average has an excellent chance of being hired."

PERKS: Each staff member receives vacation time, discounts on food/lounges/rooms, and a health care program. Local activities include hiking, skiing, swimming, camping, canoeing, and, of course, a tremendous summer of theater.

TO APPLY: Applicants should either write for an official application or send a cover letter and résumé to Lorrie LeCompte-Adderson, Assistant General Manager/Personnel, Windmill's Ashland Hills Inn, 2525 Ashland Street, Ashland, Oregon 97520; (503) 482-8310.

WINE WORLD ESTATES
(Napa Valley, Sonoma Valley, and Santa Barbara, California)
Seasonal (Summer) and Year-Round

Wine World Estates is the parent company of a group of wineries in California's Santa Barbara, San Luis Obispo, Napa, and Sonoma counties. Wine World operates the world-renowned Beringer Vineyards in the Napa Valley, the highly acclaimed Chateau Souverain in Sonoma, and Meridian vineyards in San Luis Obispo. Wine World's fine wines are produced under the brand names Beringer Vineyards, Chateau Souverain, Maison Deutz, Meridian, and Napa Ridge. Wine World Estates's best-known winery, Beringer, was founded in 1876 by the renowned German winemakers Jacob and Frederick Beringer.

SPECIFICS: Wine World Estates's various wineries employ a total of 490 year-round employees. During the crush (the annual wine grape harvest, which runs from August through October) approximately fifty additional personnel are hired. While there are a variety of seasonal crush employees, most staff employees are long-term and career-oriented. All of the wineries operate hospitality facilities for tourists and hire tour guides, wine tasting servers, retail store managers, retail sales staff, and stock clerks. The administrative departments of the wineries employ clerks, secretaries, accountants, purchasing specialists, sales personnel, computer operators, order clerks, payroll clerks, and financial directors (controllers). For those interested in working in the actual winemaking process, the wineries employ enologists (winemakers), engineers, cellar workers, vineyard workers, viticulturalists, bottling line staff, warehousemen, quality control technicians, and forklift operators. All of the above positions are long-term and year-round (with the exception of vineyard workers, who usually are off in December and January). The wineries hire additional staff during the summer when tourism is at its peak. Positions include tour guides and stock clerks. Seasonal crush employees hired from August through October include temporary lab technicians, and cellar workers.

INSIDER TIPS: The most popular non-career position is tour guide. "An ideal tour guide candidate is not necessarily someone who knows a lot about winemaking, but rather an individual with a strong interest in wines and an ability to project an idea to a group of individuals. We want guides who can size up the age and experience of their tour groups and vary their tours accordingly. Someone who simply repeats a canned narrative is not of interest to us. Teachers and former teachers make excellent guides."

TO APPLY: While each winery has its own on-site personnel manager, all applications should be routed through Wine World's main office. Applicants should send a cover letter (outlining what positions they are interested in and to which winery they would like their résumé forwarded) along with a résumé and a SARP to Human Resources Department, Wine World Estates, 2000 Main Street, St. Helena, California 94574; (707) 963-7115.

APPENDIX I
ALPHABETICAL LISTING OF COMPANIES

APPENDIX II
GEOGRAPHIC LISTING OF COMPANIES

KENTUCKY
KENTUCKY KINGDOM 346
NATIONAL PARK CONCESSIONS, INC.
   410

LOUISIANA
DELTA QUEEN STEAMBOAT COMPANY
   394
WATER TOWN, INC. 369

MAINE
ACADIA CORPORATION ACADIA
   NATIONAL PARK 190–91
BOOTHBAY HARBOR YACHT CLUB
   194–95
FUNTOWN USA 372
SUGARLOAF USA 180–81
SUNDAY RIVER SKI RESORT
   181–82
WELLS CHAMBER OF COMMERCE
   218–19

MARYLAND
ANNAPOLIS SAILING SCHOOL,
   35–36
TIMBER RIDES 366–67

MASSACHUSETTS
ATLANTIC ASSOCIATES 387
BRADLESS DEPARTMENT STORE 195
OCEAN EDGE RESORT AND
   CONFERENCE CENTER 208
PARAGON TOURS 307–8
RIVERSIDE PARK 373
STUDENT HOSTELING PROGRAM 311
TOWN OF YARMOUTH—CEMETERY
   DEPT. 196–97

MICHIGAN
BOYNE MOUNTAIN LODGE 147–48
CRYSTAL MOUNTAIN 151–52
EL RANCHO STEVENS 270
INDIANHEAD MOUNTAIN RESORT, INC.
   276
MISSION POINT RESORT 281
NATIONAL PARK CONCESSIONS, INC.
   282

MINNESOTA
BEAR TRACK OUTFITTING COMPANY
   265–66
GRAND VIEW LODGE, GOLF & TENNIS
   CLUB 272
GUNFLINT LODGE & OUTFITTERS 274
KETTLE FALLS HOTEL, INC. 278–79
VALLEY FAIR 374

MISSISSIPPI
FUN TIME USA/BEACH AMUSEMENTS,
   INC. 339–40

MISSOURI
CLIPPER CRUISE LINE 391
WORLDS OF FUN/OCEANS OF FUN
   348–49

MONTANA
BEST WESTERN BUCK'S T-4 LODGE OF
   BIG SKY 71–72
BIG MOUNTAIN SKI & SUMMER
   RESORT 142–43
BIG SKY OF MONTANA 143–44
GLACIER NATIONAL PARK HOTELS
   83–84
HAMILTON STORES, INC. 85–86
SIX FLAGS OVER MID-AMERICA 374

Do you know of other employers in paradise? Do you have comments about this book or about your job in paradise? We would like to hear from you. Write to:

Jeffrey Maltzman
Author, *Jobs in Paradise*
HarperCollins Publishers
10 East 53rd Street
New York, NY 10022